All This . . .
and Evans Too!

All This . . . and Evans Too!

A MEMOIR

by Maurice Evans

 UNIVERSITY OF SOUTH CAROLINA PRESS

Copyright © UNIVERSITY OF SOUTH CAROLINA 1987

Published in Columbia, South Carolina, by the
University of South Carolina Press

FIRST EDITION

Manufactured in the United States of America

Library of Congress Cataloging-in-Publication Data

Evans, Maurice.
  All this—and Evans too.

  Includes index.
  1. Evans, Maurice.   2. Actors—Great Britain—
Biography. I. Title
PN2598.E697A3 1987 792'.028'0924 [B] 86-19222
ISBN 0-87249-496-9

In gratitude to the actors who have
supported me and the staff that has
tolerated me during half a century of
my doing what comes "natcherlee."

Contents

contents

Photographs
A toddler (1904).
"Sunday Best" (1906).
"Sans Teeth" (1907).
Helmsman of the *Evelyn Hope* (1934).
The "Tennis, anyone?" period (1930–34).
As Richard II (1934–35).
Maurice Evans (1935).
As Romeo (1935–36).
As the Dauphin in *Saint Joan* (1936).
As Napoleon in *St. Helena* (1936).
As Richard III (1937–38).

contents

contents

As Dr. Zaius in *Planet of the Apes* (1967).

With Kenny Chase (1967).

With Charlton Heston, Leon Shamroy, Kim Hunter and friend, Linda Harrison, Roddy McDowall, and Franklin Schaffner (1967).

As Norman Thayer in *On Golden Pond* (1981).

All This . . .
and Evans Too!

I

"All the world's a stage . . ."

1. CHILDHOOD

OR AS LONG as I can remember my surname has made me fair game for the punsters—"Good 'Evans," " 'Evans above," and in America " 'Evans to Betsy," but it was left to Gilbert Miller to coin the pun for this memoir. As coproducer with the Theatre Guild of a revival of *Twelfth Night* in which I was to appear with Helen Hayes, he greeted the actors assembled for the first rehearsal with that doubtful gem. The "All this . . . ," however, seems appropriate for the record of a career which, at this moment in time, has lasted for sixty-odd years and shows no sign of calling it a day.

What an exciting journey it has been and continues to be! Even Polonius's description of the diversification demanded of an actor is an understatement: "tragedy, comedy, history, pastoral, pastoral-comical, historical-pastoral, tragical-historical, tragical-comical-historical-pastoral." To that catalogue add actor-manager (the last of the breed) and theatrical and television producer—and it is not surprising that I often wonder in which of the pigeonholes I most truly belong.

That doubt was obviously shared by a colourful cockney lady back in 1934. At the time I was the leading man at London's famous Old Vic Theatre, playing the title role in Shakespeare's *Richard II*. It was a matinee day and a bevy of autograph seekers were gathered outside the stage door—the wall behind them displaying posters advertising current and future productions: *Richard II, Richard III, Henry VIII,* and *King Lear*. The youngsters were so numerous that pedestrians were obliged to step off the sidewalk onto the heavily travelled road. One such passerby was my cockney lady, an imposing female, majestically carrying in her hand a quart jug of beer recently drawn for her at the neighbouring pub. To circumvent the fans, she was forced to step off the curb, narrowly avoiding being sideswiped by a passing bus. As she regained the sidewalk, she looked back at me over her shoulder, and in a voice

1

1901-1935

pregnant with scorn said to her companion, " 'Oo does 'e think 'e is . . . King Charles?"

As a matter of fact, who *do* I think I am, and what made me decide to become an actor? To answer that oft-repeated question, it is necessary to dredge up memories of one's early childhood. Born in 1901 in the market town of Dorchester, Dorset, I was a somewhat precocious youngster according to my father. To most children the urge to imitate comes naturally, and imitation is the actor's stock in trade. In my own case, I dogged Father's footsteps, copying his every move as he went about his quaint occupation. Like his father before him, he was an old-fashioned chemist and druggist in the days that preceded the arrival of patent medicines. All remedies had to be dispensed by the druggist's own hand following a doctor's Latin prescription—salves, ointments, liquid concoctions for every conceivable ailment, and pills galore. It was the manufacturing of pills that fascinated me the most. They started off as a medicinal paste finely ground in a stone mortar with a pestle. Gobs of this messy stuff were transferred to a marble slab and rolled into tubular "worms." These worms were then placed on a grooved metal contraption constructed on the principle of the guillotine; and once in a while I was allowed to operate the upper knife-edge, resulting in a delicious sensation as the "worms" were being transformed into neat little pills.

But there were times when Father's little helper was told to "hop it"— times when I listened at the keyhole to Father's voice counselling a customer about some unmentionable affliction. Or the occasion when I could just hear a real Romany gypsy whispering into Father's ear his recipe for his sick horse— huge pills containing a weird assortment of herbs to be administered only at certain phases of the moon. Pills bring to mind an incident caused by His Majesty's Post Office, which had a strict rule forbidding liquid to be sent by mail. It was therefore the practice of the druggists to attach to the neck of the medicine bottle a tin pillbox half filled with buckshot. Anyone checking for liquid would shake the package and be rewarded for his curiosity with nothing but the rattle of buckshot. This device caused some embarrassment when such a package had been dispatched to a dowager out of town. She wrote ordering a repeat of the cough mixture, adding, ". . . and don't forget to send the pills— they have done me a world of good."

My predilection for following in Father's footsteps was partly due to the fact that "chemists," as they are called in England, customarily wore white coats. But then white coats were *de rigueur* also with housepainters and fishmongers, the latter crowning their snowy garb with straw hats. It was to one of these highly disparate occupations that I aspired, the reason being, I assume, that white coats represented some kind of costume—the forerunner of the theatrical habiliments that I was to don when I grew up. It so happened that

CHILDHOOD

my first appearance on any stage was actually in a *dirty* white coat. The play was Father's adaptation of Thomas Hardy's *Under the Greenwood Tree* being presented by local amateurs at the Dorchester Corn Exchange. His script called for a sheep-shearing scene onstage; so, in the interests of realism, the cooperation of a local farmer was sought. He obligingly contributed the services of a couple of those woolly, mournful beasts, together with their barbers and a small boy to coax the sheep into the wings for their cue to enter. In lieu of payment to the farmers, the Amateur Dramatic Society provided them with a barrel of beer. Some time between the final rehearsal and the night's performance, the barrel became broached and the shepherd boy was discovered fast asleep, his mouth wide open, and the spigot of the barrel slowly dripping into it. Thus it was that little Maurice at the age of seven was impressed to take his place—not exactly an auspicious debut into a theatrical career.

One looks back in wonder to the days of yore when country folk, lacking other means of entertainment, contrived to make their own. In addition to the long hours at the chemist's shop, Father found time to play first violin in a string ensemble, to sit on the bench as a magistrate, to write and play the leads in his own plays. Mother, too, was no mean actress and singer; so I, along with my two brothers and two sisters, was brought up in a home atmosphere of constant bustle of preparations for the latest dramatic adventure. Still, it was not until Dorset's famous son Thomas Hardy moved into our orbit that things got into high gear. Hardy had resolutely refused permission for his novels to be adapted into plays on the grounds that professional playwrights and actors were incapable of truthfully conveying the character and speech patterns of his inimitable Dorset types. Nothing daunted, Father convinced Hardy to let him have a try, claiming that his Dorset background and that of his group of local amateurs could successfully catch the spirit of the original. I was far too young to appreciate what was going on up there on the stage of the Theatre on the Pier of Weymouth when the first Hardy-Evans collaboration made its bow. *The Trumpet Major* must have satisfied Hardy because he subsequently allowed Father to adapt *Far from the Madding Crowd*, *The Woodlanders*, and *Under the Greenwood Tree*.

My only recollection of the performance of *The Trumpet Major*, apart from its being my first visit to a theatre, was of being taken to it by Hardy himself and his unpredictable first wife. Her figure was vaguely familiar to me as the strange female one saw in Dorchester furiously pedalling a rusty bicycle with a motoring veil streaming behind her. Our exit from the Weymouth Pier Theatre placed Hardy in a dilemma. With a stiff breeze blowing from the English Channel and her motoring veil fairly whipping around, Mrs. Hardy insisted on walking perilously balanced on the very edge of the esplanade some

1901–1935

fifty feet above the rocky shore. Hardy's agonised cry of "Do be careful, dear" had absolutely no effect, but he dared not let go of my hand for fear that I would join his wife in her antics.

In London, the following notice appeared in the *Referee* on November 25, 1908:

> A dramatic version of Mr. Thomas Hardy's novel "The Trumpet Major," or, to be exact, some scenes from that novel transferred to the stage by a Mr. A. H. Evans, delighted a crowded audience at the Corn Exchange at Dorchester last week. It was purely a local affair, and, excepting always the distinguished novelist, whose fame extends wherever the English language is spoken, it was an exhibition of local talent. It was, by general consent, the "best Dorset." Mr. Evans, who had prepared the stage version of the story, appeared for the nonce not only as a dramatist, but as an actor besides, taking the part of Festus; Mr. Hardy, who was prevented by ill health from being present at the performance, had interested himself actively in the production; and although "The Trumpet Major," in the form in which it was presented, may be too episodical for the regular business of the theatre, the military humours of the scenes might well be appreciated beyond "Casterbridge," which, as all good Hardy men know, is only another name for Dorchester itself.

The other Hardy adaptations caused quite a stir. Word got around the London press that Hardy's novels were being shown as plays at Dorchester's Corn Exchange, and it became the custom for the first-string critics to come from London for the openings. It is too bad that the manuscripts of Father's works were irretrievably lost, the sad fact being that they were in storage with my furniture in London when they became the target of one of Hitler's firebombs. Now that Hardy's works are in public domain, they are being discovered by the moviemakers, but perhaps one may be forgiven for claiming that the pioneer of the dramatic potential of this author was one Alfred Herbert Evans, J.P.

This constant activity in our Dorchester home on Icen Way had little or no attraction for me. In fact I regarded it with positive hostility when I was forced to take the part of a speechless fairy in some stupid kindergarten play. I got my revenge, however, when, having spotted the bell-push that gave the signal for the front curtain to be drawn, I pushed the button thereby obliterating my fellow players from the sight of the audience.

Later, when the family moved to Stoke Newington, a suburb of London, and I was about eight, it was discovered that I had an unusually fine boy-soprano voice, a talent for which my parents' chapel—Congregational— had no use, but we kids were lugged off every Sunday by our top-hatted father

CHILDHOOD

and bonnetted mother to suffer through the interminable sermons. My younger brother, Hugh, and I alleviated the tedium by squatting on the floor of the family pew and engaging in pillow fights with the chapel's kneeling cushions.

It was something of a relief to the parents when the choirmaster of the Church of England establishment asked their consent for the two of us to join the choir of St. Andrew's. I proved to be an exception to the cooing-dove type of voice, which is the mark of most boy sopranos. As a result I was swiftly promoted to solo boy and melted the hearts of my hearers with my perfectly natural vibrato. I took all the compliments for granted, for, being of Welsh extraction (everyone sings well in Wales), I regarded singing as my birthright. So here I was once more in a white costume—the pleated surplice worn over a cassock—showing off before my first big audience. St. Andrew's was famous all over North London for its music. The choirmaster and organist was a fascinating pint-sized genius named Charles Boddington. A fine musician, he taught during the week at the London School of Organists, and on two evenings a week both gave us hell and made us laugh during choir practice. After Sunday evening service, he gave a recital at the magnificent organ, allowing me on occasion to sit near the console whilst he performed the intricate gymnastics of a Bach fugue—singing his curly head off throughout.

Watching on televison a recent royal wedding at St. Paul's recalled to me an event in my choirboy days which might very well have steered me toward a career in the theatre entirely different from the one that eventually opened up for me. News of my piping soprano had reached the ears of the St. Paul's "talent scouts" whose job it was to be on the lookout for replacements for those incumbent choristers who, with the oncoming of puberty, one day suffered the embarrassment of advertising the fact by emitting a resonant baritone note in place of the top "C" for which they were aiming. Father vetoed St. Paul's invitation for me to join the choir, fearing that my education would be neglected. A pity, really, because at the end of my soprano days and at the proper age I would have been given an easy scholarship to King's College, Cambridge, and after graduation, a social standing that would have served me well in later years. To crack the snobbish cliques of the West End theatre in those times was almost impossible unless one had Oxford or Cambridge to one's credit.

As it was, I became a solo boy in the school choir at the Grocer's Company school in London, and on account of "the voice" got away with murder as far as my education was concerned. The fact that my grades were consistently abysmal was dismissd by the teachers with an airy, ". . . Oh, Evans, M. H.? He sings!" Whenever the school's governors paid a visit, I was trotted out to sing for them and was made a big fuss of. The only memento to have survived from

1901–1935

those schooldays, and the only prize I was ever awarded, was, prophetically perhaps, a copy of Shakespeare's collected works, on the flyleaf of which is inscribed "M. H. Evans, for Singing."

Home from school, St. Andrew's church hall awaited us with a program of athletic and other activities to absorb our energies. One Christmastide, it was suggested that we try our hands at a nativity play, and it fell to me to organise it, thereby having my first taste of being an actor-manager. Father wrote the script with the aid of the New Testament, and I gave orders to my fellow actors to rifle their attics for old bedsheets and anything that could serve as costumes. I cast myself as Herod, suitably robed in my makeshift finery. The finishing touch, however, was a number of brass curtain rings that I wore as bracelets. I got the only laugh in this reverent opus when, making an authoritative entrance, I raised my arm in a Roman salute, whereupon the curtain rings slid from my wrist over my skinny elbow to nestle finally in my armpit.

No lolling about glued to television sets in those days. No radio to rob us of any appreciation of classical music or the art of conversation. Not that we were by any means the little angels we appeared to be in our surplices; we had our own brand of delinquency, but for the most part it was fairly harmless. When joining in the Lord's Prayer with the congregation, the words "Lead us not into temptation" became "Lead us not into Thames Station." But the church was the hub around which our lives centered and, by keeping us occupied, kept us away from serious mischief.

On Saturday afternoons, weather permitting, we were taken on supervised country hikes, one of which brought me close to an untimely death. A great storm had felled ancient trees all over the Hertfordshire countryside; one of them, a ten-tonner at least, had been stripped of its branches, its huge trunk reposing invitingly on the crest of a steep grassy hill. Boys will be boys, so when our supervisor was busy arranging for our cream-bun tea at a neighbouring cottage, a dozen or so of us decided to try to dislodge the treetrunk and start it rolling down the hill. My fingers were caught in the bark and before I knew it I was drawn over the tree's girth and found myself pinioned beneath its weight—acting as a sort of wedge to arrest its forward motion. It took half the population of the village to rescue me from my predicament. Had it not been for the soggy condition of the ground, which obligingly offered a depression the size of my head, I would not be here today to tell the tale. What an unusual headline it would have been—"Boy Run Over by a Tree."

These halcyon days were soon to end, although I was still singing in the choir. On rare occasions I was hired and actually *paid* to sing a sickly anthem at fashionable weddings—"Love one another with a pure heart fervently." I would barely get through the opening phrase before the bride broke into tears.

CHILDHOOD

The more elegant the wedding, the greater the flood. Even the bridegroom could occasionally be seen to dab his eyes. I was greatly mystified by this lachrymose response to my singing and came to the conclusion that the state of holy wedlock was not all it was cracked up to be. I wonder, could that early impression have something to do with the fact that in all my eighty-some years I have managed to elude falling into the matrimonial trap? It could certainly explain why, in my Broadway days, I was able to portray with such conviction, Shaw's misogynist hero, Jack Tanner, in *Man and Superman*. Quote: "Marriage is the most licentious of human institutions! I say *the* most licentious of human institutions; that is the reason for its popularity!"

It may seem very farfetched to claim that these childhood experiences had some bearing on my choice of career, but they certainly played their part in the building of my character, and it is one's character that eventually demands expression. In my case, it was acting that seemed to fill the need, so I formed a small amateur dramatic society called the Cranleigh Players. Strictly for our own amusement we rehearsed playlets in our parents' drawing rooms. We became rather unpopular with the grownups by failing to restore their furniture to its proper places and forgetting to wipe our muddy boots on entering.

One day we spotted a butcher's shop which had gone out of business and had the shutters up on the street windows. We broke into the back of the shop and surveyed the empty upper regions. A large room in the rear of the premises looked ideal for our purposes but, of course, it lacked a stage. Nothing daunted, but groaning with the effort, we stripped the shop of all the butcher's marble slabs and hoisted them upstairs to our secret theatre. With various drawers to support them, the marble slabs became our coveted stage. With all these clandestine goings-on, we were haunted by guilt, to say nothing of the fear of being caught by the police. Measures had to be taken to forestall this, so we devised an alarm system consisting of strings across the downstairs stair-treads. The strings were attached to an old-fashioned, spring-type doorbell overhead, the idea being that any intruder mounting the stairs would catch his foot in the string and set off a warning peal. We actors and actresses were all assigned bedroom closets into which we were to hide if ever the bell rang—two to a closet. With increasing frequency the playlet rehearsals were interrupted by some joker tripping the alarm system, whereupon we all disappeared to our allotted closets. If the giggles and bumps were anything to go by, it became obvious that the close proximity of two in a closet was far more popular than the suspended play rehearsal.

It was at about this period that I realised it was time "to put away childish things." The upper register of my voice having fallen victim to increasing maturity, I was relegated to the back row of the choir to sing alto. The change

1901–1935

took place at Whitsuntide. I was reaching the end of the beautiful soprano melody of the "Veni Creator" ("Come Holy Ghost, our souls inspire") but when I opened my mouth for the last high note, not a sound came out. No one had warned me that this had to happen one day, so it came as a terrible shock and cast me into the Slough of Despond. Victorian parents like mine seemed to have no idea that keeping a youngster in ignorance of the facts of life could cause the child very deep distress. It remained for the church to come to the rescue.

Up to this time, St. Andrew's had been rather low church under the pastorship of the Rev. Mr. Relton who, to judge by his sermons, was more interested in physics and astronomy than in spiritual matters. Now we had a change of vicars in the person of a high churchman preposterously named Dr. Golding-Goldingbird. He introduced far more ceremony and frills. Led by me carrying the cross, the choir now made a processional entrance all around the nave, our solemn progress sometimes becoming straggly when my naughty brother, Hugh, paused over a forced-air grill, allowing his surplice to balloon out like a parachute.

Other innovations appealed to me for their theatricality, and for that reason, I think, rather than for any deep religious feeling, I became an altar boy and thoroughly enjoyed all the genuflecting and so forth. Not for long, though. Behind the scenes, not unlike the theatre, the church is not all that glamorous and the clergy not all that devout. I resented having to serve at the altar on Wednesday mornings at 7 o'clock when Holy Communion had to be celebrated for the same three elderly ladies, whose souls were already well and thoroughly saved. Our socialising curate, the Rev. Mr. Nuttall, made little attempt to disguise his frequent hangovers, and the liturgy would be punctuated with audible burps. So, as disillusionment set in, I began to turn once more to amateur theatricals.

A group called the Hornsey Players, headed by a lad named Gerrard Middleditch, roped me in. Our leading lady, euphoniously named Bessie Butt, and I were given good parts in adult plays. It was at this point in my life, I think, that I knew for sure that acting had to be my vocation. It was further confirmed when we decided to put on a production of Shaw's *Major Barbara*. In our search for somewhere to stage it we came across an acting school in the West End being run by the actress May Whitty. For a reasonable sum she agreed to allow us the use of her small theatre, but with the proviso that her daughter, Margaret Webster, be cast as Barbara. Thus began in a very tentative way an association which, many years later, made our names familiar to American theatregoers.

In the spring of 1914 the clouds of war had gathered, and by August England had declared war on Germany—World War I, "the Great War." In

CHILDHOOD

typical fashion, the public dismissed the news, confident that their standing army of regulars could easily polish off the Hun. Life went on much as usual, though there were hints of troubles ahead. It struck home when my militant-minded brother Donald calmly announced that he had joined the army. His bloodthirsty ambition to wipe out the entire German army single-handed was promptly frustrated when it was discovered that he was an engineering student. On being called up, he was posted at the Woolwich Arsenal in South London where he spent the entire war biting his nails and tending the antiaircraft searchlights.

To digress somewhat, at war's end Donald continued to brood over the fact that he had been denied active service. The Bolshevik revolution had started in Russia and the British prime minister was calling for volunteers to form the core of an expeditionary force which, supposedly, was to back up the White Russians and put an end to the revolution—a pipe dream if there ever was one. Donald and his two mates were given the job of running army telephone wires through the forests and frozen steppes of northern Russia. His description of Russian civilization at that time was that it was three hundred years behind Western Europe. The villagers that he and his team encountered lived in domed mud huts with chickens and pigs as bedfellows. Whatever one may think of the Soviet system, the fact that it has somehow spanned a period of three centuries in one lifetime is undeniably astounding.

The fall of 1914 saw an awakening on the part of the public as to the seriousness of the war situation. Belgium had been overrun, and to everyone's horror British wounded soldiers, evacuated from the battlefields, started pouring into England. A volunteer army was hastily assembled under the aegis of the sporting figure of Lord Derby. All men of military age were required to wear a "Derby" armband on their civilian jackets to denote that they had registered. This gave rise to a cruel custom on the part of some of the female population, who made a practice of pinning a white feather on the chests of any youngster not wearing an armband. This was discrimination of the most callous sort. Many who had been excused from registration on health or other legitimate grounds were treated with the same scorn as the shirkers.

The outbreak of war resulted in many changes even in the lives of those of us who were too young for service. At school, one by one our masters were called to the colours, to be replaced by women teachers, whose lives we beastly boys made miserable. We referred to them as "Ma" this and "Ma" that to emphasise our priggish dislike over the change of tradition. One of our favourite victims was "Ma" Low. She taught us ancient Egyptian history, her diction being hampered by spectacularly protruding teeth. If you happened to be sitting close to her desk, you were the target of her liquid sibilants. Being out of range, further back in the classroom, I was able, on one occasion, by

1 9 0 1 — 1 9 3 5

covering my mouth with my hand, to disguise the presence in my mouth of an old upper set of my father's dentures. With a "now you see it, now you don't" flick of my hand, I kept the class in convulsions much to the puzzlement of "Ma" Low, who failed to understand what it was we found so funny about Tutankhamen.

We weren't very popular with "Ma" Phillips either. Instead of following her instructions in the chemistry lab, we would make up our own concoctions in our beakers, which, when placed over a Bunsen burner, emitted an eye-watering cloud smelling strongly of rotten eggs. Only one of the younger masters remained and he, poor man, though a British subject, was the son of a famous German scholar. This made him fair game for his students and we showed him no mercy; but the day came when "Beefy Bill," as we called him, got even with us when our nefarious scheme went awry. One of us, peeping through a crack in the classroom door to watch for Beefy's approach down the corridor, was to cry "Cave!" —whereupon, we were all to start beating time on our desks with our tin geometry boxes and to sing in unison:

> Beefy Bill's a German
> Beefy Bill's a Spy
> Ask the Kaiser!

It served us jolly well right when our lookout jumped the gun on us by shouting "Cave!" before identifying the approaching black-gowned figure. In the midst of the pandemonium who should come bursting into the classroom but the headmaster himself. What a dressing-down he gave us!—ending with the command, "All of you come to my study immediately!" We formed a line and proceeded to that inner sanctum where the Head now stood with a vicious little bamboo cane in his hand. One by one we bent over his desk to receive several strokes on our posteriors. The boy ahead of me in the line was a very timid character nicknamed "Skimpole." A model student in all respects, he had certainly not joined in our heartless game, but he looked at the Head with such an imploring expression that I got the giggles. I was rewarded for my levity with one extra swipe of the cane and retired notably chastened. One wonders whether or not a liberal dose of this kind of medicine might not restore the badly needed discipline in our schools today.

If our outside interests were mainly responsible for the development of one's individuality, the core of the painful process of growing up was the family. We five children were rather a strange bunch—come to think of it— having so little in common. Donald, the budding engineer, was altogether absorbed in the recently discovered science of wireless telegraphy. He built his own crystal set and wound his own magnetic coils on Cerebos Salt tins. There was many a slip, but the day finally came when his dedication to Signor

CHILDHOOD

Marconi was crowned with success. Excitedly he hollered from his upstairs den, "It works! Come and listen." We all rushed up to his hideaway and one by one were allowed to put on the headphones, and one by one we handed them back to the inventor with an expression that seemed to say, "So what?" All that was to be heard were the faint dots and dashes of the Morse code being tapped out by some ship at sea. We had no conception of the magnitude of Donald's achievement and made a very unappreciative audience. To add insult to injury, in the early days of the 1914–18 war, the Metropolitan Police seized every vestige of his precious possession, suspecting it might be the listening post of an enemy spy. Years after the war's end, a callow young policeman came to the door one day and sheepishly handed Mother a cardboard carton bursting its sides with a tangled jumble of wires and the like, and bearing a label reading "Detained for the Duration."

My sisters, May and Evelyn, were reasonably close, both being destined to become schoolteachers, as was their mother before them. I can envisage them now dressed in their school uniforms, which consisted of dark blue tunics with wide pleats all down the front. The purpose of the pleats was that they could be discreetly let out as the young ladies' busts developed. Both girls were athletically inclined and once in a while the brothers would condescend to watch one of their hockey matches. We boys, brought up to play the gentlemanly (and deadly dull) game of cricket, were secretly amazed and envious when we saw our sisters swinging their hockey sticks and cracking the shins of their opponents. No wonder that during school holidays they both joined the Women's Land Army and put the fear of God into the German prisoners of war of whom they were in charge.

Our individual interests were so disparate that, except at suppertime, an observer would find it hard to believe we were related. Mother found the lack of communication between us so oppressive that she would bring a book to the ample family dining table. Our curiosity being aroused by her contentment with what she was reading brought the inevitable question; she would say, "Want to hear some of this?" It soon became a custom for her to read aloud to us in her beautiful voice passages from Dickens, Thackeray, and others. I was never late for supper from then on, and my personal reading advanced from *Tom Brown's Schooldays* to sterner stuff.

Our musical education within the family circle was a different matter. Donald and the two girls, none of them having the slightest interest in the accomplishment, were forced to learn to play the piano. To this day I can hear echoes of the interminable five-finger exercises, the mucked-up arpeggios, and the laborious assaults on little pieces for beginners. Even the parents rebelled at the prospect of yet another child making the night hideous at the piano, so it was decided that I was to emulate Father and be taught to play the violin.

1901–1935

Ironically, I had a natural bent for the piano, and although I've never had a lesson I can still (arthritis permitting) strum quite a creditable tune. So I was condemned to the fiddle with all the torture that difficult instrument involves. I'm not one to be easily beaten by a challenge, but it seemed unfair to me that, whereas my brother and sisters had all the notes of the piano's eight octaves to choose from, my miserable violin provided me with only four strings, leaving it up to my fingers to create the rest. Scraping away valiantly, but hopelessly out of tune, my efforts to become a second Fritz Kreisler were imitated by my siblings with derisive catcalls.

Unlike most other families, ours had very few relatives. Mother had none, and Father had only four unmarried sisters—although there was great secrecy about a mysterious younger brother named Will, who must have been the black sheep of the family. Auntie Charlotte, Auntie Ada, and Auntie Milly lived together in a rambling old house in a district of London that was going downhill, known as New Cross. By way of protecting themselves against unwanted intruders, the maiden aunts kept a gentleman's silk top hat hanging on the hat rack in the entrance hall, but it rather gave the show away when one noticed it was thickly covered with dust.

The fourth sister, Auntie Jo, whom we rarely saw, was a remarkable woman. As a young girl she became a missionary and was sent to India by an organisation, preposterously named the Society for the Propagation of the Gospel in Foreign Parts. She quickly resolved to devote her energies to the amelioration of the sad lot of the untouchables in the outskirts of Calcutta— Baranoga by name. Her practicality took precedence over her piety, so she went to work setting up a compound in which these unfortunate people could live with self-respect. Instead of building a church for them, she established a workshop where they were taught to produce the typical Benares brassware. Eventually her experiment became practically self-supporting and was a great source of pride to the workers. Every three years, Auntie Jo returned to London to raise funds for the expansion of her good work. Her success as a fund-raiser was in no small measure due to her appearance; for she continued to wear the sari in London and after so many years in India strongly resembled a very beautiful native Indian woman. She had no choice when the Indian government commandeered her now flourishing workshop as World War I began, enlisting the skills of her untouchables to turn out brass shell-cases for use of Indian troops being despatched to join the British army in France. A far cry from the "Propagation of the Gospel," but one I am sure she pursued with equal energy.

Her younger sister, Milly, had the same quality of boundless energy. She was the headmistress of a Council school in a squalid London slum, and ruled it with a rod of iron. Personally, however, she was a gay and funny woman. At

CHILDHOOD

Christmastime, she and her two sisters would come to visit, but it was always Auntie Milly who brought sun into the house, and the one who shone in parlour games and charades—an incipient actress I suspected. Though no maiden aunt myself, I may have inherited some of her inclination and determination.

During our family summer holidays a kind of truce was declared between us warring children. A cottage would be rented each August in some coastal village of Dorset or Devonshire where our tempers were cooled by swimming in the icy waters of the English Channel. Father taught me to swim, and having satisfied himself that I was an accomplished dog-paddler, rode me out on his shoulders to deep water into which he dumped me unceremoniously. I needed no encouragement to strike out smartly for shore and to take refuge in the bathing machine—blue to the gills and shaking all over, but mightily proud of my aquatic prowess. This abrupt introduction to the briny deep overcame all my fear of the water and probably accounted for swimming becoming the only sport in which I excelled. Those bathing machines were really something, resembling nothing so much as an oversized privy mounted on large cartwheels. At high tide, these peripatetic vehicles would be parked high up on the beach. We would enter ours in relays to change into our demure bathing costumes. As the tide receded, an attendant would hitch his horse to the machine and it was pulled over the sand to the water's edge. By this maneuver it was made certain that lady bathers, though heavily apparelled, might be exposed to view for only a brief moment as they stepped into the surf.

Our next-door neighbours in the bathing-machine colony were two elderly spinsters. From top to toe, with the exception of their faces, there was nary an inch of bare skin to be seen as they ventured, hand in hand, into waist-high water. Taking it in turns, one clutching the other would bob up and down to the depth of her shoulders, emitting girlish squeaks of delight at their daring. The puzzling thing about this exercise was that both ladies went into the water wearing quantities of jewelry, ropes of pearls around their scrawny necks and pearl rings on their bony fingers. Consumed with curiosity, Mother dared to ask them one day, "Why all this display?" The old girls—we referred to them as "Odds and Ends"—replied, "It's for our pearls. It rejuvenates them to be reminded of the water from which they originally came."

These beach holidays later gave way to more picturesque fishing villages such as Osmington and Lullworth Cove, places that could be reached only by horse and cart on dusty country lanes. (Many years later, I volunteered to show some American friends some of the favourite spots of my youth. Alas, my dusty lanes had become broad, surfaced roads with signs reading, "This Way to the Car Park," and my jewels by the sea had lost their sparkle.) One of our family August holidays found us at a little place named Perranporth on the rocky coast of Cornwall—Camelot country, no less. A pair of massive headlands formed a barrier against big Atlantic waves, slowing their impetus to a gentle swell that finally spent itself on Perranporth's sandy shore. The rhythmic action of these waves reminded one of my sisters of pictures she had seen in a *National Geographic* magazine of South Sea islanders riding such watery steeds; so off we went to a local carpenter, prevailing upon him to make for us what turned out to be the very first surfboards ever to be launched on British waters. The occasion marked the first time my name was to appear in print. The London *Daily Mail* ran a short piece under the headline, "Evans Family Introduces New Sport." I'm told we started quite a craze locally, probably spoiling the tranquillity of our Cornish playground, but let us hope not.

I suppose similar changes have taken place on the coast of North Devon. The approach to one particularly favourite village was down an extremely steep hill, an incline of about one in seven. Some enterprising entrepreneur had salvaged a genuine old stagecoach, and it was on the driver's box of this relic that we kids delighted in riding to the village. At the crest of the hill, the coachman would descend from his perch and wedge metal shoes under the wheels. Remounting to the driver's seat, he would turn and address his passengers in an ominous voice, "And now we come to *the garshly bit!*" A flick of his whip and the horse proceeded to drag us sliding down the hill while we hung on for dear life.

In addition to his other accomplishments, Father was a fine photographer, particularly of country scenery. He was able to pursue his hobby to his heart's content on these summer holidays, but *not* to Mother's joy, however. Those were the days of bulky accordion-pleated cameras, which had to be mounted on separate tripods, and no matter how rough the terrain it was her job to carry the "legs." The summer we went to Wales she found very trying because Father had spotted an inaccessible bay, which took his fancy as a subject for marine photography. Picking her way down an uneven goat track, with the "legs" in one hand and a picnic basket in the other, did nothing to improve her disposition. We kids ran ahead in search of somewhere to picnic that did not involve sitting on prickly undergrowth. We scrambled over the rocks on the shoreline, finally lighting on a large flat rock that was out of sight from the rest of the bay and perfectly located for our lunch—so we thought. It was not until well after our alfresco repast, when our parents were snoozing and the rest of us shrimping in the pools, that one of us realised that the tide had turned and was about to cut off our retreat from the picnic rock. The alarm was sounded and a somewhat disorderly withdrawal was made by all.

In spite of Mother's protestations, Father insisted on revisiting the same spot on the next sunny day, but promised to consult a tide table in advance. So off we went once more, Mother bringing up the rear, again carrying the "legs." She staggered her way towards the corner that concealed our erstwhile picnic aerie and saw to her dismay that another family had anticipated our arrival. Her sense of the ridiculous must have deserted her, for I distinctly remember her drawing herself to her fullest height and saying, in a voice not unlike Sarah Bernhardt at her most imperious, "Are you aware that you are occupying *our* rock?" The Evanses slunk back to the top of the goat track with Mother secretly hoping that the intruders found themselves actually cut off for the day by the tide.

Alongside our substitute picnic-ground atop the cliff ran a narrow-gauge railway by which miners were brought to and from the mines and our holiday village of Llanbedrog. They rode on a sort of flatbed affair drawn by an elderly horse; their approach would be heralded by one of the miners starting to sing some traditional Welsh folksong. Within minutes his lead would be taken up by his fellows, all of them singing in improvised harmony—fading into the distance as the sun went down. Quite extraordinary, this faculty of the Welsh for untutored a cappella singing, although it did have its drawbacks if you happened to be a touring actor, arriving thirsty, in some Welsh town on the Sabbath. In those days of train journeys, there was a saying that nothing moved on the railroads on Sundays but "Actors and Fish." Emerging from the station, not a porter or a cab in sight, you trudged towards your diggings past chapels of various obscure denominations. From most of them floating voices uplifted in song—voices that undoubtedly included the missing porter's tenor and the absent cabbie's bass.

Another feature peculiar to Wales is the paucity in the variety of surnames, making it quite hopeless to trace your antecedents, if that is your object. Every other person you meet is either a Jones, a Williams, a Morgan, or an Evans. In ordinary parlance one often finds it necessary to add an individual's trade or profession to his surname to identify him correctly; for example, Morgan Evans the butcher, or Evan Williams the candlestickmaker. Welsh pronunciation of proper names is something of a challenge; try your tongue around one of the towns in Snowdonia named Pwllheli.

2. A TEENAGER'S FIRST JOB

The war, which everyone thought would last only a year at most, came closer and closer to home. Our smug reliance on the invincible British navy became a myth with the commencement of air warfare. Until then, aviation had been regarded as nothing but a dangerous sport. We used to arise at the crack of dawn and pedal our way to the Hendon Airfield to watch aviators, like Cody, barely clearing the hangar roof as he put down his wooden flying machine after an "Around Great Britain" race. A. H. G. Fokker, who made the first trans-Channel flight from France, was also a great attraction. The aeroplane, which was to play such an important part in winning the war, also brought tragedy to many of us. Like most schoolboys, I became a devoted admirer of a lad somewhat older than myself. In my eyes he was everything I hoped I could become, and no doubt I bored him with my idolatry. My admiration of him reached its peak on the day he called at our house to say good-bye. He was resplendent in uniform of a Royal Flying Corps pilot, having obtained his wings after only a few hours of flying. Twenty-four hours later his family received a telegram saying that he had been shot down over the German lines. What, up until then, had been everybody else's war was now very much my own. Nothing could console me except the prospect of eventually getting into uniform myself to avenge my friend.

As the war dragged on our family underwent radical changes. Father's chemist's shop ran into financial difficulties, food was in short supply, and rationing was in force. Our staple diet was kedgeree, a mixture of smoked haddock, rice, and chopped hardboiled egg—a dish which to this day evokes nauseous memories. Life, however, was not without excitement when the Germans started to bomb London from their Zeppelin airships. The nearest thing we had to an air-raid shelter was the massive mahogany dining table. Mother, young brother Hugh, and the girls huddled together under the table during the raids, but Father and I would go out on the street to watch the action. We decided we'd rather be bombed by the Germans than scorched to death by the gas fire in the dining room. The only time we beat a retreat was when a piece of antiaircraft shrapnel pierced the brim of Father's hat.

There was something indescribably sinister about those Zeppelins when they invaded our skies at night. They floated silently well out of range of the antiaircraft guns, but on a clear night were picked up by our searchlights—one of them manned by brother Donald. Finally the great night came when an intrepid young airman, his single-seated plane armed with nothing but a machine-gun, managed to gain sufficient altitude to pump a few rounds into the Zeppelin's gasbag. The whole airship burst into flames, depositing chunks of molten metal and charred bodies over the London environs. The tension that gripped the city during these raids resulted in an uncanny silence, but on the night of this last Zeppelin raid a cheer, faint at first, started in the east of London. Gradually the cheer was taken up street by street until it swept the entire metropolis, developing into a mighty roar like an advancing avalanche.

The daylight raids that were to follow were by conventional aeroplanes,

A TEENAGER'S FIRST JOB

taking the military by surprise during their first forays. No air-raid warning system had been set up, so there was no way of telling whether it was friend or foe overhead until the bombs began to fall. It was a Saturday morning when the Germans paid us their first visit. The female caretaker of St. Andrew's and I were in the vestry preparing for the morrow's services when all hell broke out. We rushed outside and looking skywards saw a spectacular air battle in progress. This was altogether too much for the old caretaker lady in her forget-me-not-trimmed bonnet. With a sigh of disbelief, she fainted dead away into my arms. I dragged her inert form back into the vestry, produced a bottle of the sacramental wine, of which I was the custodian, and plied her with a generous helping. This extremely intoxicating libation not only dispelled her fainting fit but, after a second swig, sent her into a deep sleep for the duration of the raid.

Bombs notwithstanding, life had to go on. My sister May became a student-teacher in one of London's poorest districts, coming home at the end of the day thoroughly disillusioned. What possible point was there in slaving to impart education to children who, at the end of their day in school, would be returning to their homes to be beaten by a drunken father or mother? There was wry humour in the accounts of some of the goings-on in the classroom. A hand is raised. Hoping that its owner is going to ask an intelligent question, the teacher asks, "What is it, Ivy?" Pointing her finger at the head of the girl in front of her, Ivy replies, "Please, Teacher, Mary Jones 'as got nits in 'er 'air." This rather unsavoury topic was the source of amusement to me under different circumstances. One day I was waiting for a bus outside a barbershop when I noticed a small Cockney boy staring intently at what was going on inside. The barber, a burning wax taper in his hand, was giving a customer a treatment for hair ends, known as a "singe." The boy called across the street to his companion, "Alfie! Come 'ere! Look at that bloke." "Blimey," said Alfie, " 'e's lookin' for 'em wiv a light!"

May's pet hate, apart from little visitors in her pupils' hair, was having to give Scripture lessons to indifferent listeners. She thought she had found a way of making the Old Testament more palatable; so, knowing of my thespic leanings, she invited me to watch her in action at her next Scripture lesson. The class consisted of tiny tots to whom she first told in her own colloquial language the story of Moses in the bullrushes. She wrapped a ruler in the blackboard duster and explained to the kids that this was the baby Moses. The incipient prophet was then hidden somewhere behind her desk. Several of the children were picked to portray the characters in the legend as she had previously described to them. Without a trace of self-consciousness and taking it all most seriously, the children reenacted the Bible story. I was deeply touched by one little girl's belief in what she was doing when, finding the baby in the imaginary bullrushes, she cradled the ridiculous ruler and duster in her arms and cooed endearments to it. Nowadays, I always tell teachers who are having trouble inculcating Shakespeare into the minds of their students, "Let them *act* it out, no matter how badly. Otherwise, the Bard, to them, is nothing but a laborious exercise in memorisation."

I became sixteen in 1917, a fateful year for me. Stoke Newington, which had been a prosperous suburb, had gone into a decline. Father's more substantial customers were moving further afield; so we followed suit by moving out of London to Surrey. The day of our move from the north of London is a blot on the family escutcheon. The parents unwisely sent us ahead to Surrey to receive the first vanload of furniture while they remained behind to supervise the loading of the second van. The embers were still glowing in a bonfire in the rear garden of our new abode in Coulsdon. As things began to be unloaded, each of us started to spot items we had been forced to live with since our nursery days. A terrible Landseer print, "The Stag at Bay," and a few sickly religious lithographs were put aside together with a smattering of Chinese and Japanese bamboo furniture that we hated, but which, today, would fetch a pretty penny in the auction rooms. As soon as the movingmen were out of sight, we enjoyed the fiendish delight of piling this junk on the embers and seeing it burst into flames. Mother didn't seem to miss the things, or, if she did, blamed herself for leaving them at the other house.

One memorable day shortly after the move to Coulsdon, Father said he had to have a private talk with me. For a moment I thought it was going to be about the bonfire episode, but then I saw by his grave expression that it was something far more serious. He told me that setting up the new chemist's shop had put such a strain on his purse that he could no longer afford my school fees and that the time had come for me to go out to earn a living. To his relief, the prospect pleased me because I had always considered school a waste of my time. This rosy outlook didn't last for long, however.

One of the jobs being offered sounded rather attractive—a position at the music-publishing house of Chappell & Co. on Bond Street in London—and that was the job I took. My visions of moving into glamorous musical circles were quickly shattered when I was informed that I was to be the new office boy, my predecessor having been called up by the army. Thus began eight years of stultifying apprenticeship in a niche for which I was ill-fitted. When not running errands, I sat on a high Dickensian stool poring over gigantic ledgers that defied my unmathematical mind. My immediate superiors, Mr. Hole and Mr. Pain, must have been relieved when after a year or two I was promoted to the cashier's department where my duties were less mindboggling. I was able to get out of the stuffy office more frequently, making trips to the bank and distributing the staff wage packets on Fridays—an exercise that gave me an unwarranted sense of superiority. In addition to being publishers of sheet music (the hit tunes of those days being such gems as "Roses Are Shining in Picardy" and "Where My Caravan Has Rested"), Chappell & Co. were the lessees of London's principal concert hall, the Queen's Hall, on Langham Place. This was the home of Sir Henry Wood's famous orchestra and his renowned Promenade Concerts.

For the "Proms" all the seats were removed from the ground floor and a circular fountain installed in the centre. Admission prices were very low for those hardy souls who had the stamina to promenade around the fountain as the concert proceeded. Being on the fringe of the management, I was allowed a free seat in the balcony when one was available. Best of all, my duties as assistant cashier called on me to pay the instrumentalists their weekly salaries. This function gave me the opportunity to play truant from the office and attend the orchestra rehearsals. Occasionally they would be interrupted by the wailing of the air-raid sirens, which would be the signal for everyone to dive for the basement with Sir Henry shouting to the concert master, "Remind me to go back to 'B.' " The raid warnings so often turned out to be false alarms that after a while Sir Henry ignored them and ploughed on with the rehearsal, even though the bombs might rival the orchestra's percussion section.

A concert devoted solely to the works of one composer was given each evening, Monday through Friday, with a Pop concert on Saturday. Anyone attending the Proms regularly was able to hear all the Beethoven symphonies (except the "Choral"), Wagner one night, Brahms, Mozart, and Bach on others. Not all of them had been adequately rehearsed; nevertheless they provided the nearest thing available to a thorough grounding in classical music. Sometimes a world-famous artist would donate his services; Feodor Chaliapin or Lauritz Melchior who, incidentally, in his younger days was a baritone, not the *Heldentenor* he later became. That splendid pianist Myra Hess was most generous in her appearances, and Vladimir de Pachmann was a great favourite at the Proms. In addition to being an outstanding Chopin virtuoso, Pachmann was also something of a comedian. Before settling down to play, he put on a regular performance about the position of the piano, his suspicion of dust on the ivory keys, and arguments about the exact height of the piano stool. He had an invariable practice of talking as he played, but it was only at the Proms with an ambulatory audience at such close quarters that he was able to give his verbosity full rein. "Listen to this!" would precede some beautifully executed run, to be followed by, "Only Pachmann can do that!"

Back at the office, things became more lively when a merger took place between Chappell's and the American firm of Harms Inc.—a most unlikely partnership. Chappell's had originally been a family concern, one member of which had had the foresight to acquire the publishing and performing rights to

1901–1935

all of Puccini's works besides the operettas of Gilbert and Sullivan, amongst others. In my time, however, the Bond Street store was presided over by a rotund gentleman whose name, Bill Boosey, aptly described him. Without actually seeing him arrive on the premises, a strong aroma of perfume mingled with cigar smoke proclaimed his presence. He was the typical Edwardian in all respects—the carnation in his buttonhole, his enormous appetite for rich food and rare wines, and, of course, the resultant gout. His scorn of any kind of modernisation of business practices was responsible for the antiquated conditions under which we worked. He stoutly refused to recognise that the singing of ballads in English drawing rooms ("Come into the Garden, Maud" and "Seated One Day at the Organ") had to give way to the new American jazz. His stubbornness allowed competitive publishers to challenge Chappell's preeminence, forcing him in the end to agree to the merger with Harms Inc. From then on, Mr. Boosey was seen less and less at Bond Street and more and more at the racecourse.

To inject new life and, I suspect, new capital into Chappell's, one of the two Dreyfus brothers, owners of Harms Inc., arrived from New York. This was brother Louis. Brother Max had the musical judgement and Louis the uncanny business know-how. They were Jewish immigrants, half-Polish and half-German. Unlike Max, who became a cultured Connecticut squire, Louis never bothered to learn to speak English distinctly. His first introduction at Bond Street, his hat on the back of his head, caused a horrified reaction, but I found his breezy manner and curious accent a welcome change from the starched propriety of our surroundings. Possibly due to my interest in amateur dramatics, I had developed a keen ear for habits of speech. At any rate, I seemed to be the only member of the staff who could understand his slurred American utterance. As a result, Louis took a shine to me and I became not only his interpreter but also privy to his financial machinations. He had come from the States with his briefcase bulging with securities of various sorts, and it was my job to trot between banks and brokers as these assets were juggled in the most mysterious fashion. His manipulative skills were amazing. For instance, having been told the name of the best tailor in London, he had me take him to Kilgour, French and Stanbury on Dover Street, where he ordered a whole wardrobe for himself. In no time at all he had bought a share in the tailor's firm, presumably getting a healthy discount on his purchases. Many years later I had my own suits made by Kilgour—some of which I am wearing to this day—but the fact that I was one of their director's favourites didn't entitle me to a single penny off my bill.

Prompted by Louis, I was to introduce several of his friends and business associates to this sartorial establishment. These included the then up-and-coming composer George Gershwin, making his first visit to England. Someone might have had the decency to warn this shy young genius that white linen plus fours and a white golfing cap with a pompom on top would make him not a little conspicuous on Bond Street. But that's the way he first appeared at Chappell's, shortly to be hurried to the tailor with instructions to modify his sporty apparel. Jerome Kern was another great American composer to whom I was assigned. Unlike Gershwin, he was a seasoned traveller and a collector of rare books, a world that I hardly knew existed. When I heard the prices he was paying Quaritch's for these treasures, I was thankful that I had to carry them only a short block away to deposit them in Chappell's safe. These luminaries of the musical scene were the first Americans to come into my ken and I took an instant liking to them. It never occurred to me that one day, in 1941, I would become one of them by taking out naturalization papers for United States citizenship, thereby spending more than half my life in the land of the free.

3. FROM AMATEUR TO PROFESSIONAL

Each time that Louis Dreyfus returned to the States, the old drudgery of the office routine reasserted itself until, one day, a girlfriend of mine asked me to go to see her acting in an amateur production in which she was appearing at the St. Pancras Peoples' Theatre. Fearing I might not like her performance, I dreaded the experience. The theatre was located in a dreary tenement district, part of an institution called the Mary Ward Settlement. Not unlike a Salvation Army hostel, it provided recreation and food for the extremely poor populace of the neighborhood. Its most successful activity, as I was to find out later, was the amateur theatre group who put on a series of plays throughout the year, the price of admission being sixpence. Going backstage after a performance can be tricky, particularly if you have reservations about what you have been seeing. (Emlyn Williams has a crafty recipe for these awkward moments. He takes you by the hand, looks directly into your eyes, and makes the totally noncommittal comment, "What about your performance!" The conceited performer thanks him profusely for his praise, whilst the modest one gets the opposite and intended message.) Fortunately my girlfriend was very good in the play, so I did not have to resort to that kind of subterfuge.

It was she who persuaded me to join the St. Pancras Theatre group, and in doing so rescued me from my Bond Street doldrums and started me on a career which flourished with extraordinary rapidity. I no longer had to bemoan my lot, because at the end of my nine-to-six imprisonment at Chappell's I was busily rehearsing or playing in some play with my new friends, or attending classes in deportment and fencing. Our mentor and director was a sprightly lady named Maude Scott, and it was she who gave me the only lessons I was ever to receive in the art of acting. It was entirely due to her that I took the giant step from amateur to professional and my indebtedness to her is incalculable.

There have been many other helping hands throughout my career; in retrospect one realises how much one took for granted on the way up and that, sixty years later, one doesn't have the decency to remember their names. One such forgotten name fills me with shame. A fellow member of the theatre group, it was she who persuaded George Bishop, the second-string drama critic of the *News-Chronicle*, to visit our theatre in his official capacity. Next morning his review appeared under the headline, "Boy Cashier Makes Good."

It was the Lenten season, during which the deeply religious sponsor of the Settlement insisted that no secular plays be presented. Consequently, it was decided to stage a cycle of eighteen playlets by Laurence Housman (later to gain recognition as the author of *Victoria Regina*) portraying the life of St. Francis of Assisi. I had the good fortune to be cast as that adorable, whimsical Saint, the "Jongleur de Dieu" as he was affectionately known. The plays traced his life from his playboy days in Perugia to the miracle of the stigmata and his death, calling for a wide range of emotional acting on my part. The final episodes shifted from prose to blank verse, a change that nearly caused my downfall. To memorise the soaring cadences of Francis's metamorphosis, I found it necessary to utter them out loud. I couldn't very well do this in the family bathroom, so I would go striding about the Surrey hills, shouting my head off. Oblivious to my surroundings, I failed to notice the approach of a long line of men and women. They turned out to be the unfortunate inmates of a nearby mental hospital being given their morning exercise. It was only by a stroke of luck that one of the warders didn't have me join the line.

My preoccupation with the preparations for the St. Francis productions made inroads on my powers of concentration at the cashier's desk, resulting in my making elusive errors in my accounts. My brain became further befuddled when I received a note from a total stranger, signed "Terence Gray." He said he had seen me as St. Francis and wished to meet me to discuss a proposal connected with the theatre. I was ushered into the presence of a tall Irish gentlemen with a beautiful curly beard and a terrible stammer. Haltingly, he explained that he was restoring a charming Regency theatre at the seat of his alma mater, Cambridge University, and was in the process of recruiting a permanent company of actors. He wondered whether I would be interested in joining the company at what was to be called the Festival Theatre. I was bowled over by his salary offer, which was exactly what I was earning at Chappell's. The thought of being paid as much for doing something I liked as

FROM AMATEUR TO PROFESSIONAL

for doing something I hated was most appealing. I asked for time to think it over, having never in my wildest dreams thought of myself as a professional actor. It was left to my father to put a damper on my news, pointing out that whereas Chappell's salary was on a steady year-round basis, the Festival Theatre was to operate only during the university term.

Next morning I was again confronted with the horrible tangle of my accounts. Although not without misgivings, I decided to toss aside the ledgers and balance sheets to take my place in the theatrical sun. Because of his love of the theatre, Father was obviously torn, but felt it his paternal duty to warn me that I was not to look to him for support if things went wrong. I took up the challenge and vowed to myself that somehow or other I would contrive to be independent; a vow, I'm pleased to say, I was able to keep to the letter.

My employer, Mr. Gray, was a rich dilettante with forward-thinking notions, not all of them exactly practical. Although the restoration of the front of the house was impeccable, retaining as it did the characteristics of the original operetta theatre, the stage appurtenances were something else again. His design was ideal for the initial production but lacked flexibility for the realistic plays that were to follow. His innovations included a thrust stage, a permanent plaster sky-cyclorama onto which scenery and clouds could be projected, and a revolutionary lighting system by the German pioneers, Schwabe-Hasseit. These novelties caused a sensation on the opening night of our first production, the occasion being a presentation of the Aeschylean trilogy, *The Oresteia*, newly translated from the Greek by Professor G. M. Trevelyan. It was all very impressive: the atonality of the music, the severity of the scenery, and the masked actors. There was nothing realistic about the masks; on the contrary, they were impressionistic to a degree. Made of papier-mâché, their features were modelled in geometric planes. One had only to tilt one's head in varying directions for the masks to give the illusion of the emotions demanded by the text.

In order to achieve these effects, it was necessary to wear the masks at rehearsals, their fragility requiring us to treat them gently. Whereas the rest of us carefully removed our masks for the tea and coffee breaks, Miriam Lewis, who played Clytemnestra, stoutly insisted on keeping hers on, with the result that the hot liquids softened the papier-mâché. One could frequently catch her in the act of dabbing fiercely at Clytemnestra's oral orifice with a napkin until there was more and more of Miriam visible and less and less of Clytemnestra.

In Greek tragedy the movement of the chorus is always a hard nut to crack. They usually resemble a bunch of ubiquitous women who alternate between the behaviour of a flock of lost sheep and the frenzied movements of anxious females running to catch the last bus. In our production all this was changed, the services of a first-rate choreographer having been employed to design the actions of the chorus. This was the choreographic debut of the founder of today's Royal Ballet, Dame Ninette de Valois. The London drama critics attended the opening and were lavish in their praise, not only of Ninette's contribution but of the acting as well. This being my very first appearance as a "pro," it was surprising and gratifying to read in the *London Sketch* of December 1, 1926, this tidbit: "Mr. Maurice Evans was the Orestes. One day we will find that Mr. Evans has flown from Cambridge. Look to it that you see him before he becomes famous."

In this, my one and only season at the Festival Theatre, I played a wide variety of parts ranging from Maurice Maeterlinck's *Monna Vanna* to the original melodrama *Sweeney Todd, the Demon Barber of Fleet Street*. Most plays are associated with some mishap and the two just mentioned were no exception. In the former, wearing a jerkin with a lot of metal buttons on the sleeve, I had to play a passionate love scene with her ladyship whose hair (the actress's own) fell to below her waist. I broke away from a hot embrace only to find that a strand of madam's hair was inextricably wound round one of my buttons. Unaware that we were tied together in this umbilical fashion, she was mystified by my insistent proximity, which was not in the least what the scene called for. After several vain attempts to disentangle myself, I realised there was nothing for it but to resort to the ungallant action of yanking at the poor girl's tresses. It obviously hurt and for a moment I thought she was going to hit me or at least report me for being drunk and disorderly, but I managed to ad-lib an apology and to indicate the bits of hair still on my cuff. So all was well.

In *Sweeney Todd*, I played the Demon Barber's victim, Mark the Mariner, who is shot down a trapdoor to be converted into a meat pie in the adjoining cellar. One evening an overeager stagehand let the trapdoor go too abruptly, whereupon my barber's chair came off its moorings and the back of my skull made noisy contact with a brick wall. For a dazed moment I thought I had actually *become* that juicy pie filling.

Our repertoire included plays by George Bernard Shaw, Lady Gregory, and William Butler Yeats, not to mention an Egyptian drama by Terence Gray himself. This last epic, in which I played a prince who had married his sister, marked the only time I was prevented from taking a curtain call at the end of a performance, and for a rather curious reason. What the prince had done to deserve it, I don't recall—it can't have been punishment for marrying his sister, a custom that was all the rage in those days—but in the final scene of the play I had to be mummified alive, smothered with evil-smelling unguents and strapped to a board from head to toe with strips of linen wrappings. I was then carried out in solemn procession as the curtain began to descend. Immediately the curtain was down, the other actors lined up to take their bows, a courtesy that was denied me due to my immobilised condition as a mummy. My bearers propped me unceremoniously against the offstage wall where I was obliged to wait for someone to unwrap me—I had the odd sensation of being a parcel. I've often wondered what would have happened if a fire had broken out at that moment—a premature cremation, I fear.

Rehearsing one show all day and playing in another at night began to take its toll. A double bill of Shaw's *Androcles and the Lion* prefaced by a fey piece by W. B. Yeats entitled *On Bailie Strand* was seriously underrehearsed, particularly the Yeats one-acter. To our dismay, it was announced that both authors were to attend a matinee. When the day arrived our alarm reached fever pitch. Yeats, being almost blind and partially deaf, asked for the loan of a copy of his play so that, with the aid of a magnifying glass and a flashlight, he could follow the dialogue. Only Torin Thatcher, playing the lead, had memorised the text with any accuracy, the rest of us improvising our dialogue in a manner that must have puzzled the poet. We were rather relieved when he told us afterwards that this was the first performance of the play to his knowledge. That, added to the fact that it was full of obscure Celtic mysticism, allowed us to speculate that he was probably as confused as we were, begorrah!

The company was in better shape for the Shaw play, which was just as well, because G.B.S. came onstage after the audience had departed to demonstate the action he had in mind when the lion chases Caesar. Incongruously dressed in his customary Norfolk jacket and knickerbockers, and carrying his years like a youngster, he leapt about the stage in the character of Caesar, mounting steps and jumping from one level to another, all the while shouting to the actor playing the lion, "Get hold of my toga!" It's fortunate that Shaw wasn't in the Hollywood studio when, many years later, the motion picture of *Androcles* was being made—with me as Caesar. In this same scene I was doubled by an animal trainer, and the toothless old MGM lion, Jocko, was replaced by a beast straight from the circus. All the camera crews were safely ensconced within wire cages, and on the word "Action" the doors of the royal box were supposed to burst open to reveal a terrified Caesar being chased by the lion down the steps. Instead of which the circus lion got in first, so that one had the ridiculous sight of Caesar chasing the lion. "Retake, please!"

4. THE WEST END

It was a very difficult and more daunting flight of steps that confronted me at term's end at Cambridge. I found myself on the very bottom rung of the thespian ladder with no prospect of mounting any further. Then, as so often happened later in my career, a ministering angel came to my rescue. Though only a minor actress in the company, Peggy Calthrop was nevertheless well known in London theatrical circles, and it was she—bless her heart—who urged me to strike out for the big time in the West End.

A letter of introduction to Peggy's friend Owen Nares (the reigning matinee idol of the day) started me on my way. He in turn gave me a note to a producer named Leon M. Lion, who had just taken a lease of Wyndham's Theatre where he planned to put on a series of plays. He had recently concluded a long run in a pseudo-oriental drama for which his diminutive stature suited the part. It proved a handicap, however, when it came to casting himself as the leading man of his own company at Wyndham's, so he wisely restricted himself to parts that suited his inches. In addition he planned to direct the plays as well as cope with the managerial chores. He had hoped to form a permanent repertory company, but this got no further than putting four actors under long-term contracts, all the others being hired for each individual production. This was where my luck and Owen Nares's recommendation came in, for I was engaged as one of the four permanent members. The others were a character man, Frank Lloyd; an ingenue, Maisie Darrell; and a comedian who lived up to his unusual name of Archibald Batty.

My contract, postdated to whenever Mr. Lion would be ready to start his season, was to spread over a period of three years with options on the management's side to renew or cancel at will. It also conferred on the management the right to lease out my services to other employers, half of my salary for such engagements to go to Mr. Lion! In the meantime, my stipend was to be 2 pounds, 10 shillings per week for the first year; 5 pounds for the second; and 8 pounds for the third. I had burnt my bridges as far as Cambridge was concerned and here I was in London with no specific date for the commencement of my new job. After a lot of scurrying around, I finally auditioned for and secured an engagement in a comedy-mystery called, *The One-eyed Herring*, written, for reasons best known to him, by Lt. Col. Sir Frank Popham-Young, Knight Commander of the Bath. In this short-lived offering, which the London *Times* described as "a medley of ghosts and electric torches, pistols and prussic acid," I understudied nine roles and played a one-line part as a London bobby, P. C. Andrews. Appearing at the landing atop the stairs, I had to say, "Mr. Belton, sir, there's something up here I think you ought to see." Needless to say, there was no mention in the press of this, my West End debut, on August 25, 1927.

Finally Leon M. Lion had marshalled his forces and was ready to go with a political mystery melodrama, *Listeners*, in which he was to star, as well as to direct and produce it. At long last I was on the payroll only to find myself relegated to the understudy stable once more, besides playing a bit part. It was assumed that should Mr. Lion ever be prevented from appearing due to illness, the play would be suspended until he recovered. Thus there would never be any question of his understudy substituting for him. At rehearsals I noticed he was making no effort to memorise his lines, and that directing his fellow actors was his main concern. I knew the day would come shortly when he would want to sit "out front" to observe his handiwork. Something told me that no man could function in the triple capacity he had undertaken, so I had subtly asked to be allowed to understudy his part. By dint of hard work and the burning of much midnight oil, I succeeded in becoming letter-perfect in his role. I don't think Mr. Lion was aware of my existence, but came that fateful day when he saw me playing his part quite creditably without a script in my hands—and it was obvious that I was no longer to be ignored.

By dress-rehearsal time, the poor man was still floundering around in a morass of unlearned lines. I learned afterwards that, unknown to Mr. Lion, the author had, in a moment of panic, suggested that I replace the star on the opening night. Fortunately this idea was promptly vetoed, otherwise my sojourn in what we had named "The Lion's Den" would surely have been summarily terminated. Somewhat sobered by the tepid reception given by the press to *Listeners*, Mr. Lion closed the play and went into retreat to consider what his next vehicle should be.

In the meantime, and without his assistance, a slight comedy of reclaimed love, *The Stranger in the House*, was put on to fill the gap. The star in this production was Sybil Thorndike, that very fine actress and wonderful person whom I had long worshipped from the peanut gallery. It was a great thrill to work in the same play with her, and to learn from her that modesty about oneself and consideration for one's fellow players were the key to integrity in one's own work. Sybil was mostly identified with Shakespearean heroines, so it was fascinating and extremely edifying to see how smoothly she was able to make the transition from, say, Lady Macbeth, to the gentle realism of our domestic play. In praising her performance, the London *Times* (April 5, 1928) had the generosity to end its review with this heartwarming bouquet: "Miss Maisie Darrell, Mr. Wallace Geoffrey, and Mr. Maurice Evans likewise did very well what their parts plainly required of them."

Presumably Maisie Darrell and I were being paid identical salaries, and thereby we discovered that a meager 2.5 pounds a week made life a pretty tight squeeze, even though we each continued to live with our respective parents. We took it in turns to pay for our dinners at the Express Dairy. Because it was cheap and filling, our order was invariably the same: two poached eggs on baked beans and a glass of milk. I don't think we could have lasted the first year out on that kind of diet had it not been for the Arts Theatre Club, to which we each belonged. It consisted of a small tryout theatre, a big lounge-bar, and a spacious restaurant on the top floor. Most of the actors working in the West End would congregate there to talk shop and eat, if one could afford it.

It was here that Maisie and I met our saviour. He was a Mr. Mower, the chief representative in England for Electrolux. That a possible empathy existed between the theatre and vacuum cleaners it was hard to imagine, but, fortunately for us, Mr. Mower was rich and hopelessly stagestruck. He delighted in nothing more than to take a big table in the club's dining room and invite anyone who looked like an actor to join his repast. I think the first time I met Laurence Olivier was when we gorged ourselves side by side at this table. I'm afraid we all took shameless advantage of the old man's generosity, but he didn't seem to mind, and we were always hungry.

It was during the run of the Sybil Thorndike play that I had to school myself in the discipline of the lesson hardest for actors to learn, that of disguising the boredom caused by repeating the same words and actions eight times a week, including two matinees. One had constantly to remind oneself that no two audiences were alike (the difference between them often being distinguishable only by the levels of their coughing); still, they had paid their money and were entitled to one's best. The old saying "The play must go on" is no cliché. No matter what personal problems one has—family bereavement, a reluctant girlfriend, or even just a bad head cold—the actor is obliged to grit his teeth and get on with the job.

I was to find, also, that the most effective medicine against boredom was to keep busy with some activity connected with the theatre; and this was where another of my unsung helpers came to the fore: Mrs. Green, Mr. Lion's personal secretary. On some pretext or other I would invade her office about the time I knew she would be having her "elevenses" (coffee break) before the boss showed up. In a corner of her room I espied a pile of play manuscripts one day, many of them in unopened envelopes. In answer to my enquiry, Mrs. Green said that they had been lying neglected in Mr. Lion's office for ages. It seemed that when Mr. Lion announced his plans for his tenancy of Wyndham's Theatre, every budding playwright in the country started submitting scripts for his consideration. How they were ever to get read was, in Mrs. Green's opinion, a mystery. To which this eager beaver answered, "How about letting me make a start on them, writing a short précis for Mr. Lion's information?" "Help yourself," said Mrs. Green, "and good luck!"

Little did I know what I was letting myself in for; almost all the plays were amateurish disasters, but had to be ploughed through willy-nilly. Most of this laborious reading I did on the train to and from our Surrey home. One day, deep in the pages of a particularly hopeless manuscript, who should enter the

THE WEST END

train compartment but Mrs. Green herself. Unknown to either of us, we were practically neighbours in Coulsdon.

From then on Mrs. Green was my ally, seeing to it that Mr. Lion took notice of my labours and of their source. Now I was persona grata and almost the confidant of the man of whom I had stood in awe. I'm not sure whether it was his original thought or an old maxim, but he cautioned me that in judging a play the acid test was to ask oneself, does it have conflict? "There is no drama without conflict" was his summing up. Yes, I thought, and not only in drama—for the basis of comedy, too, is conflict. All the best jokes are at the expense of someone else's discomfiture.

I seem to have been more critical regarding Mr. Lion than I intended in what I have written in these pages. As I got to know him better, I found that, under the posturing, there was a sensitive likable man. Why the posturing? It was no longer fashionable for actors to take pride in being looked upon as "rogues and vagabonds." Instead they aspired to membership of the Garrick Club and to be assigned a special table at the Ivy Restaurant—the "in" establishment for the theatrical mighty. On occasion at the Ivy an excess of wine would accompany luncheon, to the detriment of the afternoon's rehearsal. Although Lion indulged to some extent in these class-distinctive habits, beneath it he was a simple soul. This quality in his nature had been discovered by no less than the famous author-playwright John Galsworthy.

To redeem himself from the unfortunate start of his Wyndham's venture, Mr. Lion decided to revive two of Galsworthy's plays—*Justice* and *Loyalties*. In the former, he played Falder, the pathetic figure of a man imprisoned due to a miscarriage of justice. The revival suffered from the fact that the original production had aroused such public indignation that many of the most flagrant injustices had been corrected by changes in the laws. Thus Falder's predicament was no longer as heartrending, and Lion, or any other actor, had difficulty in winning the full sympathy of his audience. I, on the other hand, was cast in one of those legendary actor-proof parts, the counsel for the defence. It is very hard to fail in a courtroom drama, particularly if you are defending a wronged party, and apparently I was no exception to the rule. E. A. Baughan, the respected critic of the *News-Chronicle*, had this to say about me: "Mr. Maurice Evans, an actor unknown to me, made an emphatic success as the counsel for the defence. He will bear watching." What Mr. Baughan also didn't know was that many years earlier, as the young drama critic who used to come to Dorchester to review my father's adaptations of Thomas Hardy, he may even have been present on the occasion of my first appearance on any stage.

To play in *Justice* at night and to star in and direct *Loyalties* by day was too much even for Mr. Lion's ego, so he had the good luck to persuade Basil Dean, the director of the original production, to direct our revival. Dean was a terror to work for, using sarcasm as his favourite instrument of torture. He was reputed to detest actors as a whole and some in particular, regarding us as nothing more than pawns. Of course he had to modify his abusive manner when addressing Mr. Lion, but he made up for that by taking it out on the rest of the cast. On the whole, Lion was at home in the part of the Jewish outsider striving to be accepted in snobbish English society, although again his lack of stature told against him. For the rest of the case he spared no expense in rounding up a distinguished aggregation of actors whom Basil Dean proceeded, metaphorically, to strip naked. I shall never forget his cruel treatment of a dear character actress, Miss Mary Jerrold. She had been told where to sit for the scene in the first act; plumping herself down in the chair indicated, she promptly produced from her handbag her knitting.

"Put it away, Mary," ordered Dean in his ugly nasal drawl.

"Put what away?" said Mary.

"That stuff in your lap," he replied.

"You mean my knitting?"

"That's right, put it away."

"But, Basil, you know I *always* knit in a play."

"Not in this one you don't!"

Not that he had to be so blunt, but Dean knew exactly what he was up to. By stripping actors of their mannerisms and stale tricks, he produced a freshness of approach to their characterisations, which was beneficial to the play and to the actors themselves. I found it fascinating and instructive to see actors, who had previously relied solely on flaunting their personalities, suddenly actually getting into the skin of the Galsworthy characters. It was a lesson that I tried to apply to my own work from then on.

In *Loyalties* I played two minute parts, those of Augustus Borring and of Edward Graviter; but small as they were, I was not to escape Dean's envenomed tongue. He had shown no mercy to each and every other member of the cast, but had said nary a word to me. I bore his silence uneasily until we reached the dress rehearsal, at which time I stupidly put my head on the block.

"Was I all right, Mr. Dean?"

From him came a withering, "Yes. But don't *act*, Evans, this isn't a spy play."

Another lesson I was to learn was to beware of selfish performers. In the almost invisible part of Graviter there was one opportunity for a laugh, if I got my timing right, but the other actor in the scene considered all laughs to be his sole prerogative. I couldn't understand why I was losing the laugh until I noticed that, just as I was about to say my line, the other actor was producing a white handkerchief from his breast pocket with a great flourish. I foxed him

THE WEST END

finally by varying the timing so that he was never quite sure when to display his linen.

At the end of the run of the Galsworthy plays, Mr. Lion was informed by the French government that if he could arrange to bring them to one of the state theatres he would be awarded the Légion d'honneur. The wearing of that bit of red ribbon in his buttonhole was irresistible to Mr. Lion, so we were told that we would appear briefly in both plays in Paris at Théâtre de l'Odéon. The company duly assembled at Victoria Station to embark on the London-to-Paris boat-train. To our surprise, who should be on the platform but the fabulous Mr. Mower. How dear of him to come to see us off, we thought. He seemed to be overdoing it a bit when he entered the train to wish us Godspeed. The departure whistle blew, but Mr. Mower stayed where he was. It was only then that we realised the old boy had decided to come with us to play host to us during our visit to Paris. And what a host he proved himself to be! Night after night, at the end of the performance, either a chartered bus or a fleet of limousines would be at the stage door ready to whisk us off to some choice restaurant for a delicious supper.

Théâtre de l'Odéon was our first experience of a nationalised theatrical institution, and not a very happy experience at that. The management was supposed to have reproduced the scenic designs of the London productions of *Justice* and *Loyalties*, but, what with the confusion between British feet and inches and the French metric system, they got it all wrong. Basil Dean nearly had a fit when he saw the French idea of an English drawing room. Not only the decor, but the doors and windows were in quite the wrong positions. Frantic efforts were made to sort all this out when everything came to a dead stop. Very solemnly a brigade of firemen, their brass helmets glistening in the stage lights, proceeded to go through their noontime drill on the stage. "For God's sake," said Dean, "they've sent us the whole bloody French army!" The firemen, having gone through the ceremony with their hoses and axes, finally retired.

"All right," Dean bellowed, "let's get on with it." Dead silence. "Now what's up?"

"Sorry sir," from the stage manager, "The stagehands have all gone to lunch."

There were fewer errors in the sets for *Justice*, which received a favourable press. I treasure the only "notice" in a foreign language that has ever come my way. Referring to my performance as counsel for the defence, *Paris Soir* said I was "plein de chaleur." I don't know about my acting being "full of fire," but I certainly *do* know my head was full of the stuff after the closing-night party. I was led astray by my elders, who took me to a nightclub where the rage of Paris, Josephine Baker, was appearing. They plied me with what must have been gallons of that sickly sweet champagne so dear to the French palate, an indulgence that I was to regret next morning. Where we went after the Josephine Baker show is a veiled memory, but I have a distinct recollection of sitting on top of a taxicab singing on the Champs Elysées. I'm told, too, that as the dawn broke I was discovered sleeping peacefully under a tree in the Bois de Boulogne, being rescued only just in time to gather up my belongings at our hotel and catch the boat-train from Paris to London. Needless to add, the Channel crossing was something too distressing to be recalled here.

Back in London, Mr. Lion decided to rest on his laurels for the time being. To keep Wyndham's active, he had the bright idea of mounting a production of William Congreve's *The Way of the World* starring Edith Evans. She had already been seen as Mrs. Millamant in this Restoration comedy at the relatively remote Lyric Theatre at Hammersmith Broadway, for a limited run. Now her dazzling performance was to delight audiences in the West End and make theatrical history.

Up to this point in her career, Edith had been associated in the public mind mainly with rather drab characters. The role of Millamant required her to be the most glamorous, the most provoking, teasing, witty character that Congreve ever created. Edith had all these qualities to perfection and some to spare. It was all the more amazing because she, in person, was far from being any of these things. In fact, to us youngsters, she was a forbidding, unapproachable individual, so we made no attempt to get to know her.

In the company of my fellow understudy Peggy Ashcroft, I would go "out front" night after night to watch the miraculous transformation that Edith achieved upon her first entrance. Her cue was given by her would-be lover on stage: "Here she comes, I'faith, full sail, with her fan spread and her streamers out, and a shoal of fools for tenders." At this point, on sailed the most beautiful creature one had ever set eyes upon. The audience gasped, and no matter how many times we watched her entrance, Peggy and I gasped right along with them. We would ask each other, "How *does* she do it?" The nearest we could guess at an answer was that her mumblings in the wings prior to her entrance were reaffirmation of her Christian Science belief that perfection is within the reach of us all.

One passage in the Congreve play stays indelibly in my memory as an example of Edith's captivating way with words. In a voice running up and down the scale from soprano to contralto, and each syllable fairly oozing hauteur and impudence, she answers an enquiry about letters from Mirabell, saying: "O, ay, letters—I had letters—I am persecuted with letters—I hate letters—Nobody knows how to write letters, and yet one has 'em, one does not know why. They serve one to pin up one's hair."

Beyond renting out his theatre to the producers of *The Way of the World*,

THE WEST END

Mr. Lion had nothing to do with the production. Consequently, it was only a fluke that I was allowed even to understudy in the importation. It seemed an awful letdown at the time, but I tried to console myself with the fact that I was being given the opportunity of observing a group of experts displaying their techniques in a style of period acting of which I had no previous knowledge—the lace cuffs, the snuffboxes, the affected patterns of speech, and so forth. Another advantage of being reduced to understudy status was that it gave me plenty of free time; amongst other things, time to question whether Mr. Lion was going to be able to hold out much longer with his Wyndham's venture, or incidentally, with my contract.

We young actors were fortunate in those days not to be burdened, as the modern young actor is, with the misguided paternalism of a trade union ostensibly protecting one from being "exploited." We gladly subscribed to one of several Sunday-night tryout organisations, the Stage Society or the Repertory Players for example, in order to be on their roster of actors more than willing to work without payment, thereby to be "exploited" in one of the tryouts. There was no guarantee that one would be retained in the cast should some manager decide to buy the play, but we were quite content to take our chances. Many young playwrights owed their start to these showcase Sunday nights, and many an actor, too.

The Arts Theatre Club also fell into this category and it was in its little world, in October 1928, that, as some magazine of the day wrote, I "first burst upon the London public" in a neglected play by John Van Druten entitled *Diversion*. It was transferred later to the Little Theatre in the Adelphi, an opening night not to be forgotten. Serving one's apprenticeship in the English theatre is not an overnight task, and the press is hesitant to go all-out and say one has "arrived." In the case of my impersonation of the ill-starred lover in *Diversion*, the approval of the critics was unanimous, but nearly all of them left my artistic future to further proof. For instance: "Mr. Maurice Evans put the agonies of frustrated passion on the plane of tragedy. The capacity of this young man for emotional acting is quite remarkable. *He is an artist who should be watched.*"

Perhaps the English critics have the right idea. In America, I think, we are too free with laurel crowns. It must be terribly embarrassing for a budding author, on the strength of a single work, to be hailed as the writer, the poet, the dramatist of the century. Anything more calculated to smother creativity is hard to imagine. The same is true of actors—we need room to make our mistakes, and a keen ear for mere flattery in our successes.

I think I managed to keep a level head when I had to start receiving visitors in my dressing room, most of them admiring strangers who took it for granted that I would know who they were. This is where dear Cathleen Nesbitt came to my rescue. She was my vis-à-vis in *Diversion*, the femme fatale, and the cause of my attempted suicide as the young lover. Offstage she was always a darling. After the visitors had left, I would knock on her dressing-room door and ask her to identify the departing figures.

"Who was that rather gushy man?"

"Oh, that's Sir George Arthur, who was aide-de-camp to Lord Kitchener of Khartoum. He collects celebrities as others do precious stones, so you can now consider yourself his latest find. He will see to it that you meet all the *right* people—you poor boy!"

And he did with a vengeance. He and Lady Arthur, who was lady-in-waiting to Queen Mary, lived in the Boltons in Kensington, in a house which, I believe, was occupied in later years by Douglas Fairbanks, Jr. I would find myself at one of their dinner parties seated between Gladys Cooper and the Bishop of London; and on one occasion, playing charades after dinner in the drawing room with Princess Alice, the Countess of Athlone. We were required to depict a couple enduring a Channel crossing in a rough sea. I doubt whether Queen Victoria would have been amused to see her granddaughter acting out the scene with great verve. At one point, she thrust a wastepaper basket into my hand, saying, "Do you need the bucket?"

The Arthurs also introduced me to less affluent royalty in the person of a cousin by marriage of Queen Mary, Lady Dorothy, the Marchioness of Cambridge. We became good friends and I had an open invitation to drop in for tea at any time. On one of my visits, I discovered Dorothy sitting on the floor of her drawing room sorting out a pile of rather hideous clothing. She explained that the garments had just been sent over from Buckingham Palace for her to take her pick and pass on the rest. They were from the clothing exhibits at the recent British Industries Fair and had been presented to the Queen. Amongst them were several peignoirs, which the manufacturers obviously had thought suitable for Her Majesty; the front of the robes were securely fastened together at the bottom hem so that there was no possibility of the royal ankles being exposed to view.

From time to time Queen Mary would invite herself to tea at the Cambridges, sometimes at very short notice. The children had to be spruced up in a hurry and Lord Frederick summoned home from the Coutts Bank where he worked. Another routine duty for Dorothy was to hide all her best porcelain objects. The Queen was an avid collector of porcelain, and was wont to cast envious glances at other people's private collections. It was not unknown for her to hint what a pity it was that some little ornament amongst their treasures was almost certainly one of a pair, its fellow being in her own possession. Unless precautions were taken, the owner had no option but to become a secretly unwilling donor. It shouldn't be concluded that all Her

THE WEST END

Majesty's acquisitions were obtained in this manner. Far from it. She was a frequent customer of numerous little antique shops tucked away in unlikely towns and villages, and on those occasions her equerry paid hard cash on the spot. She could hardly go in person to bid for items at Christie's or Sotheby's, but there was one oriental emporium on Bond Street that she couldn't resist. A few years earlier, from my perch at Chappell's, it was not unusual for me to see the royal Daimler pull up outside the very expensive shop, Yamanaka. Often she would leave the establishment empty-handed, presumably having failed to strike a bargain!

I'm not sure that Lord Frederick altogether approved of my visits or those of another chum of his wife's. He was the Prince of Wales's personal pilot, and his Royal Flying Corps peaked cap and my fedora would be hanging side by side on the hat rack, catching the eye of his lordship as he came home from the bank. In a caustic moment, he once said to Dorothy, "How would you feel if you came home one day to find me closeted with that aviatrix, the Duchess of Bedford, and Miss Tarrara Bunkhead?"

Flattering as were the attentions of these exalted people, I began to miss the company of my theatre buddies. It is a common failing of actors to prefer to associate almost exclusively with members of the theatrical profession, talking interminable "shop." My dressing-room visitors were preponderantly "pros," their approbation meaning much more to me than the compliments of the general public. I could hardly believe my eyes one night when the door opened and who should walk into my room but the absolute idol of every actor in the business, Sir Gerald du Maurier. We, his worshippers, would scrape up the money to go watch his acting in plays with Gladys Cooper at the Playhouse Theatre. His technique was utterly marvellous and indeed unique. Try as one might to analyse the secret of his method, one came away none the wiser. No pin-up beauty—he had something of the Jason Robards look about him—he nevertheless exuded personality and sex appeal to an extraordinary degree, and yet it was done with complete ease and believability. His individual trademark as an actor was his way of treating the opposite sex. Whereas any other actor playing a love scene would caress his inamorata incessantly, du Maurier made love at arm's length. This physical stand-offishness kept women in his audiences in agonies of suspense.

Du Maurier's instincts as an actor were matched by his expertise as a director. Gladys Cooper told me of the unexpected turn that his dissatisfaction with a scene they had to play together took at one performance. The script called for them to be lolling about on a bed, indulging in idle chatter. Without warning, departing completely from the author's lines, he barked at Gladys, "How many brothers have you got?" Under her breath, she murmured, "Gerald!" He repeated, "You heard me, how many brothers have you got?"

Stunned, Gladys ad-libbed, "Ahh . . . two." "All right," said du Maurier, "This is for both of them," and he slapped her vigorously on the side of her face. Gladys had a sore jaw for a week, but the scene had come to life; a modified version of the slapping business was retained and the ailing box office was besieged.

The Cooper-du Maurier partnership was a happy one, though most of the plays they did together were of little consequence. However, Sir Gerald was an inveterate practical joker and this was apt to cast a shadow on their relationship from time to time. Not realising it was April the First, I went to a matinee of one of their shows in which a friend of mine, Derek Williams, was playing the juvenile. He was the first to appear when the curtain rose, ushered in by the butler, who was given the time-worn line, "I'll tell her Ladyship you are here, sir." Derek ambled over to an armchair, picking up a newspaper en route. As he opened the newspaper, a clockwork butterfly flew out—Sir Gerald's without doubt! Then Gladys entered, resplendent and elegantly gowned. Applause! The script called for her to move to the sofa and to sink gracefully into it. Not on April the First, however! Sir Gerald, in league with the property man, had removed all the springs from the sofa with the result that Gladys's bottom hit the floor with a resounding thump while her knees went up to her chin.

Practical joker or not, to me it was a god who had walked into my dressing room unannounced that night. Actors of his eminence were not in the habit of making backstage visits, especially to meet young novices. Even less likely were they to say, as Sir Gerald did to me, "Who the hell taught you to stand still and listen as you did tonight?" I was struck dumb. Could it be that my idol was confessing that he had actually had difficulty in learning this precept? It had never occurred to me to do anything else *but* to stand still and listen until it came my turn to speak. But it was thanks to Sir Gerald that I was made conscious of the habit, and, I hope, continued thereafter to obey the dictum.

The du Maurier imperturbability on stage was the envy of all us young actors, so I found it unbelievable when Gladys let me in on a closely guarded secret about him. She said he had always been self-conscious about his hands, never quite knowing what to do with them. Plunging them into his trouser pockets was not the solution, since it contradicted the suave demeanour; so, for his stage clothing, he had his tailor make jackets for him with deep outside pockets where the awkward hands could take refuge unseen. Even the mighty have their weaknesses. Gladys herself was certainly no exception. In her managerial capacity at the Playhouse, she was energetic and well organised, but as an actress she took a most casual view about learning her lines, taking the optimistic attitude that everything would be "all right on the night." All right for her, perhaps, but not for the nerves of her fellow players.

THE WEST END

Later, during her Hollywood days, Gladys developed an airy lack of concern about her career. A telephone call came one day in London—a prominent West End manager wanting to know whether she would be available for a play he was proposing to produce that December, and might he send her the script for her consideration. "Oh, that isn't necessary," said Gladys. "I'd love to be with the children at Christmas anyway." She had rather the same blithe disregard to speed limits and so forth. She thought nothing of driving her open sports car to and fro between New York and Los Angeles, with or without a valid licence. She regarded it as a personal insult when, on arriving in California on one occasion, a traffic cop pointed out that her operator's licence had long since expired and that before a new one could be issued she would have to take a driving test. She protested that she had been driving automobiles practically since they were invented, and that for her to have to be subjected to a test was utter nonsense. The long-suffering cop politely handed her a copy of the California Highway Code, advising her to study it. Memorisation not being her strong suit, she ignored the cop's advice and when she went for her test, failed it ignominiously. She did no better on her second try, but scraped through somehow on the third.

To be a passenger in Gladys's car was a hair-raising experience because she never seemed to look at the road. A friend of hers relates that as Gladys drove her into the driveway of her Pacific Palisades home, she was so busy talking that she forgot to apply the brakes as they approached the garage. Fortunately the building was of flimsy construction, since they ploughed right through the rear wall with Gladys still talking. It always amazed me that this woman, who was the epitome of feminine beauty, had so much of the tomboy in her, and yet when there was need for money to prop up her theatre, she didn't hesitate to make capital out of her reputation as England's most glamorous daughter. She allowed her name to be used as the brand name of a line of cosmetics—face creams, lipsticks, and so on. The monologuist Elizabeth Pollock used to include in her program a funny imitation of Gladys supposedly giving a sales talk about her miraculous salves and lotions. The spiel ran—"I wake up in the morning—I look in the mirror—and I say to myself—Gladys, WHY?" On more occasions than I care to remember, these words have come to mind when I looked in my dressing-room mirror to face the task of repairing the ravages of the night before.

To descend from the heights to which the du Mauriers, the Coopers, and their kind had already reached and to which I most humbly aspired, the problem uppermost in my mind was "Where does one go from here?" In my case, "here" was my dressing room at the Little Theatre, and further than that I espied no future. Since the aforementioned Leon M. Lion was walking off with half of my salary, money was a worry, too. It was small comfort when an elderly woman, who was attending our matinee, sent back her card asking that she might visit. Her name, Florence Waters, meant nothing to me, not even when she explained that she was a second cousin of my father. In some strange genealogical fashion this meant that I was distantly related through her to her equally distant relative Eva Turner. "Cousin" Florence had discovered Eva, then a Lancashire millhand, when she was auditioning in a radio competition. Tracing their relationship, Florence undertook to sponsor the training and career of the great mezzo-soprano Eva Turner, the most famous Turandot of her day. It was good to learn that there was at least one other struggling artist in the family, but Florence seemed convinced that I had already "arrived." I bade her good-bye and promised to visit her in the country as soon as the play closed.

The words were no sooner out of my mouth than the newsboys were tearing down the Strand hollering, "The King is ill! Read all about it." George V was seriously ill with double pneumonia, causing fears for his life. Crowds gathered outside Buckingham Palace to read the doctor's bulletins, and the crowds that normally would be going to the theatre simply evaporated. Although the King finally recovered, the hiatus at the Little Theatre box office dealt us a deathblow, causing the closing of *Diversion*.

I learnt afterwards of a funny incident connected with George V's illness. In his youth he had been a midshipman in the British navy and emulating that other seafaring man, Long John Silver, he had acquired a talkative parrot on one of his tours of duty. My Buckingham Palace informant—as the columnists say—told me that the King insisted on having the bird in his bedroom at all times, even during the period of his illness. Lord Horder, the royal physician, was emphatic in his disapproval of the parrot in the sick-room, and it was only with great difficulty that he obtained the King's grudging consent that the bird be removed forthwith. His royal patient made it a condition, however, that it was to be temporarily lodged in Queen Mary's boudoir. The cage was duly transferred, as ordered, but without the Queen's knowledge. The change of surroundings was not at all to the parrot's liking. He became totally disoriented, dreaming that he was once more in the wardroom of H.M.S. *Invincible*, having his vocabulary enlarged by some joker to include a plethora of four-letter words not to be found in the dictionary. Queen Mary, entering her boudoir, took the cover off the cage, only to be greeted with a stream of colourful abuse mainly directed at the world's female population. My informant was unable to tell me how the story ended, but it's fun to speculate.

At the onset of a national crisis, the theatre is often the first to suffer. The illness of a head of state is usually accompanied by a falling-off of business at the box office. This was true at the time of the King's illness, and the coup de grace was administered to a number of plays that were nearing the end of their

THE WEST END

runs anyway. Another factor, peculiar to the English theatre, contributed to their demise, that being the annual invasion of the Christmas Pantomime. These extraordinary extravaganzas were, and to a lesser extent still are, the staple diet during the festive season. Many a family of children are given their first taste of the theatre by attending one of these travesties of "Cinderella," "Jack and the Beanstalk," or "Puss in Boots." "Puss in Boots" was my own introduction to a West End theatre. We stood for hours in a long queue outside the Lyceum Theatre in the freezing cold waiting to be admitted to the pit or gallery, but once inside it was all enchantment. In Christmas Pantomime it is the inescapable convention that the hero—known as the Principal Boy—be played by a girl, who usually indulges in a lot of slapping of her ample thighs. I don't know what Sigmund Freud would have made of it, but I invariably fell madly in love with the reigning transvestite, in spite of the awful rhymed couplets which the he-she was given to utter. For example, at the finale of "Puss in Boots" my charmer was required to walk to the footlights and say to us:

> We thank you all for your laughter and your hoots,
> And hope you'll come-again-soon to see Puss in Boots.

Having been dispossessed of our theatres by these "Pantos," quite a lot of us found ourselves out of work. It was in circumstances such as these that our Sunday-night tryout organisations came to our rescue. The Stage Society announced that they were planning a two-performance tryout of a play about the Great War entitled *Journey's End*, to be directed by James Whale. The author, R. C. Sherriff, an insurance salesman who had experienced life in the trenches, was making his first stab at playwrighting. His script was overwritten and too sentimental; in addition, this was now 1928, ten years after the war's end. Managements to whom it had been submitted were of the opinion that audiences were unlikely to have any appetite for an all-male war play, so the script was returned with polite rejection slips. We out-of-work actors, however, had nothing to lose by giving it a try, and it so happened that a group of us who were suited to the parts were fortuitously "resting" at the time. It became obvious at the play's first reading that an ideal cast had been assembled by sheer chance.

It only remained for the script to be given the blue-pencil treatment—pretty ruthless cutting in which I took a hand—and the rehearsals got under way. It was at the Apollo Theatre on Shaftesbury Avenue on the night of Sunday, December 9, and a matinee the next day, that *Journey's End* was to receive its two tryout performances. In rehearsal the actors, under James Whale's meticulous direction, had fused into an enthusiastic team. Laurence Olivier, George Zucco, Melville Cooper, Alexander Fields, Robert Speight,

1 9 0 1 – 1 9 3 5

H. G. Stoker, and I were united in our belief in the play, and we had visions of managers vying with each other for the opportunity to put it on for a regular West End run.

Alas, our convictions were not confirmed by the review in the *Times* (London) of December 11, which made the captious comment that whereas the acting could not be faulted, the play itself was "a patch and not a core of life." The critic's confused summary appeared to suggest that this shortcoming, though forgivable at the moment, would militate against any substantial future for the work. A few managers who had already rejected the script came to the opening, presumably to confirm their skepticism, and seeing the performance did nothing to make them change their minds. Normally, at the end of a play's run, there is a closing-night party to which the actors hie themselves. Not so in our case, however. We just stood around on the stage, a forlorn cast of actors, watching the stagehands tear down our scenery—"A Dugout Somewhere in France"—to be hauled off to some warehouse, never, we thought, to be seen again.

Among the skeptics who attended our second and final performance was my past mentor and critic, Basil Dean. He came backstage with two playscripts, one for Larry Olivier and one for me. The purpose of his mission was to forestall any ideas we might have been harbouring about sticking with *Journey's End* should a transfer be in the offing. Dean's impressive talents had been so far restricted by the limitations of the small St. Martin's Theatre. Now he was about to spread his wings by mounting an elaborate production of *Beau Geste* at His Majesty's, and wanted Larry to play Beau and me his brother. Whether it was because I was being asked to play second fiddle or, rather, that my experience of play-reading in the Lion office had sharpened my judgement, I'm not sure. Anyway, I still had faith in a future for *Journey's End* and thought *Beau Geste* a clumsy hotch-potch, so I said, "No, thank you" to Mr. Dean. Larry felt differently about it and went off to the greener pastures of the Foreign Legion. The play was poorly received, but Larry made a resounding success in it and remained with Dean thereafter for a number of other productions.

My contract with Mr. Lion was still in force though Wyndham's was dark and he had nothing for me to do. The inactivity finally prompted me to take matters into my own hands. I rounded up the remaining members of the *Journey's End* tryout cast and volunteered to put up 100 pounds towards capitalising the transfer of the show if they would do likewise. The response was unanimous, though how we were going to raise the rest of the money was anybody's guess. I then had the impudence to go to Mr. Lion to ask if he would consider renting Wyndham's to us for a short term in order that we might test the drawing power of the piece with the general public. To my delight he said Yes, but added that we would have to hurry up about it and meet certain

THE WEST END

guarantees. However, no one had ever heard of a dozen or so actors going into business for themselves, so our attempts to raise the necessary capital met with only a modicum of success. Even though the stagestruck Mr. Mower agreed to chip in, we were still 200 pounds short of our goal—at which time we lost heart and gave up the whole idea.

My own disappointment was all the keener because, at the urging of my actress friend Jeanne de Casalis, I went to see a Sunday-night tryout of a play in which her boyfriend was to appear. She knew that if our efforts succeeded, a replacement for Larry, in the role of Captain Stanhope, would have to be found and she promised it would not be a wasted evening. Sure enough, onto the stage, in a trashy comedy, walked Colin Clive, a relatively unknown actor, who immediately won my vote as the new Stanhope, should the need arise. His accent, his military bearing, and his whisky voice were exactly what the part required.

Since the prospects for *Journey's End* seemed to be a dead issue, I clutched at a chance to break into the motion-picture field. Leon Gordon's play *White Cargo* was to be made into a movie, and I was chosen to play the part of the young man, Langford, who, due to the damp-rot of the tropics and the wiles of the dusky maiden Tondeleyo, comes to a murky end. It was a silent movie, of course, with a fine cast and tiptop camera work. The principal male role was played by Leslie Faber. In my book he was by far the most skilful actor of his time, but for some reason or other he was never a top drawing card at the box office. It sometimes happens like that; the type known as the actor's actor is not necessarily the public's favourite.

When it came to acting in a silent movie, Faber was not the disciplined performer he unfailingly was on the stage. With nothing to go by but the director's description of what the scene in question was concerned with, the cast were expected to invent their own dialogue. To set the mood, and to approximate the music which would accompany the film when it was exhibited in the movie theatres, it was customary for a pianist and a violinist to be stationed close to the set. If it was a love scene in which a couple were required to exchange sweet nothings, the music was supposed to inspire the actor and actress to portray deep devotion, even though one of them might have garlic on the breath. Faber was incapable of treating this kind of situation seriously, taking delight in making up dialogue that was totally inappropriate to the scene being shot. A blushing production secretary did her best to record in shorthand the licentious inventions issuing from Faber's mouth, but finally gave up the task in shock. His schoolboy behaviour was not discernible on film and did much to relieve the tedium of the dumb-show acting we were engaged in, but it was a tremendous problem for the producer later on. The film was completed and ready for distribution when it was announced that Alfred

1901–1935

Hitchcock had succeeded in incorporating sound into his picture called *Blackmail*.

The day of the microphone had arrived and the death-knell of silent pictures sounded. *White Cargo* and many other ambitious films became obsolete overnight. After weeks of cogitation, our producers decided to salvage their expensive film by adding to it a sound track. This gave rise to the necessity of voices matching the lips of the images on the screen, a process known as "dubbing." It also involved hours of interrogation as to our recall of the dialogue we had employed at the time of the silent shooting. The problems were further aggravated by the tragic news of Leslie Faber's sudden death. We had done most of his dubbing but some crucial scenes still lacked his voice. Those of us who had been involved in the missing episodes were recalled to the studio to be quizzed as to what words Faber had used. It took great ingenuity to substitute inoffensive words for the unprintable phrases he had, in fact, uttered. We all pitched into this somewhat macabre task, and some of us, including me, did our best to imitate his voice in the dubbing.

There was one important scene in the picture in which for some reason the silent version was inadequate. There was nothing to be done but hire a studio and reshoot the scene with live sound. Seemingly dogged by ill fortune, on the day that Gypsy Rhuma (Tondeleyo) and I were called to the Whitehall Studios at Elstree, the thermometer dropped to an unprecedented low, freezing up everything in sight, including the heating system. Gypsy and I sat on the verandah of my tropical bungalow, she in a fur coat with nothing on underneath but a sarong and a bra, and I wrapped in heavy blankets. Our teeth chattering, we went over the emotional dialogue of our scene of parting. Our outer coverings were removed and the cameras started to turn. We had barely started to speak our lines when the director called, "Cut." It appeared that whenever either of us spoke, clouds of frosted breath issued from our mouths and nostrils. By then we were so cold that we had started to vibrate in every limb; brandy was sent for to warm us up, but its only effect was to make our frosted breath more noticeable. "Try breathing *in* as you speak," said the frantic director. We tried, but the harder we tried the giddier we became. Shaking in our sandals, we demanded more brandy. Fortified by a generous helping of the stuff, we plunged into the highly emotional farewell scene, playing it with torrid passion even though our articulation lacked clarity.

Early in 1929 my prophecies regarding *Journey's End* were to be rewarded. Out of the blue, in this case the environs of Chicago, there arrived in London Maurice Browne, the manager of a community theatre. He had come with two purposes in mind. One was to launch a production of *Othello* with Paul Robeson as the Moor, himself as Iago, and Peggy Ashcroft as Desdemona. The other was to search for playscripts, preferably those by new authors.

THE WEST END

The realisation of his first ambition—the less said about that the better—made severe incursions into his exchequer besides leaving him with a lease of the Savoy Theatre. In his quest for playscripts he was luckier, for *Journey's End* had been brought to his attention. For Maurice Browne this was a life-saver: a tenant for his unexpired theatre lease, a physical production tucked away in a warehouse, and, with the exception of Olivier, a cast willing to go to work at a moment's notice. I felt so strongly about the vital importance of the part of Stanhope being properly cast, and was so convinced that Colin Clive would be the answer, that I had the temerity to say that my participation would be conditional on Colin being given the part. Neither the author, the director, nor Maurice Browne had ever heard of him, so I realised I had really stuck my neck out. They had no option but to interview Colin, and an appointment was made for a week thence. I spent the intervening days closeted with Colin and the script, drilling into him all the values I knew the director would be looking for, and rehearsing the Stanhope-Raleigh scenes in preparation for his audition. He came through with flying colours, was hired next day, and made a big hit with the press when the show finally opened for its record run.

During the first few weeks at the Savoy, I was still working in *White Cargo* at Elstree and barely making the journey back to London by curtain time. The program cover with a picture of Colin and me in our "tin helmets" was witness to this, because instead of a little down on Raleigh's upper lip the camera clearly showed me with a stubbly beard. This was the way I had to look as Langford in the film and there was nothing to be done about it except to put on Raleigh's makeup with a heavy hand.

That opening night at the Savoy is burnt in my memory, particularly the audience's reaction to the final scene of the play. Raleigh, mortally wounded, lying on his cot in the dugout, breathes his last. Stanhope, crushed by his sorrow, drags himself wearily up the steps. As he disappears to the trench above, a direct hit by an enemy shell demolishes the dugout, burying Raleigh where he lies. Slowly the curtain was lowered to the accompaniment of machine-gun fire. There was total silence in the theatre. Our stage manageress, Madge Whiteman, was perplexed; was the absence of applause the sign of approval or condemnation? Should she or should she not raise the "rag" for the customary curtain calls? The actors settled the question for her by giving a few claps, loud enough to be heard "out front." That was enough to dispel the tragic mood in which the audience had been held, giving way to thunderous applause and bravos.

The press next day were equally enthusiastic, so there was much joy in our dressing rooms. On the second night, Maurice Browne summoned us onstage. With tears of gratitude in his eyes, he made a rather embarrassing speech about the indispensability of the present cast of the play. When the time came for a company to be sent to America, we, and only we, he vowed, would be allowed to go there as "Ambassadors of Empire!" Gilbert Miller soon talked him out of that and within a matter of weeks started to recruit his own company for the Broadway production. So much for promises!

It was unreasonable on the part of us holdovers from the Stage Society tryout to nurse a dog-in-the-manger envy of Maurice Browne's good fortune. We had got cold feet about the last 200 pounds, so had only ourselves to blame for letting the property slip through our fingers. I've often thought since that our loss was actually a blessing. Imagine what would have happened to us as individuals if, in addition to acting in the play, we were splitting between us the vast profits that started to pile up. All ten of us would probably have started arriving at the stage door in our chauffeur-driven Rolls-Royces, and our acting would have gone down the drain. As it was, we were well paid by Mr. Browne and were able to settle down to the comfort, and the tedium, of an assured long run and the possibility of Hollywood offers in the future.

Such offers did come for Colin Clive and me to play our parts in the motion-picture version, which James Whale was to direct, but we were still doing sellout business at the Prince of Wales Theatre, to which the show had been transferred. The management baulked at giving leaves of absence to both of us simultaneously. They felt that, since my name was at the top of the billing, it would be less noticeable if Colin was the one allowed to go to Hollywood while I continued to hold the fort in London. Even though a tight limit was set on the length of his absence from the play, I was not too happy about it. Still, I consoled myself with the thought that whereas in the theatre I was managing to be convincing as an eighteen-year-old boy, the probing camera might very well disclose the fact that I was actually ten years older than that. As it turned out the picture was made far too hurriedly, so all in all I was well out of it.

There is always a danger of one's performance becoming stale and mechanical after a time. It did me good, therefore, to have to re-rehearse with Colin's temporary replacement, and the play continued to command the audience's absorbed attention. There was an unusual yardstick for measuring the extent to which we were holding them, which differed from the average play. Ordinarily with a hit show, there is no lack of visiting friends in the dressing rooms. Not so with Journey's End, however—particularly women friends. It was not unusual for them to telephone the following morning to apologise for not coming backstage, explaining that they had been so affected by the play's ending that their mascara had run and that they were really not fit to be seen; meant as a compliment, of course, but rather a bore when one had reserved a supper table somewhere.

5. A HOME OF MY OWN

It was about this time that my retaining contract with Mr. Lion lapsed, so I was no longer being docked half my earnings. The terms of that contract were seemingly extremely harsh, but upon reflection I had to admit that when he signed me up I really didn't have any other choice. In my case, he was investing in an unknown instead of putting a bet on an outsider in a horse race. None of the three other actors he had hired at the same time brought him profits from being sublet to other managements as I had done. In other words, he had taken a gamble on a human instead of horseflesh, and was entitled to his winnings even though they had come out of my pocket.

With a full salary coming to me each week, I had money in the bank for the first time in my life, and it was time to have a home of my own. I was able to rent a top-floor flat in John Street, in a building known as the Adelphi, immediately opposite the Little Theatre, which had housed *Diversion* not long before. Just off the Strand, and within easy walking distance of the theatre district, it was an ideal location, quiet yet accessible. Strolling through back alleys after the show, I would often stop at my favourite fish-and-chip shop. An order of "filleted plaice" (British for fillet of flounder) with two penn'orth of chips would be wrapped in newspaper. I had difficulty in controlling my salivary glands until reaching home, usually appeasing them with a few chips on the way.

Furnishing my flat was a fascinating task. I became a frequent bidder at the auction rooms, acquiring some good eighteen-century pieces and a very fine Bechstein grand piano. With the assistance of a Scots girlfriend, I also spent time poking around such places as the Caledonian Market for the odd item. Thus the John Street flat was made very cosy.

In those palmy days before domestic service became a dirty word, I was able to hire a very dear woman, who had been my mother's right hand at Stoke Newington years before. She had watched me grow up there, always addressing me as "Master Maurice." Now I was promoted to "Mr. Maurice" and she made an enormous fuss over me. Mrs. McQuinn, affectionately known as "Quinney," had only one stubborn streak; she refused to go home in the evening until she had served my supper, seen me off to the theatre, and washed up the dishes. This meant that she put in a ten-hour day, six days a week, and made me feel like a slave-driver. She was a dear and I don't know what I would have done without her. By way of company, I had one goldfish and a pair of West Highland Terriers. The Westies were the beginning of a long-lasting love affair between me and this incomparable breed of dog, but my feelings for the goldfish were more temperate. It was the cause of the only disagreement I ever had with Quinney. We had run out of fish food and I couldn't be bothered to go out to buy more, so, figuring that the fish would not know the difference, I put a pinch of Quaker Oats in the water. Quinney caught me in the act and gave me a withering look.

"Not Quaker Oats, Mr. Maurice!"

"Why not?" said I.

"Everyone knows that Quaker Oats is ever so heating to the blood," she replied and off she stalked to the kitchen, the fish bowl clutched to her bosom.

The Adelphi boasted some distinguished neighbours. George Bernard Shaw was just around the corner from me, Cedric Hardwicke right opposite, Edmund Gwenn a few doors down the street, and a frequent sight was the diminutive figure of Sir James Barrie, resembling one of the lost boys from his *Peter Pan*, trotting down to the post office.

Living in the Adelphi was almost like being in a village. You were on intimate terms with your postman and milkman, and, since Covent Garden market was so close by, a hawker pushing his barrow would ply his vegetable produce on John Street once a week. To attract attention, he would give vent to a centuries-old street cry. Although I tried with all my might to make out the words, the nearest I ever got to understanding them was "Apples a pound pears seedy or plum." Going back to London many years later, I saw to my sorrow that Number 9, John Street and the adjoining buildings had been replaced by a concrete monstrosity called the Shell-Mex Tower.

Glad as I was to have the security of a sucessful play and the comforts of John Street, I had periodic yearnings for the lovely English countryside. When you are country-bred, as I was, you never get the desire to rusticate out of your system, so I invested in a Riley sports car. In this, my pride and joy, I would invite a chum or two to go on weekend forays with me.

One such chum was Derek Williams, who had finished his job with du Maurier and Cooper at the Playhouse, and was waiting for Gilbert Miller's summons to report for rehearsals in New York where he was to play my part of Raleigh. I had earned a week's vacation from the play, so, having loaded up the car with collapsible cots, a tent, and other camping equipment, Derek and I set out on a fishing trip to Devonshire, albeit somewhat unwillingly on his part. We pitched our tent on the banks of a trout stream on Dartmoor, which was much to the liking of the Westies, who came along with us. It poured rain most of the week, not the most suitable condition for dry-fly fishing. I fear we spent more time in the nearby pub than we did on the trout stream. It soon became apparent that Derek had none of the Boy Scout in his background, so it fell to me to cope with all the cooking over a Primus stove. One evening I rebelled and announced that in spite of the rain I was going out with my rod even if I had to cheat by putting a worm on the hook. "Very well," said Derek,

A HOME OF MY OWN

"*I* will cook the supper." I had just coaxed a trout to take some interest in my line when there was an explosion from the direction of the tent. Running as fast as my legs would carry me to see the cause, I was greeted by the sight of Derek, the two dogs, the bedding, and even the tent itself liberally plastered with spaghetti and tomato sauce. My self-appointed chef had placed two cans over the naked Primus flames without having pierced them! The dogs licked each other's coats with relish, but our job of cleaning up the mess was somewhat more complicated.

After the Devonshire fishing expedition, all Derek was willing to do was to play the occasional game of golf with me—a sport that I have found tends to bring out the worst in one. I think it was best described by Lord Curzon when he said, "Golf is a game in which one is required to push a very small white ball around a very large quantity of very green grass with instruments *entirely* unsuited to the purpose!" Having joined the Stage Golfing Society, which had its headquarters, including a bar, over the Café Anglais in Leicester Square, I dropped in there one day to drown my sorrows after a particularly disastrous round of golf. I found Rex Harrison in equally morose spirits, and he said to me, "Why the *hell* won't somebody give me a job in the West End instead of all this everlasting touring!" A crystal ball would have given Rex needed assurance at that moment.

Although not a fortuneteller, the club's barman was the epitome of his profession, lending a patient ear to the beefing of members about their golf scores, their professional setbacks or whatever, even encouraging them to look on the brighter side of things. He had a remarkable faculty for making one feel welcome, sometimes to a degree that he seemed to be endowed with subliminal powers. Reginald Gardiner, the inimitable actor-monologuist, told me years later that, revisiting the club for the first time following a five-year successful sojourn in Hollywood, the barman merely planted a glass on the counter, saying, "Same as usual, Mr. Gardiner?"

As one grows older, how enviously one regards the attribute of unerring identification such as that of the club's barman. The story is told of Benjamin Disraeli's inherent shortcoming in that respect; he never forgot a face, but frequently had momentary difficulty in putting a name to it. Deft politician that he was, he would take the hand of the individual with the familiar face, look the person straight in the eye, saying most solicitously, "And how's the old complaint?" By the time the individual had given him a rundown on the most recent attack of lumbago or whatever, the elusive name had usually come to mind and his honour was saved.

Probably more than in any other profession, a theatrical career depends on chance happenings: the people you happen to meet, a recommendation by someone you don't even know, and sometimes the pure accident of resembling

1901–1935

some established performer. The choice you make of opportunities resulting from such chance encounters can completely govern the direction of your career.

An instance of this came about when I called at our theatre one morning to pick up my mail. I heard voices coming from the stage and popped my head in to see what was going on. To my surprise it was a rehearsal of *Journey's End* but with an unfamiliar cast. I was told that this was a company of actors who were about to set forth on a tour of India and other remote parts of the world with a repertoire consisting of *Hamlet, No, No, Nanette,* and *Journey's End!* I thought this was too good to be missed, so I sat down to watch some of the rehearsal, expecting the worst. The moment arrived for Raleigh to make his entrance down the steps of the dugout. Onto the stage came a young man who proceeded to give a performance that was infinitely better than my own, absolutely perfect in all respects. I sat glued to my seat throughout the rehearsal and at the end went backstage to meet the Raleigh.

"Who are you?," I asked, "and where did you come from?"

"My name is John Mills," he replied.

"Now look here," I said, "you don't want to waste your time going to India and all that. Our management is hunting for a replacement for my understudy; just say the word and I'm sure the job will be yours." Here was a case of an actor forced to make a choice, and I have to hand it to Johnnie that, as much as he would have preferred to stay in London, he felt he was morally committed to his present employer.

It turned out that Johnnie made the right decision because, in the course of his Indian tour, his talent was recognised by the vacationing Noel Coward, who spread the word of his "find" on returning to London. Thanks to Noel's introductions, two important parts were awaiting Johnnie when his tour finished, starting him on his distinguished career in the theatre and films.

In England alone three touring companies of *Journey's End* were on the road while we continued our stint at the Prince of Wales, but the end was finally in sight, even for us. I hadn't given a thought to the future, foolishly believing that, once word of the impending closure got out, other managements would be clamouring for the services of the actor who had headed the cast of such a long-running production. On the contrary, they had forgotten about my very existence, and I was reduced to the indignity of doing the rounds of agents' offices, only to be told that one of the Raleighs from the touring companies had captured a part I was interested in. Only then did I realise that Larry Olivier had stolen a march on me by declining *Journey's End.* While I was at an artistic standstill, he was repeatedly being seen by the critics and enlarging his scope as an actor. For me, it was almost like starting all over again, and I felt desperately discouraged.

A HOME OF MY OWN

Agents are of little or no help in these circumstances. If in your last job you had played, as I had, a Second Lieutenant in the British army, then the agents would sit back and wait for someone to write a play calling for a Second Lieutenant in the British army. This is exactly what happened to me, even though it was the French army this time. A translation from the French had been made of a play by Maurice Rostand entitled *The Man I Killed*. It was about a young man who, on the eve of the armistice, had shot a young German soldier and was suffering an acute case of remorse. Having pocketed the dog tags of the German boy, Herman, the young man seeks out the parents in Germany now that peace has been restored. His offer to make any reparation within his power cuts very little ice with Herman's father—played by Robert Lorraine—or his mother—played by Sara Allgood with her lilting, but inappropriate Irish brogue. His penitence gets a warmer reception from Herman's girlfriend—played by Jean Forbes-Robertson—who suggests an approach that might soften the hearts of the obdurate parents. Herman, it seems, was an aspiring violinist—a talent conveniently shared by his executioner—so all the Frenchman needs to do is to play a few notes on Herman's violin and the father's anger will be appeased. How's that for a plot!

Perversely, the audience's sympathy was all with my character and not with the grumpy Papa, and this was not at all to the liking of the leading man, Robert Lorraine, who proceeded to do something about it. I noticed that at the commencement of our engagement in Birmingham he played his part with a slight tremor of his hands; by the time we reached Glasgow, however, his affliction had developed into raging palsy, so that when the tear-provoking moment came for him to make me a gift of Herman's violin, it required considerable dexterity on my part to get a firm hold on the instrument.

If that wasn't cause enough for mirth, Lorraine's uncalled-for curtain speech certainly was. With the whole cast onstage, he walked down to the footlights to thank the audience, though for what, since the Scots' applause had been barely discernible, it was hard to say. Not to be dissuaded, he asked the audience, "Might there, perhaps, be present tonight, some playgoers who had also been present on the occasion of my last visit to this estimable city of Glasgow?" No Glaswegian response was forthcoming. "Then let me remind you," Lorraine continued. "That time it was in a play by the father of tonight's author, Edmond Rostand [dead silence] *Cyrano de Bergerac!*" (You could hear a pin drop!). Raising his voice by several decibels, Lorraine tried a new tack. "The time before *that* . . . ," and on and on he went with a chronological recital of his past apearances, but he still failed to arouse his dour hearers. This was just too much for Jean and me; we both got uncontrollable giggles and had to leave the stage, whereupon we both proceeded to split our sides laughing.

Fortunately this Gallic caper was abandoned out of town, so we were spared the scrutiny of the London press. However, I continued to live under the play's shadow for some time thereafter, being offered nothing but plays adapted from the French! It was rather like having an obstinate head cold that refused to be shaken off.

A welcome change of pace came in October 1930, when Colin Clive was summoned to Hollywood to fulfill a previously made commitment. Following the demise of *Journey's End*, he had been appearing with Edna Best and Herbert Marshall in Ferenc Molnár's *The Swan*, a production that had only one more month to run. He felt awful about leaving Edna and Bart in the lurch, but the studio left him no choice. Was there any chance, he asked me, that I would agree to step into his shoes as the royal fencing-master, Dr. Agi? I sensibly buried my pride and said Yes. For me it turned out to be one of the most stimulating months I have ever spent in the theatre: a good tragicomedy to play, a pair of eminent actors to work with, and a beguiling drama to boot.

In December of that year, *Who's Who* tells me, I found employment in a light comedy by E. M. Delafield called *To See Ourselves*. I have only the dimmest recollection of this piece, which is strange, because for the first time I seem to have broken down the reserve of the London *Times* critic, who wrote, ". . . the younger generation for once represented with insight and intelligence." The generally conservative *Saturday Review* critic really let himself go, however, stating flatly, "Mr. Maurice Evans is the best young actor on the London stage today." It was all very flattering to have this sort of thing said about one, but it did curiously little to advance one's career. If nothing else, it must have given me courage to turn down translations from the French and "Tennis, anyone" parts, because my credits at that point seem to be mainly concerned with films.

6. "TALKIES"

In the early days of "talkies," American technology outstripped British efforts; thus the country was flooded with the Hollywood product. The government, in an effort to prop up the British film industry, passed a law which stated that for every thousand feet of American film imported so many *hundred* feet of British film had first to be *made*. Overnight, there appeared from nowhere every two-bit agent in the country with papers purporting to be a script in one pocket and sufficient money in the other to rent a sound studio for six days. This was purely, or rather impurely, a device to get around the law. The exhibitors had a steady supply coming to them from the States, but had to go through the pretence of renting the British product to keep the American films in the pipeline.

We actors had no compunction about appearing in these six-day quickies, known as "Quota Films," being convinced that they would never be shown. Most likely they would remain in the can in some dishonest agent's office, just in case proof had to be available that the footage had actually been shot. Of course, none of us had the prescience of the coming of television, otherwise we would have had nothing to do with them. To this day, people will occasionally say to me, 'I saw you on the tube last night," naming a title that rings the faintest of bells. Once someone said to me, "I thought you looked rather old in that movie," and I remembered that the action of that particular film looked as though it had been photographed by candlelight.

The scripts, too, were unbelievably bad. One of them, a mystery story, was so convoluted that when we started shooting on a Monday no one, least of all the author, had the faintest idea how the story finished. We had to vacate the studio by midnight on Saturday, so that fateful morning an emergency script conference was called, which, as the precious minutes ticked by, was joined by everyone on the set—actors, carpenters, and property men— all of us trying with no success to suggest a credible finale. As the hands of the clock crept toward the witching hour, the director went before the camera for a big close-up. "Who *did* steal the jewels?" he asked. "The answer lies in the sequel to this exciting melodrama . . . don't miss it!"

An agent called me one day to say that a ten-day quickie, called *Path to Glory*, was about to start shooting on the morrow and that he would meet me at the Walton Studios in an hour's time, if I were interested. He briefed me that it was a costume picture set in Outer Bosnia or somewhere of the sort, and that a beautiful girl, named Valerie Hobson, was to supply the love interest. It sounded all right, so I jumped in my Riley and drove down to meet the director.

While waiting for him to appear, I took a look at the set, quite an impressive representation of the Bosnia village's main street, and casually noticed a stack of old bicycles in a corner. The director was most affable, explaining that I was to play the part of a conquering hero returning in glory to the village of his birth. As an afterthought, he said, "You do ride, of course?" Remembering the bicycles that had previously caught my attention, I replied, "Sure. Not that I've been on one for years."

The next morning, all decked out, I waited for someone to bring me the bicycle on which I expected to ride down the street. At that moment, the big loading doors swung open and through them came a huge dappled-grey horse, snorting with fury. "Never been in a film studio before," said the beast's groom. That piece of information did nothing to still my apprehension, but I felt that the misunderstanding about my equestrian inadequacy was my own fault. There was nothing for it but to bluff my way through the scene. However, while I was behind the set being helped into the saddle, the director, without my being aware of it, instructed the village maidens lining the street not only to cheer but to take off their scarves and wave them vigorously as I rode past. Needless to say, this scared the daylights out of the horse, who took off as fast as his hooves would carry him, demolishing pieces of scenery before he was caught. Later, when I saw the film, it was hard to judge who looked the more terrified, the horse, or me—the conquering hero!

For all their lack of integrity, these Quota Films offered opportunities for young actors and actresses to get a foot in the door. When being interviewed for parts in regular productions, they could truthfully claim to have had previous experience and that footage existed to prove it. In one such quickie, we had a young dancer, named Marjory Robertson, being given her first chance to show that she could also act. Herbert Wilcox, the well-known producer, happened to get a glimpse of her work on our set. He immediately put her under contract, groomed her into stardom, and eventually married her. That eager young girl became the renowned luminary of British films and the stage as well, Dame Anna Neagle.

Quota Films had the advantage of keeping me busy after a fashion and stopped me from accepting unsuitable theatrical offers. One such offer, I confess, had a most irresistible appeal because it implied a possible career on Broadway. A very persuasive American producer, named Jed Harris, nearly succeeded in getting his claws into me, but when I heard his grandiose plans for establishing a repertory company on the Great White Way, I decided to steer clear of his cultural ambitions.

I was to have another near miss about going to the States. Lee Shubert was in London shopping for attractions to fill his Broadway theatres. Amongst others, he picked on the J. B. Priestley and Edward Knoblock play-with-music *The Good Companions*, then playing at His Majesty's. Provided I could make myself ready to leave for New York within a few weeks, I was to play the juvenile lead. Terms were agreed, and while Shubert took off for a European tour, I took off to a tailor in Bond Street and ordered, quite recklessly, six suits, an overcoat, and other accoutrements to enhance my wardrobe for New York. I became uneasy as the weeks went by and the contract from Shubert failed to materialise. It was purely by accident that I learned that Valerie Taylor, whom he had signed for the female lead, had made it a condition that her husband be hired to play my part opposite her; thus my salute to the Statue of Liberty was indefinitely postponed. In contrast to the shoddy behaviour of Lee Shubert, the tailor behaved like a true gentleman in allowing me to pay for

A toddler (1904).

"Sunday best" (1906).

"Sans teeth" (1907).

Helmsman of the *Evelyn Hope* (1934).

The "Tennis, anyone?" period (1930–34).

As Richard II (1934–35).
"I wasted time, and now
time doth waste me."

"The apparel oft proclaims
the man" (1935).

only one suit at a time. It was a matter of years before I acquired the final garment.

The goodwill of the tailor was cemented by my introducing to him another customer in the person of Robert Donat. After stepping into my shoes at the Festival Theatre, Cambridge, Bob had landed firmly on both feet in the West End. Wearing the dress uniform of an army officer and playing a romantic role, he looked the acme of sartorial elegance. In his street clothes, however, he was a disappointment, not only to his admirers, but to the agents and Hollywood talent scouts who had their eye on him. The head of an Adonis was attached to an unusually long neck from which sprang shoulders at an angle of forty-five degrees. His preference for casual everyday clothes did nothing to disguise these imperfections. Our mutual agent asked me to take him to my tailor, who made him a jacket with exaggerated shoulder pads and a high collar. Although Bob vowed he would wear it only for job interviews, it did the trick for him and he was off to Hollywood before you could say "Jack Robinson."

Although the theatre was, and still is, my first love, motion pictures do have a special advantage. They can take their actors to a variety of places in the world, which otherwise the actors might never visit. But for a movie entitled *The Queen's Garter*, I might never have seen pre-Hitler Berlin, for instance. It was made at the UFA Studios on the outskirts of the city. The film was under the direction of the famous German director, Erich Pommer, who was trying his hand at a new gimmick. The script was especially designed for the unusual talents of Lilian Harvey. Although of English origin, she possessed enchanting linguistic accomplishments. Her English had a distinct Cockney flavour, her German was an attractive Mittel-Europa, and her French adorably quaint. Pommer's idea was to shoot the picture in those three languages with Lilian Harvey starring in each version. This meant she had to be surrounded by three different casts of supporting actors, who appeared in scenes with her that were shot in succession. As soon as I finished a scene, Heinz Rhumann stepped in to do the German version. Charles Boyer doubled in the English and French versions and Conrad Veidt played Boyer's role in the German version. It was not considered cricket to watch the other fellow playing "your" scene, a courtesy which, needless to say, was blithely ignored by all the French actors except for Boyer.

Berlin was a very stimulating city in those days and although, to begin with, I blanched at the huge quantities of restaurant food put before me—to say nothing of the steins of beer—after a few weeks I was asking for seconds and refills.

Back in England, and on a strict diet, I was sent for by a recently arrived Hungarian director who was about to make his first full-length feature film in

Britain. The picture was *Wedding Rehearsal* and the director, Alexander Korda. Stories have been written depicting him as the ruthless tycoon of the British film industry, a portrait that bears no resemblance to the Korda I worked for. At that time his knowledge of English was sparse and his opinion of English food far from complimentary. Modesty and courtesy, I would say, were his outstanding characteristics. He and his brothers, instead of lunching in the studio commissary, had a long trestle table set up for them on the sound stage. Their lunch consisted of innumerable cans of anchovies and highly spiced Hungarian food swimming in oil. They would invite members of the cast to join them for coffee, over which we discussed the work ahead. Looking down the table on a busy day of shooting, one would see Roland Young, Lady Tree, John Loder, and a number of other important actors. Often at the other end of the table, looking rather overawed to be in such starry company, would be me and two young, inexperienced actresses, one of them Joan Gardiner, and the other Merle Oberon—both of them destined to marry into the Korda family later.

My recollections of the script have faded into the past, but one scene does stand out in my memory. It was an episode in which Lady Tree, almost speechless with embarrassment, was endeavouring to educate Merle and Joan about the facts of life. Whereas any other actress might have fumbled with a handkerchief in her lap to indicate nervousness, Lady Tree went one better. Seated in an elbowchair, searching for innocent words suited to the delicate subject, she started to wind her handkerchief around the chair's arm. Then, in her attempts to evade the awful truth, she tied and untied knots with the hanky, finishing with a bowline that defied all efforts to release it.

How greatly acting techniques have changed with the coming of wide-screen projection! I doubt whether audiences realise that in a close-up the performer's face is about twenty feet in width when projected onto such a screen, and that, consequently, the flick of an eyelash is apt to look like overacting. I loved Alec Guinness' reply to a questioner's "What do you *do* to seem so natural?" Said Sir Alec, "I do *nothing*."

Bridging the gap between silent and sound films was a formidable transition for any actor to accomplish. For those trained in the theatre it was second nature to pitch the voice so that it was clearly audible in the far reaches of the top gallery. In the silents no attention was paid to the vocal volume because the dialogue would never be heard; thus the theatrically trained actor spoke as though in the theatre. With the coming of the microphone in the motion-picture studios, the actor's vocal chords became the property of the sound engineer whose job it was to do the recording. It was that technician who modulated the voice to match the image on the screen, not the actor. The "mikes," such as they were, had a very limited range, making it necessary for

"TALKIES"

a veritable battery of them to be concealed behind such items as coffeepots, flower vases, and so forth. It was quite a trick for the actor to be sure to be within range of the right coffeepot or flower vase before uttering a line.

Later, of course, the microphone "boom" was invented, enabling an operator to follow an actor's movement from place to place with a single microphone suspended over the performer's head. Although this contraption put an end to the "hunt the slipper" gyrations made necessary by the stationary mikes, it too created problems for the actor. Being unconscious of this bird of prey hovering over one's head, one was apt to revert to projecting the voice as if in a theatre. Even Ethel Barrymore had difficulty in adapting to what I like to describe as the "saliva" school of acting. In her first Hollywood talkie, she was booming away until her brother Lionel cautioned her that her merest whisper was all that was required. I'm told she took him so literally that her somewhat heavy breathing was more eloquent than her speech.

The sudden onslaught of the talkie made victims of many a silent-picture performer because of vocal deficiencies. They were replaced more and more, not always for the better, by theatre actors who possessed the necessary vocal attributes. There were exceptions, of course, among the stars of the silent screen who switched without difficulty to the new medium. Handsome Carl Brisson was one of the fortunate ones, although he did have difficulty of another kind in an early talkie being shot close to his home at Elstree. The script was an adaptation from a novel by Elinor Glyn (author of such gems as *Six Nights on a Tiger Rug* or something of that sort) and she was frequently present at the studio to be sure that no one tampered with her deathless prose. On one occasion, however, she felt constrained also to assist the director in overcoming a difficulty that had brought the production to a halt.

Her story called for the presence of a parrot on its perch in the hero's living room, but the bird supplied by the animal farm was uncooperative. Whenever the hero (Carl Brisson) entered the room, the parrot gave forth with a stream of ear-splitting squawks. Half a morning had been wasted in attempts by the sound engineer to eliminate Polly's interference, all to no avail. At this point, the author, her patience exhausted, marched up to the perch, looked the parrot straight in the eye, and in her most commanding voice said, *"This is Elinor Glyn! You will cease this noise at once!"* That was the parrot's cue to dig deep into its repertoire for sounds that far outdid the earlier performances. It remained for Carl to suggest a solution to the problem. He owned a pet parrot that was his constant companion; let everyone take a tea break, he suggested, and he would run home to fetch the bird. To the relief of all and sundry, the newcomer took to the perch without so much as a peep, giving rise to the hope that he or she might be mute. The camera started to roll, Brisson made his entrance, and advancing towards his friend on the perch, mouthed one of those inane things one habitually says to parrots. To everyone's distress—and amusement—the discreet bird gave vent to the one and only phrase it had ever been taught (by its master, some said): "Pretty Carl! Pretty Carl!"

From the actor's standpoint it took, and in fact still takes, little crises like these to dissipate the boredom of an average day in the studio. Apart from the writer, the only truly creative people involved in the business of canned entertainment are those behind the camera, not in front. Contrary to the impression given by those who write about their glamorous careers before the camera, the truth is that they are only one cog in a very intricate machine. Their usefulness is largely measured by their ability to obey the industry's sacred tenet—"Theirs not to reason why." The actor must trust the director implicitly, the director being the person who is thinking in terms of the cinematic result. Suppose the scene being shot is one in which you have been utterly captivated by the beauty of a girl passing by. It is now time for your close-up registering that emotion, but instead of gazing at a beautiful girl you are staring directly into the faces of the husky camera crew. In order to get the reaction needed from the actor, the director may ask, "What do you most fancy for lunch—chicken or meat balls?" The actor's face lights up as he opts for "meat balls"! "That's it!" exclaims the director. "Just look into the lens and think lovingly of meat balls. . . . Okay, cut. That was great, luv. Go to lunch and I'll pick up the tab."

7. "JEUNE PREMIER"

From a personal standpoint, I found that working in the studios made fewer demands on my time as compared with the theatre's rigid routine and uncertain survival. A film contract named an exact starting date and a guaranteed amount of salary; whereas a play, after three or four weeks of rehearsal (unpaid in those days), could open on a Monday and close the following Saturday. With that lovely movie money in your pocket, you were in a position to indulge in different forms of recreation. What a much-abused word that is—"recreation"; it really means being re-created by being in touch with art and the wonders of nature. In the intervals between film jobs, I would dragoon a friend to accompany me on hiking trips abroad. On one such jaunt we walked, on blistered feet to begin with, all the way from Zurich to Lausanne, scaling nine mountain passes en route. Fifty years later I clearly remember every inch of our progress, the *albèrgos* we stayed in, the bread-and-cheese and beer lunches in our haversacks, the incredible variety of wild-flowers, and the streams in which we bathed our poor feet. A couple of

"JEUNE PREMIER"

weeks of that sort of life and you returned to foggy London, well tanned and thoroughly refreshed. Many years later, I made automobile trips through Switzerland, but, unlike my hiking expeditions, they have left no impression on my jaded mind.

Tom Helmore was in *White Cargo* with me, playing the part of the fresh-faced youngster who arrives to replace my swiftly disintegrating character—too much booze and too much Tondeleyo. He and his wife, Evelyn, lured me into taking an interest in sailing. Between us we bought a sailing dinghy in which to learn the mysteries of navigation. The boat leaked like the proverbial sieve, to which our soaking-wet bottoms testified when we came ashore, but it taught us how to handle a sailing craft and prepared us for what was to come later. We became the proud owners of a forty-foot sailing ketch, which we kept on its buoy in Poole harbour in Dorset. It made no pretensions of being a racing craft, but was wide-beamed and consequently very comfortable below decks. Most weekends, with the assistance of our temperamental auxiliary motor, we would snake our way out of the harbour before hoisting sail in the tricky waters of the English Channel.

Neglecting to study tide tables before casting off can result in a receding tide sweeping you halfway to France. Although knowing perfectly well that there are no whales or porpoises in the English Channel, we were convinced on one occasion that we had run into a school of them. Closer investigation, however, revealed that the fountains of water springing up around our bow were caused by artillery shells being fired into a target area that we had unknowingly entered. A hasty retirement was made with all sails set.

A cardinal rule when sailing is to trust your charts rather than the advice of local boatmen. Departing from this basic precept when sailing very close to shore off Fowey harbour in Cornwall, we almost lost our precious boat, a disaster for which I would have been mainly responsible. Tom had carefully studied his charts, which showed the channel we were in to be sufficiently deep for our draught. To my unschooled eye, the channel looked dangerously shallow, so I did the unpardonable thing of hailing a party of fishermen who were anchored not far from our course. I asked them if we were all right to keep going; their spokesman thought not, and advised us to head out to the deeper water marked by a bell buoy. Rather reluctantly, Tom swung the helm sharply to port, whereupon within minutes we struck a rock. With a four-knot tide running out, the rounded surface of the rock soon became visible, making it inevitable that in no time at all we would be perched high and dry on its slimey face. By the time we had unlashed the dinghy, the yacht was lurching to a perilous angle and there was nothing for it but to abandon ship. Evie already had one foot in the dinghy when she remembered that her purse was still in the cabin. Somehow or other she clambered back on board and retrieved it, even though she risked her life in doing so. It wasn't until we pulled mournfully away from our stranded yacht that I realised how deeply attached I had become to our water-borne home. The sight of it, helpless and abandoned, had all three of us with tears in our eyes. Our spirits rose noticeably when a passing coal barge kindly sent a man aboard with a hawser, but our hopes were dashed once more when the yacht refused to respond to the efforts to dislodge it. Waving our thanks to the bargemen, we reached the shore and started on foot to the nearest pub. At the doorway we turned for a farewell glimpse of the *Evelyn Hope*, as she was named. Suddenly, lo and behold, she righted herself, and with her copper bottom apparently intact, she slid off the rock and with her mainsail still set she started slowly moving due south. No lifeboat has ever raced to a rescue with more speed than we put on in our little dinghy. Back on board, we did a swift turnabout and were soon safely in Fowey harbour where quite a crowd had gathered to cheer us. It was drinks all round that evening, by which time our little escapade had assumed the proportions of some historic maritime adventure.

While waiting for another film job to turn up, I was able to do some theatregoing, an opportunity that I was denied when working in the theatre myself. I was intrigued by the announcement of a production of Nikolai Gogol's *The Inspector-General*, starring Claude Rains and directed by Komisarjevsky. It was to be presented, strangely enough, at the Gaiety Theatre on the Strand, which was invariably identified with musicals and gorgeous show girls. I decided to try my luck for a ticket on the opening night, but a sold-out house meant climbing up to the unreserved top gallery, which I did.

The curtain rose on Komisarjevsky's sombre scenery, all of it mounted on a vast turntable that rotated most bewilderingly to accommodate the demands of the episodic drama. I became aware of the fidgeting of a man seated on the hard wooden bench of the row in front of me. He wore a cloth cap and a kerchief and looked the most unlikely customer for this very Russian, very esoteric entertainment. It then dawned on me that he had come to the Gaiety expecting the usual fare of flesh and fun and couldn't for the life of him figure out what was doing onstage. After about an hour he could bear it no longer. During a silent moment in the acting, he rose to his feet and, facing us seekers after culture, said in his loud Cockney accent, "Well, goodnight all!" Succinct criticism in a nutshell!

In June 1931 I was prevailed upon by John Van Druten to renounce my vow regarding translations from the French. It was John's *Diversion* that had first put me on the West End map, so I could hardly do otherwise. In any case, the play he had adapted was currently enjoying the second year of its run in Paris and contained an attractive leading role for me. *Sea Fever* was the English title John gave to Marcel Pagnol's delightful *Marius*, and after going twice to

"JEUNE PREMIER"

Paris to see the play I fell head over heels in love with the idea of appearing in it. Pierre Fresnay was Marius, the sea-fevered son of the old barkeeper in the *vieux port* of Marseilles. Raimu, as the father, gave a stunning performance. He had one wordless scene of at least five minutes' duration in which, clad in his nightshirt and carrying a candle, he has left his bed to check whether or not his errant son has returned home. Half drugged with sleep and yawning cavernously, he gave the impression of having forgotten why he had come downstairs into the bar. To help clear his mind he scratched his tousled head, but that merely prompted the idea of widening the area to be scratched. With perfect discretion and not a hint of vulgarity, Raimu, in his tickling nightshirt, had most of the audience scratching along with him—a masterly bit of mime.

Watching the Parisian production, I found that my schoolboy French left me far behind in appreciating much of the humour. It was explained to me that to a Frenchman the Marseillaise accent and sense of humour is what Cockney is to an Englishman or Brooklynese is to an American. John Van Druten made no attempt to find an English equivalent to the French patois, which turned out to be a mistake. Marius's girlfriend, Fanny, was played by Peggy Ashcroft in her perfectly cultured diction, in spite of Fanny's occupation of fishmongeress, and my Oxford accent was even less suited to the bartender I was playing. Raimu's part of the father was assigned to a fine actor, Norman McKinnel, whose natural Scots accent seemed just as incongruous.

However, none of this diversity of speech seemed to bother our preview audience or, in fact, the owner of the New Theatre, Bronson Albery. He came to my dressing room after the preview full of enthusiasm, going so far as to ask what colour I preferred for the redecoration of the room, predicting that I would be its occupant for many months. That was on a Sunday night; we opened on Monday to a tepid reception, but we were not too concerned about that.

Being in the habit of not reading my press reviews until after a show has closed, I arrived at the theatre in blissful ignorance of the dismal notices that had appeared that morning in most of the papers. I did not have to wait long to learn their contents, because the show was withdrawn after only eight performances, and my dressing-room walls were denied their fresh coat of paint. Two years in Paris—one week in London!—*C'est la vie!* Determined to justify our original faith in the play—and in the absence of the adapter, who had left town—Peggy Ashcroft and I played the last four performances in Cockney accents; it made all the difference, as witnessed by the audience's laughter and applause.

Who's Who in the Theatre is seldom wrong, so it is probably true that in August 1931 I appeared at the Criterion Theatre on Piccadilly Circus in something called *Those Naughty Nineties*. It's probably just as well that I have absolutely no remembrance of that entertainment, but I do recall vividly the Criterion Theatre, since it was the only time I ever appeared on its stage; also, because it was there that I was privileged to be presented to a member of the royal family.

Queen Mary was an avid matinee-goer and, due to some poor recommendation on the part of one of her ladies-in-waiting, had decided to patronise our skittish-sounding offering. I can only guess that Sir Nigel Playfair's presence in the cast lent it some dignity. That same lady-in-waiting had an unusual duty peculiar to the Criterion, which, unlike other theatres, possessed no royal box or retiring room. Thus, when the Queen attended a performance a temporary "loo" had to be erected behind one of the regular boxes. Her lady-in-waiting on those occasions was required to carry in a handbag a chamois-leather cover for the seat of the loo, thereby ensuring that Her Majesty's derriere would never come in contact with that plebian oval. The Queen never smoked in public, but thanks to the temporary loo, she was able to enjoy a few puffs on a cigarette during intermission. Having been notified that the coast was clear, we actors all trooped back to be introduced. The Queen was graciousness itself, apologising for summoning us during the interval, explaining that her husband insisted on her serving him his tea herself, which meant that she had to be back at Buckingham Palace by 5 o'clock.

A reference work credits me with having been involved in a series of frothy comedies of intrigue and mistaken identities in 1932 and 1933. An ill-starred attempt at playwriting by Beverly Nichols and three additional translations from the French did nothing to advance my career, although they brought me in close contact with people who would influence my later fortunes in America. I had lost touch with Margaret Webster since our amateur days, but found her again when I briefly joined another Van Druten play, *After All*, in which she was playing a small part. By now the show was booked into a few suburban theatres to which I offered to drive Peggy in my Riley. After the show, on our way home, she would often invite me to join her for supper in her parents' flat, which was in St. Paul's Churchyard. With her mother, Dame May Whitty, presiding at the groaning mahogany dining table and her handsome father, Ben Webster, ensconced in a fireside armchair, we would talk shop. One by one other actors started dropping in—John Gielgud with some of his cronies, Robert Harris, and others—all of us rather earnest creatures intent on the state of our souls, to say nothing of our pockets. The Websters regaled us with stories of their days with the two famous actor-manager companies that had been regular institutions in the past in London. By alternating between the companies of Sir Henry Irving at the Lyceum and Sir

"JEUNE PREMIER"

Herbert Beerbohm Tree at Her Majesty's, the Websters in their younger days had received steady employment.

In the flat below the Websters' had dwelt an elderly lady who had been the belle of the Irving Shakespearean productions—the famous Dame Ellen Terry. By the late 1920s she was practically blind and not too steady on her feet, but she still retained the merry disposition she had displayed when playing Beatrice to Irving's Benedick. There was no elevator in the Webster-Terry building, so Dame Ellen would ride up to her flat in the parcel lift, her legs dangling over the edge as she laughed happily while ascending to the upper regions.

I listened to the tales of those days with something approaching envy, comparing them with my then unrewarding imprisonment in the vapid trifles that seemed to have become my destiny. May Whitty was a very positive lady. She told me that the only way for me to get out of that rut was to show the critics and the public that I was capable of (as she put it) "taking off my stays" and doing the big classics. I listened to her advice with much skepticism, not believing I was equipped to enter a field in the theatre to which I had an aversion. Dare I confess that my schoolboy introduction to Shakespeare had implanted within me what amounted almost to a hatred for the poet? Not only did he represent the drudgery of memorising—without understanding—speeches from his plays, but on one occasion I was drafted to appear in a school production of *A Midsummer Night's Dream*. The older boys, monitors and prefects, made up the cast; but when it came to the fairies they were obliged to impress someone who could sing the lullabies. Thus was I forced into playing Peaseblossom. They dressed me in a blonde, bobbed wig and flowing pink tulle, and the ribbing I got from my classmates left a mark on me that I have never forgotten.

However, at May Whitty's insistence I did pay a visit to the Old Vic, where Ion Swinley was playing *Hamlet*. It is quite extraordinary that I had reached an age of discrimination without ever having seen the play. I believe it is traditional to consider that one's *first* Hamlet can never be bettered, and it was certainly true for me. Ion Swinley, a greatly underrated actor, was masterly in his interpretation of the Prince of Denmark. His performance struck a spark of hope that one day I might be worthy of acting in the plays of Shakespeare. Nevertheless, I was full of doubt about my ability to meet the demands of the classics and, while thanking May Whitty for her advice, I said that I thought it was premature to make such a drastic change of direction.

It really served me right that my timorous attitude landed me in yet another disastrous translation from the French, entitled *The Heart Line*. This entanglement was due to the urging of my old friend from *Journey's End* days, Jeanne de Casalis. I was spending a weekend at her country cottage in Kent, mainly for the purpose of reading the play, for which she had already been signed. Jeanne, however, was preoccupied with another more important matter. In the patio of her lovely Elizabethan cottage stood a dovecote. Its occupants had been purchased at a pet shop and came with instructions to wire them in for a couple of weeks to encourage their homing instincts. My arrival, and that of her young neighbour, Vivien Leigh, coincided with the day that was to see the termination of the doves' incarceration; they were to be set free to circle gracefully around the roof.

Not a bit of it! The wire removed, the silly birds refused to budge. Jeanne, in her entrancing French accent, tried coaxing them with endearments and handfuls of birdseed—with no success. Her Gallic frustration reached such a pitch that she finally mounted a stepladder and seized one of the doves. The feathered friend still stubbornly refused to spread its wings, so she carried it to the top floor of the cottage and, appearing with it at a leaded attic window, launched the bird into space. Unlike elephants with their proverbial long memories, a dove, it appeared, found two weeks too long to remember how to fly, for this one plummeted to the patio with a loud thump, but was otherwise unhurt. The telephone call to the pet shop that followed was hysterically funny to Vivien and me. Jeanne, alternating between French and English, upbraided the owners for having sold her incapacitated birds. Eventually she calmed down and we got around to reading *The Heart Line*. It was a sore disappointment. However, since Komisarjevsy was to direct, and the cast, besides Jeanne, also included Ann Todd, I decided I couldn't say No. The fate of the play was, I regret to say, like the dove's—a flop.

It was little comfort to me that I continued to receive good notices from the critics in spite of their indifference to my material. I had to begin to admit that I was in a very precarious profession and that it was time to look to the future. My yachting friends, the Helmores, having similar views, had decided to do something practical about it. They looked around for a business activity having nothing to do with the theatre, and in doing so struck gold. An acquaintance of theirs from New Zealand had arrived in England with a machine that was to revolutionize the trade of dry cleaning.

Until then, the only existing facilities were provided by a firm called Pullars of Perth, which had numerous receiving shops all over London. Garments intended for dry cleaning were deposited in these centres and from there were sent all the way to Perth in Scotland to be cleaned. The reason for this journey was never apparent, but the patient British customers simply assumed that Pullars knew what they were up to. Needless to say, it was weeks before one's things were returned, often requiring repeated visits to the receiving centre before being able to claim them. The New Zealander's invention was designed to explode this myth; but how to convince the public that they could actually have the work done in one day? The Helmores had the bright idea of installing the machine in the window of a shop near Victoria Station and hiring pretty, uniformed girls to operate it. The novelty was an instant success and the Helmores were soon opening branches in other parts of the city.

Not to be outdone, I decided to follow suit by opening a similar establishment, picking Bloomsbury as the ideal site for my venture. In all of London, this was the area most favoured by American tourists. They were accustomed to quick dry cleaning at home and had a right to expect the same service in their travels. In theory this was a sound choice on my part, but in practice it couldn't have been worse. We opened the doors for business on the very day that the American banks closed in the depths of the Great Depression. The tourist trade evaporated practically overnight, with the result that our only customers were Bloomsbury residents. My theatrical friends all rallied to get the business off its mark, but their custom was insufficient to meet the payroll of quite a large staff.

I was to learn, also, that cleaning other people's clothes was a distinctly uninspiring occupation and, on one occasion at least, extremely hazardous. An actress friend was one of our first customers. She had just bought at Worth's in Paris a stunning dress made of a synthetic material that none of my staff had previously encountered. On the first night she wore the new dress, she had the misfortune to spill tomato juice down the front. I assured her that we could remove the stain in a jiffy, which indeed we could and did. After the cleaning process, the routine was to iron by hand or to steam garments on the trouser press. Steaming was thought to be the appropriate finishing method in this case. The operator placed the precious dress on the press and applied his foot to the steam pedal, whereupn the dress shrank to the size of a man's cravat. No amount of pulling and stretching made the slightest difference to what now resembled a dishrag, and no amount of apology from me could console the furious owner. We paid up, of course, but it was an ominous beginning.

On another day, there was quite a stir outside the shop when an electric landau—a relic from the past—drew up at the curb. A footman handed down from its interior the grandest of grande dames of the theatre, Dame Madge Kendall. Amidst much bowing and scraping from the staff, she deposited on the counter a voluminous silk nightdress that she wished to have cleaned. Thanking her profusely for her patronage, I escorted her to the landau whilst assuring her that the nightdress would be delivered to her residence on the morrow. After the garment had been given the dry-cleaning treatment, it was noticed that a stain was still visible. A second run through the machine and it was still there. Judging by its location, we were bound to conclude that the Dame had suffered a little accident in the night. Our only recourse was to send it out to a regular laundry from whence it came back stainless, but a whole week later. To compound the felony, when the errand boy finally delivered it to Dame Madge's house, he demanded cash on the nose or no nightie!

In the summer months there used to be a mass exit from London at the weekends. The male members of the population bent on country pursuits took with them two pairs of flannel trousers, one grey to go with their sports jacket, and the other white for the tennis court or the cricket pitch. Our rapid cleaning service was a godsend to them, except on the all too frequent occasions when the identity tags came off the trousers in the machine. When that happened, the fat man arrived in the country with the thin man's trousers and vice versa—the weekend being thus ruined. Coward that I was, I used to avoid being present in the shop on Monday mornings until the storms had blown over.

I spoke earlier of the large degree that chance plays in an acting career, but that fortune's wheel should spell out a connection between a dry-cleaning business and the Theatre Royal, Drury Lane, was too preposterous to be believed. Nevertheless, it came about that my ex-employer at Chappell's, Louis Dreyfus, was coproducing a musical comedy at that venerable playhouse, and was searching for someone to play the *jeune premier*. His wife had kept track of my diversified doings in the theatre and jogged Louis's memory about my existence. Some eight years had elapsed since I had quit the Chappell's job but, Louis's curiosity being aroused, he made enquiries amongst some of the staff who had been colleagues of mine at that time. "Does anyone know how I could get in touch with that Maurice Evans who used to work here?" he asked. One of the girls told him she had no idea where I lived, but that she had recently sent a dress to be cleaned at my shop in Bloomsbury; thus contact was made and I got the job!

Not a translation from the French this time, but, what was worse, an adaptation from a German operetta entitled *Ball at the Savoy*. The English "book" was concocted by Oscar Hammerstein II, a fact that, mercifully, is not chronicled amongst his theatrical credits. An Hungarian duo of comedians imported from the Berlin production, and the American singer of Gilbert and Sullivan fame, Natalie Hall, were the principals. Not since my choirboy days had I sung in public, but here I was in 1933, at 8:15 each night, lying in a gondola with Natalie before a backdrop of the Grand Canal of Venice, lifting my voice loudly enough to be heard over a full orchestra. My character was a very restless young man, constantly hopping from one fashionable resort to another. The stagehands had their work cut out to keep the scenery in comparable motion, and Oscar was obliged to write me absurd cue lines such as, "Come on, girls—let's all go to Monte Carlo!" The show was certainly nothing to shout about, but the thrill of working in that gorgeous theatre made up for it. The flunkeys with their powdered wigs who "paged" the house curtain as it fell, the dressing rooms with fireplaces for the wintertime, the Green Room, and everyone standing at attention on stage for the national anthem at the end of each performance—all these made for a glamorous atmosphere lacking in other theatres.

The glamour, however, was somewhat tarnished by my extracurricular activities. I was still stuck with the dry-cleaning business and had to divide my time between Bloomsbury and Drury Lane. The cleaning trade continued to be slack, a condition I attributed partly to the poor demonstration techniques being employed by the girls who operated the machine in the shop window. To correct this, I got into the window to show them how to go about it. In no time at all I had a considerable crowd of girls on the pavement outside watching my showmanship. "You see how simple it is," I boasted to my assistants, to which one of them replied, "Them girls is fans of yours . . . they come up 'ere to get a close look at you."

This was my cue to be less in evidence at the beastly shop, but in order to keep the wheels turning I had persuaded the Drury Lane wardrobe mistress to award us the cleaning contract for the *Ball at the Savoy* costumes. This was a financially rewarding but time-consuming operation that demanded my constant supervision. The inescapable necessity of getting the costumes back to the theatre in time for the performances would sometimes cause me, the show's glamour boy, to arrive at the stage door in the shop's delivery van, much to the amazement of the autograph seekers gathered there.

On one occasion, making a dash for the theatre, this time in my car, I was faced by a traffic jam. I had no option but to go into reverse and take an alternative route, which, unfortunately, was a one-way street. I made the stage door by the skin of my teeth, double-parked the car, and fled to my dressing room, my two West Highland Terriers in pursuit. I congratulated myself that I got away with my driving infraction until I made my entrance in scene 2. Looking towards the opposite wings, I espied the figures of two helmeted policemen, who must have been on my tail without my being aware of it. This being strange territory to the two "bobbies," they were so engrossed with the musical goings-on that it gave me time to enlist the help of two of the prettiest chorus girls. Both representatives of the law were so bewitched by the attentions of the girls that they let me off with a caution.

It required considerable resourcefulness to achieve my nightly transplantation from the grounds of commerce to the sphere of art—even though our Germanic operetta hardly fell into that category. There was an awareness that I was treading the boards on the site of an earlier playhouse where the mighty had once strutted—Garrick, Macready, and a host of legendary actors. Superficially there would seem to be little similarity between the acting techniques employed in these unrelated media. Conversely, it was my experience that the openness of the stage settings in the Drury Lane, the freedom of movement, and the need for vocal projection were all to serve me well in my future classical undertakings. Just as a performance of *Hamlet* would be prefaced by a flourish of trumpets, so a musical would be preceded by an overture. In both cases, these musical introductions not only alerted the audience, but got the adrenalin flowing in the veins of the actors. None of that "here we go again" attitude that makes it so difficult to get into gear in a straight play, but a feeling of being on one's toes right from the start.

If *Ball at the Savoy* did nothing else for me, it seemed to have made a convert of the London *Times* critic, who had been sparing with his praise in the past. It was such a feather in my cap at the time that perhaps I may be forgiven for quoting him:

> Mr. Maurice Evans is the best "jeune premier" that there has been in musical comedy for some time. He can act, his dialogue is as good as his songs, and his charm has no relation whatever with that of a tailor's dummy or of an advertisement for toothpaste. In brief, though musical, human. [*Times*, September 9, 1933]

What was intended to be a prudent sideline was developing into a full-time headache, so I put a manageress in charge of the shop and was, consequently, able to give almost undivided attention to my professional affairs. I couldn't shake off the yoke entirely, however. Occasionally, as I was about to take my place in the gondola, a chorus girl would stop me to complain that she had sent a pair of white gloves to be cleaned, and that we had returned someone else's brown ones. From time to time there were crises that the manageress felt unable to cope with; for instance, one of the girls whose job it was to operate the cleaning machine in the shop window seemed to be overcome by the fumes given off by the cleaning chemical. I was called in to check the ventilating system, which I found to be in perfect working order. However, descending unexpectedly to the boiler room in the basement, I discovered the ailing young lady firmly clasped in the arms of the errand boy— an exercise that seemed to suggest a form of "vapours" other than the cleaning fluid.

8. THE OLD VIC

Thanks to *Ball at the Savoy*, the increased breadth I had achieved in my work encouraged me to revise my negative evaluation of my capacity to tackle the bravura of the classics. With the closing of the musical, I made a point of going to the Old Vic to watch other actors at their labours. Once I made the

THE OLD VIC

mistake of picking a matinee, the audience being composed of nothing but schoolchildren. On one wall of the auditorium there was a large sign with an arrow and the word "Boys"; on the other, its duplicate marked "Girls." Throughout the matinee there was an uninterrupted stream of visitors to these regions, making one wonder whether the author, William Shakespeare, would have considered these calls of nature to be a silent protest over having to sit through his drama. "Forewarned is forearmed," so when I joined the Old Vic later on I made it a condition in my contract that my understudy substitute for me at all school matinees. Two of these unfortunates made distinguished careers later on; one of them, Marius Goring, and the other, Alec Clunes, playing parts that otherwise would probably never have come their way.

Any out-of-work actor is a pitiable sight, and I was a particularly pathetic specimen at this juncture. When the two weeks' notice was posted on the Drury Lane notice board, I was convinced that it signaled the end of my theatrical career. Thoughts of plunging from the deck of the *Evelyn Hope* into a watery grave were dispelled in the nick of time by an offer to me to join the supporting cast of a trifling romp especially designed for the deservedly popular actress Yvonne Arnaud. Her craftily exaggerated French accent and bubbly personality made her quite irresistible both on and off stage. She had one scene at the end of the first act of this farce in which, accusing her husband of unfaithfulness, she commenced to pack her bags to leave him forever. Turning a deaf ear to his pleadings, she went frantically from one wardrobe closet to another, from tallboy to chests of drawers—emptying them in preparation for her threatened departure.

I was not involved in these antics and on a warm matinee day would climb the stairs to the stage door to get a breath of fresh air. One afternoon I was joined by a perspiring policeman who seemed to be in the mood for a gossip. He called my attention to two young ladies-of-the-town parading on the opposite side of the Soho back street. "Takes all sorts to make a world, don't it, sir?" he exclaimed. "Do you know what those girls just told me? A bloke come up to them a few nights ago and asks them, 'You two girls like to come home with me?' 'What, both of us?' says one of them. 'That's right,' he says. And do you know, sir, when they got to his place, all he wanted them to do was to take off their clothes, crawl round on their hands and knees, while he threw *jam* at them! Funny, ain't it?" When I told Yvonne of this fantasy, she went off into peals of laughter, saying she couldn't wait to dine out on the yarn.

After the matinee, the stage manager and I visited a grocery store where we bought a quantity of small pots of jam. Before the evening performance, we secreted a jam pot in every one of the drawers that Yvonne had to empty in the course of her indignant departure scene. She didn't notice anything unusual about the first couple of drawers, but by the time she reached the third it began to dawn upon her what we had been up to. Thereafter she was unable to keep a straight face; in fact, as the curtain descended, she was helpless with laughter. She vowed to take her revenge, but alas, the play came off shortly after, dealing me the punishment I deserved.

I had got out of the habit of dropping into the Webster flat, but now that I was out of work once more I resumed my visits. May Whitty welcomed me back with the news that she was about to go into rehearsal in a revival of an interesting play by Harley Granville Barker entitled *The Voysey Inheritance*, and that to the best of her knowledge no one had been cast as the son, Edward Voysey. It was to be the first legitimate production to be staged at the recently restored Sadler's Wells Theatre, an offshoot of the Old Vic, representing years of determined fund raising on the part of the Old Vic's visionary manageress, Lilian Baylis—of whom, more later.

All in all, it struck me as being a good way of dipping a toe in the Old Vic waters and to do so in a contemporary play. It had the added attraction that Granville Barker had agreed to come out of retirement to direct the play, and his name was one to conjure with. Some years before this he had turned his back on the English theatre, which had failed to give him his due. His brilliant theories about Shakespearean production, his notable presentations of Bernard Shaw's plays, and his own stature as a playwright (e.g., *The Madras House*) were never fully appreciated. I think he felt that Sadler's Wells deserved the kind of encouragement that he himself had been denied.

The rehearsals for *The Voysey Inheritance* were awesome for me in particular, because Barker himself had played my part in the original production. Very occasionally, in order to demonstrate a value he wished to emphasize, he would show me how he had delivered the lines at that point. It took considerable restraint on my part to refrain from letting him see that I considered his style of acting sadly out of date—but as long as he stayed put in the director's chair, he was of enormous help.

The play centres around the solid, genial, respected lawyer, Mr. Voysey, who announces quite brazenly to his family one day that he has been using clients' trust funds for his private speculations. The burden of the sins of his father fall upon young Edward—an interesting Hamlet sort of part to play. My stone-deaf mother was May Whitty, and very funny she was in the role. Passing the open door of her dressing room one night, I was commanded to enter. "You are very good in this play, but it's still collar-and-tie stuff. Whether you like it or not, I'm going to tell Lilian Baylis she ought to engage you for her next Old Vic season." And so, at last, the day came for me to enter the inner sanctum to discuss terms.

Much has been written about Lilian Baylis, but only by working for her could her full flavour be savoured. Paralysis of the muscles on one side of her face contributed to the individuality of this fearless lady. People imagine her to have been a fanatic devotee of William Shakespeare, whereas in actuality opera was her first love. It must have been quite a shock to Charles Laughton when he arrived with money donated by the Pilgrim's Trust and poured it into the willing hands of the goddess of the Old Vic. His season immediately preceded mine, and Lilian agreed to allow Laughton to recruit his own Shakespearean company. At his first meeting with her, he was profuse in his promises to make his season a high-water mark in the theatre's history, adding that he had recently been sleeping with a copy of the works of the Bard under his pillow. "That's all very nice, dear, but can you learn his lovely lines?" was typical of her protective attitude toward her two theatres and her reputation.

Another example was the famous occurrence when she was being driven by her secretary, Mrs. Clark, to the newly opened Sadler's Wells. Her means of transport was an extraordinary conveyance known as a "Trojan." It was propelled by a motorcycle engine connected by a long rubber belt to one of the vehicle's rear wheels. As a result, the car resembled a crab when it was in motion. On this day a traffic cop signaled Mrs. Clark to an abrupt halt, which resulted in the Trojan turning turtle and pinning Lilian beneath it. Mrs. Clark, having been thrown clear in the accident, approached the policeman, breathlessly exclaiming, "Officer, officer, do you know who is under that car? Lilian Baylis of the Old Vic!" A voice beneath the Trojan echoed, "*And* Sadler's Wells, dear."

The addition of Sadler's Wells to Lilian's operation turned out to be a blessing for her drama companies. Hitherto they had had to alternate with the opera season at the Vic, which had made for discomfort of a very special kind. When the final bill of the opera company happened to be *Lohengrin*, the dramatic actors taking over the stage from the singers of the previous week would be seen scratching themselves. It appeared that Lohengrin's swan was infested with fleas and, despite a liberal coating of "size" to glue them in, many of them escaped the painter's brush and took refuge in the actor's costumes. "To be [*scratch*] or not to be [*scratch*] . . ." could hardly pass as a new interpretation of the soliloquy. By the time I joined the Old Vic, the opera company had removed itself and its companions to the Sadler's Wells, where it alternated with Ninette de Valois's ballet company. Dancers, it seemed, were less inviting hosts to the pests; either that or a more sanitary swan had finally been invested in.

On September 17, 1934, the Vic curtain rose, together with my hopes, on a production of *Antony and Cleopatra*. A Bostonian actress, Mary Newcombe, was the enchantress of the Nile and another non-Shakespearean, Wilfred Lawson, the Antony. Both seasoned performers were also taking their first dip

1901–1935

not only in the Nile but in Shakespearean waters. Consequently, my baptism as Octavius Caesar aroused fewer goose pimples than would otherwise have been the case. A pat on the back by the *Times* critic for my portrayal made me feel I had survived the first plunge and could look ahead with increased confidence.

Due to an inadequate budget, the production suffered from rather sketchy scenery. Painted backdrops were employed to create the frequent transitions between Rome and Alexandria. At one hilarious performance, the "flyman," whose job it was to raise and lower the drops, had been indulging in another sort of "drop" at the local public house, with the result that he mixed up his ropes. In the middle of an Alexandria scene he started to lower the panorama of Rome. The passionate lovers, realizing that they were about to be cut off from the audience's view, scuttled downstage to continue the Alexandria scene, now unaccountably taking place in Rome. Frantic signals from the prompt corner to the flyman caused Rome to disappear and the lovers were once more in Alexandria.

The mishap of another performance had nothing to do with a stagehand but, rather, with an actor's lapse of memory. It is the final scene of the play— Cleopatra is dead on her throne, the asp clasped to her bosom—her serving girls, having breathed their last, lie at her feet. Enter Dolabella (played by that seasoned Shakespearean actor, Abraham Sofaer). Surveying the tragic scene, "Sofie," for some reason, proceeded to spout a long speech from *Julius Caesar*. Realising that something more than her "crown" was "awry," Cleopatra's corpse opened one baleful eye in an effort to dam Sofie's loquacity, but it required an imperious early entrance by me to staunch the flow.

Although we supporting players were favorably mentioned by the critics, they maintained certain reservations about the principals. None of the reviewers, however, waxed as opprobrious as they did about two other Cleopatras: John Mason Brown's famous summing up of Tallulah's impersonation, "Miss Bankhead barged her way down the Nile—and *sank*"; or the convoluted appraisal of Eugenie Leontovitch's attempt, "If Miss Leontovitch's performance did nothing else, it settled once and for all the Bacon-Shakespeare controversy, for now a Royal Commission has only to open both graves to see which has been most turned in!"

No promises had been made as to what parts I was to play during the season, and I assumed I would be the second string to some more experienced actor's bow. Instead of which, overnight I was promoted to the onerous status of leading man and was told that my next assignment was to play the title role in *Richard II*. Knowing that I had only three weeks to rehearse while playing Octavius Caesar at night, I hurriedly read the play and blanched at the prospect. I was on the verge of begging the management to relieve me of the

THE OLD VIC

task when, one morning, I encountered John Gielgud on the steps of the Midland Bank where we both had accounts—or overdrafts as the case might be. Aware that he had played the wayward king during one of his Vic seasons, I told him of my dilemma, adding that I really didn't think much of the role of Richard. "Don't be ridiculous!" he said. "It's the most wonderful part in all Shakespeare for a young man." Here was another instance of a helping hand, and in this case, one that had the deepest influence in my career.

A bare three weeks of rehearsal and I was to put his recommendation to the test. This was a woefully short time in which to find the clue to Richard's capricious character, but the search was tremendously assisted by a remark made by our costume designer, David Ffolkes. He said he thought that just because the character was a king, it was utter nonsense for him to wear a crown at all times. "Very uncomfortable on the pillow," he added. So David designed for me a series of saucy, bejewelled hats to be worn in the early portions of the play, with Italianate costumes to match. This not only gave me the key to the wilful nature of the young monarch, but made a telling point when I postponed wearing a crown until the time had come for Richard to surrender it to Bolingbroke—"Here, cousin, *seize* the crown." So typical was this of Richard's love of histrionics that a progressive characterisation emerged of a playboy king who grew in stature only in adversity.

In the brief time given me for preparation, I'm sure I left much to be desired on opening night, but must have got into my stride once that was over. Departing from custom, Miss Baylis revived the production six months later for an additional two weeks' run. It was then that my watchdog on the *Times* had this to say:

> It's the special grace of Mr. Evans' performance that, as it has matured, it has made clear the distinction between Richard in prosperity and Richard thrown back upon his own resources. At the Old Vic Mr. Evans has greatly increased his reputation, and is now to be recognised as one of the few actors who, knowing how to distinguish between good tradition and bad, does not hesitate to take a new line when his reason and his art are prepared to justify it. [*Times*, April 6, 1935]

With two dramatic roles under my belt I was then to have my first experience of playing Shakespearean comedy, an assignment that usually signifies one of his clowns. You have to be born with a special talent to be anything but tiresome in a part such as the gravedigger, Sir Toby Belch, or Sir Andrew Aguecheek.

Not being endowed with such qualities, I was spared the embarrassment of falling on my face attempting to be clownish. The company boasted two actors (one of them Alan Webb) who had the method at their fingertips and were a joy to watch. Thus for my introduction to Shakespearean comedy I was cast as the boastful Benedick in *Much Ado About Nothing* opposite Mary Newcombe's Beatrice. Our scenes together were great fun to play although, like all our predecessors in the parts, we became rather lost in the ramifications of the plot of this somewhat muddled comedy.

Mary Newcombe had made it a condition of her joining the company that a production of George Bernard Shaw's *Saint Joan* be mounted for her benefit. In doing so she couldn't possibly have known that out of all dramatic literature she had picked my very favourite play.

Years before, seeing an announcement of its premiere at the New Theatre with Sybil Thorndike as the Maid of Orleans, I had stood in the queue for a seat in the top gallery. That evening made an indelible impression on my young mind, doing more than anything else to nourish in me a passion for the art of the theatre. The scenic splendours by Ricketts, a fine aggregation of actors, and Sybil's luminous Joan added up to theatre at its finest hour. I left the theatre in a daze with her agonised plea still ringing in my ears—"How long, O Lord, how long!" In this state of enchantment, I wandered up St. Martin's Lane and into Leicester Square with the intention of going home on an Underground train. Quite unconsciously, I descended the steps to what, in my bemused condition, I thought to be the station, only to find my way barred by an indignant female—bucket and mop in hand. I had inadvertently strayed into the entrance to the "Ladies" instead of the Underground. My musings were quickly banished by the attendant's obvious suspicions of my intentions in invading her forbidden territory, and I beat a shamefaced retreat into the upper air.

Since those days, I have seen a number of actresses playing Shaw's Joan, but none of them, I feel, could hold a candle to Sybil's portrayal. She gave the farm girl a strong hint of the androgynous in her characterisation. She used the north-country accent indicated by Shaw in his text, and was the sort of girl who in this day and age would be a militant advocate of women's rights. Most other Joans play the part as though Joan knows from the start that it is her destiny to be burnt to a crisp. Mary Newcombe was not allowed to fall into any such error, due largely to the presence at our rehearsals of Bernard Shaw himself. It was an inspiration, of course, to know he was "out front" even though he sometimes dropped off to sleep during the lengthy tent scene between the clerics and the Earl of Warwick. During his waking moments, it behooved us to be word perfect, strictly avoiding any tendency to paraphrase. I was lucky to be cast as the Dauphin, the lacklustre heir to the throne whom Joan impertinently insisted on addressing as "Charlie." Shaw seemed to like what I was doing in the role and suggested a piece of business that brought down the house, namely, the moment when the Dauphin, with Joan as his ally, quite unexpectedly advances tentatively upon a bullying courtier and snaps his fingers in the courtier's face. This caused one aisle sitter to write, "Mr. Maurice Evans plays the Dauphin as a deflated youth with one superb moment of inflation."

Contrary to what one might deduce from Shaw's writing and strange political opinions—he once startled America by saying there was no hope for the United States until it tore up the obsolete Constitution and started all over again—personally he was a courteous and considerate gentleman. He put me at my ease to such an extent that I had the nerve to ask him whether, in the play's epilogue, we might cut a heavy-handed joke he had written about the statue of St. Joan being a traffic hazard in downtown Rheims. Instead of flaying me for my presumptuousness, he said merely, "My boy, I write very long, boring plays. I know pretty well when the audience is about to go to sleep, so I put in a joke. If I can think of a good one, so much the better; if not, even a bad one has to do." The Irish pixie came out in G.B.S. when Mary Newcombe wanted him to suggest what kind of attitude she should strike as the final curtain fell. "No attitude, my dear," he said, "just jump into bed with Charlie."

Not content with sitting through a long dress rehearsal, Shaw came up on the stage when he saw photographers were about to take routine pictures. It was revealed to our surprise that he was an avid and accomplished amateur photographer. He insisted on posing us for the photographs, oblivious of our urgent desire to get done with the picture taking, so that we could dash home for a bite to eat and back again for that evening's performance of *Much Ado*. To distract him from his preoccupation with the camera, I told him, since we were neighbours, that I'd be happy to drive him back to the Adelphi. He glanced at his pocket watch and said, "No, thank you, I'm late as it is," and he strode on his long legs out through the stage door. He was halfway across the Waterloo Bridge when I drove by him; and by the time I had fought my way through the congested traffic on the Strand, he was probably sitting down to his unappetising vegetarian supper.

On New Year's Day of 1935, James Agate, the doyen of the London drama critics, went early to the Old Vic to cover the first night of *The Taming of the Shrew*, with Cathleen Nesbitt as Katharina and me as Petruchio. His review in the *Sunday Times* bore the headline "The Taming of Eugene Onegin." It appeared that, while waiting for the performance to commence, he had dozed off, but when the curtain rose, instead of the sun-drenched streets of Padua, he found himself looking at a scene of snow-capped mountains. Someone had omitted to tell him that at this point in our Vic season we switched with the opera company, and thus our opening was at Sadler's Wells.

1901—1935

Although he wrote a very deft and amusing piece, we were never to know what he would have thought of us.

Cathleen and I had a romp in *The Shrew*, and although I was required to treat Katharina pretty roughly, it did not reach the extremes of our previous association in *Diversion* when I had to strangle her. Years later, in the early 1980s, this beautiful actress, in spite of or because of her ninety-four years, was playing Rex Harrison's mother in *My Fair Lady*. I asked a friend, who was attending the show, to go backstage and give Cathleen my loving remembrances. He called me up afterwards to tell me he had delivered my greetings.

"Was she surprised?" I asked.

"Guess she must have been, because all she had to say was, 'Maurice Evans! Is *he* still alive?'"

Reliving those Old Vic days of constant study and rehearsal, I sometimes marvel that I did survive. I very nearly reached the end of my tether when, during the energetic run of *The Shrew*, I had to memorise the difficult lines of Iago. Whereas I had comparatively little trouble in learning Shakespeare's blank verse—due, probably, to its insistent rhythm—my brain rebelled when it came to the prose. It was handy for me that Abraham Sofaer (Othello) had played Iago in a previous production and was, therefore, able to correct me when I made mistakes. All the same, it was grossly unprofessional to rely on a fellow actor to do this service. On my way to the theatre on opening night, I had to admit to myself the awful truth that I really didn't know the part. In the hope of gaining a little courage, I broke my strict rule of never drinking before a show, and dropped in at an Oyster Bar in the Strand, where I washed down half-a-dozen oysters with a split of champagne.

That first performance of *Othello* was a nightmare not only for me but for poor Sofie, who spent half the time prompting me instead of concentrating on his own performance. To add insult to injury, a lack of perception on the part of James Agate (the self-styled infallible critic) caused him to misjudge my fumblings as deliberate inventions: "This was a boyish, eager Iago . . . vivid and full of variety, making you feel that his words were the coinage of an ecstasy now first minted, and not the measured delivery of something conned and pondered."

It was my devout hope that Sofie would be mollified by Ivor Brown's review in the London *Observer*, which praised his Othello and assured him that I was not out to steal his thunder:

> Mr. Maurice Evans gave us the real Iago; a man of twenty-eight,
> brusque soldier, quick of wit, attractive, seemingly honest, moving with
> a hearty application to the pleasures of revenge. He was part of the
> play. Too often Iago has been a middle-aged gentleman, with his name
> in lights on the doorstep, who seems to say, "This is my night out.

THE OLD VIC

Just watch me act Othello off the stage." Mr. Evans, an open-faced, chuckling rogue, and not a "star" demonstrating the importance of being sinister, persuaded me to believe in Iago's action more than any I have seen in the part. [*Observer*, January 27, 1935]

Sofie was an unusually fine Othello, having it greatly in his favour that, being half-Arab by birth, he had no need to "black up" as the Moor of Venice, since nature had made him the genuine article. I've always thought Othello a thankless role because jealously is its motivation; although almost all human beings at some time in their lives have been torn apart by jealousy, when portrayed on the stage it fails to arouse sympathetic response from audiences. The average reaction is, "For heaven's sake, snap out of it!"

It would be a misnomer to describe *Othello* as a comedy, but it got perilously close to it at one of our performances. At the rear of the auditorium, the Old Vic had a coffee-and-buns snack bar that boasted a small food elevator. Lilian Baylis had given strict orders that the theatre's black cat was to be shut up in this contraption during performances, but came the night when her order was neglected. Onstage, I had just entered for the first of the three scenes wherein Iago pours poisonous thoughts into the ear of Othello, and was greeted by titters from the audience, which seemed strange. When that happens in a modern play, one's automatic reaction is to check one's fly, but no such vent exists in Elizabethan doublet and hose, so I walked offstage none the wiser as to the cause of the mirth.

The upstage area of the setting was a slightly elevated platform open at its offstage ends. As I made my second entrance, I became aware that Othello and I were not alone. Unknown to me, the black cat had apparently followed my first exit and hidden under the platform, but had now decided to be my constant companion. Unrestrained laughter broke out as Blackie rubbed passionately against my leg while, just as passionately, I resumed corrupting Othello's nature. By then, Lilian Baylis, doing her accounts in the stage box, popped her head through the heavy velvet drapes to see what was going on. She rushed backstage just as I was making my second exit with Blackie close on my heels. Lilian made a grab for the cat, who again darted under the platform. Down went Lilian on her hands and knees and out of the corner of the good side of her mouth made foolish sucking noises alternating with "Pretty pussy, pretty pussy!"—all to no avail. I heard Othello's approaching cue for my final entrance and prayed that Lilian and her cohorts would somehow immobilise the intruder, but no such luck. On I stalked again with my "familiar" at my side, this time to be greeted by howls of laughter and applause. "Enough of this," I thought, walking Blackie down to the apron stage part of the orchestra pit. Careful of my aim, I administered a resounding kick to Blackie's rear end sending him sailing through the air to land with a mighty

1901–1935

crash on the orchestra cymbals. Cheers broke out to mark the end of a beautiful friendship, but it remained for Sofie and me to restore order and decorum.

Another salient memory of this production concerned the dry-cleaning shop, which, incidentally, had become more prosperous. The driver of our delivery van, for reasons that escape me, also acted as my dresser at the theatre during the run of *Othello*. Towards the end of the play, it will be remembered, Iago does not appear for a considerable time—the hiatus being amply filled by Othello's protracted smothering of Desdemona. While I relaxed in my dressing room, my dresser posted himself in the wings to watch the action. He had orders to inform me when the tragic scene reached its climax, so that I might ready myself for my entrance. His manner of conveying this intelligence consisted of his knocking on my door and saying in his delightful Cockney accent "Okay, sir, 'e done 'er in!"

In the bitter cold of February, while we were rehearsing for Shaw's *Major Barbara*, I played Euripides' *Hippolytus*, in a scanty leopard-skin tunic—and goose pimples. As in my amateur days, I was again cast as Barbara's chilly swain, Adolphus Cusins, and, although some fifteen years had elapsed since my previous encounter with the role, I was glad to find that I still remembered most of the dialogue. The interlude thus provided afforded me the badly needed time to study for my next formidable assignment. John Gielgud and Michael MacLiammoor had each been acclaimed for his Hamlet in that same season, and now it was my turn to enter the Elsinore stakes. Lilian Baylis decreed that the best way to avoid odious comparisons was for the Old Vic to present the uncut, four-hour text, billed as *Hamlet—In Its Entirety*. I privately thought she was out of her mind to risk the sufferance of the critics already satiated with the Dane, but with her good eye on the box office she wouldn't say No. Her uncanny sense of what constituted a "draw" was rewarded by the *Times* maintaining that "One sees it as a play that no one can be trusted to cut."

It was just as well that the man on the *Times* wasn't around for our first matinee, however. Although I had, somehow or other, managed to master the lines of the "Entirety" (or the "Eternity" as one critic described it), the cut version had to be employed for the afternoon performances. There had been no time to rehearse the elisions, so I just kept on going until someone onstage coughed, stomped his foot, or made a discreet throat-slicing gesture. In the Queen's closet scene, Shakespeare has given Gertrude a number of short phrases aimed at stemming her son's torrent of abuse, but, although no cuts were made in that particular scene, she stood ready with an armoury of quotes that she or others could employ elsewhere in the play—lines such as, "O speak no more"..."No more, sweet Hamlet"..."No more!!" At Lilian Baylis's

THE OLD VIC

insistence we were required to give three performances a week of the truncated text and five of the "Entirety"; only in this way could her precious matinee receipts be preserved regardless of the strain it put upon us poor actors.

I suppose it is every actor's cherished dream to play Hamlet at some time in his career, but in my case there was no chance to dream because the opportunity simply dropped in my lap. I was thirty-four when my chance came, though I'm told I looked considerably younger. The youthful aspect and innate energy that had condemned me to perennial juvenile roles in the commercial theatre then proved advantageous; these qualities were compatible with my rooted conviction that Shakespeare never intended Hamlet to be portrayed as suffering from mental dyspepsia. The appellation of the "Gloomy Dane" had tripped up many an actor before me and was a connotation that I strove to avoid at all costs. Until he has played the part in the "Entirety," an actor is apt to fail to observe that, in addition to revealing the indecisive side of Hamlet's characters, he is obliged to drive the plot bowling along. Four hours is a long span in which to hold audience attention, and neglecting the more mercurial aspects of the Prince's nature is asking for trouble. My emphasis in keeping the ball in the air caused Ivor Brown to remark in his *Manchester Guardian* review:

> Mr. Maurice Evans, who played the part tonight, had masterly memorised it all, and was eager to demonstrate the light touches of Hamlet's wit as well as to unpack his heart with the words of anger and chagrin. Mr. Evans had completed a season of extremely heavy parts with a brave shouldering of the longest. From six-thirty till close upon eleven he was continually in action, passing from a deft delivery of the quips to a strong show of passion when the times to declare it made their call upon his spirit.

The critic of the *Daily Mail* threw aside all restraint by declaring me to be "the finest Hamlet of our time!"

This being the final offering of the season, I was again beginning to say to myself, "Where do I go from here?" The answer came in the form of a visiting card sent backstage one night. It bore the name "Guthrie McClintic" with an address in New York, but I'm ashamed to say that it meant nothing to me. I displayed even more unforgivable ignorance when he came to my dressing room asking me if I would be interested in going to America to play Romeo to his wife's Juliet. I did my best to hide my provincial naïveté and asked for time to think it over. Before leaving, he enquired whether, by any chance, I was related to Edith Evans who, he explained, had been playing the nurse in his production.

He had no sooner left than I was on the telephone to Edith, asking the name of Guthrie McClintic's wife. "You mean to say you've never heard of the First Lady of the American Theatre—Miss Katharine Cornell? How dare you!" She then informed me that up to the time of her own husband's death, she, Basil Rathbone (Romeo), and Brian Aherne (Mercutio) had all been in Katharine Cornell's company during the New York run of *Romeo and Juliet*, but were prevented by other commitments from staying with her for the tour in the fall of 1935. Although I didn't in the least resemble Basil—Mrs. Patrick Campbell once described his visage as "a couple of profiles slapped together"— nor was Ralph Richardson a look-alike for Brian, we were both being asked to step into their shoes.

Several circumstances made it tempting for me to accept Guthrie McClintic's proposal. In the first place, I felt that, having been on display at the Old Vic for almost a year in a variety of splendid parts, I was entitled to receive some attention from West End managements, but their continued silence was anything but golden. Secondly, I had just received notice that most of the Adelphi, including my flat, was shortly to be demolished to make room for the concrete palace known as the Shell-Mex building. Finally, the idea of putting the Atlantic Ocean between me and the dry-cleaning shop had a magnetic attraction. These cogitations very nearly wrecked the following evening's *Hamlet*, forcing me to set them aside until after the show's imminent final performance.

It was a long-standing custom for the last night of the Old Vic season to be given over to excerpts from the plays presented during that year, plus guest appearances by some past favourites such as Sybil Thorndike and Lewis Casson. The "fan club" supplied a large cake, slices of which were handed across the footlights to us exhausted actors. We were then expected to join sticky hands with the audience in the singing of "Auld Lang Syne." The crowning moment of this questionable ceremony was the entrance on stage of *Doctor* Lilian Baylis resplendent in mortar-board, hood, and gown. After thanking the audience (while cajoling them to attend in greater numbers the following season), she called on each member of the company to make a brief speech, standing close behind us herself as we did so.

When it came my turn, I decided to forgive and forget the occasional grievances she had caused us, by saying that the season had been an harmonious experience and that we had worked together as one happy family. This admittedly fulsome remark was greeted by a grunt from her ladyship and an audible aside of, "Oh, what a liar!" It would not be fair to describe it as having been a season of discontent, but the atmosphere had not been all sweetness and light. We were all miserably underpaid and overworked, but we were young enough to survive. An occasional tongue lashing by Lilian had the salutary effect of cutting some of us down to size—preparing us, in the future, to "bear the whips and scorn of time" and of obtuse writers, directors, and assorted producers.

One of Lilian's shrewd stratagems was to admit a number of American students to swell our numbers, a privilege for which they paid a substantial fee. They were seldom given more to do than backstage chores, carrying spears and sometimes a minor understudy assignment. I'm told that in a previous season the Horatio was taken ill and was unable to appear. No understudy had been appointed or rehearsed, so one of the student members bravely volunteered to "wing" the part. He was wrapped in a voluminous cloak, which hid a copy of *Hamlet* that he carried, as well as a flashlight. His noble effort, which succeeded in keeping the curtain up, received short shrift from one quarter, however. No "flights of angels" sang *him* to *his* rest that night. On the contrary, all Miss Baylis had to say was, "Well, dear, you had your chance . . . *and* missed it!"

With the finish of the Vic season, I took a badly needed rest, lounging about the deck of the *Evelyn Hope* and getting familiar with *Romeo and Juliet*. I have to confess that it was not a case of love at first sight, but I came to the conclusion that if Guthrie McClintic deemed me suitable—and he had given me a month's grace to make up my mind—it was not my place to reason why. In any case, the American tour was limited to four months after which I fully expected to return to England to find the dry-cleaning shop disposed of and a change for the better in my theatrical fortunes. A cable of grateful acceptance was despatched to New York, after which I settled down to enjoy two months of leisure. These were interrupted only by preparations to vacate my flat, store my furniture, and pay my tailor's bill.

It had been a year since I had been able to do any theatregoing, so I made up for lost time by seeing as many plays as I could, amongst them having my first exposure to Henrik Ibsen. For years Bernard Shaw's championship of Ibsen had failed to arouse the British public from its apathy. Now the cudgel was taken up by J. T. Grein, another Ibsenite. A special matinee of *Ghosts* was to be put on at my old stamping ground, Wyndham's Theatre, starring Mrs. Patrick Campbell and John Gielgud. I went to the performance full of expectation, only to be sorely disappointed by Mrs. Campbell's rotund Mrs. Alving. Towards the end of the play she was supposed to sit stock still in the conservatory at the rear of the stage while John played, beautifully, his "give me the sun" scene. Not Mrs. Pat, however; she became seized by paroxysms of coughing and handkerchief waving, which drew attention to herself, quite spoiling John's "moment."

At the end of the performance I went backstage to congratulate and commiserate with John, only to be confronted by Mrs. Campbell (whom I had never met) with a Pekinese dog at her bosom. Thrusting the creature into my arms, she said, "You've got a kind face, take Wung Wung-Woosh Woosh for a walk." Obedient to her command, I paraded up and down the stage-door alley, but the recalcitrant Peke took so long to make up its mind that I never got to convey my condolences to John.

Mrs. Pat's dogs were constantly getting her into trouble. She told me much later of a time when, hoping to evade the quarantine law, she smuggled one Peke, called "Moonbeam," into England. "I had Moonbeam safely tucked away under the front of my fur coat, but just as I was going through customs, she let out a little yip. I hoped the customs officer would think I had a barking tumor, but I couldn't fool him, so they put my little pet in quarantine." Then, of course, there was the New York taxi story which, in spite of being attributed to Mrs. Fiske and others, I still believe to be a Campbell original. Emerging from a taxi with Moonbeam on a leash, she was hailed by the driver as she crossed the sidewalk. "Hey, lady, did your dog do that in my cab?" "Not at all," came the reply, "I did." And on she swept.

Farewell parties were given for me in advance of my sailing to New York in September 1935. One of them, if I remember correctly, was at Cedric and "Pixie" Hardwicke's flat across the road on John Street. An amateur palmist was one of the their guests and, in spite of my skepticism, I agreed to have my future read. Her prediction was most optimistic, including a prophecy that I would receive a substantial inheritance from a relative. This I dismissed as nonsense, since no rich relatives showed up on our family tree. Not many months later, when I was in the States, I received a letter from the solicitors to my father's second cousin, Florence Waters—the lady from *Diversion* days— telling me that she had passed away. To my great surprise, the old dear had remembered me in her will, having made a bequest to me of some real estate that she owned. Her generosity gave me a sense of financial security, to a large extent curing me of a tendency to be convinced that a single day's unemployment spelt disaster.

Had I known at the time of my departure for the States that this nest egg was in the offing, I would have embarked with a greater sense of security as I set forth to engage in the feud between the Montagues and the Capulets.

II

1935–1942

"... *their exits and their entrances ...*"

1. THE NEW WORLD

ARLY IN SEPTEMBER 1935 I boarded the *Berengaria* at Southampton. As the coastline of my birthplace, Dorset, faded into the distance, doubts began to assail me. At the age of thirty-four what business had I to think I could be convincing as the teenaged Romeo? There was some comfort in knowing from *Who's Who* that Miss Cornell had already proved that at a ripe thirty-six she was entirely believable as Juliet. Even so, I felt at sea in more senses than one.

Such knowledge as I had of America was limited to the impressions I had gained from Hollywood movies; so, in outfitting myself for the journey, I supposed I should resemble the screen's image of a Shakespearean actor battling his way through the winter snows of the eastern seaboard. To achieve such an appearance I had purchased at Moss Bros. a second-hand, floor-length, fur-lined overcoat with a beaver collar. I think I donned this absurd raiment only once during the forthcoming tour and that was for an inquisitive photographer in Chicago. By then I had settled down in the States, but was eager to have a picture of that garment to remind me of my earlier apprehensions.

I didn't have much time to enjoy the amenities of the venerable Cunard liner, due to the formidable task that awaited me at the end of the Atlantic crossing. To be replacing another actor is always an unenviable stint, and I had to follow Basil Rathbone's Romeo. The least I could do was to be word perfect in the part, knowing that my fellow actors would expect it even from an overaged juvenile. With all the will in the world, the original players would not be able to resist saying, "Basil used to move away from me on that line," or, "Is *that* my cue?" I steeled myself against this probability and concentrated on studying the text.

81

1935–1942

I had done a considerable amount of research on previous productions of the play and came to the conclusion that I should be on the lookout for pitfalls. Romeo seemed to have come off poorly in the past, disappointing audiences, who generally come to the play with the notion that he is the ideal lover of all time. They are quickly turned against him by his oddly unsympathetic behaviour. He falls in and out of love and is directly responsible for the killing of his friend, Mercutio, by Tybalt. He must sob like a child when he takes refuge in Friar Lawrence's cell ("blubbering and weeping, weeping and blubbering"), and must leave the newly wedded Juliet to face the consequences of their sudden marriage and his banishment. How to make this boy credible? My watchwords throughout my career have been two "C's"—clarity and credibility. No problem about "C" number one, but what to do about "C" number two? Before leaving London, I had written to Granville Barker begging for help. His prefaces to Shakespeare had been, and still are, my credo, but I wanted more from him than the printed word: "*Romeo and Juliet* is a lyric tragedy, and this must be the key to its interpreting." All very true, but it didn't solve my problem. Thus I asked him, "What about the contradictions inherent in Romeo's conduct?"

On the wall of my ship's cabin I pinned up this reply: "Always bear in mind that Romeo is a hot-blooded Italian. No polite duelling with Tybalt—fight him like a tiger, and stab him with your dagger once he has fallen. Cling to his prostrate body and keep on stabbing and stabbing until you are dragged apart by sheer force." Referring to the balcony scene, he had this to say, "It must be acted with the unconscious naïveté of children. Whether the players are sixteen or sixty they must assume an innocence and ingenuousness for this interlude that is absolutely required by this text." Moral: Don't behave like a lovesick swain. Instead, and without sacrificing the lyrical mood of the scene, play it with uninhibited exuberance. I should almost literally be standing on my toes, like a ballet dancer.

With these thoughts churning around in my head, I spent most of my eight days on the *Berengaria* locked in my cabin, studying my lines and rehearsing them at the top of my lungs. What my neighbouring shipmates thought of this, they were too polite to say, but my steward took care to keep my cabin porthole firmly locked, just in case he had some nut on his hands. There was a note of relief in his voice when he announced that we were scheduled to dock in New York early the next morning.

I was up on deck at dawn to see what, on subsequent crossings, I came to regard as one of the most exciting views in the world—the sun rising over the cloud-capped towers of Manhattan. On this initial introduction, however, I was stunned. From the distance, the city looked to me like nothing so much as a house of cards, divided by cracks, which, from where I stood, looked about

THE NEW WORLD

half an inch in width. It seemed inconceivable that human beings could actually *live* in those forbidding canyons, but, as the tugs nudged us closer to the island, I realized it was the long-distance perspective that had lent it so little enchantment.

The tedious immigration formalities made me impatient to get ashore to see what the place was really like, consequently I descended the gangway in rather unseemly haste. A stentorian voice rang out, "Watch your step!" I turned around to see who had issued this somewhat startling welcome to a stranger in his land. To my insular eyes the speaker was a curiosity—an immensely tall black official. It now seems hard to believe that in 1935 the only members of the black race we ever saw in England were occasional jazz-band musicians and nightclub entertainers. Though my greeter's pigmentation was a novelty, I took his cautionary instructions to heart. In the ensuing weeks, I took care to follow his advice when I spied a crack in the sidewalks of New York.

Emissaries from the Cornell-McClintic office were on the dock to meet me and were overflowing with cordiality. They put me in a Checker cab with my steamer trunk on the rack on the back, and told me they would see me at the hotel. In a matter of minutes I found myself replying to a barrage of personal questions fired at me by the driver of the cab in an accent I was later to learn was typical of denizens of the Bronx. After the uncommunicative manner of London taxi drivers, this struck me as friendly but strange. If all New Yorkers talk in this manner, I thought, they won't understand one word I'm saying. Leslie Banks had warned me in advance that on his first visit he had some difficulty in developing an ear for accents. On his first night at the Algonquin Hotel, he asked the operator for a wake-up call the following morning at 8 o'clock. Leslie was duly awakened from a deep sleep and, wondering where he was, croaked an "Hello" into the telephone, to hear the operator saying in her painfully bright tones what sounded to Leslie's unattuned ear like. "Good morning Ada Clark."

"Afraid you have the wrong room," he said.

Not quite so brightly the operator repeated, "Good morning Ada Clark," several times over.

Exasperated, Leslie finally said, "Listen! I am trying to get some sleep after a long journey, and my name is *not* Ada Clark, so I'm hanging up." Glancing at his bedside clock as he did so he saw that, instead of being in the wee hours, it was actually 8 o'clock. "Make a mental note," he said to himself, "eight o'clock equals Ada Clark."

To get used to the sounds, the smells, and the sights of New York made my first day abroad in the city a fascinating experience. It was one of those rare Indian summer days when the thermometer shot up into the nineties, which, for an Englishman, was like being on the equator. I had promised to look up a friend of one of the Old Vic American students, so took advantage of this day to pay him a visit. Drenched in perspiration, I eventually found my way to Greenwich Village and knocked on the door of his flat on Bank Street. "Come in," said a voice. I entered to be confronted by the sight of a young gentleman seated in a chair, stark naked, with his feet in the refrigerator. An electric fan aimed at the fridge was, I assumed, for the purpose of cooling the rest of his anatomy. It was a very informal atmosphere in which to make an acquaintance. With his business suit on he became my guide for the next few weeks to the places of interest, the restaurants, and the night life of Manhattan.

I counted myself lucky that the Great Depression was on the decline and that Prohibition was no longer in force, particularly the latter. Actors returning to England from the States had told me stories of the days of the Volstead Act—the speakeasies, the bootleggers, and bathtub gin. One friend assured me that it was not in the least untoward when my old friend Dame May Whitty invited him to pay her a farewell visit at the Algonquin, adding, "Bring an empty bottle or two." This dignified lady's show had just closed and she was about to return to London. During the run of the play, she, like most of her colleagues, had been in the habit of brewing her own gin. Now that it was time to go home, she was distributing what was left.

On the first day of rehearsals, I always feel as though I am enduring the agony of the new boy at school, and *Romeo and Juliet* was no different. With the exception of Ralph Richardson, whom I knew only by sight, the rest of the company, though well known to each other, were total strangers to me. This feeling of being a rank outsider was quickly dissipated by the arrival at rehearsal of Katharine Cornell and her secretary, Gertrude Macy—both of them radiating warmth and good cheer. Guthrie McClintic had a way with him, too, which instantly broke the ice. That morning he had a fund of jokes and gossip to impart, after which he said reluctantly, "Well, I suppose we'd better do a bit of rehearsing." We all gathered round a table and introductions were made. It was only then that, in addition to many other adjustments, I was fated to endure a second christening. It is typical of the British insularity deliberately to mispronounce names that are foreign in origin, the theory being that once they have come into common British usage they must be made to sound as if they are home-grown. Thus my charming French Christian name of "Maurice" is perversely pronounced "Morris" in England. I found it refreshing, if somewhat confusing, to hear myself being introduced quite properly à la française, even though Ralph Richardson stoutly refused to conform. One other member of the company had a first name that was new to me; he was a youngster who was to play Romeo's companion, Benvolio, and

As Romeo (1935–36).

As the Dauphin in *Saint Joan* (1936).

As Napoleon in *St. Helena* (1936).

As Richard II (1937–38).
"We will ourself in person to this war."

MAURICE EVANS as KING RICHARD II

As Richard II, drawn by Lupas (1937–38).

MAURICE EVANS as Hamlet

As Hamlet, drawn by Lupas (1937–38).

As Hamlet, with Katherine Locke
as Ophelia (1938).
"I did love you once . . . ."

As Hamlet, with Henry Edwards as Claudius and Mady Christians
as Gertrude (1938). "Madam, how like you this play?"

THE NEW WORLD

who bore his famous theatrical heritage as Tyrone Power II—called by his friends "Ty" for short.

It is relatively easy to tell at the first reading of a play whether or not it has been felicitously cast. And it was quite obvious from the start of our rehearsals that we were in for a successful production. Katharine Cornell had already established herself as an entrancing Juliet. Ralph, dancing his way through the part, was going to be splendid as Mercutio, and I was going to try my hardest to acquit myself with honour. We were particularly anxious to be at our best because this tour was, for the most part, a kind of missionary venture on Kit's part. Our schedule called for visits to towns all over the country that, during the depression, had been starved of theatre of any kind. Her publicity agent, Ray Henderson, had invented for her the title of "First Lady of the Theatre," so we were about to make a triumphal progress throughout the land.

First stop—Baltimore, Maryland. With no regular theatre in existence there, the Lyric Symphony Hall had to do. The dress rehearsal was, for me, unmitigated hell. Although it was only October, there was a slight nip in the air—much like the mild autumn weather I was accustomed to in my native land. The steam-heated auditorium, however, was something else again. Apparently Kit Cornell had a fixation about warmth being beneficial to her vocal chords and had instructed her advance agent to order adequate heat wherever we were to play. Taking her at more than her word, the engineer at the Lyric had the building so hot that the very walls were fit to burst.

On the opening night, the body heat of a packed house raised the calorific count by several degrees, so that, by the time we reached the balcony scene, the sweat from Juliet's brow was cascading onto the doublet of Romeo as he stood in the courtyard below. His "Call me but love, and I'll be new baptized" seemed a superfluous remark in the circumstances. The wetter I got, the harder I tried to convince myself that damp courtships are not unusual in Verona, and that my sodden condition would be accepted by the audience as a brilliant directorial invention of Guthrie McClintic's. The balcony scene over, I was in the grip of mild heat prostration. Offstage, Florence Reed (Juliet's nurse) stood fanning herself. I grabbed the fan from her hand, hoping that it would cool my fevered brow; with my brain fairly reeling I very nearly made my entrance into Friar Lawrence's cell with the damn thing still in my hand. Even without such an incongruous object, my appearance and my speech brought alarm into the good Friar's expression, which mounted to absolute panic when I jumped from the dialogue of Act I, scene 3 to a speech belonging to Act III, scene 3.

If my odd behaviour perturbed the Friar, it literally upset Guthrie McClintic. Following a lobster dinner at Miller's restaurant, he was watching the show from the rear of the orchestra, and when he heard me floundering around he beat a hasty retreat into the street where he and the lobster parted company. All my good intentions of playing Romeo with intense energy had been brought to naught on this tropical opening night. Seeing no possibility of improving my performance under such debilitating conditions, I begged Kit and Guthrie to release me from my contract as soon as they could find a replacement. They wouldn't hear of it, and promised to turn down the thermostat from then on; so off we went the following week to our second stand, the National Theatre in Washington, D.C. There the conditions and the temperatures were far more normal, but becoming acclimated continued to have occasional surprises.

One of these surprises arose on account of the ghastly wigs that Ty Power and I had been required to wear in Baltimore. The distance from downtown Baltimore to downtown Washington is no more than 45 miles but the journey was long enough for the hairpieces to become permanently mislaid, and nowhere in the nation's capital could substitute wigs be found, so we were both sent to a women's hairdressing establishment to have our hair curled— a demeaning experience. In those days, individual ringlets were somehow attached to strings that passed through pulleys suspended from the ceiling of the beauty parlour, causing considerable tension on the scalp of the victim below. However, it was not until the drying process commenced that the operation assumed torture-chamber proportions. That was the moment when an electric dryer resembling a handgun was aimed at one's coiffure by an otherwise harmless-looking girl. My torturess, sad to say, was armed with a dryer that had a loose connection in its evil interior. Every time it sparked I jumped, and every time I jumped my ceiling-entrapped hair was nearly torn out by its roots. Blushing self-consciously, Ty and I emerged from this strictly feminine establishment to be greeted by a chorus of wolf whistles from the crew-cut attendants of a gas station across the street.

Wearing hats thereafter, we "did" the sights of that impressive capital city and were royally entertained. Francis Biddle was a particularly generous host, and a tea party at Alice Longworth's was an occasion to be remembered. I thought she showed poor taste, however, in inviting us, and a number of youngsters who were present, to smirk over her collection of old photographs of Eleanor Roosevelt as a young girl. Granted, protruding front teeth are not exactly an aid to feminine beauty, but that anyone, particularly a relative, should have kept a scrapbook of the actual First Lady's handicap seemed to me to be unworthy to say the least.

Following a stimulating two weeks in Washington, our next stop was Pittsburgh, to which we travelled in private Pullman cars on the Pennsylvania Railroad. It was a lovely fall day, and having checked out early from our hotel, we had time to kill before going to the Union Station. Across the road from

THE NEW WORLD

the hotel was one of those little parks that abound in Washington; children and dogs were scampering around while their elders sat on benches soaking up the sunshine. All the benches being occupied, Ty Power and I lay down on the grass to luxuriate in the balmy weather. Within minutes a hefty member of the District of Columbia Police Force towered over us.

"Get up off that grass," he said in no uncertain terms.

"I beg your pardon," said I, in my most lofty manner.

"You heard me—get up off that grass!"

Ty obediently scrambled to his feet, but I, thinking I was still in England where politeness is the hallmark of the police, drew from my pocket my diary and a pencil, saying, "You will kindly give me your name and your number."

His answer came in flash: "My name's Patrick O'Connell, my number's 88304, and you can stick that up . . . !"

I was outraged and demanded that Ty take me to the nearest police station to report this insulting officer. Pullling me to my feet, Ty patted me on the back, saying, "Relax, old boy, you'll get used to us in time."

What the Alcoa Company in Pittsburgh have turned into a pyramid of glass was then the delightful old Nixon Theatre, by far the most handsome playhouse on our itinerary—all red plush and gilt. It was to the stage door of this famous theatre that the Lunts reportedly arrived one night in a rowboat, the Monongahela and Allegheny rivers having overflowed their banks into downtown Pittsburgh. The vagaries of the elements are apt to restrict one's freedom when touring in the winter.

In the course of this journey, I spent more time in movie theatres than ever before and even took up bowling for a change of pace. Kit's eminence in the profession kept her in constant demand for newspaper interviews and radio stints, but, since Ralph and I were nonentities as far as the American theatre was concerned, we had more than enough time on our hands. Our wizard publicity man, Ray Henderson, arranged athletic-club guest cards for me wherever we played. Frequent steam baths and gym workouts saved me from having to request our wardrobe mistress to let out Romeo's doublet at its seams, but the temptation to overindulge in clubs like Pittsburgh's Duquesne made life a running battle for the duration of the tour. That I succeeded in winning the contest appeared to be confirmed when many weeks later the *Nashville Banner* printed a review that I have ever since treasured.

It is extraordinary how Mr. Evans reminds us of another British actor now to be seen in Nashville on the screen—Freddie Bartholomew. Of course, comparisons of stage and screen are odious, but in this case Mr. Evans must regard this as a big American compliment.

Since Master Bartholomew was in knee-pants at the time and I a hoary old thirty-four, the compliment belonged, rather, to the stretch of the reviewer's imagination than to my portrayal.

In another respect, Nashville was a highlight of the tour. Such theatres as had once been available had been turned into movie palaces, so the only building capable of housing us was an abandoned revivalist chapel known as the Ryman Auditorium. The late Mr. Ryman had been the operator of a notorious showboat on the Mississippi who one day got religion. As a penance he applied his profits from demon rum to the building of the chapel. When Mr. Ryman went to his doubtful reward, an enterprising matron, Mrs. Knaff, snapped up the edifice, despite the fact that it was constructed entirely of wood and was, therefore, a dangerous firetrap. In booking an attraction to play there, she at the same time booked a fire engine to be on duty outside the premises just in case.

Apart from a makeshift stage—the ploughed surface of which was the terror of visiting ballet companies—the auditorium remained as it had been since its inception, the chapel pews in a horseshoe pattern, and "God is Love" written on the balcony rail. A large sheet of canvas with a rectangular opening served as a proscenium arch. At its sides, the canvas concealed the area where the pews not occupied by the audience were reserved as our "dressing rooms"—boys on the right, girls on the left, and one diminutive hideaway for Miss Cornell. It was all delightfully informal. Sitting in my pew to put on my makeup, I inadvertently dropped a stick of greasepaint on the chapel floor and it rolled out of sight under the canvas. An obliging occupant of an audience pew lifted the canvas and handed me back the errant cosmetic saying, "Yours, I believe."

I had staked my pew claim earlier in the afternoon while making a tour of discovery of this shrine in Thespis. I noticed that the "orchestra" pews down front extended to the side walls of the building, but assumed that they would not be sold to the public, since not a glimpse of the stage was vouchsafed from those locations. My attention was next drawn to a coating of white dust on many of the more favourably situated pews together with occasional chunks of what a glance heavenwards showed to be ceiling plaster. A very old, very black cleaning man was taking his time removing the evidence when in came a bosomy lady like a dreadnought at full steam. The fabled Mrs. Knaff, for this was she, said authoritatively to the old man, "Sweep up good, Joshua, that stuff makes the customers nervous." I asked whether we could expect a big audience that night, and she said, "Sure thing, not a pew left."

"What about those?" I asked, pointing to the ones at the extremities.

"Oh, those we give to the blind folks and sell the rest cheap with a warning."

I followed Mrs. Knaff to what had been the chapel's vestry, but now

THE NEW WORLD

served as her office. She then busied herself writing customer's names on the reverse of some of the tickets and, having rolled them up, stuck them in her hair; others she pinned all over her ample bosom. At showtime it was a case of, "Oh, Mrs. So-and-So, I've got your ticket here somewhere." Her box-office procedures were simplicity itself—two cigar boxes, one for the torn tickets and the other for the money. At the end of the performance, she would hand both boxes to the show's company manager, saying, "That's all you get." Our chap told me that in his experience this primitive countup had always come out right to the penny.

That evening at Nashville was full of surprises, one of them not at all funny. Kit was waiting for her entrance atop the balcony when the heavy velour backing parted company with the Ryman's rotted ropes and came crashing down, missing her by inches and severely injuring our head carpenter. Another novelty was that the only backstage convenience was in Kit's so-called dressing room. This meant that only when Juliet was onstage could the rest of the company avail themselves of her throne—quite a line of "penny-spenders"! It was even more awkward for the audience. Unlike at the Old Vic, there were no signs on the walls of the auditorium pointing to "Boys" and "Girls." How the "Girls" managed was a mystery, but at intermission an usher would direct the "Boys" to turn right at the fire engine where they would find some bushes.

I once told Gertrude Lawrence of these weird goings-on, which she suddenly remembered when she was about to play a closing date in Toronto. She called up her producer, John Golden, in New York, and practically commanded him to book their show into Nashville for a final one-night stand. When he protested that moving by rail from the snows of Ontario to the hills and dales of Tennessee was an impossibility, Gertie merely said, "Not if they put on a special train." John berated me roundly when I next saw him for ever having breathed the name of Nashville to his star.

Mercutio, it will be remembered, is polished off in Act III, leaving two long acts to go. With nothing more to do but to take his curtain call at the end of the show, Ralph considered it beyond the call of duty to have to sit idle in his pew for another full hour; so he wheedled permission to skip curtain calls on this and future one-night stands. By then I knew Ralph's eccentric nature and thought the management had made a rash concession. I had visions of him getting lost in strange towns and missing trains, and so forth. I took the rather pompous attitude that, being the only Englishmen in the cast, it was up to us to conduct ourselves diplomatically. It served me right that I ended up being Ralph's nanny—coaxing him to retire at a reasonable hour, giving him wake-up alarm calls, and having a taxi waiting to rush us to the stations. It was in Memphis, Tennessee, that I finally resigned from my self-appointed nursemaid situation.

We played our one-nighter there in a vast municipal auditorium, the stage of which was back-to-back with a boxing arena, divided by only a flimsy partition. The enthusiasm of the supporters of that manly sport was hardly the appropriate accompaniment to Shakespeare's lyric tragedy. In fact, I found it hard to keep a straight face when delivering Romeo's familiar lines, "O, that I were a glove upon that hand—that I might touch that cheek." After this unsettling evening, and knowing that we had a very early train call next morning, I hurried back to our hotel where, greatly to my surprise, Ralph had kept his promise to meet me in the lobby. I led him towards the elevators with a lot of nauseating remarks about getting our beauty sleep and so on, and reminded him to be down in the lobby at 7 A.M. on the dot. "Don't wait for me," he said as the elevator doors opened. "I want to buy a few cigars—see you in the morning." Came the dawn, but no Ralph. I called his room. No reply. "Must have gone ahead without me," I thought; so I jumped into my waiting taxi and sped to the station with only seconds to spare. "Where's Ralph?" everyone said accusingly. Not being at my best at 7 o'clock on a rainy morning, I said I hadn't the faintest idea and that I was not responsible for him. After a heated consultation with the stationmaster about holding the train, the company manager grabbed a cab to the Peabody Hotel, where Ralph was still sleeping soundly after a night over which it is best to draw a veil. The unshaven truant eventually arrived at our waiting train with jacket and trousers pulled over his pyjamas, but otherwise he was quite unconcerned. "Catching American trains is all too easy," he said, "like shooting a sitting pheasant!"

In retrospect, I realise how fortunate it was that my introduction to the States took the form of a coast-to-coast tour. In no other way could I have covered so much ground in such a short time, and become familiar with the widely diverse accents and outlooks of the people of this vast continent. Of course, my impressions were based mainly on the cities we visited, but, from my Pullman berth, I could keep track of the smaller towns on our route. With a map on my lap, I would spot names that offered promise of something spectacular—Athens, Cairo, Paris, Berlin, and not-to-be-forgotten Bugtussle, Oklahoma. Mostly they were so insignificant that they didn't merit so much as a toot by our engine driver, but, for me, they were all part of a fascinating panorama.

Compared to today's nerve-wracking mode of travel by air with its delays, lost luggage, and all the rest—what heaven it was to travel by train! Arriving at our destination in the early morning, our Pullman cars would be quietly shunted into a siding and hooked up to the heating or cooling systems as required. Coffee was served by the car attendant, and porters were waiting to handle one's baggage whenever one felt inclined to set off for the hotel. On one occasion, the Pullman even served as our hotel. Without warning our reservations at the Des Moines hotel had been taken over by a Shriners' convention, thereby putting us in the same dilemma as the Holy Family's "no room at the inn" situation. The town was swarming with gentlemen wearing headgear that to my untutored eyes identified them as visitors from Istanbul. I was assured that there was nothing foreign about them excepting, possibly, their nocturnal habits, and that we should count ourselves lucky to have a Pullman roof over our heads for what would otherwise have been a sleepless night.

I was grateful for those peripatetic months, not only for their geographical education, but because they gave me ample time to experiment with the inherent difficulties of the role of Romeo. I knew that as a climax to the tour I was to stand or fall in the judgement of the New York critics, since we were scheduled to play at the Martin Beck Theatre for a couple of weeks at Christmastime. Thus I looked in vain for some guidance from the provincial aisle-sitters. Owing to the scarcity of theatrical productions, which the depression had brought about, few of the local journals had regular drama critics on their staff. Therefore the job would be delegated to the sports writer or the social columnist, resulting, in the case of the disastrous Baltimore opening, in my being described as "amounting to no more than a stooge for Miss Cornell in the balcony scene." The word "stooge" did not appear in my Oxford dictionary, so I was none the wiser, but I misread it for the sobriquet usually reserved for dull food—"stodgy."

If I was being accused of inadequacy, I felt I had a legitimate excuse. Juliet's balcony was situated upstage, dead center, and she, needless to say, was bathed in a flood of flattering amber light. My poor Romeo, however, was obliged to play the scene with his back to the audience, lit only by the dark blue light of the moon. It took some maneuvering on the sly as the tour progressed, but I finally coaxed our electrician to cut holes, the size of silver dollars, in the moon's blue gelatin so that, in addition to my rear end, the audience could have a fleeting glimpse of my face from time to time.

Romeo and Juliet opened in New York on December 23, 1935. The next morning I, somewhat apprehensively, turned to the drama page of the *New York Times*, heaving a sign of relief when I read the following:

> Mr. Evans making his debut in the part on this side of the water, became last evening excellent as the scenes moved along. Both he and Mr. Richardson appeared at first to be a shade harassed—perhaps by Forty-fifth Street and its similar tenant of a year ago—but that wore

away.... The experts last night applauded vigorously, and so the Messrs. Evans and Richardson were voted in.

Later in the day, John Mason Brown of the *New York Evening Post* had this to say:

> Seldom has a production of such a drama as Romeo and Juliet mellowed and matured as magnificently as has Katharine Cornell's revival of the play. Last year's production, admirable as it was, was merely a glowing outline compared to the superb performance last night. Mr. Evans's Romeo is indeed the best, the most persuasive, the most likable, and most understandable that I, at least, have ever seen. His Romeo may speak faultless English and speak it capably, but he has a hot Italian soul. He is a dynamic extrovert, an impromptu poet whose reactions demand instant utterance. Most fortunately of all, Mr. Evans's Romeo is—as all Romeos should be and very few are—a man of many moods. "Fortune's fool" that he is, he turns from the vehemence of his frenzied stabbing of Tybalt to the lyric enchantment of his leave-taking from Juliet with the same ease that his affections show in switching from Rosaline to Juliet. By keeping his Romeo volatile and violent, by draining each of his moments of the emotion which then possesses him, and by taking a proper pride in the glories of the verse that falls his way, Mr. Evans redeems this baffling Montague and adds a story-telling interest to the production at the Martin Beck.

Delighted as I was with these critical Christmas presents, I felt the need to celebrate in some way or other. Robert Benchley, who was then the witty drama critic of the *New Yorker*, said he would be pleased to join me after the show for a night out on the town. So off we went to a multiplicity of imbibing establishments where he was very much persona grata. Standing at their bars and drinking only one beer at each of them, I finally lost count of the joints and also, alas, the quantity of beers consumed. One of the midtown spots into which we weaved had no bar so we were ushered to chairs in close proximity to the jazz band. The big hit that season was "The Music Goes Round and Round," but my chair being immediately below the trombone and its player's salivary glands being overly active, I was obliged to shift my glass round and round to save my beer from becoming diluted.

From this hole-in-the-wall, Bob conducted me to Harlem in the very wee hours. We went to the homes of several of Harlem's foremost musicians, wonderful performers who were in the habit of getting together after their nightclub stints for jam sessions, improvising fascinating rhythms and harmonic innovations. I hated to tear myself away but my conscience was beginning to prick me about the morrow's performance. I dared not ask Bob what time it was for fear of embarrassing him. Earlier in the evening he had told me that it was well known that when he was witnessing performers whose talents were only skin deep, he had an involuntary habit of glancing at his pocket watch. To produce his timepiece in answer to my enquiry could be misconstrued as boredom with our present entertainer, so I contented myself with quoting Romeo's opening question in the play, "Is the day so young?"

The scheduled two-week engagement at the Martin Beck Theatre was marred by an accident I sustained during the twelfth of the sixteen performances. Jo Mielziner's setting for the ballroom scene consisted of handsome draperies. To prevent them from blowing about, heavy chains were concealed in their bottom hems. As Juliet made her shy, hurried exit from the ballroom, I chased after her at full speed and, in doing so, trod on one of the hidden chains. The result—a broken bone in my foot. Hobbling with the aid of a cane, which I did my best to hide under my cloak, I managed to struggle through the remaining four performances; though audiences must have been bewildered by this immobile Romeo, particularly in the sword fight with Paris in Juliet's tomb.

Incidentally, that rapier-and-dagger death stuggle put Kit on her mettle, since one of the rapiers was apt to break at the peak of the fight. On a couple of previous occasions, one half of the weapon flew high in the air immediately above the supposed corpse of Juliet. It was a tribute to Kit's professional discipline that she continued to keep her eyes firmly shut when she heard the "ping" of the breaking rapier, wondering on what part of her anatomy the jagged piece of steel would fall. On my incapacitated last nights, she had no such worry, however, since Paris and I looked as though we were out to murder each other with butter knives.

Stage sword fights are notorious for the unreliability of the weapons. A story is told of the famous Macready playing the hunchback, Richard III, on the gaslit stage at Drury Lane. From bitter experience, he had learnt that his trusty steel had a temper of its own. He therefore made it a practice to order a property man to stand by in the prompt corner with a substitute sword just in case of an accident. He was instructed to be in readiness to present the sword, hilt forward, to Mr. Macready on seeing him advance to the corner. On this one occasion, however, the property man gently took hold of the end of the blade in his right hand and laid the rest of the sword across the crook of his left elbow, completely unaware that the hilt was hovering over a naked gas flame. Advancing to the prompt corner, Macready reached for rapier number two with a grand gesture to be proffered what was, by then, a scorchingly hot hilt. The un-Shakespearean dialogue that followed was not recorded, alas.

After a considerably protracted wait for my broken foot to mend, I bought a second-hand, very showy automobile. It had a retractable canvas roof, a rumble seat, running boards, and a compartment to stow one's golf bag.

1935–1942

It was a LaSalle. The application form for a driving licence caused me some trouble. It required me to answer personal questions such as "Any visible distinguishing marks?" and "Color?" I took the latter to mean the colour of my eyes and duly answered "brown." It puzzled me that the next question repeated the enquiry about my eyes, but I answered it nevertheless, refraining from writing "hazel" just for the sake of variety.

In my newly acquired vehicle I made my first visit to Kit and Guthrie's house overlooking the Hudson River at Sneden's Landing, a charming collection of rentable cottages owned by the Tonetti family. I had not been told in advance that the style of living at Sneden's was most informal and somewhat Bohemian; so I made the mistake of arriving at the McClintics in my city suit and highly polished shoes. To say that my hosts and their other friends were casually arrayed would be an understatement; in fact, they all looked comfortable but sloppy.

It did nothing to ease my own discomfort when, after an off-the-lap luncheon, Gert Macy (Kit's secretary) announced that she would accompany me on a stroll along the riverbank to view the waterfall—the local sight on the Palisades to which all newcomers were expected to pay their respects. On second thought, after glancing at my burnished footwear, Gert said, "The path is awfully muddy—you can't go in those—half a jiffy, you've got small feet—I'll get you an old pair of Kit's. When she produced a battered pair of loafers I couldn't very well give voice to my apprehension, so we sallied forth on the quagmire. One step into its glutinous surface and off came the First Lady of the Theatre's shoe. It was obvious that the borrowed shoes were a full size too big for me. Determined to keep going, I reached the waterfall, much to Gert's amusement at seeing me waddling like a duck. We never breathed a word of this to Kit, and I consoled myself with the thought that if audiences were conscious of our feet rather than our faces a lot of us would never have made the grade.

The ambience of Sneden's Landing was quaint, to say the least, but when Gert offered to make arrangements for me to rent one of the Tonetti cottages I gladly accepted. She warned me that the previous tenant, being overawed by famous neighbors like the McClintics had shied away from calling Mrs. Tonetti's attention to certain shortcomings in the amenities of his rented home. When he met her for the first time as she emerged from her house, her unusual appearance emboldened him to speak up. She was wearing odd stockings, a red one on the left leg and an off-white one on the other. In one hand dangled a cabbage, but she greeted him warmly with the other, asking why, unlike previous tenants (Burgess Meredith for one), he had not voiced any complaints. He professed himself satisfied with everything except, perhaps, one rather perplexing feature of the bathroom:

THE NEW WORLD

"Whenever I flush the toilet, steam comes out."
"That crazy plumber," she said, "doesn't know his hot from his cold."

It is amazing how many flukes, how much happenstance goes into the building of an actor's career. In my case, the outstanding example of such a fortuitous occurrence was during my foot convalescence at Sneden's Landing. Although I was now living practically in the McClintics' backyard, neither Kit nor Guthrie had let me in on their plans for their next Broadway production. One Sunday, however, Guthrie called up asking me to come to lunch right away. Meeting me at their door, he thrust a Western Union cable into my hand, which read, "If you can find him get Maurice Evans," signed G.B.S.

It didn't take much imagination to conclude that Shaw was referring to *Saint Joan*, and that at last Kit's long-cherished desire to appear as the Maid was to be realised. A revival of *Saint Joan* was to be their next production and casting ideas were being sifted through with meticulous thoroughness. What had somehow escaped their attention was that I had played Charles, the Dauphin, in the Old Vic production under the critical eye of Shaw himself and that, judging by his cabled response, I must have won the dramatist's approval. Shaw's eminence as a writer was matched by his notoriety as a canny bargainer. It would not have surprised me if he had dunned me for an agent's commission of 10 percent of my Dauphin salary, but in this instance he was in a charitable mood and content to give his recommendation gratis. It was such a far cry from Romeo to the hopeless freak who, thanks largely to Joan, was to become Charles II of France, that it was not surprising that it did not occur to Kit and Guthrie to offer me the part.

There must have been moments of regret that they had chosen me once we started rehearsals. Try as I might, I could not resist interfering with Guthrie's direction when I saw that his staging differed from what I knew from experience to be Shaw's intention. I had enough sense to refrain from offering hints and tips to Kit herself, but otherwise I believe that I was able to contribute some ideas which paid off. It was only when the play had opened and she felt secure in her performance that Kit confessed to me that she ran out of breath in the Rheims Cathedral scene and wondered if I could suggest a remedy. Harking back to my choirboy days, and at the risk of shocking her, I told her that since speech and singing employ the same physical machinery— the same bellows, the same pipes and chords—it follows that declamatory speech demands the use of singing techniques rather than the less vigorous ones of polite conversation. Unfortunately for the actress, however, this requires her to obey the golden rule of singing, namely, to dig her heels firmly into the floor of the stage and, just as firmly, to squeeze her buttocks together.

The result of this indelicate action is to place the diaphragm in the appropriate position to allow the lungs to expand to their maximum capacity.

The following night in the Rheims coronation scene, Joan, dressed in her soldierly chain mail with a blue tabard covering her from chin to mid-thigh, knelt at my feet, saying: "Sire, I have made you king; my work is done." To which I had to reply: "I would not go through it again to be emperor of the sun and moon. The weight of these robes! I thought I should have dropped when they loaded that crown on to me. And the famous holy oil they talked about was rancid, phew!" As I spoke, I noticed that Kit was getting her bellows working in preparation for her two-page speech that was to follow. As she launched into it, I found it very touching when, taking a squint at her back as she turned away from me, I could clearly see from the pulsing movement of her tabard that she had taken my advice.

Although Guthrie McClintic had serious shortcomings in working with other actors, he was Kit's Svengali. In common with so many of today's disastrous theatre directors, he himself was a disappointed actor, but unlike them he shunned imprinting the McClintic hallmark on his productions. He surrounded himself with a topnotch staff so that his name on the bill was a guarantee of a first-class cast of actors, lavish costuming and decor, and the extraordinary beauty of his "First Lady" wife being shown to its best advantage. Not for him the modern perversions of the classics—Hamlet in a "T" shirt and Ophelia in a bikini. He was content to allow his well-chosen actors to receive the kudos while he kept a wary eye on the box office and paid particular attention to the maintenance of Kit's public image. This last endeavour was not easy, because Kit was a very private person. Dependent as she was on Guthrie's guidance in professional matters, their marriage appeared to be more like congenial partners than husband and wife. Of course, I crossed their path only in their maturity, and for all I know in earlier years their relationship may have been far closer. As it was, one was adopted either by Kit's coterie or by Guthrie's somewhat raffish clique, and I didn't seem to fit into either.

There is a popular belief that a great spirit of camaraderie exists among the actors appearing together in a play. It is true that during rehearsals and out-of-town tryouts, we have the common bond of anxiety about the show's prospects, and sometimes a mutual dislike of the director or an interfering author. But once the show has opened and the critics have given us their blessings, all the anticipatory excitement evaporates. The foreseeable future consists of repeating the same dialogue in the same theatre eight times a week. Consequently, the last people one wants to spend one's free time with are the other cast members.

There are, of course, exceptions, and in the cast of *Saint Joan* there was a

THE NEW WORLD

notable one. It was Brian Aherne, a Britisher like myself but, unlike me, one who had long since made America his home. Possibly on account of our similar background and ages we easily struck up a friendship during the pre-Broadway tour and were even civil to each other during the run. This may, to some extent, have been due to the fact that Brian's splendid Earl of Warwick and my ineffectual Dauphin were not required by the author to play a scene together. Amongst other shared pursuits was our mutual admiration of Kit's secretary, Getrude Macy. A very rare person was Gert, equally popular with both sexes and always fun to be with. If you had a problem, Gert would solve it for you in a jiffy.

Gert's terrific sense of humour got us into an awkward fix on one occasion concerning Brian. The organiser of a Madison Square Garden benefit for Jewish orphans was soliciting "name" performers such as Brian to grace the gala by putting in an appearance on the big night. The round-up was conducted through Western Union telegrams delivered to the various stagedoors. The first of these appeals was brief and to the point, but, as the day of the event neared, the organiser became more and more eloquent. He resorted finally to a two-page night letter beseeching and imploring Brian not to disappoint the poor little orphans in need. Not having committed himself, Brian showed Gert and me the last of these passionate communications, which arrived during the matinee of our show—the big evening at the Garden being that night. Gert and I were convulsed by the missive but Brian took it all most seriously and wanted our advice as to whether he should oblige with his presence. I noticed a wicked twinkle in Gert's eye as she assured him he should consent. She took me aside, saying, "Let's send Brian another telegram." Like a couple of naughty kids we hied us to the Western Union office, composing our counterfeit message on the way. We should have known better than to play a practical joke on Brian, of all people, and this one certainly misfired

Sure enough, when we got to the theatre that evening he had just opened our telegram. "Good God!" rang out from his dressing room, "here's another of these damn things!" He came barging into my room brandishing our message, and proceeded to read out loud to me and my conspirator, Gert, the following:

A THOUSAND ORPHANS WILL BLESS YOU FOR BEING ON OUR STAGE AT THE GARDEN TONIGHT (STOP) A FIRE ENGINE WILL AWAIT YOU AT YOUR STAGE DOOR AT CURTAIN FALL TO TRANSPORT HITHER (STOP) PLEASE WEAR JOCKSTRAP AND HELMET (STOP).

It was immediately apparent that he didn't realise it was a put-on; so we tried to convince Brian that the telegram was a fake, but he wouldn't listen. He blamed Western Union for a typographical error, saying that the word "jockstrap" should read "jockey" and that in the fifteenth century a nobleman's page was called his "jockey." Thus, he reasoned, as the Earl of Warwick in *Saint Joan* he had such a page and he was being asked to come to the Garden on a fire engine accompanied by his page. Gert and I confessed, at this point, that we were the guilty authors of the telegram, but Brian brushed aside our protestations. Our misplaced attempt at humour was further compounded when, at the end of our performance that night, I heard Brian say to his dresser, "Just take a look to see if there's a fire engine outside the stage door, will you?"

If Brian ever realised that we were indeed the guilty parties, at least he didn't hold it against us. Thanks to him I was introduced to many of his New York friends, amongst them Brooke and Buddy Marshall. At the time, they were the owners of the famous Castello Brown in Portofino, which was then a delightfully simple Italian fishing village. Later, Portofino was invaded by various Hollywood luminaries and became quite spoilt, but when I was there as a guest of the Marshalls (and their tenant for later summer vacations) it was an experience which I treasure. One dined by candlelight on the castle battlements overlooking the Mediterranean—a truly spectacular view. This was the same castle from whence Richard Coeur-de-Lion set forth on his Crusade. There was only one discordant note about those halcyon evenings and it came from the church in the village square below. For some reason or other it had an unusually active belfry. Not content with simply summoning the faithful, the bells would peal out the time of day or night. This would not have been of consequence except for the fact that the pattern of the campanology was identical to the first eight measures of the signature tune of the then popular Laurel and Hardy comic films.

My dear friend Helen Hayes once discovered in some obscure London second-hand store an out-of-print book entitled *Old Vic Drama*. It deals, in part, with my own season there, including *Saint Joan*, and it is the only reminder in my possession of that production. In this autobiography I am trying to avoid pontificating about my own theories concerning the parts I have played. It seems to me more reliable to quote from the impressions I have made upon professional critics and other writers, favourable or otherwise. Accordingly, here are a few lines from Helen's birthday present:

> The Dauphin is a part that tends in performance to overstep the border line into farce; but Shaw emphasises the sharpness under the weak impudence, and Maurice Evans, playing the character as a shrivelled monkey of a man, brilliantly underlined the shrewd wit while preserving the ineffectual pathos.

Shaw's own stage directions describe "Charlie" Dauphin in somewhat similar terms:

THE NEW WORLD

He is a poor creature physically. He has little narrow eyes, near together, a long pendulous nose that droops over his thick short upper lip, and the expression of a young dog accustomed to be kicked, yet incorrigible and irrepressible. But he is neither vulgar nor stupid; and he has a cheeky humour which enables him to hold his own in conversation.

To Shaw's prescription I added an inability to pronounce any "R's" and persuaded the costumer to lower the belt of my tunic so that it gave the impression that my waist was approximately at the level of my knees. A putty nose and flat feet helped to mirror Joan's introduction of him to the Court: "Here is the King for you! Look your fill at the poor devil." That the portrait was authentic seems to have been recognised, and again I quote, this time from John Mason Brown writing in the *New York Evening Post*:

It is difficult to believe at the Martin Beck these nights that the same actor who is at present giving such a richly comic performance as the Dauphin in Miss Cornell's memorable production of "Saint Joan" was only recently to be seen on that same stage as the unusually successful Romeo. Everything that was lusciously romantic in his Romeo has shrivelled into something dryly comic in his Charles. The voice is different. The walk has changed. The personality has undergone a complete reversal. The actor playing the two parts seems to have as little in common as a pomegranate has with a cactus.

The *Saint Joan* production was an agreeable interlude for me. With Romeo behind me, I no longer had to watch my weight and nurture my vocal chords. I was able to relax and to make friends. New York was a fascinating city in those days and I took full advantage of it. I was greatly helped by Brian and also by the only other actor, besides me, held over from *Romeo and Juliet*—Ty Power. He played the small part of Bertrand de Poulengy, or "Polly," in the opening scene of the play and, like me, spent a lot of time in the dressing room because neither of us was involved in the two lengthiest scenes in the play.

Ty came into my room one night in a state of great excitement. The New York office of Twentieth Century Fox had been persuaded to give him a film test a week thence, and please would I take him through the lines of the short script that he had been given. The material, if I remember correctly, required him to impersonate a rather stylish drawing-room type of young man—a sophisticate, a quality that Ty as a person lacked at that time. Actually he was quite a gentle soul, not in the least boastful, and well aware that he lacked experience as an actor. For the film test, he thought all he had to do was to recite the lines he had memorised, looking straight at the camera. I dissuaded him from any such delusion, and rehearsed him in the brief scene, giving him bits of action and movement. By the end of the week, I had to admit I had failed to effect much improvement in his rather wooden performance. I wished him luck, while privately thinking that he sorely needed it.

The weeks went by and no word from Fox came to Ty. On the other hand, I was similarly propositioned by Fox to make a test. Brian, an old hand at the ways of Hollywood, advised against it in no uncertain terms. He said that the California studios had warehouses packed to the roof with New York film tests that nobody had ever bothered to look at. "Never do tests for anyone until after you've been hired," Brian said.

But the New York office wouldn't take No for an answer. Getting quite impatient with them, I finally said, "I've been told on good authority that your tests are treated with scorn at the studios."

"Not at all," they replied. "Our tests are held in high respect."

"All right," I said, "I'll put *you* to the test! Show me a test you made some weeks ago of a young friend of mine named Tyrone Power."

"With the greatest of pleasure," they replied. "Any time at your convenience." Later that day I was ushered into the projection room and in a few minutes the screen lit up and on walked Ty looking extremely handsome and acting out his tiny scene with unbelievable self-assurance and personality. It wasn't long before he was signed up by Fox. I had to admit to being a poor judge of what it takes to make a film star.

Before going on tour with *Saint Joan* we took the summer off. Kit went to her beach home on Martha's Vineyard and I decided to go back to England for my vacation. Gert Macy planned a holiday in Europe, so I suggested we go on the same transatlantic liner. We booked passage on the German liner *Bremen*, being told at the ticket office that we had the option of eating three overhearty meals a day in the dining saloon or cashing in our meal tickets. The brochure had informed us that the *Bremen* boasted a Cordon Bleu restaurant on the top deck and we figured our meal-ticket cash would meet the cost of a least one dinner at night if we chose sensibly. This we did, though we couldn't resist the plates piled high with caviar. The good food and a melodious dance band made those evenings a delight. The only trouble was that by noon of the following day we found ourselves ravenously hungry. One day Gert's eye lighted on a tray of canapés that a party of beefy Germans were tucking into across the bar where we had rendezvoused. Our mouths watering with envy, we ordered the drinks we thought most likely to sustain us until our evening meal. Two black velvets—Guinness's Stout and champagne—were brought to our table and, to our joy, a huge tray of canapés compliments of the management. The German idea of an appetiser included generous slices of beef and so forth, enough for a regiment. And so in this way each noontime thereafter, our hunger was appeased, giving us renewed energy to dance into the wee hours each night.

THE NEW WORLD

Those were the days when holiday-making Americans were accompanied by their automobiles on transatlantic trips, and Gert was no exception. When she disembarked at Cherbourg I waved her good-bye as she drove her Ford convertible off the dock on her way to the Olympic Games at Berlin. It was typical of this remarkable girl that the lack of a ticket for the stadium didn't faze her in the least. With nothing to identify her except a windshield sticker of the American flag, she parked on a side street just off the main thoroughfare that the opening-day parade was to traverse. She let the bands and the soldiers go by, but when the crowd started to cheer she thought that some bigwigs were approaching. Sure enough, the recognisable countenances of Hermann Goering and Heinrich Himmler were to be seen as they rode in their open limousines, to be followed by other Nazi dignitaries and finally by Hitler himself. Seconds after the Führer passed from her view, Gert tooted her horn at the people blocking the entrance to the parade route. Seeing the U.S. flag on her car, the respectful German civilians and police assumed that no one but a diplomatic personage would dare to order them in such a peremptory manner to make way. They dutifully stood aside, enabling Gert to join in the parade all the way to the stadium.

Back with my family outside London, the pangs of homesickness from which I occasionally suffered in the States quickly disappeared. In fact, I found myself reminded of the short shrift I had been given by potential London employers before going to the States. I couldn't help comparing that with the instant acceptance I was receiving in New York under the Cornell banner, and was eager to get back there after a few weeks at home. It was at this time, when rummaging through old papers and photographs, that I began to wonder whether there was the faintest chance of my persuading some Broadway producer to take a flyer with *Richard II*. Pretty unlikely, I thought, but Mother disagreed. Unbeknownst to me, she had kept a scrapbook of my doings at the Old Vic and elsewhere and insisted that I take it with me to New York. As it turned out it's just as well that I did, for otherwise I might never have made my real mark in America.

The *Saint Joan* tour got underway and, having nothing better to do, I went to the theatre at our opening stand to watch the crew unload and set up the Jo Mielziner scenery. His design was a permanent set in the style of a gothic triptych—three soaring arches served to frame dropcloths depicting the various localities of the action. It struck me that the basic concept of the scenery would be equally suitable as a way to stage *Richard II*; so I coaxed our head carpenter to lend me a set of the blueprints. In my hotel room I made copies of the triptych and drew a series of very amateurish sketches of the types of backgrounds needed for the swift scene changes essential in any

1935–1942

Shakespearean historical play. If nothing else, this occupation relieved some of the boredom of touring while keeping alive my wishful thinking about finding a management willing to present the play.

My memories of much of the tour seem to have faded away; it largely consisted of visits to cities that I had already seen on the *Romeo and Juliet* itinerary. We did, however, go to two places that were new to me: San Francisco and Los Angeles. I shall never forget our early-morning arrival at Oakland, by train, and how out of the mist shrouding the bay the beauty of San Francisco revealed itself. The train tracks ended in Oakland, and one transferred from the train to a ferry boat, which chugged its way across the bay slowly, giving its passengers a gradually closer view of the sparkling city. As we stood in the bow of the ferry, drinking it all in, Kit suddenly let out a cry, "Gert! Where are the dogs?" Sure enough, in her haste to get on board, her two dachshunds had been left behind in the drawing-room compartment of the train. Arriving at the ferry terminal, poor Gert had to run like mad to catch the next boat leaving for Oakland to rescue the animals. The luck of Gert Macy was being put to the test and it did not fail her. Our train was still at the Oakland platform, and unconcernedly snoring under a blanket in the drawing room were the missing hounds. In the meantime, I was getting my first ride in a cable car and savouring my first delicious meal in Chinatown. Most of us were comfortably lodged in the Huntington Hotel on Nob Hill which, in those postdepression days, was glad to accommodate a troupe of rogues and vagabonds. Those with suites had proper kitchens, so we took it in turn to give after-theatre supper parties. My culinary expertise, not being what it is today, caused me to cheat by serving meals prepared in Chinatown's "take-out" restaurants. The show did sellout business and was well received by the drama critics. One resident of San Francisco did not, I suspect, join in the general acclaim. I was in Kit's dressing room after the show one night when a visitor, in the person of that very fine actress Ina Claire, was announced. Not only was she an outstanding performer but, as I was to discover, an expert in diplomacy. Without uttering one word of congratulation about Kit's performance, she embarked on a torrent of praise for the elegance of the First Lady's legs—"I'd give anything to have legs like yours," and so on without ceasing for about fifteen minutes, all about legs!

I thoroughly enjoyed this initial visit to San Francisco, as I did each time future tours included it on our route. Only once did its traditional hospitality fail me, but that was in 1942 when I had exchanged doublet and hose for the uniform of a captain in the army of the United States. I had been posted to the Central Pacific Command, but due to some screw-up in my orders no quarters at San Francisco's Fort Mason had been assigned to me while I awaited transportation to headquarters in Hawaii. The city was jam-packed with

NAPOLEON AND RICHARD II

service personnel of all sorts, and I counted myself fortunate that, having been a regular guest at the Huntington Hotel over the years, I was in clover. Shouldering my knapsack and other gear, I strode into the hotel lobby confident that I would be greeted as of yore. Sad to relate, the desk clerk took one look at my uniform and gave me the treatment reserved for anyone under the rank of general—"No room at the inn!" It was the same humiliating story at all the hotels and I finished up sharing a room with a drunken major in a rooming house run by Jehovah's Witnesses.

By contrast, I hated to leave San Francisco at the end of the *Saint Joan* engagement, though our next stop being Los Angeles, another enjoyable experience seemed guaranteed. I looked forward to renewing old friendships with members of the English colony in Hollywood and to being taken to the movie studios. Instead of this, I was informed that the show was to play the Biltmore Theatre in the cultural desert that was downtown Los Angeles. There were no freeways at that time and Los Angeles, Hollywood, and Beverly Hills were separated by acres and acres of waste land. It took a very important Broadway star to entice the denizens of movie land to make the wearisome journey down the entire length of Sunset Boulevard with its multiplicity of traffic lights. Fortunately for us, Kit was one of the few with the necessary magnetism, but even so the Hollywood crowd appeared to be more interested in being photographed in the theatre lobby than in taking their seats for the performance. The opening night was a disgrace in this respect. It made Kit so angry that she gave orders that at all future performances no one was to be seated during the first scene of the play. Gert was appointed to see that the rule was obeyed and thoroughly enjoyed causing the laggers and the latecomers to cool their heels. Over the years I have noticed that people involved in the motion-picture industry take a very condescending attitude towards the labourers in Broadway's vineyard, as much as to imply that only they are the true vintage. They gobble up our plays and, more often than not, make a hash of them on the screen, but, to them, the originators of that material are very small potatoes.

2. NAPOLEON AND RICHARD II

Back in New York following the *Saint Joan* tour, I found my luck still holding. The producer Max Gordon sent me the script of a play about Napoleon. I was delighted to see that the authors were old friends of mine— R. C. Sherriff, of *Journey's End* fame, and Jeanne de Casalis. *St. Helena* was its title and Max's accompanying letter quoted some laudatory reviews of its London production. I instantly knew that the Emperor was a superbly observed role, a part that would either make or break me; so I said Yes. Max was wearing two hats at the time, one of them being to act as playscript spotter for Metro Goldwyn Mayer. Those Hollywood giants, lacking judgement in their own staff, decided as a precautionary measure to finance a Broadway production of a script before committing themselves to picking up their motion-picture option. Max had been impressed by *St. Helena* when he saw it in London and was given the go-ahead by Metro, it being agreed that they were to have no say in his Broadway production.

I was dumfounded when, having extracted such a major concession, Max proceeded to toss the casting of the play into my lap. He argued that the play could not succeed unless I was surrounded by a supporting cast of my own choosing. I felt totally incompetent for such a responsibility; I could see myself making the most horrific gaffes by asking established Broadway actors and actresses innocent questions about their previous experience. I consented to undertake the vetting job provided Max would bring my friend and the coauthor of the play to the States and permit her to be the final arbiter.

Jeanne de Casalis duly arrived and auditions for the bit parts and interviews for the principals commenced for what must have been a record for haphazard casting. Nevertheless, we somehow made satisfactory selections and a date was set for the show to go into rehearsal. It was far enough ahead for Jeanne to take me in hand—and thank the Lord she did. We burnt the midnight oil in our suites at the Gotham Hotel ($19.00 per day at that time!), where she drummed into me fine points on tackling the part. Not only had she done an enormous amount of research on Napoleon's character, but, in the writing, had included many of her own father's idiosyncrasies. He, like Bonaparte, was a Corsican and bore a strong resemblance to him in many ways. Without Jeanne's insight, I'm sure I would have given the stereotyped portrait of the great man in decline. There's more to it than just wearing a forelock and sticking your hand in your waistcoat. Jeanne made me aware of the complexities of the man, the variety of his moods, and his stature as a statesman.

The modern theory that the wallpaper at Longwood, the house the British had assigned to Napoleon on St. Helena, contained a poisonous substance gives credence to the belief that the Emperor's deteriorating health, and ultimately his death, was due mainly to this factor rather than to a common liver complaint (the previously held view). Whatever the cause, Napoleon's failing health was gradual and all the more tragic for that reason. It made the part in the play a most gratifying one for the actor. The slow enfeeblement of the character gave him progression, even though on a downhill course. It offered me a challenge to avoid self-pity in the portrayal.

NAPOLEON AND RICHARD II

This is the snare that constantly awaits any performer in a situation of this sort. If I succeeded in evading the trap it was because I was following a golden rule of all acting, tragedy and comedy alike: "Never play the *result!*" When you are playing the part of Hamlet *you* as a person know what his fate is to be, and so does the spectator. But as an actor you must convince yourself and your audience that you haven't the faintest idea in advance that "flights of angels" are going to "sing thee to thy rest."

Some of the critics took exception to the episodic structure of the play, but they must have approved of Jeanne's tutelage of me, because I arrived at the Lyceum Theatre for the second performance to see my name up in lights over the title. It didn't hurt, either, to read Brooks Atkinson's review in the *New York Times* that morning (October 7, 1936), which said in part:

> Mr. Evans' third appearance on the New York stage confirms a first impression that he is an actor with the soul of an artist. He has force when he needs it; he can roar with enough passion to terrify an army; but he is also an actor of quick sensibilities, who knows that pride wounds a man inside where he and we feel it most keenly. His dignity is not an ailment but an attribute of character.

Although Richard Watts in the *Herald-Tribune* was congratulatory about my performance, he was the foremost critical dissenter in regard to the play. The gist of his review implied that if you could sit through a play that called upon your sympathies for the man who "butchered half of the youth of Europe and set the pattern for dictators like Hitler and Mussolini, then you have a different outlook than myself."

Max and the rest of us felt that this was not legitimate dramatic criticism, but it became clear after a few weeks of a sluggish box office that Watts's opinion was shared by the theatregoing public. I reminded Max that the London production had also suffered its vicissitudes until Winston Churchill came to its rescue. He had seen the play when it had its premiere at the Old Vic and thought so highly of it that he wrote a letter to the London *Times* urging theatregoers not to miss the play. As a result, *St. Helena* transferred to the West End at Daly's Theatre. His *Times* letter was blown up and pasted on the theatre billboards and resulted in a successful run. When I suggested to Max that he use the same promotional gimmick at the Lyceum, he said that it would be generally thought that the signature was that of an American novelist, bearing the name of Winston Churchill, whose last book was published in 1919. In Max's opinion this would hardly constitute a drawing card.

I was bitterly disappointed, of course, but was encouraged by an unsolicited person-to-person crusade that developed. The mystique of Napoleon had created fans devoted enough to telephone their friends urging them to see the show, resulting in some increase in attendance. The cast couldn't have been more loyal. We all volunteered to cut our salaries to Equity's minimum compensation, thereby giving the show a little longer run during which the good word could be spread.

It was entirely due to that temporary reprise that the most important step in my career took place. We were in the last week of our extended run when I received a telegram from a total stranger, Joseph Verner Reed. The message read:

YOUR PERFORMANCE AS NAPOLEON QUITE EXTRAORDINARILY MOVING (STOP) BROADWAY NEEDS YOU SO DON'T GO TO HOLLYWOOD LIKE ALL THE REST ARE DOING (STOP) GOOD LUCK (STOP)

I tucked this friendly telegram into my pocket and at supper that night showed it to my old friend Derek Williams, who was prospering on Broadway at the time. "Well, I'll be damned!" said Derek. He then enlightened me about the sender. Joseph Reed was a wealthy dilettante who had burnt his fingers very badly when he indulged a whim to finance and manage his own Broadway repertory company headed by that strong-willed actress, Jane Cowl. Later he wrote a book, *The Curtain Falls*, that described the frustrations of the impractical venture and his determination once and for all to turn his back on the theatre. In spite of this vow, Derek was of the opinion that Joseph Reed was incurably stagestruck and that I'd be missing a great chance if I didn't get to know him.

Hurriedly reading the Reed valedictory, I then hunted up the author's address, in Greenwich, Connecticut, and wrote him a letter. After thanking him for his complimentary wire, I injected a note of regret that the imminent closing of *St. Helena* left me no option but to join the general exodus to Hollywood, abandoning the plans I had in mind for my next Broadway appearance. A day or two went by, then a second telegram was delivered, this time to my hotel. It stated that the Reed family would be passing through New York the following day and suggested I join him in the bar of the Gotham Hotel at noon. He turned out to be a pleasant enough person, but rather restless and inattentive when I got onto the subject of *Richard II*. It seemed to register when I told him that for some inexplicable reason there had been no American production of the play since 1884, when Edwin Booth had appeared in it for three performances at the McVickers Theatre in Chicago. Mentioning short runs caused our conversation to switch back to *St. Helena*, and any further discussion of *Richard II* became impossible.

Very downhearted, I returned to my hotel room. The following morning, as I opened my bedroom door to pick up my newspaper, I noticed an envelope that some bellboy had slipped under the door. I assumed it was my hotel bill and didn't open it immediately, but when I did I was in danger of suffering a stroke. The envelope contained a note written on a Gotham Hotel telephone pad and read: "Hope this will help you to go ahead with your plan. J.V.R." Unfolding the other piece of paper in the envelope I could hardly believe my eyes when I saw it was a cheque for $35,000. Such things just don't happen, I thought—not even in America! To have found a willing backer on such slight acquaintance made me feel that I was living in the time of the Medicis.

The saga that followed the windfall was equally staggering. There I was with all that money—in those days enough to produce two drawing-room comedies—a scrapbook containing high praise for my Richard at the Old Vic, and photographs to whet the appetite of some Broadway entrepreneur. Guthrie McClintic would not, I felt sure, be interested because there was no part for Kit. It was too soon to expect Max Gordon to take another gamble on me. Beyond those two, no other producers had come within my ken. I knocked on Gilbert Miller's door and laid my situation before him, but, as I had been warned, his field was the importation of ready-made London productions. He referred me to Brock Pemberton, who had a more adventurous spirit. But when, in addition to showing him the Old Vic material, I whipped out a cheque for all that lovely money, Pemberton obviously thought there had to be something fishy about the whole proposal—and that was that.

With Joe's cheque still burning a hole in my pocket, I wrote to him at his Palm Beach home telling him of my frustrating search for a producer. He wrote back, saying that he had no use for any of the merchants of Broadway, but that, if I were prepared to take a chance on a newcomer, to get in touch with the son of an old family friend named Robinson Smith. Only recently graduated from university—Yale, I think—he was an avid theatregoer, but that hardly qualified him for the rough-and-tumble of Broadway. However, I liked him instantly and he responded in a like manner. He had breeding, and the fact that his family and the Reeds were close friends made his involvement in my enterprise attractive. If things should go wrong, at least I would have someone to share the blame! The odds on a mishap were almost a dead certainty. After years of neglect of the Bard, there was suddenly a rash of Shakespeare on the Great White Way. John Gielgud was packing them in with his *Hamlet*. At the same time, Leslie Howard made the grave mistake of trying his hand at the part in a rival production just around the corner. It had also been announced that the husband-and-wife team of Philip Merivale and Gladys Cooper were to appear in both *Othello* and *Macbeth*, this too proving to be an error of judgement.

Nothing daunted, Bob Smith and I were game to go ahead with our project. He had some contact with the Astor Estate, the owners of the St.

James Theatre on 44th Street, one of the few large playhouses that had not been shuttered by the depression. He was told that the theatre, though vacant, was under lease to a song-and-dance man named Eddie Dowling, and that he was the person we would have to deal with as tenants. Full of blarney (although he had never set foot in Ireland), Eddie exhibited little interest in our project, but finally agreed to mention it to his unnamed partner. It later emerged that there was a sinister figure in his background—a mysterious White Russian named Boris Said—who wished to remain anonymous even though he was the controlling power. No shrinking violet was Boris, as we were to find to our cost. If a bear can have a taste for music and theatre, then Boris had some, but his regular business was that of an importer of furs and so forth, an occupation that he pursued with rapacious determination. When his covert dealings were in need of a helping hand, he believed in going to the highest echelon no matter how tortuous the route. His association with Dowling was typical of his stratagems. It was common knowledge that for some years Eddie had been Franklin D. Roosevelt's court jester and unofficial purveyor of entertainment at the White House. Consequently, Boris offered to underwrite Eddie's precarious situation at the St. James and in return was to be in a position to get his foot in the door of the executive mansion—the fount of the favours and waivers his business dealings required.

My introduction to Boris caused me to thank my lucky stars that in Robinson Smith I had a partner who could relieve me of all the haggling over the terms that Boris's personality promised. If the show was to have any chance of recouping Joe Reed's investment, there was no time to spare. My job was to get the show on the road, a formidable task from the artistic standpoint alone. I was in no mood to argue when Bob Smith told me of the iniquitous contract that the Russian demanded. In addition to the usual 30 percent share of the box-office receipts, Boris was to receive 50 percent of the profits, if any. He put up no investment in the show, but gave an undertaking that if we ran out of money during the preproduction period, he would stake us for the balance in order to get the curtain up on opening night. He also made a condition that Eddie Dowling be credited as coproducer with Robinson Smith. Eddie was invaluable when it came to publicity and union contracts, but he had absolutely nothing to do with the creation of the production. Our lawyer had recommended that Bob Smith and I form a corporation for the operation. Even so, I must confess that I was somewhat startled when, called on to sign our agreement with Boris, I saw myself described in the document as a partner in "Richard II, Inc."

We were making these negotiations toward the end of 1936. In those days of no air conditioning it was customary for Broadway to shut up shop by

NAPOLEON AND RICHARD II

June at the latest; so it was essential to get things rolling well before spring if the show was to be given a chance for a respectable run.

My first move was to bring from England David Ffolkes, who had been our scenic and costume designer at the Old Vic. Having told him I wanted the basic triptych design that had worked so well in *Saint Joan*, I practically chained him to his drawing board. The dear fellow worked like a fiend, but when we submitted his designs to the scenery shops, the estimates were astronomical. The agonising process of pruning many of his flights of fancy fell to me. I was ruthless. Even so, there was little capital left for the costuming.

Some sympathetic soul told me that in the not too distant past Dennis King had produced and starred in Gordon Daviot's *Richard of Bordeaux* on Broadway, using duplicates of the costumes by the designer, Motley, which John Gielgud had employed in his production of the same play in London. The show did not find favour in New York, and my informant suggested I contact Dennis King to find out how he had disposed of the wardrobe. I unearthed the name of his manager, who gave me Dennis's telephone number on Long Island. To my joy and amazement, Dennis said the entire wardrobe was stored in one of the stables on his estate and that he would be delighted to sell it to me, all except his personal costumes. This one proviso soothed David Ffolkes' feelings; at least, he would be responsible for covering *my* nakedness in regal splendour. When the time came to interview actors for the supporting roles, it was difficult to refrain from letting one's choice be influenced by their physical proportions. Ideal for the part under review, but would he or she fit the Motley costume?

No one was more surprised than Dennis's manager when the critics attributed some of the success of the production to the lavish costuming. This man proceeded to make a perfect nuisance of himself by instituting legal action against "Richard II, Inc."—claiming that having supplied us with Dennis King's telephone number he was entitled to 10 percent of the show's profits. I hasten to say that he was no longer working for Dennis, who was furious when he learnt of his former employee's conduct. The suit was thrown out by one court after another, but poor Bob Smith was obliged to be present at all the hearings. This was my first, but not by any means my last, contest with the law in New York. I was to learn the hard way that, simply by reading the estimated profits of a show in *Variety*, anyone with a grudge, or just anybody greedy enough, was easily induced by some shyster lawyer to fabricate a suit with the object of securing from the management a settlement out of court. I found it particularly galling in a future trumped-up suit to be advised by my lawyer that, since it was a jury case and the plaintiff a woman, I had best swallow my outraged pride and make a settlement.

Fortunately there were no such legal hassles during the preparatory stages of *Richard II*. Things seemed to be progressing smoothly. Bids for the building of the scenery had been accepted and contenders for the leading parts interviewed. I then began to realise that, although I knew exactly how I wished the play to look and be performed, it would be a serious mistake to occupy the director's post myself besides playing the leading role. During rehearsals of any play there must be a spirit of teamwork, and I felt that no such atmosphere could be achieved if my fellow actors were conscious of my being their employer and their mentor. Directors with Shakespearean background simply did not exist in New York, but an English friend of mine, Alan Wheatley, who had been a member of the *St. Helena* cast, came up with an idea that pleased me. He reminded me that our mutual friend, Margaret Webster, was a Shakespearean authority, having played in Ben Greet's outdoor touring company on almost every English football field. I put in a call to her in London and asked her whether she would consent to taking over the reins of what was really a ready-made production. I was delighted when she said Yes and even more delighted when she arrived and showed herself to be so knowledgeable and easy to get along with.

Over the years I had lost touch with Peggy, though I knew that as an actress she had not made much advancement. This was partly, I think, because her mother, Dame May Witty, wouldn't let her plough her own furrow. I seem to remember Peggy telling me that when she was about to be born her mother, who was in Washington, D.C., at the time, rushed to the British embassy to ensure that she would give birth on what, technically, was British soil. If the mother feared that the baby would be tainted by arriving in a foreign land, her daughter certainly showed no signs of it when she came to work for me. Peggy adapted so quickly that it was hard to believe that she had ever been near the British embassy.

Leland Hayward, my theatrical agent at the time, had recently married Margaret Sullavan and had moved from his flat in the Rockefeller Apartments into her more capacious quarters. He kindly put his vacant flat at my disposal, and it was there that all the final planning for *Richard II* took place. Peggy had barely caught her breath after her journey, when I had her on her hands and knees studying the blueprints, which covered the floor of the living room.

"Where are the drawings of the Duke of York's Palace?" she inquired.

"Oh, I forgot to tell you, I've cut those scenes out of the play entirely."

"Won't the critics pounce on you for that?" she asked. I explained that, in America, Shakespeare was not regarded as holy writ, and that it was unlikely that any critics would spot the excision—which indeed they didn't. Futhermore, I am convinced that the York subplot was added as padding when Queen Elizabeth I forbade the inclusion of the scene of Richard's abdication. The very mention of such a possibility was an abomination to her. If I were guilty of taking liberties with the text, at least I didn't go to the same lengths as my coproducer, Eddie Dowling. His first acquaintance with the play was made at our initial runthrough, after which he seriously asked if I couldn't "do something to build up the girl's part"—meaning Richard's Queen.

When the casting started, Peggy and I were in the fortunate position of being able to say, with honesty, that as strangers in the land we had never had the pleasure of witnessing any of our candidates for the supporting roles in action, and we therefore hoped that they would not be offended if we asked them to read a few lines of the verse. But needless to say, we stopped short in the case of Ian Keith, who had a classical background and was to be our Bolingbroke. A fine actor with a commanding presence, he truly looked the part. His perfectly spoken performance and impressive stature made him a powerful contrast to the playboy King.

It took weeks of auditions to fill the minor roles, one of them being the small part of Green, a favourite courtier of Richard's. We listened patiently to dozens and dozens of hopefuls trying to deliver an important message to the King in a voice that would make his presence at Court believable. The speech reads, "The Duke of York hath broke his staff, resigned his stewardship." One hopeful after another assailed our ears with the Irish "A" and the German "U," so that the sentence sounded like this: "The DOOK of York hath broken his STEHFF, resigned his STOODSHIP." We practically broke into cheers when, finally, a young actor read the message in the King's English.

With that awesome day of first rehearsal coming near, Peggy and I made a pact as to how it and all future ones should be conducted. My chief concern was to dispel any feeling on the part of my fellow actors that, because I had done the play in London, I was in some way superior to them. I couldn't have asked for a better ally than Peggy. She created a free and easy atmosphere, encouraging everyone to experiment with their own ideas—turning on the heat only when someone was really off on the wrong foot. I think it helped that I could without false modesty claim that, as far as New York was concerned, I was almost as much an unknown quantity as the humblest spear-carrier. Although there were signs of my becoming the critics' pet, that didn't mean my name could sell the tickets. In my opinion there are only two categories in the acting profession—those who can draw money from the pockets of the public and those who can't. At that early stage in my American career, I belonged in the second classification. Living up to my theory of an actor's worth, I signed an Equity minimum contract, as did the spear-carriers, and looked to the hoped-for profits to supplement my stipend.

At rehearsals I made a point of never interfering, but, during the lunch break and again in the evening, Peggy and I had long postmortem sessions about the day's work, followed by my outline of how I wished the next day's action to be staged. Fortunately, for the most part, we saw eye to eye, the result being a thoroughly gutsy production. This redounded enormously to Peggy's credit, people in those days finding it hard to believe that a young woman could conjure up such virility from her actors. Our press representative, Dick Maney, latched onto the woman-director angle with glee. At the time, he was also the publicist for Billy Rose's *Jumbo*, so he was well equipped to trumpet Peggy's arrival on Broadway. Neither he nor anyone else in show business had any faith in our prospects. It was assumed that we were a fly-by-night organisation, which had been booked into the St. James Theatre on the heels of the Gielgud *Hamlet* just to fill in a few dark weeks. I dropped into the back of the theatre on the closing night of *Hamlet*; the ovation greeting John was no surprise, but what followed was something only he would think to do. After thanking the audience, he exhorted them to be sure to extend the same warm welcome to Maurice Evans in *Richard II* as they had to him. This was indeed a most generous gesture from one artist to another.

I went to rehearsal next morning more determined than ever to justify John's recommendation. Things were progressing well, and I realised how lucky we were to have inherited from the collapse of an attempted Shakespeare repertory company in Chicago a number of actors with the necessary background. Arthur Kennedy, later to make his name on Broadway and in Hollywood, was one of them. His careless habit at the end of a performance of stepping out of his snow-white costume and leaving it on the dusty dressing-room floor caused him to be dubbed "Droopy Drawers" by the wardrobe mistress. We were fortunate, too, to have Isadora Duncan's brother, Augustin Duncan, as John of Gaunt. His total blindness prevented him from coming on tour with us in the ensuing season. His replacement, Lee Baker, though not similarly handicapped, did startle me at one performance with a lapse of memory. It was towards the end of the famous apostrophe to England: ". . . this earth, this realm, this England, . . . Is now leas'd out, . . . Like to a tenement, or pelting farm." The word "tenement" eluded him, and, fishing for a three-syllable substitute, he made this strange pronouncement, ". . . Is now leas'd out, . . . Like to a *gramophone*, or pelting farm."

Surprises were the order of the day when the scenery was loaded into the theatre one historic morning in February 1937. As it was erected piece by piece I marvelled at what David Ffolkes had accomplished. He had been trained as an architect; his pillars and gothic arches were not only solid—no flimsy canvas and paint—but to give them an appearance of antiquity he had had the brilliant idea of covering them with velour that had been weathered with spray-guns. From "out front" it appeared very authentic, but a closer look at the backside of the rich canopy over Bolingbroke's throne revealed the scenery-shop's legend in large letters: BOLING & BROKE. Amongst other

NAPOLEON AND RICHARD II

scenic innovations David had provided an apron stage over the orchestra pit. It not only served as a hideaway for the musicians, but enabled me, when seated on it during the "Death of Kings" soliloquy, to lower my voice almost to a whisper and still be heard, so close was I to the audience. The apron stage also had two flights of stairs linking the main acting area with what our prompt script designated the "bargain basement." As the lights dimmed on the stage proper, others were slowly brought up to full while the participants in the following scene made their ascent from the basement. These swift transitions were invaluable in permitting us to skip nimbly over the purely plot interludes, and gave the whole production the fluidity of the motion-picture dissolve.

The costumes, too, were stunning, most of them being in what, in the trade, is referred to as "early dressing-gown" style of the Middle Ages. The various lords were easily identifiable by the strongly contrasting colours of their robes, although to one of our actors, Anthony Ross, the prodigal use of the palette was of no assistance because he was colour-blind. In the Westminster Hall scene, he and five other lords, all wearing gauntlets to match their robes, were in the midst of a regular donnybrook, culminating in their challenging each other by hurling their gauntlets into the ring. To stop the hullabaloo, Bolingbroke commands them to retrieve their gauntlets. Being unaware of Tony Ross's handicap, Peggy had directed him to make the first obedient move towards the pile of gloves. There was much unseemly giggling on the part of the assembled Court when, instead of picking up his own royal-blue gauntlet, Tony grabbed one that was bright emerald-green. Peggy soon set this to rights.

David Ffolkes went to town on my clothes. As at the Old Vic, he put me in silk tights, bejewelled robes, and rakish hats for the early scenes of the play, and even towards the tragic end my clothes were more elegant than anyone else's. I received several letters from good ladies begging permission to have copies made by their dressmakers, but I couldn't see myself starting a couturier revival of the fashions of the 1300s. The only garment I wore that put no strain on David's talent was the drab affair I assumed in the final prison scene. This, with the addition of a saintlike beard, emphasized that to the bitter end Richard was still acting a part in life and dressing accordingly.

Another Ffolkesian inspiration was the scenery for the Pomfret Castle dungeon where Richard was murdered. It was imperative that the dungeon fade away instantaneously to reveal the crowned Bolingbroke on his throne weeping crocodile tears over Richard's corpse. This David achieved by utilizing three black-velvet arches, one of them having a shaft of silver light painted on it, giving the illusion of a slit high up in the prison wall. One flourish of trumpets and the blacks were flown out of sight—leaving the dead King lying at the foot of the throne. On opening night this transition "brought down the house." What an opening night that was!

In providing the steps from auditorium level to stage level, we did not foresee the purpose they would be put to by many members of the audience on our truly extraordinary opening night. Not content with innumerable curtain calls, a standing ovation, and a speech from me, this bevy of enthusiasts swarmed up the apron steps, through the split in the house curtain, and onto the main stage. It was ironic that I was unable to enjoy this flattering demonstration. I had already retired to my dressing room, where I lay flat on my back with a hot-water bottle pressed to my face in the mistaken belief that it might appease the agony of an abscessed tooth. Although I knew this to be the most important night of my life, my whole being was focused on my aching jaw. I was beyond caring about anything that had happened on that auspicious evening. I just wanted someone to find a dentist who, in spite of the late hour, would put me out of my misery. My prayers were finally answered and the beastly molar and I parted company.

Until the telephone started waking me the next morning, I was sure my preoccupation with my throbbing molar had caused me to blot my copybook beyond redemption with the critics. One after another, the callers were as ecstatic as the reviews they quoted at length. The torrent of panegyrics was so overwhelming, that I asked Dick Maney to read just the first and last lines of the critiques, which appeared on February 6, 1937.

Brooks Atkinson, *New York Times*

He has wrought a glorious piece of characterization. . . . It dismissed us from the theatre with a feeling of high excitement and a conviction that there is nothing in the world so illustrious as drama and acting.

Richard Watts, Jr., *New York Herald-Tribune*

It is a thrilling and memorable performance that Maurice Evans contributes in the title role of "King Richard II." . . . His final curtain was greeted with cheers, a spontaneous and merited outburst from an audience experiencing an exalted evening in the theatre. If he isn't the finest actor now to be found on the English-speaking stage, then he will have to do until one comes along.

John Mason Brown, *New York Post*

In Maurice Evans, the English-speaking theatre possesses by all odds its finest, most accomplished actor at the present time. . . . As Richard he may lose his crown, but in doing so he gains another as an actor which is no less full of glory.

NAPOLEON AND RICHARD II

When the evening papers were on the street it was the same gratifying story, but it was John Anderson's piece in the *Evening Journal* that really made the box-office treasurers sit up and take notice:

> It is a brilliant spectacle, handsomely turned, deeply moving, richly imagined, superbly executed. It is blinding to confront a Shakespeare play as if it had never been played, for that is how "King Richard II" must stand.

All the huzzas in the world couldn't counteract acute worries about Richard II, Inc.'s financial situation. Joe Reed's bounty, though sufficient for us to get the curtain up on schedule, was not enough to pay off outstanding balances on the scenery and other debts. However, on the strength of the notices, our creditors proved more optimistic than we were, and in a few days long lines at the ticket windows justified their trust. We were able to get the production in the "black" in jig-time and could relax as the profits began to pile up in the ensuing months. It took considerable footwork to keep my promise not to disclose Joe Reed's identity even to a now smiling Boris Said. Joe himself, though glad to recoup his investment, studiously stayed away from the opening night in order to keep the secret. He must have felt proud on October 14, 1937, however, to read in the theatrical columns that *Richard II* at its 168th performance had set a new run-of-the-play record for Shakespeare in New York. Some of its popularity was undoubtedly due to the fact that for the theatregoing public it was virtually a new play by William Shakespeare, having been entirely neglected within living memory. It didn't hurt, either, that at that time memories were fresh of Edward VIII's descent from his throne; though I thought it going a bit far when one publicist claimed that the show had "abdication appeal."

Richard, like Edward VIII, was forced from his throne by his counsellors. He never cared for the job of being King except for the privileges and "perks" that accompanied the position. Half poet and very much a romanticist, he loved life and was never understood by his ministers. He was a young man centuries ahead of his time, who would have been thoroughly at home in today's age of permissiveness and neuroses. There can be no denying that Richard, as King, was a hopeless procrastinator, but the fascination of the play lies in the conflict between his inherent love of pleasure and gaiety and his imaginative and poetic nature, on the one hand, and the solid practicality of his rival, Bolingbroke, on the other. Shakespeare draws both figures with impeccable impartiality and, although at the end of the play you feel the better man has won, your heart goes out to Richard. A spoiled brat, a poseur, and as vain as a peacock was Richard; nevertheless, I think I was able to make the viewer understand his fall and wish that he could have done something to prevent it.

Looking back on those days, I still marvel that it should have been a character so entirely at variance with my own nature which brought me to the fore. I think I can truthfully say that, unlike the average mummer, I haven't a speck of vanity in my makeup. I sometimes wonder whether that is why I recall my amateur-acting experience with such affection. Then it was a stimulating avocation, free from intrusion on one's private life. Hand in hand with a professional career, however, goes the necessity not only to advertise your current activity, but to titillate speculation about your personal conduct. Many performers of both sexes build successful careers mainly on their extra-curricular habits; good looks, a dash of charisma, and a liking for public inquisitiveness about one's premarital and other sexual peccadilloes can cover what may be a multitude of shortcomings in one's talents. In the case of motion-picture actors in particular, it is not generally realised that the handsome salaries they can command is a mere fraction of the sum spent by their employers on promoting their "images." No matter how grotesque a caricature the publicity-mongers invent, that is what the artist must live up to.

I suppose everyone who yearned to be in show business was, in the beginning, motivated by some inner urge to show off. But there is a world of difference between those who are personal exhibitionists—lovers of the limelight and the fan mail—and those who shun the trimmings. Those of the first category are apt to cultivate mannerisms of speech and bearing so that their identities are permanent fixtures, even though they may, in fact, be modelling themselves on some successful predecessor. The other breed, to which I think I belong, finds satisfaction only in becoming immersed in the characteristics of the individual he or she is engaged in portraying. Ours is a different form of self-obsession, demanding a large measure of self-effacement in the pursuit of versatility. One's life becomes a compendium of the habits of Homo sapiens—how people walk, how they talk, and which specimen under observation most closely resembles the part one aspires to play. The total absorption required in the preparation period for a new role makes one a thoroughly antisocial beast as far as family and friends are concerned. One gives the impression of being wrapped up in oneself whereas, in actuality, one is painfully endeavouring mentally to fit oneself into the skin of another human being. At the outset of my Broadway career, what with Romeo, the Dauphin, Napoleon, and then Richard II, it is a wonder that I was left with a friend in the world.

Of recent years a trap has been set for the unwary practitioners of our approach to our profession. In America, and for all I know elsewhere, hosts of charlatans have sprung up spuriously claiming that they have a magic "method" for transforming competent actors into geniuses. All they succeed in doing is to rob them of whatever confidence they have in themselves and in their work. The "method" causes them to be so introverted that what they are up to out there on the stage or in front of the camera is a confidential performance for the benefit, not of their audience, but of their egos. We all know what happened to Marilyn Monroe when she got into the "method" clutches, but a more graphic example was the innocent student who signed on for a trial run at one of these phoney establishments. The proprietor-cum-wizard questioned the boy about his ambition to become an actor. His naïve enthusiasm was quickly dampened when he was told to "go into the corner over there, and think yourself a milk bottle." When the class broke for lunch, he intercepted the wizard, saying, "I'm awfully sorry, but I still don't feel like a milk bottle." "Oh, what a pity," came the reply. "That will be five dollars, please."

3. SHAKESPEARE IN AMERICA

Are you, my reader, wondering why, after all this emphasis on privacy, I am writing this memoir? The reason is simple: in the past, when I have told journalists about myself and my activities, my comments have been twisted to conform with their preconceived ideas about me, and my likes, and my dislikes. Interviewers persist in describing me as "shrewd," a term that in everyday parlance to me implies "cunning"—although the dictionary allows less opprobrious definitions of the word. To this summing up I plead not guilty. If they call me a realist about matters theatrical and life in general, I am the first to admit it. I have no faith in the existence of a life hereafter, considering such faith to be the cause of most of the world's ills. A myth that promises you a second chance in another world is an invitation to neglect your opportunities in the first one. Shakespeare expresses it succinctly in the imprisoned Richard's self-searching cry: "I wasted time, and now doth time waste me." I lean towards the Shavian view that mortality is a kind of relay race during man's brief existence. Immortality is vouchsafed him only if he strikes a creative spark during his lifetime that lights a small flame in the soul of another human being who, in turn, passes on the torch of enlightenment to others. If you have artistic ability your little spark can, in the long run, cause a conflagration of the spirit. Better than all the rave reviews are the occasional encounters with people who declare that something they saw you doing in the theatre gave them a whole new outlook on life. Granted, the art of acting is a subsidiary craft, but it has the power to illuminate the playwright's intention or to obscure it beyond recognition. Assuming that one has the necessary equipment to speak Shakespeare's verse, it is incumbent on the actor to remember that in every audience is a sprinkling of people who are witnessing a play by the Bard for the first time. It is up to the actor to make converts of the doubters, not by playing down to them, but by unfolding for them imagery and word-music that is unparalleled in the English language.

If the prophets in this age of computerism are to be believed, the day is not far off when the printed word will be a collector's item. If Shakespeare were writing tomorrow, instead of scratching with a quill pen as he did orginally, he would dictate his immortal words into a machine capable of translating them into a printout in the form of a minute capsule. The reader would purchase an edited copy of the capsulized work, feed it into his video contraption, press a button, and the printout of the text of Hamlet would light up his screen. If anything faintly approaching this prospect actually comes into being, surely it will be the actors who will have to save Shakespeare from oblivion. There is no reason to suppose that the Bard would not be as careless about his capsules as he was about his manuscripts, in which case only the acted versions of his plays would survive. I shudder to contemplate the ultimate connotations of the electronic revolution. When the sole function of the brain of man is to tell him which button to push, surely that fabulous human organ will atrophy in the same way as any immobilised member of the body.

Looking on the bright side, brainless man will not have the wits to invent further substitutes for endeavour, and, like the dinosaur, he will become extinct—and it will serve him right! Novelty is not necessarily progress and, in the theatre, novelty for novelty's sake is a sin—a pronouncement that, though lacking in profundity, prompts me to dip a toe in the sensitive waters of drama critics.

It may seem a case of biting the hand that fed you to say that, in spite of all the praise which has from time to time been showered upon me by the critics, I take their compliments with a grain of salt. Occasionally I read in their same columns similar encomiums for actors I suspect to be no more than gifted amateurs; they are the kind of performers who, lacking technique, live by the philosophy "I'll be all right on the night." They vary their performances according to the mood they happen to be in, and, in the case of comedians, put the blame on the audience if their jokes fall flat. Mistaken credit being bestowed upon directors has brought about a sorry state of affairs in the theatre. It has contributed to making dictators of directors, opening the door to individuals whose egomania has no limit. Some sympathy is due the critic who is condemned to review his umpteenth *Hamlet*. He has run out of adjectives regarding the Prince of Denmark: sardonic, princely, poetic, manly, introspective—all these he has previously worked to death. So his attention focusses on any innovations he is able to detect, and, in doing so, encourages

SHAKESPEARE IN AMERICA

the modern director to give pure rein to his perversities. Actually, unless the critic had a spy at the rehearsals, it is quite impossible for him to know whether such "improvements" originated in the brain of the director, the actor, or even the producer.

Not so long ago I was coproducer with Robert Joseph of a revival of Shaw's *Heartbreak House*, and in that instance Bob persuaded me to agree to the appointment of a director who was also a respected writer on theatrical subjects. In this directorial job he was so inept that the entire cast rebelled, despite the fact that he had directed a number of notable productions, all of which must have got by in spite of, not because of him. One of his most famous productions was *The Member of the Wedding*, starring the deeply religious black actress, Ethel Waters. On opening night, just before the curtain rose, she gathered the company on stage to join her in a prayer that must have puzzled the Almighty: "Dear Lord, look kindly on our efforts tonight and don't let Harold Clurman come back and fuck things up!"

I had a near miss with one such inspired director when he decided that the time had come to revive *Richard II* in a manner calculated to throw scorn on my own production many years earlier. On this occasion it was suggested that it would be a gracious gesture on my part to play the insignificant role of the Duke of York in support of the up-and-coming Richard Chamberlain's King. I was not averse to the idea, but was prevented by another engagement from fitting it in. Very glad I was when I heard that Dr. Jonathan Miller, for, yes, it was he, had arranged for a false floor to be installed over the regular floor of a theatre in Los Angeles. The stage sloped up from the audience at such a steep angle that on opening night one of the actors (it could have been me) fell into the orchestra pit. It is welcome news that Dr. Miller has decided to devote more time to the field of medicine where, let us hope, his experiments will prove less hazardous.

I trust I am not giving the impression that styles of acting should not change with the times. Shakespeare's playhouse, open to the sky, and Garrick's candle-lit theatre called for totally disparate techniques, as does today's open-space stage. Neither do I subscribe to the view that the "good old days" were really all that good. My father used to tell me about the turn-of-the-century Shakespearean productions starring Henry Irving and Beerbohm Tree—"a lot of realistic scenery was the background for a lot of unrealistic acting." Father also had reservations about Sarah Bernhardt's portrayal of Hamlet but greatly admired her contemporary, Isadora Duncan. His preference between the two ladies led him to swallow as gospel a story that was going round at the time, which was hardly complimentary to the Divine Sarah. It was alleged that on her frequent American farewell tours, she insisted upon taking baths in champagene in her hotel suites. In her manager's opinion this was reckless extravagance, so he conspired with her maid to rebottle the fizz after the ablutions without letting on to Madame. His calculations were upset, however, when the maid carried out the rebottling order only to find that there was considerably more liquid in the bathtub than there were bottles to contain it.

One hangover from the Victorian theatre still existed, in my early years in the West End, that was not conducive to proper teamwork. We supporting actors were never given an unabridged copy of any new play when it went into rehearsal. Instead, for study purposes, we were given what were commonly known as our "sides." These consisted of several pages bound together on which were typed one's own speeches, prefaced by the last few words spoken by another actor, which served as one's cue. It was, therefore, quite possible for an actor to attend a first rehearsal without having the faintest idea what the play was about or to whom one's words were being addressed. These abbreviated aids to memorisation had the advantage of fitting easily into one's pocket so that one could unostentatiously produce them for study while travelling. They also came in handy if one was rehearsing a love scene calling for an embrace. Carrying full-sized script in one hand made passionate contact well-nigh impossible, whereas, encumbered only with "sides," one could get on with the job with conviction! "Sides" were invaluable to actors who toured with a repertoire of plays and felt the need to brush up on their part the night before each change of bill. A favourite story, though probably apocryphal, concerned the theatrical team of Mr. and Mrs. Charles Kean, she a typical *grande dame* and he a somewhat timid spouse. Ensconced with his wife in a double bed at some provincial hotel, Charles forgot that she was to play Lady Macbeth on the morrow. Summoning up his courage, he ardently claimed a husband's rights. "Very well, Charles, if you must! [*sigh of resignation*] Only hand me m'part." A diverting tableau, if ever there was one!

Of necessity, the theatre is a thoroughly undemocratic institution. It tolerates no division of authority. One supreme boss must make all the final decisions—an onerous task for which few are qualified and none very popular. In the case of *Richard II*, I found I had the responsibility of everything that happened onstage thrust upon my shoulders. It spoke well of Peggy Webster's forbearance that she was content to carry out my wishes to the letter. This singleness of purpose gave the production a perfect sense of unity, contributing much to its success. As arbiter in chief, I was fortunate, in this my first experience of the kind, to be taught a lesson that stood me in good stead in the future. No matter how flattering the reviews and the word of mouth, after four consecutive months of playing a classic to standees, you've had it. Unlike a contemporary play, which experiences a gradual tapering off of audiences towards the end of its run, the public support for a classic is apt to evaporate

SHAKESPEARE IN AMERICA

completely after a run of from twelve to sixteen weeks, and *Richard II* was no exception. Seeing the number of unsold tickets in the June box-office rack, Bob Smith and I decided to close the show on May 29, before the onset of a nonair-conditioned New York summer. At the same time, we announced that it would reopen at the end of September for five weeks before setting forth on a long tour.

In the meantime, I took a badly needed holiday, returning to England to gird my loins. I put on my best bib and tucker figuring that there would be reporters at Southhampton as I disembarked. I needn't have bothered, however. There were plenty of reporters all right, but word had reached them that Douglas Fairbanks and Mary Pickford were on board. The news-hounds swarmed up the gangplank and almost knocked me over. Under what breath I had left in me, I murmured Macbeth's reflection, "To be thus is nothing, but to be safely thus." It was rather the same when I got to London. Except for intimate friends, nobody seemed to know or care about my Broadway conquests—I even had to fill in my family on the subject. All in all my homecoming was a disappointment. Although it hurt my pride, it proved a salutary thing to be moved down a peg or two. It forced me to take stock of my professional future, as I was reminded that, with the exception of *Richard II*, my gradual ascent of the Broadway ladder had been by courtesy of established American producers. Reaching the top is one thing; remaining there is quite another.

Before leaving New York I had put in my briefcase a research study of every recorded Shakespearean production seen in that city since 1890. I was amazed to see that out of the small total of sixty presentations, most of them performances in repertory, only four productions were credited with passing the 100 performances mark: *Taming of the Shrew* (Lunt and Fontanne—128); *Romeo and Juliet* (Jane Cowl—157); *Hamlet* (John Barrymore—103); and *Hamlet* (John Gielgud—132). In addition, my *Richard II* tied with Gielgud's *Hamlet* at 132 performances. The nearest contenders had been Edwin Booth and Lawrence Barrett, who had racked up eighty-four performances of *Julius Caesar* in 1875–76. Going down these fascinating statistics, my eye lighted on *Henry IV (Part One)*, to be informed that in 1883 it had been performed by somebody named John Jack and since then totally neglected, except for a one week's reading by members of the Players (New York). I had never read or seen the play, but knew vaguely that historically it was the sequel to *Richard II*. I got hold of a copy of the play and what a revelation it was! Not only a stirring drama, but one that traced the fortunes of Bolingbroke, of the earlier play, after he occupied Richard's throne as Henry IV. The period, costuming, and the scenery were almost identical, and the size of the cast comparable. To crown it all was the challenge it offered me to make an attempt at a startling change of pace in the part of Sir John Falstaff.

Even so, I had severe doubts whether or not an American audience would have much use for all the political wrangling and pitched battles that are the substance of the play. Better, perhaps, to use it as just an exercise in the course of the *Richard II* tour that lay ahead. It would relieve the tedium of long journeys and give the understudies and spear-carriers a chance to show me what they were made of. In the meantime, it offered me something to think about besides my Richard alter ego and the indifference with which I was being greeted in London. There, my American exploits were treated in theatrical circles with the condescending air of "it couldn't have happened here."

I took umbrage at this attitude until, one day, it occurred to me that when I had first arrived in the States in 1935 I, too, had indulged in a superiority complex. It required a firm verbal punch from a fellow actor in the Cornell company to make me aware that I was being thoroughly offensive. "If you find us so backward and our customs so objectionable," he said, "why don't you go back home?" Another incident, which brought me to my senses, happened on a night when I was dining in a hotel restaurant while on tour in one of the southern states. The restaurant door suddenly burst open admitting another Britisher who, without so much as removing his hat, surveyed the assembled diners and, in a voice audible a block distant, shouted "Monkeys!" and then staggered out the way he had entered.

My old friend David Ffolkes had recently returned from the States, as well. He and I discovered we shared a mutual discontent with the tepid reception that had been accorded us; so we decided to go on a motoring tour in Europe to improve our dispositions. Since we were both visiting Italy for the first time, David's architectural training made him an ideal companion, although his insatiable appetite for churches and cathedrals was a bit wearisome. There was no disagreement, however, about the mountainous platters of spaghetti that we consumed with equal relish at various trattorias where we refuelled ourselves for further expeditions. In the course of one of these meals I broached the subject of *Henry IV*, giving David a copy of the play, which I had brought with me. I told him I was planning an out-loud reading of *Henry IV* by the *Richard II* cast, the better to judge its potential. In the questionable event of their reading being good enough, could David see a way of designing the extra bits and pieces of scenery that would be essential if, at some time during the forthcoming tour, I decided to sneak in a couple of tryout matinees of *Henry IV*? That night he read the play and at breakfast next morning made some rough sketches on the tablecloth of an idea for the Boar's Head Tavern.

Florence, Padua, and Assisi were on our route, all of them associated with my theatrical past and thrilling in themselves. Then over the mountains to Salzburg and finally to Munich, or at least that was our destination. However, on the approaches to Munich, we were summarily confronted with signs reading "Absolut Halt" and beneath them a posse of bully boys wearing brown shirts and swastika armbands. No cars were permitted to enter the city limits that night; we had to leave ours at this checkpoint and make the journey into town by taxi. Arriving at our hotel we asked the concierge why we had been stopped at the outskirts and why all the bunting on the streets. "Oh," he said, "didn't you know? The Führer is coming here tomorrow and there is to be a big parade." We didn't say it out loud, but thought to ourselves, why all this fuss about a politician with a ridiculous moustache? We were much more interested to find out what was playing that night at the Residenz, a famous building, which David was anxious to see. To our amazement we learned that the current bill was, of all things, *Richard II* by William Shakespeare. Neither of us had a word of German, but this was something not to be missed.

As we entered the beautiful little playhouse, we noticed that the house curtain had been substituted with a drop on which was painted a very decorative family tree of the Plantagenets. For those unfamiliar with English history it was, we thought, a good idea to prime the audience concerning Richard's forebears and his kinship with John of Gaunt and Bolingbroke. However, by Act II the family tree became the subject of unseemly mirth to David and myself. Between scenes the family tree was lowered and, in the course of the preceding action, John of Gaunt had died; so someone had applied a sticker across his name reading "Todt." This was so typical of the German lack of a sense of humour that it helped to explain later why they saw nothing comic about their Führer or why they lost two world wars in a row. We were still chuckling when we returned to the hotel, and the concierge was obviously puzzled that we had found the tragedy so hysterically funny. Nevertheless, he said if we had enjoyed ourselves, we had another treat awaiting us next afternoon. He had two tickets left for the grandstand on the parade route and we really should purchase them.

Anything for another laugh was our reaction, so we took our places on the morrow in the beautiful spring sunshine. The stands were crammed with eager spectators, all in their Sunday best and most of them chewing on something. What we took to be policemen lined the route and were facing towards the stands. Afterwards we were told they were members of Hitler's elite guards—the Schutzstaffel (S.S). Bands started to play at the far end of the route and, for what seemed hours, a procession of floats passed by—the most elaborate tableaux glorifying Germany's past in the arts and sciences. These were greeted with polite applause from the occupants of the stands. Then, suddenly, the sound of martial music struck our ears. As if on a command,

1935–1942

everyone but us two stood upright peering down the avenue. In the distance soldiers appeared carrying poles with gilded German eagles on top, and others with even larger swastikas. In their wake were the troops, all of them shouldering the dummy wooden rifles which, ostensibly, conformed with the Treaty of Versailles's restriction on armaments. I've seen supporters go mad at football games, but they were tame compared with the wild hysteria of that Munich crowd. The S.S. troops were trying to calm the people down, but to no avail. It was an ugly and sobering sight, and we had no desire to see the climax when Hitler himself would appear. His visit, by the way, was the famous occasion when, in opening the new Munich art gallery, he made the pronouncement that he would forbid any picture to be hung there unless its blue skies were blue and the green trees were green.

We scuttled back to England as fast as we could, both of us going to our respective families to report what we had seen. "Pack your bags," I told mine. "There's going to be a war and you're coming to America to sit it out." I might have saved my breath. "What utter nonsense," my mother said. "Sounds to me as though you've got the American jitters." I think it was the way she pronounced "American," as though there was an unpleasant odour in the air, that really offended me. Anyway, I decided to return to the States as soon as possible where I knew I would not be treated as an intruder.

I am frequently, and I fear justly, accused of going about any occupation with the same ferocity as one of my beloved West Highland White Terriers in pursuit of a rat. It's the same with my hobbies, such as they are. I love to work with my hands—carpentry, gardening, and cooking—but I'm always in too much of a hurry and sometimes make a botch of things as a result. Lately my daubing with oil paints has demanded a slower tempo. I am also an inveterate hoarder, a failing that is useful when one is also the handyman of the establishment. I save jam jars as though they were jewels, and in them I put sundry nails, screws, and whatnot. When there is some household emergency, I know exactly what jam jar contains the requisite item for repair—just like my father before me.

It was a pity that this quality of good husbandry was overtaken by rash optimism in my approach to the forthcoming tour of *Richard II*. I assumed that word would have spread nationwide of our success on Broadway. Instead, it became apparent that even a big city such a Pittsburgh was too far from New York for us to be recognised. In a huge country, such as the United States, the word of mouth taken back home by the visiting theatregoers is paramount. Our end-of-season limited Broadway run had missed out on such spreaders of good tidings, but I was determined to keep a stiff upper lip. I even refused to take it seriously when Eddie Dowling showed me a telegram he had received from a theatre-manager friend of his which read:

SHAKESPEARE IN AMERICA

IN TEXAS WE'VE ONLY HEARD OF ONE BILL SHAKESPEARE AND HE IS A BASEBALL PLAYER

Undaunted, we set forth on our thirty-five week tour on October 18, 1937, which, at the outset, seemed promising, since we had not then strayed too far from home base. We couldn't have asked for better commendation from the local press, though one particular member of the public had a quaint way of expressing her approval. A note left at the stage door read, in part, "When you spoke that poetry, the lilt in the lines just sent me to sleep."

Quite a number of replacements for the original cast had become necessary and, in picking them, Peggy and I did so with an eye to experimenting with *Henry IV* during our travels. Preliminary rehearsals of this play had already taken place in New York before we started out, but there was much gruelling work to be done for the show to be presentable at the two matinees that were already announced for the Forrest Theatre, Philadelphia, in November. To rehearse Falstaff by day and play Richard at night was no mean undertaking. Consequently, I dumped the preparation for *Henry IV* in Peggy's capable lap. She was a purist about the Bard, and it took quite a bit of argument before she would swallow my idea of incorporating a scene from *Henry IV (Part Two)* in our production. It gave Falstaff a little more scope by including the very funny interlude when he musters recruits for the army— Wart, Mouldy, Feeble, Shadow, and Bullcalf. Peggy feared we would be accused of poaching, but I was able to assure her that there was no record of the play ever having been seen in Philadelphia so that the audience would be none the wiser. Once she had agreed to go along with this emendation, I gave her her head with the production, attending only the rehearsals that involved the fat knight. I don't remember enjoying rehearsals of any part more than I did Falstaff—imagining his appearance, his voice, and his wit. But when the day arrived in Philadelphia that I first donned the padding, the wig, and the putty nose, I had a radical change of heart. It was unmitigated torture, and at the end of the first of the two matinees I was so dehydrated by the suit of lamb's-wool padding that emergency medical assistance had to be called. How I managed to get through *Richard II* that same evening is one of those "the show must go on" mysteries. It was some comfort that, in spite of my distress, the play itself was an undoubted success and provided me with a tour de force. Nevertheless, my duty was to forgo indulging in more whims and to stick solely to completing the *Richard* tour—all thirty more weeks of it.

It quickly became obvious that the routing of the tour was ill-advised. Owing to the unwieldy amount of scenery we were carrying and the hours it took to truck it from the railroad yards to the theatre and back, we were obliged to follow quite an unsuitable itinerary. Although the railroads cooperated by putting on special trains for us, it would be 2 o'clock in the morning before we were loaded up and ready to roll to our next scheduled town. This resulted in our stopping at places where theatregoing, apart from the cinema, was completely unknown.

One such unfortunate halt took place when the distance forced us to play the then undeveloped Austin, Texas. Recently I visited Austin to work with the drama students at the University of Texas and was amazed to find there the best-equipped and by far the finest theatre complex in the United States. In 1937, however, it was a different story. Somehow or other, our indomitable crew managed to squeeze enough of our production on the inadequate stage of a movie house to make a performance just possible. I dressed in the boiler room, and everyone else dressed under the stage by the light of a single ceiling lamp. Before the doors opened to the public, I followed my usual practice of taking a look at the front of the house to gauge how much projection would be needed. In the lobby I introduced myself to the movie-house manager, finding him something less than cordial. In fact I suspected he was distinctly miffed about having to suspend the run of a popular film to make room for our classical monster. He seemed, however, to be resigned to making the best of a bad job. As we were chatting, the boy who ran the candy concession came into view, a tray slung on his shoulders displaying the sort of goodies favoured by moviegoers. The manager stopped the boy and, critically surveying the contents of his tray, said, "Listen, boy, throw out the Baby Ruths, the Lovenests and the chewing gum—this is a class show!"

The tour involved a lot of painful education, which I benefited from on future jaunts, but at the time it wasn't pleasant. It was madness to think that I could draw audiences in the Katharine Cornell manner, when her name had become a household word. Our industrious advance agent had difficulty in getting the local papers to print his momentous news that *Richard II* was coming to town. Once we arrived in the smaller towns, the press changed its tune but too late to be of any help to the box office. At one point, our fortunes looked so dim that I decided emergency measures would have to be taken to overcome this apathy. I quite seriously suggested that in future a team of horses be awaiting us at each railroad station on our route. Having changed in our Pullman cars into our Plantagenet finery, we would then make a procession down the main street, scattering flyers as we proceeded to the theater. However, the local police made some fuss about who was to clean up the calling cards of the horses, so the brilliant scheme was dropped. Who knows—it might have worked—it does with circuses!

Somewhere along the route I had another encounter with the police. In those segregated days it wasn't practical to travel with a black valet, so, much to my sorrow, I had to leave mine behind in New York. In his place, I hired a

SHAKESPEARE IN AMERICA

white Cockney who ran foul of the law in some obscure town in the Middle West and had to be dismissed. By a lucky chance, there was a small-part actor in our troupe named Emmett Rogers, and he volunteered to fill the gap for the remainder of the tour. He proved so valuable that, except for the war years, he became my right-hand man in business affairs through 1955, going on to become a producer on his own.

Apart from the ups and downs of the tour, I had much else on my mind, the foremost worry being about my next professional step. After having made such an auspicious start in New York, it was a crucial decision to have to make. The simplest solution would have been Falstaff, but something told me that, although I might come off all right personally, the play itself invited second-best opinions in comparison to *Richard II*. The only sensible alternative seemed to be *Hamlet*. But there was a danger that the recent Gielgud and Howard productions had given both public and critics their fill of the tragedy for the time being. I was about to abandon the idea when it occurred to me to look up the records to see if and when the entire text of *Hamlet* had been seen in New York. The answer, I was delighted to see, was "never"—except for one performance as described by Yale's associate professor of playwrighting, Walter Prichard Eaton:

> I once before saw all of Hamlet. I forget the year, but it was around 1904 or 05 or 06. E. H. Sothern, peeved because no two critics agreed on what should be omitted, said he would put on the entire play and we must all come. We came. It was a Saturday night. We were in the old Garden Theater (on Madison Square) 'till about 2:30 Sunday morning. I thought I never wanted to see the play again.

This threw a totally different complexion on the venture, giving it something of the same novelty that *Richard II* had enjoyed. As Brooks Atkinson of the *New York Times* was to write later on: "one can say that no one has really seen 'Hamlet' until he has sat enthralled before the uncut version." It was one thing to have conceived, but quite another to endure the labour pains. What bothered me most was our accountant's forecast that, at the rate *Richard II* was limping along, and by the time Joe Reed had recouped his money, and Boris Said had taken his slice of the cake, there wouldn't be a penny left in the kitty. This prediction turned out to be almost correct, so I was faced with the necessity to start from scratch to finance *Hamlet*—In Its Entirety.

Joe Reed, being quite indifferent to profits, came up trumps and I also made a substantial investment out of my own pocket. There was, alas, a Russian fly in the ointment; Boris Said insisted that the St. James Theatre would be made available in October only if he became a member of the board of the producing company. He had not interfered with the *Richard II* preliminaries and I assumed he would keep his hands off our new enterprise, but how wrong I was! No sooner was his condition met than he started to throw his not inconsiderable weight around. Amongst other things, Boris took the implacable view that no one in his right mind would sit through four hours of *Hamlet*. If Joe and I insisted on the "Entirety" then the limit should be one performance per week, with the others a cut version. As Boris thumped my desk to emphasize his conviction, Joe Reed started to pace up and down the office with obvious distaste. At one point Joe noticed on my desk an antique pistol that I used as a paperweight. Unseen by Boris, Joe picked up the pistol, aimed it at the enemy's head, and clicked the trigger. Waving an airy goodbye he handed me the weapon and left the office, never to attend another board meeting. This left it to me to argue with the Russian until we reached a compromise of two cut versions each week alternating with "Entirety" at the other performances.

Thoroughly exhausted, not only by the thirty-five-week tour, but by my new partner as well, I took off for England for the last of my sailing holidays aboard the *Evelyn Hope*. The rumblings in Europe were becoming so menacing that I told my two Helmore shipmates I thought they should dispose of the yawl and join me in America as soon as possible. Before returning there myself, the three of us went to Portofino for a thorough rest, to be broken briefly when Peggy Webster and David Ffolkes joined me for a *Hamlet* planning conference. Towards the end of our Italian holiday, I noticed something that I had not observed on my previous visit—lots of young men in uniforms of a sort and sporting very fancy, plumed hats. Our housekeeper at the Castello seemed reluctant to talk about them, but when I pressed her she said they were Boy Scouts. From other informants, however, we learned that they were members of the Young Fascist organisation. This reinforced my feeling that Europe was no place for Britishers to be disporting themselves, so we decided to make ourselves scarce.

It was good to be back in the States, particularly as I had another exciting challenge in the offing: the scenery and costumes for *Hamlet*. David Ffolkes and I decided that, since Leslie Howard had gone towards a Danish flavour and the McClintic-Gielgud production had a very fussy James I decor, we would do well to stay with a Tudor style. I wanted audiences to be reminded that this was an Elizabethan play written for the lusty Elizabethan appetite for gore, sword fights, and murders. The floor plan of our production should bear a certain geometric affinity to the stage of an Elizabethan playhouse. The familiar "Words, words, words" scene dictates such consideration. Hamlet, reading a book, must be in view, walking a while, when the Queen says, "Look, where . . . the poor wretch comes reading." (Who was the well-known actress who spoonerized that line into, "Look, where the poor reed comes retching"?)

HAMLET—IN ITS ENTIRETY (1938)

Polonius then says, "Away, I do beseech you, both away!" (The King and Queen don't budge.) "I'll board him presently." (They still stand pat.) "O, give me leave." (They exit.) The scene is no good if the actors are looking off into the wings at an advancing Hamlet, nor is it right if Hamlet has not been near enough to notice the conspiratorial atmosphere. It seemed to me certain that, at the Globe, Hamlet had made his entrance, whilst reading, from the "inner above" level and that he did not reach the main stage until the King and Queen had left it. That he has seen and heard these exchanges with Polonius explains his mocking attitude in the "Fishmonger" dialogue which follows. In keeping with this, David gave us a gallery at the rear of the main hall of the castle, which served this and many other scenes to perfection.

Never in my wildest dreams had I pictured myself as one day having the enviable privilege of playing the Prince in a production over which I had total control—for good or for evil. I purposely gave myself six months of uninterrupted concentration on the preproduction details. These included minute supervision of the scenic plans and the costumes, sifting out ideas for casting and the *entrescène* music. Without the familiarity with the play and the part that I had gained at the Old Vic, I could not possibly have undertaken so much responsibility. Even with that previous experience, I felt the need to restudy the play and the character. Having set David on his course, I thought it best to leave him alone to do his sketches.

4. HAMLET—IN ITS ENTIRETY (1938)

New York was in the grip of one of those intolerably steamy-hot summers that take all the stuffing out of me. I was told that about the only cool part of the country within reasonable proximity to the city was the Adirondack Mountain area of upstate New York. The nights would be cool, I was assured. So, armed with everything I could lay my hands on in regard to *Hamlet*, I set forth on the night-train to Lake Clear Junction. My accommodation was a quiet inn by the shore of Upper Saranac Lake. The ambience was ideal for my purpose of calm consideration for the task ahead, besides providing the privacy I needed to recapture my memory of the actual lines spoken by Hamlet.

One day, paddling slowly in a canoe around some of the small islands dotted about Upper Saranac Lake, I hailed a fellow on the dock of one of them asking him if I could have a glass of water. He invited me ashore and took me into the kitchen of his log cabin to slake my thirst. I instantly fell hook, line, and sinker for everything about his tiny island, and asked whether he knew of any others like it which might be available for rental the following summer.

"You can have this one if you like, Mister."

"How much?" I asked, breathlessly.

"Ayah . . . how about a hundred dollars a year?" came the reply. I seized him by the hand by way of closing the deal.

The next day I authorised him, at my expense, to add a bathroom to the cabin and to install a second-hand farm generator, which he promised would give me a thirty-two-volt electric supply. It all seemed too good to be true, which indeed, it turned out to be. When I came to take possession of the island and its added facilities the following summer (1939), the man greeted me with a confession. Although he had been using the island for years, he was not the owner but merely a squatter. Due to unpaid New York State taxes, the property was about to be put on the block. In order to avoid losing my bathtub and its essential companion, I was represented at the sale. To my satisfaction the property became mine, though the back taxes demanded were substantial. Norway Island, as it is named, has continued to be my summer retreat to this day, and through the years has been the birthplace of nearly all my subsequent professional ambitions.

That summer of 1938, however, I had to force myself back into the Hamlet groove and forget about my future island. My thoughts reverted to my introduction to the play. It was the first time I was a member of the audience at the Old Vic in 1924. It was not uncommon for one to believe that one's first Hamlet is far and away the best. Ion Swinley never became a top star in the London firmament, but in my book his Hamlet has never been excelled. That is a broad statement from someone who later saw Barrymore, Gielgud (three different productions), and the Olivier celluloid version. Maybe Swinley's use of the uncut text made the performance so memorable; if so, I had my work before me to match his stunning interpretation.

In these pages it is not my object to write a dissertation on Hamlet's madness; whole volumes have been written concerned solely with this subject. I am, on the other hand, in a position to quote a summary of the controversy. A woman, attending one of my matinees of the play was overheard saying to her companion, "You see, dear, he's not mad at all—he's just very, very annoyed—and with good reason!"

I worked like a beaver at Saranac, making periodic trips to New York to check on David Ffolkes's progress and to acquaint Peggy Webster with the overall scheme I had in mind. We agreed that in staging any of Shakespeare's plays it is essential to take into account that he was not writing for posterity but to be *acted*, loudly and clearly, by a particular group of actors to whom he was attached. Unlike our modern pampered institutions subsidized by the taxpayers, his theatre had to pay its way, though sometimes with the assistance of royal patronage. Still, his plays had to appeal to the commoners in the pit as well as to their lordships. In regard to the fashioning of my own performance, Peggy was wholeheartedly in agreement with the opinion of that man of the theatre, Harley Granville Barker: "The actor is bound to reconstruct the character in terms of his own personality. He realises himself in Hamlet, and if he did not his performance would be lifeless."

I returned to New York with an overriding determination to present the full text as an exciting show above all else. Peggy and I concentrated on assembling a fine cast. She had convinced Mady Christians that her slight German accent would not preclude her from being most effective as Queen Gertrude, which indeed she was. I arranged for Henry Edwards to come over from England and play Claudius, Whitford Kane was to the the first gravedigger, and George Graham made an excellent Polonius. As Ophelia, Katherine Locke, who had just concluded a long run as the Jewish ingenue in *Having Wonderful Time*, had to bridge the not inconsiderable gap between a Catskill holiday camp and the castle of Elsinore. At Peggy's suggestion, Lehman Engel was commissioned to write the score and conduct the pit orchestra.

At last we were ready to take the plunge, and I was more resolved than ever to prove Boris Said in the wrong about the "Entirety," so I conceived the idea of giving the audience an unusually long intermission after the first half. Sardi's restaurant, only a few doors down the street from the St. James Theatre, was not the prosperous bistro it is today, and Sardi himself was delighted to cooperate in arranging a buffet supper to be served during our intermission. It worked like a charm and made quite a sensation on 44th Street when we sent out our orchestra trumpeters onto the outside balcony of the theatre to recall the diners for the second half. Sardi told me later that this novelty had put his establishment back on the map after the lean years of the depression. To express his gratitude on opening night, he sent a waiter to Mady Christians's and my dressing rooms with trays containing splits of champagne and chicken breasts. Both of us were dying of hunger and overexcited by the tremendous reception accorded to the first part, so we tucked in recklessly. The result was the most flatulant performance of *Hamlet* on record. "Mother" (*hup*), "Mother" (*hup*), "Mother" (*grrr*)! Possibly this is why one critic made the observation that I "lacked natural melancholy."

Thanks to Peggy's well-organised schedules and her good-humoured way of handling actors, the rehearsals started as planned. I left the decisions about the text entirely to her, knowing that she had at her fingertips the choices between the three Quartos and the First Folio. She had decided that the intermission should come after the scene nearly halfway through the play containing the "To be or not to be" soliloquy and ending with the King's words, "Madness in great ones must not unwatched go" (Act III, scene 1). This suited my approach extremely well, that soliloquy coming shortly after the point in the play where for the first time Hamlet expresses some doubt about the apparition of his ghostly father—"The spirit that I have seen may be the devil; and the devil hath power to assume a pleasing shape." The audience, having recently had that bee put in its bonnet, would go to Sardi's for the buffet supper, returning to the theatre later to find Hamlet far less irresolute— in fact, in a holiday mood with the band of Players and relishing his plot to "catch the conscience of the King." Particularly when the uncut text is employed this is the logical moment to divide the play. The second half, dramatically speaking, has a cops-and-robbers flavour in contrast to the mournful atmosphere of the first part. The mounting excitement of the action produced an amusing comment by one spectator towards the end of one of our performances. Standing at the back of the theatre in the company of Dick Maney, our press agent, was Toots Shor, the proprietor of a popular restaurant on 52nd Street. As the play drew towards its close, Dick whispered to Toots that it was time for him to get back to his customers. "No hurry," said Toots, "I want to see how this thing comes out."

The demands made upon the actor playing this title role increase in intensity in the latter half of the play, requiring him to conserve enough energy and sufficient vocal power to meet the demands of the graveyard scene and the rapier-and-dagger finale. He must possess faultless technique to stay the course even though he runs the risk of being accused, as I have been in my time, of sacrificing depth of feeling for technical proficiency. I found, even as we rehearsed, that I had to watch myself like a hawk to make sure I didn't abuse my vocal chords. Serious damage can result from allowing the "rogue and peasant slave" soliloquy to run away with you—"Bloody, bawdy villain! Remorseless, treacherous, lecherous, kindless villain! O, vengeance!" That passionate crescendo must be orchestrated in such a way that one avoids laryngitic consequences. I remember even such a master as John Gielgud urging me, if I were coming to the play, to do so on a Monday night, as he was finding that by the end of the week he was as hoarse as the proverbial crow.

Any actor aspiring to tackle the "Entirety" should know in advance that he is condemning himself to a life of strict austerity. He will find, as I did, that his doctor wasn't kidding when he warned him to remain totally silent from curtain fall each Saturday night until it rose again the following Monday. At weekends he must abjure use of the telephone, and communication with his fellow man must be by means of a pad and a pencil. His household pets, being denied his customary endearments, will slink away from him in disgust.

It spoke well for Peggy Webster's tact that she arranged rehearsals so that I was given periods of rest, whereas she had set herself the unremitting duty of being glued to her director's chair for every minute of every day. Any fatigue we were feeling was instantly swept away when we moved from the rehearsal room into the theater where our scenery was being set up. The great hall of Elsinore Castle was already in position, and what an impressive sight it was! The imagination of most scenic designers is carried away by the opening scene on the battlements of the castle. Ignoring the fact that they are in use only in Act I, they impose an inevitable stage wait before the exterior can give way to the interior where the majority of the play takes place. No such flight of fancy had struck David Ffolkes, however. In fact he had made it possible for Gertrude and Claudius to be already in their chairs of state during the ghost scene, but invisible to the audience. As with *Richard II*, no mechanical considerations interrupted the swift flow of the tragedy.

Through no fault of David's, however, there was one performance during the run when the handling of the scenery caused me to fly into a rage. For the graveyard scene he had designed a series of tombstones set in front of a painted canvas drop depicting the exterior. As I was handed poor Yorick's skull, I became aware that the pictorial drop of Elsinore's battlements was slowly rising into the air. Suspended momentarily in that position, it then started to descend, but in doing so a draught caught it, causing it to become festooned over the tombstones. The scurrying legs of sundry stagehands were revealed, by then, to a tittering audience. To make matters worse, some helpful soul commenced to poke at the drop with a broom handle in an effort to dislodge it, no doubt fearing that when it was flown out at the end of the scene it would ascend heavenwards, tombstones and all. Those were the days when an employer could reprimand an employee face to face. I ordered the entire crew to line up at the end of the show, and demanded an explanation. The union delegate then informed me that after the sixteenth performance of a Broadway show a rotation system came into force. One regular member of my crew was required to stand down at one performance weekly to make room for an unemployed substitute. (This, of course, ensured the delegate of the substitute's vote at the next union election.) In practice, it was impossible to entrust a man with vital duties of which he knew nothing; so one kept the regular man at his job and told the substitute to sit quietly in a corner doing nothing. Knowing this to be the case, the union sent its oldest and most decrepit members to fulfill this hypocritical task.

On the night of the graveyard catastrophe, the union had sent an old fellow named George, who was assigned to the fly rail. He had much difficulty mounting the ladder, but once safely aloft his mates told him to make himself comfortable. In the case of a play of ordinary length no problem would have arisen, but the four hours of *Hamlet* proved too much for George's bladder. Unable to get to his feet without something to hold onto, George grasped the rope nearest the place where he was seated and hauled himself up. Unfortunately, the rope he had chosen was attached to the graveyard backdrop, causing it first to rise and then to lower once he was upright. George was unrepentant for the onstage contretemps he had caused and blithely pocketed his $4 for his night's work at Elsinore.

Unlike *Richard II*, which defied comparisons with previous productions, *Hamlet* could not hope to escape them, nor I to emerge unscathed. Like it or not, our fate was in the lap of the gods, if drama critics can be regarded as members of that hierarchy. On the morning of October 13, 1938, these were some of the words handed down from Mount Olympus:

Brooks Atkinson, *New York Times*:

The uncut Hamlet is no cultural chore, but the grandest play ever written. It is a headlong play of vital scope in the ample text of the second quatro. That is the fresh spirit in which Mr. Evans takes it. He acts it at the top of his compass. On the negative side, he has abandoned the posturing, the school-book melancholy that tradition has imposed upon Hamlets, and he does not interpret the business fearfully. On the positive side, he acts as Hamlet of modern sensibilities who does not love words for their own sake but for their active meaning. This is a Hamlet of quick intellect who knows what is happening all through the play. He dominates by alertness. He is frank; and, above everything else, he is lucid. Probably the Elizabethans played Hamlet in this fashion before the scholars burdened the drama with problems. It is refreshing and exciting to see it played for sheer drama. Margaret Webster's staging and direction have created what is virtually a new play. Only the dopes will stay away from this one.

Richard Watts, Jr., *New York Herald-Tribune*:

Mr. Evans' "Hamlet" is one of the great and satisfying events of the modern theatre.

John Mason Brown, *New York Post*:

Unlike most recent Hamlets, Mr. Evans is not a neurotic princeling with a pale visage who strikes despairing poses under spotlights. He is the first entirely masculine Hamlet of our time. He has wit, gaiety, vitality, and charm. Watching him, one understands what the King means when he describes Hamlet's spirit as being "free and generous"; why dueling should be something at which he excels; and why Fortinbras insists after his death that "the rites of war speak loudly for him."
Mr. Evans' Dane is, in other words, not the introvert Mr. Gielgud disclosed so brilliantly. He has a consistency Mr. Gielgud's Hamlet never dreamed of achieving, and a brilliance of his own which is no

less rewarding. Mr. Evans, moreover, is an actor who does not lose control of himself. His performance shows careful planning and is always in hand. He saves himself for his more torrential outbursts and realizes them superbly. His voice is a beautiful instrument, capable of doing justice to the magnificent beauty of the lines he speaks. Exceptional as he is throughout, in such moments as the scene with Ophelia which he turns into a heart-breaking love scene, or as in the tempestuous excitement of the "play-within-a-play," or as in the glorious tension of his closet scene with Gertrude, Mr. Evans proves himself to be the finest actor of our day in a production which is by all odds the most satisfying and most moving "Hamlet" has received within not-so-recent memory.

This man Evans is a superlative performer, a genius the stage is fortunate in claiming as its own. What Flagstad is to grand opera he is to the theatre. Should proof be needed nowadays of the theatre's greatness and of the fact that great acting has not vanished from the earth, this proof can be found in abundance at the St. James these late afternoons and nights in the person of Mr. Evans and his revival of "Hamlet" in its entirety.

It was somewhat ironic that the only daily newspaper that didn't join in the general enthusiasm was the London *Times*, whose correspondent's dispatch of October 28 had this to say:

Mr. Evans has attained his new triumph in a "Hamlet" played in its entirety. The presentation begins at the ungodly hour of 6:30 P.M., and an hour and a quarter later an interval is provided for dinner—a half-hour's interval. "Hamlet" will doubtless be productive of indigestion, as well as of poetic excitement. The latter it certainly has in full measure. The tragedy is played admirably, as well as at length, and Mr. Evans was, on the opening night, almost blasted from the stage by "bravos." The reviewers caught the spirit the next day and superlatives knew few bounds, the moderate agreeing, conservatively enough, that Mr. Evans is now the foremost Shakespearean actor of our day. In this jubilant chorus not to use the word "great" became niggardly. Your Correspondent, however, cannot use it, feeling that the actor's playing is always very fine and sometimes electrifying, but on the whole somewhat uneven—uneven, of course, on an unusually high plane.

The morning after our opening, the St. James box office was besieged by ticket buyers. The treasurers did their level best to push the two scheduled matinees of the cut version, but there were no takers. The same was true of the ticket-brokers who were falling over themselves to be assigned blocks of seats, none of them for the shorter matinees. For the first and only time during our partnership, Boris Said admitted he was in the wrong and, after two wobbly matinees of the truncated version, they were not to be seen again. The weekly magazines gave additional impetus to the public demand for the "Entirety," though some of the more sober monthly articles had their reservations.

Rosamund Gilder, *Theatre Arts*, December 1938:

Mr. Evans' presentation is vigorous, free, remarkably expert. His reading, beautifully cadenced, harmonious and delightful to the ear, avoids subtleties. There is no sense of lacerating inner conflict in his Hamlet. His prince is capable of noble anger, of overwhelming depression, of violent grief, but the profounder depths of the part are left unexplored. At no moment in the play do we see in him the stigmata of the experience which makes Ophelia describe him as one "loosed out of hell to speak of horrors." The flashes of insight, the devastating moments when often, without speaking a word, John Gielgud revealed Hamlet's naked, tortured soul are not in this picture. It is, deliberately, the portrait of a young man "most generous and free from all contriving," whose frank wooing of Ophelia in the nunnery scene is entirely in keeping, and who can undoubtedly ride, fence, write poetry and eventually "kill a king" without too much inner havoc. As in his Richard II, Mr. Evans presents a technically fluent and assured performance. It is a joy to watch his masterly handling of an arduous role. He is always alert, alive, vigorously present, keeping pace with the tempo of swift-moving events.

It is indeed fortunate that an incident at a later performance did not occur on the opening night. In the first scene at the Court, after dismissing the ambassadors, Claudius turns his attention to the sulking figure of Hamlet with the line: "And now my cousin Hamlet and my son." Sad to relate, our Claudius (Henry Edwards) had an ill-fitting lower denture, which on one occasion left its anchorage on the word "son." Miraculously, he caught it in midair and restored it to its berth. It sent the assembled courtiers into poorly disguised stitches, and I'm not at all sure that I was audible in Hamlet's reply: "A little more than kin, and less than kind." I was too busy wondering what would have happened to the plot if Claudius had missed the catch and Hamlet had been obliged to pick up the errant teeth and politely hand them back to their hated owner. I dreaded the rest of that evening, for each time Claudius and Hamlet met in a scene there seemed to be some oblique reference to teeth—"I eat the air, promise-cramm'd," or Claudius's "Hamlet, this pearl is thine."

5. FALSTAFF AND MALVOLIO

In the light of continuing sold-out houses, it was difficult for me to hold to my conviction that after four months or thereabouts the pot would go off the boil. But stick to it I did by putting into rehearsal *Henry IV (Part One)*, even though I was still playing *Hamlet* at night. This double duty made it impossible for me to supervise the production, but, with the tryout Philadelphia matinees behind us, I felt it was safe to entrust everything to Peggy and David and to confine myself to putting in an appearance only when the Falstaff scenes were scheduled. We had given ourselves a mere nine days between the closing of *Hamlet* and the opening of *Henry IV*, too fine a margin, I was to find out. When the scenery was brought out of storage it refused to fit the limited depth of the St. James stage. David had made an error in his measurements and Peggy had failed to detect it.

The first of the two dress rehearsals was a shambles, so much so that the company was dismissed. The two culprits, the entire stage crew, and I lay on our bellies on the stage floor trying to discover where the error was in the blueprints. We were at our wit's end on that night of January 28, 1939, knowing that the opening was irrevocably set for the 30th. It was then that our heaven-sent stage manager, Eddie Dimond, came to our rescue. Ignoring the measurements controversy, his solution involved jettisoning some of the scenery, then tearing down the remainder and repositioning it in workable order. The crew volunteered to accomplish this by working right through the night, and we were told to go home to bed. By the time I got to the theatre next evening, that loyal gang had practiced a dry run of the scene changes and all had gone well.

It was not only the scenic problems that had been solved. Ever since the Philadelphia tryout, when the heat prostration caused by Falstaff's padding had nearly finished me off, I had been seeking some less distressing alternative. One day, passing the old Metropolitan Opera House, I noticed a poster announcing a forthcoming production of Verdi's *Falstaff* with Lawrence Tibbett. I sought out the opera wardrobe master and asked him how Mr. Tibbett coped with the enlarging of his girth. The wardrobe master proudly produced for my inspection his very own invention. It consisted of a series of crinoline hoops which hung by tapes from one's shoulders—light as a feather and allowing air to circulate freely. A flared jacket could be draped over this bird-cage contraption and, providing I held Mistress Quickly at arm's length when embracing her, it would look as though it were solid fat and not air that was separating us. Grateful as I was for the Met's assistance, I nevertheless doubted that I could sustain the part for any length of time, so a limited engagement of four weeks only was announced.

I felt bad that my *Hamlet* confreres had taken the pains to study and rehearse their roles for such a short reward. Henry Edwards as King Henry and Mady Christians as Lady Percy had both agreed to stay on, and a newcomer to our company, Edmond O'Brien, was to play a fine Prince Hal. The best tonic for an actor who has been steadily playing tragic characters is suddenly to hear the blessed sound of laughter. It cured all my fears about what, in advance, had seemed mostly a test of endurance, and it took little persuading, after I read the reviews, to extend the engagement for an additional five weeks.

Brooks Atkinson, *New York Times* January 31, 1939:

It is a play of high excitement and valiant people, with some roaring low comedy seasoning the martial dish, and a fit successor to the uncut "Hamlet" and the compassionate "Richard." From the rueful Hamlet to the exuberant Falstaff is no chore at all for Mr. Evans. Buried under a mountainous costume, he lards the lean stage as he walks along. Clumsy, begrimed, heavy of foot, white of hair, jolly of nose, he is a most engaging rogue with convivial humor and a bar-fly's wit. Out of all the gallimaufries of Shakespeare's comedy Mr. Evans has constructed an intelligible character whose cowardice and knaveries are logical parts of a man every one is instinctively fond of. Mr. Evans never forgets that Shakespeare was human and wrote with a racy quill for the pleasure of human beings.

Richard Watts, Jr. *New York Herald-Tribune*, January 31, 1939:

Mr. Evans gives him all the humor, all the richness, all of the strange perverse lovableness of the man, providing him with a strange kind of inner dignity of a decayed gentleman, who has found that life is the greatest of all desirable jests. I am certainly no enthusiast for Shakespearean clowns, but no one can mistake Falstaff for a Shakespearean clown. He is one of the great creations of literature and Mr. Evans can prove it to you.

The correspondent for the London *Times*, February 22, 1939:

Mr. Evans plays the part in what appears to be a bale of cotton-wool. No actor in years has looked more ponderous, or played with more inward agility and lightness. . . . Falstaff, of all great characters, is one of the most sapless in the library. Mr. Evans fills in abundantly with sap—fills him with a humour which comes as much from a bubbling inner appreciation as from the lines, makes him far more than the coarse clown he appears so often in the playing, gives him the stature of humanity at its least regimented.

FALSTAFF AND MALVOLIO

Delighted as I was by such encomiums about Falstaff, I was even more surprised by the reception given to the play itself. Of course, it was greatly in our favour that as the curtain rose on Act I it revealed Bolingbroke, now King Henry IV, enthroned in the same surroundings that he had previously been seen in at the close of *Richard II*. It must have seemed like old home week to the faithful in the audience. But they were to find this play far less of a biography about the central character; many others are given their innings—Prince Hal and Hotspur, for instance, having some memorable verse passages. They could wonder, too, at the leave-taking scene between Hotspur and his wife, beautifully played by Wesley Addy and Mady Christians, and sounding as though it were fresh from the pen of Noel Coward rather than the Bard of Avon.

I suppose it was the unfamiliarity of the play which caused some of my Falstaff inventions to be taken for granted. There were two ideas which I particularly liked. One was in the Boar's Head Tavern scene where, after the previous night's roistering (when Falstaff had caught a severe cold), I was discovered seated with my feet in a mustard footbath and an icepack on my head. This picture seemed to me to suit the dialogue: "Bardolph, am I not fall'n away vilely since this last action? Do I not bate? Do I not dwindle? Why, my skin hangs about me like an old lady's loose gown! I am withered like an old apple."

The other legitimate touch was in the battlefield scenes. No matter what part of the melee he found himself in, Falstaff always carried over one arm a folding campstool (on which he overflowed) to rest whilst the others fought, and from which he could deliver the famous "Honour" speech. "Honour pricks me on," says Falstaff, adding, "Yea, but how if honour pricks me off when I come on? How then?" Later, when we did the play in repertory, it wasn't easy for me to give that speech its full cynical flavour, for Hitler had marched into Poland, and Great Britain had declared war on Germany. Military conscription came into force for all males between the ages of eighteen and forty-one; and there I was at thirty-eight, and a British subject, making outrageous fun of the honour of serving one's country.

About this time I was given an opportunity to change the entire direction of my career, and I often wonder what would have happened to me if I had made a different decision about it. I imagine it was on the strength of my Falstaff that Max Gordon and Sam Harris sent me the script of the George S. Kaufman-Moss Hart comedy *The Man Who Came to Dinner*, saying that they wanted me to play Sheridan Whiteside—the part that made Monty Woolley famous in America and Robert Morley throughout the rest of the globe. If at any time I harboured the delusion that I was a good judge of a play, this one proved how fallible I could be. To me it read as nothing but a comedy of bad manners, and I couldn't for the life of me believe that it would be entertaining. Whiteside struck me as a boor to end all boors and, in spite of an intensive campaign by the management—"You can write your own ticket" and all that—I would have none of him. I have to confess that when I saw the play later on I was surprised to find I was thoroughly enjoying myself. It was curious that the casting of Whiteside in America fell to amateur actors. Monty Woolley, the bearded stranger from the academic world, played the part in New York and in the film version, while the road company was headed by the vitriolic drama critic Alexander Woollcott.

With the possibility of America eventually becoming embroiled in the European hostilities, which in late 1939 were daily appearing more ominous, I was not much in the mood for trifles. It had been by pure accident that I entered the United States in 1935 on an immigration visa. I had been given the choice of either a visitor's permit (which meant reporting periodically to the proper authorities and notifying them of any change of address) or an immigration visa (which permitted freedom of movement). The latter also conferred upon me the right to become a naturalized American citizen after a prescribed interval. The time was now approaching when I was obliged to make a declaration of my intention, or to let the opportunity go by. A change of citizenship is not undertaken lightly, and I found it a matter for much soul-searching. On the one hand was the undeniable fact that by letting me slip through its fingers, the English theatre had done me a tremendous favour. On the other hand, however, it seemed excessive for me to feel that I ought to throw away my American career in acknowledgement of their generosity.

The idea I had of forming a repertory company in New York had to be shelved in view of the uncertainties. I badly wanted to be seen as Iago, Shylock, and King Lear, but these would have to wait until the world settled down one day—a day, I may say, for which I am still waiting. According to Who's Who, from April 1939 through June 1940 I did nothing but revivals of the four plays in my repertoire, either on Broadway or on tour—obviously a sign that I was too apprehensive about the state of the world to embark on any new venture. The critics, instead of sending their deputies to the revivals, paid us the compliment of attending them in person and reiterating their earlier enthusiasm. Before returning to New York with the touring company of Hamlet, I had decided to put myself to the test by giving eight performances weekly instead of the seven that were all that I had dared to do in the original production. On matinee days this required me to be in the theatre for ten consecutive hours, seven of them being actually on stage. Somehow or other I survived, giving credence to the old maxim that hard work never hurt anyone. The final total for Hamlet was 136 performances in New York and 151 on tour.

FALSTAFF AND MALVOLIO

The tour was not without its lighter moments, particularly when the matinee audiences included numbers of school children. The Hanna Theater in Columbus, Ohio, had a second balcony, which, at one matinee of *Hamlet*, was crammed solid with children who had been told that if they bought a ticket for the show they would be excused from school that afternoon. Needless to say, there was a rush to the box office, and the gallery was occupied by more than a hundred spitefully minded brats who were determined to have a good time no matter what was in progress on the stage. While waiting for the curtain to go up, they filled in the time by making paper darts out of their programs, which they launched from their aeries in the direction of the apron stage. Heavier missiles, such as balled-up gum wrappers, were apt to miss their target, landing on startled occupants of seats on the orchestra floor. When our company manager reported the state of affairs, I realised that we were in for a lively afternoon, and rather dreaded the juvenile reaction to Ophelia's mad scene. Because there were no ushers in peanut heaven, I suggested a policeman be requisitioned to keep order. There happened to be a traffic cop about to go off duty outside the theater and, his curiosity piqued, he agreed to oblige. By the time he had been talked into it and had climbed the many stairs, the play had got under way. No more talking or singing, no more paper darts. Polonius entered and delivered his first comedy line, whereupon the children joined in the laughter along with their elders. The traffic cop, not knowing his Shakespeare as well as he should, emitted a stentorian "Quiet!" and the poor actor playing Polonius couldn't get a laugh all afternoon.

Although in those distant days Tulsa, Oklahoma, was very much a cow town, we were surprised to find that it had not only a theatre but one with a stage that actually boasted a "grave trap," surely a relic from the times when other companies had toured with *Hamlet*. This enabled us to inter Ophelia's corpse with more dignity than in some of the theatres on our route. However, it was midwinter in Tulsa and the theatre's heating system was the forced-hot-air variety. When the lid was taken off the grave trap, a blast of air shot upwards, bearing on it the delicious aroma of coffee being brewed by the wardrobe mistress in the basement below. The hot draught caused untold mirth on the part of the mourners when Queen Gertrude attempted to scatter flowers into the grave. In a suitably tearful voice, Mady Christians said the line, "Sweets to the sweet! Farewell!" As if on cue, the hot-air blower cut in and Mady's paper flowers flew back at her no matter how hard she tried to beat them into submission.

These were strenuous months for me, for having closed *Hamlet* on tour, I returned to New York for a successful revival of *Richard II*. This was followed by a West Coast tour of the play in May and June of 1940. Although the tour was rewarding, these weeks were not very happy ones because they coincided with the British evacuation at Dunkirk and the fall of France. Furthermore, I was still in a vacuum as to my intended change of citizenship. It was reassuring, however, when I was in Los Angeles, to be instructed by the British consul general that it was the wish of His Majesty's government that all British subjects (especially members of the English colony in Hollywood) remain in the States until further notification. In the meantime, we were to take every possible opportunity of convincing our American cousins of the need for their support in the war effort. The meeting with the consul general took place at Boris and Dorothy Karloff's house in Beverly Hills; the older members of the English colony, under their leader, C. Aubrey Smith, looked mightily relieved, and the young fry were noticeably harassed.

With no plans for the future except to wait out developments in Europe, I hied me to my Adirondack island for the summer months of 1940. My English yachting friends, Tom and Evelyn Helmore, joined me there and helped enormously in getting the place in shape. Evie, who later became Mrs. Boris Karloff, had picked out furniture and draperies for me at Macy's in New York. More than forty years later, the same furniture and curtains look as good as new, thanks to the clean mountain air. I can't truthfully say the same of the antiquated personal clothing, although some of it is still serviceable. I attribute my long and healthy life to those idyllic summers on Upper Saranac Lake. It is close to the Canadian border and Montreal, and, being that far north, sundown does not come until 10 o'clock at night in July. The sunsets are so spectacular that it is hard to leave one's rocking chair even though something is boiling over in the kitchen. Norway Island is minute—you can walk around its perimeter in ten minutes—and that is one of its charms. We have built platforms, which project over the water at all points of the compass so that it is breakfast facing east, luncheon south, cocktails west, and sunsets north. Sitting on the porch with a drink in hand and good music on the record-player, one feels one is on shipboard with eleven miles of lake stretching ahead. Tiny though it is, the island abounds in conifers of various sorts and blueberry undergrowth—everything about it peaceful. The trees made a useful shelter for me on the occasion that a bevy of canoeing Girl Scouts from a neighbouring camp came paddling around the island shouting, "Hiya, Hamlet." They were sternly forbidden by their Scout mistress to repeat their indiscretion.

The squatter, known as "Doc," having installed my bathroom, had emigrated to a nearby island taking his down-the-garden-path privy with him. For the most part, living was surprisingly civilised and included daily delivery by boat of foodstuffs and mail. No refrigeration, of course, but an old icebox on the kitchen porch was all we needed. In the winter, mainland neighbours had teams of horses pulling large blocks of ice, which had been cut from the lake, to be stored in an icehouse under layers of sawdust. They kindly saw to it that my icebox and my martinis didn't go wanting. Most important of all was the fact that we were able to persuade the telephone company to run a cable under a mile of water from the mainland. It was one of those crank-handle affairs on a very verbose party line, but at least it enabled me to keep in touch not only with New York but with my family in England during those anxious days.

It was thanks to this means of communication that my next professional move was made. Word had reached me that the Theatre Guild and Gilbert Miller were planning a fall production of *Twelfth Night*, starring Helen Hayes, and that Peggy Webster was to be the director. After several arguments with sundry camp caretakers around the lake, I managed to get exclusive use of the telephone long enough to call the Theatre Guild. I told them that if they were prepared to take the risk of my being called up for British military service I would like to be their Malvolio. What Peggy thought I don't know, but I strongly suspect she lacked enthusiasm about finding herself once more under my shadow. She didn't have to worry, however, because, apart from my own interpretation of Malvolio, I had nothing to say about the production, and was resolved to keep my mouth shut. There was one awkward moment when Helen Hayes, whom I knew only socially, took me aside at the first rehearsal and, in all innocence, asked me my secret for speaking in iambic pentameter. I was afraid Peggy would suspect a conspiracy between Helen and me but mercifully our tête-à-tête was interrupted by the arrival of Gilbert Miller's portly person. Thus I was spared the necessity of confessing that I hadn't the faintest idea of any magic formula. As the rehearsals got into gear, I became more and more impressed by the speed with which Helen adapted to verse speaking without hints and tips from me or anyone else. More than any other I have had the pleasure of working with, Helen is her own sternest critic during rehearsals. Her Viola was a case in point; her first reading of a scene seldom satisfied her, so she would ask if she could try a different approach in a second or even a third reading, each one quite unlike its predecessor. I have never encountered a performer with such rare variety of techniques or such unfailing professionalism of behaviour. Illyria and *Twelfth Night* were virgin territory to Helen and me, which made it a stimulating journey for both of us.

Suffering somewhat from an overdose of revivals, I was particularly elated to be tackling something new. I don't recall having seen a production of the play and I've found no record of a sustained Broadway production since 1870. I have a framed poster on my study wall issued by the Globe Theatre, Boston, announcing a performance "For the first time in America, by this company, of *Twelfth Night*." This was a production starring Mr. Henry Irving and Miss Ellen

Terry. A footnote certainly suggests the date of 1884; it reads, "Carriages may be called at the Essex or Washington St. entrance."

I had read so many of Shaw's withering opinions of Irving's acting that it wasn't hard to avoid his reputed style. The only notion that occurred to me was the probability that, at Shakespeare's Globe, Malvolio and Falstaff had been played by the same actor. Like myself, that actor would want to differentiate between the two characters as much as possible. It therefore followed that, as I had played the fat knight as a gone-to-seed gentleman, the thing to do was to portray Malvolio as a commoner of humble beginnings desperately trying to be even more genteel than his masters. I was greatly helped by the charming scenery and costumes devised by Stewart Chaney. For me he created a fantasised tuxedo and overlong shoes, which told the story of a butler's fallen arches.

To discover if I managed to bring Malvolio to life, I must turn once more to the aisle sitters:

Brooks Atkinson, *New York Times*, November 20, 1940:

An old hand at Shakespeare, Mr. Evans is superb. He is acting a Cockney Malvolio, which is an amusing idea. As usual, he has designed the character with imaginative detail, never forgetting the point of the scene he is playing. Without truckling to the customers for easy laughs, he can catch pomposity in the tiniest suggestion of a strut or in the fulsomeness of ceremony. A master of Shakespearean dialogue, he can speak it for sense without losing the rhythm. "Run?" he inquires politely when Olivia bids him run after the Duke's messenger. It is only one word. But somehow Mr. Evans puts into it the disdain, the fastidiousness, the vanity and alarm of a fatuous underling. Put that down as acting.

John Mason Brown, *New York Post*, November 20, 1940:

Mr. Evans brings all of his excellent endowments as a character actor to Malvolio. He does not burlesque the part by turning him into the clownish steward Mr. Sothern—an admirable Malvolio—was tempted to do. He plays him as a time-pleaser, sick of self-love; a pathetic, quiet, entirely human being who is more ridiculous inside than out. His Cockney accent, which he does not overstress, is the most felicitous of comic innovations.

Sidney Whipple, *World-Telegram*, November 20, 1940:

It is Mr. Evans, however, who spares neither himself nor tradition nor the play itself, to provoke sound and honest laughter. This Malvolio of his is a magnificent anachronism, a deliberated, cheerfully brazen

FALSTAFF AND MALVOLIO

metamorphosis of a medieval majordomo into a twentieth century cockney butler, pompous, witless and more often than not in comic difficulties with his pronunciation. And whether or not you may be bothered by the relation of such a character to the formal court life of Shakespeare's Illyria, it is his Malvolio that dominates the entire play.

Even Rosamund Gilder, who had previously had her reservations about me as a tragedian, seemed to have buried her hatchet for the time being, saying in *Theatre Arts* January 1941:

Mr. Evans as Malvolio has enough [style] for a whole cry of players. His entrance in the pompous black of his steward's office, his gold chain about his neck, his high flared collar setting off a face unexpectedly adorned with goatee and sideburns, his high-soaring eyebrows expressing a noble self-complacency, an invisible hauteur, is an event in itself. He registers at once Malvolio's enormous conceit, his high seriousness, his disapproval of frivolity. In order to break away from the ordinary pattern of Shakespearean speech, and from the confines of his own successes in it, Mr. Evans has provided Malvolio with a genteel cockney accent. He scans his speech with care, avoiding h's where they do not belong, breathing upon them lovingly in their right places. This amusing trick keeps his voice well away from the music of the bard's blank verse with which his audiences have associated it so closely during these last years. The accent makes Malvolio's dream of Olivia's favor more ridiculous than ever and it adds yet another note to the chorus of colloquial speech with which American productions of Shakespeare are afflicted, but it is justified by Mr. Evans' use of it as a comic device. His performance is sprinkled with genuinely witty moments, as for instance, when Olivia bids him:

> "Run after that same peevish messenger,
> The county's man: he left this ring behind him . . ."

Mr. Evans interjects a "Run!!" which is as full of comment as a whole speech could be. In that one word he expresses his outraged dignity, his shock, his surprise and disapproval of the whole procedure.

How I managed to get away with rewriting Shakespeare was something of a mystery, and only now do I dare own up to my sin. The interjection of the word "Run" was an involuntary reaction to Olivia's command at one of the rehearsals. It broke up everybody and bets were laid that none of the critics would spot the slight liberty taken with the text.

6. BECOMING AN AMERICAN AND BECOMING
MACBETH

After 128 performances in New York, *Twelfth Night* embarked on a long tour that lasted until June 1941. Our engagement in Chicago was to last for a month, which allowed time for some relaxation. Helen was astonished when I had to confess that I had never witnessed a baseball game. She was a devoted fan of the Chicago Cubs and insisted that I accompany her to a game. I didn't dare say it, but baseball appeared to me a tame sport compared with the English preparatory-school game called "Rounders." Granted we played with a soft ball, but it required accurate aim to hit a boy with the ball as he ran from base to base. Unlike me, Helen was thrown into transports of delight when one of her Cubs scored a run; this caused her, each time, to dig me fiercely in the ribs with her rather sharp elbow. I was black-and-blue by the time I got back to my hotel and not much wiser about the manly sport.

Beyond keeping myself in shape at the Chicago Racquet Club, I had little to do with my leisure time except to brood on the misfortune of wartorn England. Communication with my family was now almost impossible, particularly as I was on the gypsy trail. About all I could do was to send money and food parcels and hope for the best. To take my mind off these worries I formed the habit of going to the movies once a week. A terrible Hollywood opus came to a local film palace with the intriguing title of *Lady Scarface*. What was even more surprising was that it starred Judith Anderson. Her performance would not have won her any Oscar, but her appearance gave me exactly the impetus I needed at the time. I had been toying with the idea of taking a crack at *Macbeth* as my next Shakespearean role, if and when circumstances permitted it. However, I had failed to think of an established actress who, as my vis-à-vis, would match me both physically and vocally. I called her in Hollywood and found her most receptive to the idea of Lady Mac. She hadn't appeared in New York since her success in *Family Portrait* in 1939 and was eager to do something to erase the image which Hollywood had thrust upon her. I knew that she had essayed the part in 1937 at the Old Vic, opposite Laurence Olivier, in a production which was dogged by the misfortunes traditionally associated with the play. The opening had to be postponed owing to Larry's loss of voice, and the Old Vic's famous Lilian Baylis died during the engagement. Not one to be put off by theatrical superstitions, Judith was game to have another try under more propitious circumstances. It suited her Hollywood commitments to wait until I had completed the *Twelfth Night* tour and taken a summer holiday.

And so, back to my beloved island in July to study *Macbeth* and to find out exactly what I was letting myself in for. I became convinced that the mood of the tragedy was suited to the times and that it certainly agreed with my own mental state. By then the Blitz was in its full brutal swing and the steps I had taken earlier in 1940 to ensure the safety of my parents had misfired. At that juncture, in what was known as "the phoney war," I had persuaded Father and Mother to join my sister May, who lived on the Channel Island of Guernsey. No one could possibly have foretold the suddenness of the German conquest of France and the consequent vulnerability of the Channel Islands, which are closer to the French coast than to the English. As it turned out, I had unwittingly chosen for the parents the only piece of English territory that fell into German hands throughout the war. It must have been a ghastly moment for the old folks and my sister's household when, early one morning, the police knocked on their door telling them that the Germans were coming. They were offered the options of sitting out the war under German occupation or, with only one suitcase per person, to embark immediately on a small steamer awaiting final departure at the dock. My brother-in-law, being the headmaster of the local school, had to leave his family to their own devices while he rounded up all his pupils for the exodus. My mother, bless her heart, managed to win over the harbour master to disobey his order concerning pet animals. She told him that her son was in America and that she had given him a solemn promise to take care of his West Highland Terrier, Hamish, in his absence; so there could be no question of her leaving the dog behind in Guernsey. It probably meant that a precious Jersey cow had to be taken off the passenger list, but "stowaway" Hamish couldn't have cared less, since milk was not on his diet. The family had a rough time of it when they landed. They and the schoolchildren were given temporary shelter in Weymouth's docklands warehouses and were eventually dispersed all over England. My brother-in-law's pleadings to be allowed to keep his youngsters in one unit were refused by a government totally immersed in the national crisis. Although he had weathered World War I with distinction, this rejection was more than he could bear, costing him a nervous breakdown and finally his life. My sister behaved like a veritable Trojan through horrendous misfortunes, while caring for Father and Mother and providing for her children. This was to last for the duration of the war.

While we were in Los Angeles with the *Twelfth Night* tour, the plight of other English children was brought sharply to our minds. Peggy Webster's mother, Dame May Whitty, called to say that she had received a cable from the chairman of the British Actors' Orphanage reporting that a German bomb had been dropped in the grounds of the institution and the Board of Governors wanted to evacuate the orphans to America if sufficient persons could be rounded up to sponsor their support. We formed a committee and invited all the resident Britishers to attend a meeting at the Chateau Marmont.

1935–1942

Nigel (Willy) Bruce—Dr. Watson to Rathbone's Sherlock Holmes—was one of those present, giving voice, in his Colonel Blimp manner, to his doubts about the evacuation. "What will their parents think about it?" asked Willy.

"But Willy, dear," said Dame May, "they are *orphans!*"

"Ohhhhh . . . ," responded Willy. Somehow we didn't think he was quite convinced.

We had a hard time prying out the money despite the many thousands of dollars in pledges. Charlie Chaplin, for instance, gave us a cheque on his London bank, which took two years to collect. There was also great difficulty in persuading the donors that their idea of taking the orphans into individual sponsors' homes was not workable. The children had to be kept together as a group except, perhaps, during school holidays. Noel Coward took over the responsibility at the New York end of things, and Gertrude Lawrence took the credit which was *his* due. He had persuaded the Gould Foundation in the Bronx to house the kids, and the rest of us signed up for their keep. Any sentimental feelings we may have harboured for the refugees were dissipated within a few days of their arrival from England. They were taken in busloads for a tour of Manhattan, and on foot to visit Times Square, including a visit to Woolworth's five-and-dime store. On their return to their new home in the Bronx, it was noticed that most of the little darlings were carrying articles they had shoplifted on the trip. The following day they were marched back into Woolworth's to return their loot with suitable apologies.

With the orphans off my mind, I had no valid excuse for not concentrating on *Macbeth*, but the deeper I got into studying the play the more aware I became of the difficulties inherent in the part. The bugbear of producing a classic in the professional theatre is that one can never start with a clean slate. Even in the case of the less familiar works of Shakespeare there is no escaping the portraits conjured up by the illustrators of the plays. Engravings, woodcuts, and even photographs of the characters are apt to fix themselves in one's consciousness from schooldays onwards, and woe betide the actor or producer who fails to live up to those images. This applied particularly to *Macbeth*, whose lithographed appearance was invariably that of a gigantic bruiser. Obviously my five-foot-nine-inch stature couldn't approximate anything of that sort; so from that standpoint alone I sensed trouble ahead. I hoped that, somehow or other, audiences and critics might relate the action of the play and the neuroses of the protagonists to the personalities currently turning Europe upside down. It could be argued that the world's troublemakers have frequently been physically insignificant, but that was not apparent to their followers, nor did it lessen their dictatorial ambitions. Thus I felt, and hoped that others might think, that what mattered was the guts of the Thane, not his height. To quote Lord Acton's famous aphorism, "Power corrupts, and

As Falstaff in *Henry IV (Part One)* (1939).

As Malvolio, with Helen Hayes as Viola, in *Twelfth Night* (1940–41).

As Macbeth, with Judith Anderson as Lady Macbeth
(1941).

With Yehudi Menuhin (*left*) (1944).

As the G.I. Hamlet, drawn by Lupas (1945).

Hamlet in Oahu's Jungle Training Center, drawn by Sergeant Bill Beynom (1943).

THE GI AUDIENCE in Hawaii, as everywhere else, was wowed by *Hamlet* as acted by Major Maurice Evans and his soldier-actors.

The G.I. Hamlet (1945).
"He poisons him i' the garden."

The G.I. Hamlet (1945)
"Begin, murderer; pox, leave thy damnable faces,
and begin!"

absolute power corrupts absolutely." That, to my mind, was the nub of the play and was to be the basis for my interpretation.

Having at least found a starting place for a much more detailed study, I felt confident enough to put production plans in the works. This meant, in addition to the artistic side of things, arranging for new financing—and once again the fates were on my side. Word quickly got around New York that I was back in business, for the time being at any rate, and that *Macbeth* would be the offering. I had barely checked into my New York hotel when I received a telephone call from a Wall Street lawyer asking if he could call on me. Mr. Lloyd Almirall duly arrived—all six-foot-four of him—and from that moment I knew I had found a guide, philosopher, and friend. He was acting in the same capacity for Flora Robson, and his mission was to suggest her for Lady Macbeth, a role she had played at the Old Vic some years earlier. I had to tell him that I had already promised Judith Anderson the part. Lloyd agreed that Judith would be a splendid choice, and over a couple of drinks we arrived at an understanding that he should perform the same service for me as those he was engaged in for Flora and a number of other actors. Only an incurable theatre buff could fill the bill, and in that respect Lloyd was a confirmed addict. I no longer needed an office because he took over the financing of *Macbeth* and all my subsequent productions. In addition to drawing up all contracts, he became the custodian of my personal money affairs—a job about which I am hopelessly incompetent.

It was during this trip to New York that Peggy Webster came once more into the fold. In spite of the fact that at one time she, like Flora, had played the Lady at the Old Vic, she welcomed the idea of directing Judith, and agreed to join me at Norway Island later in the summer to confer on a production scheme. No sooner had I returned to the island than I received a summons to appear at the Court House of the Southern District of New York on August 21, 1941, to be sworn in as a naturalized citizen of the United States of America, for that had finally been my decision. In a sober mood I attended as directed, expecting to appear before a judge in his chambers. Instead of that, I was ushered into a huge room absolutely jammed with hundreds of other applicants, their complexions being a kaleidoscope and their speech equally diverse. It was the hottest of hot days and dozens of circulating fans made such a racket that it was quite impossible to hear what the presiding judge was saying. At one point the multihued people down front raised their right hands, so we at the rear did likewise. It was only on the way out that I was told by an official that the raising of my hand signified that I had renounced my British nationality and, without being aware of the actual moment of its occurrence, I had become a naturalized American citizen, pledged to defend the country against all its enemies.

1935–1942

Although over three months were to elapse before the Japanese attacked Pearl Harbor, shortages were already making themselves felt in the United States. The theatrical costumers were unable to obtain the kind of materials our designer, Lemuel Ayers, wanted for *Macbeth*. To achieve a sense of uniformity, he was obliged to employ upholstery fabrics to resemble the heavy woollen garments of his designs. The tartans would not have passed muster in Scotland, but at least they looked warm. We had to cut corners, too, on the construction of Sam Leve's scenery, but succeeded in getting a reasonably solid Inverness Castle, which would be practical under touring conditions. I worked out the ground plan, telling Sam to give his sketches to Peggy who would bring them to me at the island. Peggy and I worked harmoniously on the production details during her stay at Upper Saranac Lake, and finally the two of us set out for New York to put them on the fire. Little did I dream, as I rowed Peggy across the lake, that it would be several years before I would see my island again.

One of our first tasks was to obtain estimates for the scenery and the costumes from three different firms in both departments. The neglect to take competitive bids in that manner is one of the principal reasons why production costs today are so astronomical and why, in turn, admission prices are so high. We were not very popular with the designers, who favoured only one of the competitors, irrespective of cost. I remember a particularly difficult session at the costume house of Helene Pons. Lemuel Ayers was displaying his sketches with poetic descriptions of how he envisaged the final product—the shoulders to be like those of a football player, the belts to be studded with metal, and so on and so forth. Peggy sat beside me with her costume chart checking off the items of clothing from top to toe and marking down Helene Pons prices. She interrupted Lemuel in the midst of one of his most eloquent passages, saying, "Very nice, but does he wear a hat and, if so, how much?" Realising that she was up against a couple of determined customers, Helene Pons cut her estimates to the bone and I am happy to say was awarded the contract. Though this may seem to be a nitpicking method, it has been, in fact, the root of my success as a producer. It has to be remembered that before the war the best seat for a legitimate play cost $2.50 until city and other taxes raised the price to $3.50. To finance the mounting of a production, Lloyd Almirall corralled a handful of "angels" who, by the expedient of making individual loans to me, recouped their investments and received a 100 percent profit for their pains. Whereas other Broadway producers calculate the share for their "angels" at 50 percent of the profits, I have always given my benefactors a healthy 60 percent. In this way they have trusted my methods completely and have reinvested automatically in all my productions. We never had to go through the humiliating device of backers' auditions, nor was it necessary to seek investors by a public offering. Of course, there were the occasional slip-ups, which threatened the operating costs in terms of labour, but mercifully they were few in number.

One such boo-boo occurred in the "blasted heath" scene in *Macbeth*, which contains Shakespeare's casual stage direction "The witches vanish." The designer had invented some complicated machinery for this effect, which refused to function. It became clear that efforts to remedy the fault were just a waste of precious dress-rehearsal time; so I sent out an assistant for some fireworks powder and an armload of photoflash bulbs. Concealed within crevices in the rocks on which the witches were perched, the powder in smokepots provided "the fog and filthy air" and the photoflash bulbs, when activated, blinded the audience for the split second it took for the three hags to drop, unseen, to the floor behind the rocks. A simple trick, but the illusion was complete. It was just as well, however, that the audience was unaware of the funny sight of the three weird sisters crawling into the wings on their hands and knees. At a performance much later on, my invention took its revenge. Without my knowledge, a spark from the smokepots landed on and set fire to my tartan cloak. A member of the audience shouted, "Mr. Evans, you are on fire!" I tore the garment off my shoulders and with the point of my sword tossed it into the stage prompt corner. That happened in 1941, but it was not until I was at a Phi Beta Kappa luncheon honouring Walter Cronkite in 1980 that a woman introduced herself as the person who had shouted the fire alarm that night.

We took a few liberties with the text, cutting entirely the Hecate scene and disposing of the fight between Macbeth and the shadowy character of Siward, Jr. It was also thought prudent to do without Shakespeare's stage direction at the finale, "Enter Macduff, with Macbeth's head." Much better, Peggy and I thought, to finish with the fight with Macduff, at the climax of which he forced his fatally wounded adversary over the walls of the battlements to the moat below.

[*Trumpets, cheers—enter young Malcolm*]

So thanks to all at once and to each one
Whom we invite to see us crowned at Scone.

[*Flourish. Curtain*]

There is always some constraint during rehearsals when one of the two leading players is playing his or her part for a second time. It took a large measure of diplomacy on Peggy's part to dissuade Judith from her determination to be seen in bed with Macbeth at some point in the play. She was reluctantly won over when she was reminded that Shakespeare was unlikely to have envisaged such goings-on when Burbage was Macbeth and a boy-actor his spouse. Judith was splendid in the part, and true to form for this particular play, Macbeth himself came in second best.

The short tryout in New Haven and Boston that preceded Broadway gave us time to iron out the rough spots and gave me a chance to become relatively secure in my difficult role. Notices were good and the response at the box office was encouraging to all except one latecomer to our first matinee.

"Sorry, ma'am, standing-room only," said the treasurer. Suspecting some skulduggery, the woman enlisted the help of a policeman to question the treasurer.

"Look for yourself, Sarge, not a ticket left in the rack."

"That's right, ma'am," said the sergeant, "it's completely sold out."

"But it *can't* be," said the woman. "It's *Shakespeare!*"

When we opened at New York's National Theatre on November 11, 1941, I did not expect, nor did I win, unadulterated approval for my portrayal of the murderous tyrant. The same magazine critics repeated their previous accusations of my being "as much a rhetorician as an actor" ... "more directly on contact with the audience than with the other characters on the stage" ... "he does not sustain the impression of overwhelming mental tension." It is curious that one critic who detailed his objections to my performance finished his review by writing, "Nevertheless, I think I enjoyed this 'Macbeth' of Mr. Evans' more than many who admired it; there is something about his Shakespeare that he achieves and projects—perhaps it is the words." If to be easily understood is a sin, then I am proud to plead guilty, though I can appreciate the resentment by the bardolators when a psychological passage is delivered with crystal clarity for the benefit of those less cognizant. I believe the wide support given to my productions was largely due to what some experts regarded as a shortcoming. Our predecessors had managed to squeeze out a mere sixty-six performances of *Macbeth* (Lynn Harding and Florence Reed); an all-black cast only sixty-one; and Philip Merivale and Gladys Cooper a modest six. By the time Judith and I had completed our tour, our scoreboard totalled 225—surely an indication that we were adequate exponents of our material.

George Bernard Shaw has written somewhere that the sum total of philosophy propounded by William Shakespeare could be written on the back of a penny stamp; Irish whimsey perhaps, but a modicum of truth nevertheless. The genius of Shakespeare rests in his poetry, his love of words; neglect to recognise this as an actor and you do so at your peril. If you strip Shakespeare of the cadence and beat of his verse, the magical image, the tonal colours— you reduce him to the dubious philosophy of his own era, which, with extraordinary genius, he made the servant of his various characters, and set, as it were, to an appropriate tune. As it happens, Macbeth is a particularly thankless role, written in verse of a singularly monotonous beat. Furthermore, it contains a good deal of overwritten lyricism, such as Macbeth's rhetorical question, "Will all great Neptune's ocean wash this blood clean from my hand? No, this my hand will rather the multitudinous seas incarnadine, making the green one red." The Queen's similar line, "All the perfumes of Arabia will not sweeten this little hand," is much more telling.

Fortunately for us, on the morning of November 12, 1941, we were to discover that, by and large, the dramatic jurymen were on our side.

Brooks Atkinson, *New York Times*:

Mr. Evans and Miss Anderson are well matched in this play. They are not a team of conspirators. They are united by something deeper than mutual advantage, and the crimes they spatter across the face of Scotland are sensual as well as political. Mr. Evans' clarity of mind and speech make Macbeth's character a lucid portrait of a man in process of disintegration from the poise of nobility to the weakness of remorse and the confusion of defeat.

John Mason Brown (*New York World-Telegram*) said of the play: "By all odds this is the most successful production of 'Macbeth' our contemporary theatre has known." He then went on to say:

Mr. Evans may not resemble a general as Macbeth, but he is a capable major. He is an intellectual Macbeth; a man of conscience capable of thinking and saying what Mr. Merivale and Mr. Harding only looked. His is a performance, moreover, which—in spite of what it may leave to be desired in the way of physical prowess—shows once again how extraordinary a player Mr. Evans is. His Thane bears no resemblance— bodily, vocally or spiritually—to his Hamlet, his Richard II, his Romeo or his Falstaff. It is a new creation, slow in starting but deeply passionate, highly uxorious, exciting in its murder scenes, effective at the banquet, admirable in its second meeting with the witches, very fine in its delivery of "Tomorrow and tomorrow and tomorrow," heartbreaking when robbed of its belief in the prophecy of the three weird sisters and spirited in its final duel.

Burns Mantle, *New York Daily News*:

That Mr. Evans would prove an impressive Macbeth was certain. No actor of our time is more complete master of vocal sounds than he, and when it comes to fury he can roar you a defiant scene or fight you a flashing duel with the best of them.

He is not a tired old actor, as most of our Macbeths have been. He is a young man in his vigorous thirties. And while he is not by

1 9 3 5 – 1 9 4 2

temperament entirely suited to the ferociousness that is necessary to
carry the Macbeth program through, once he is reluctantly started and
held to the sticking place by her ambitious ladyship's urging, he is so
good an actor, and so earnest, that he is able to assume a ferocity that
entirely serves the purpose.
Evans is inspiring in the soliloquies, topping his evening's work with
the sound and fury conclusion.... He is tender with his lady wife,
which is more than she deserved, but commanding with his soldiers,
and it is not an easy transition for one of his stature.

Richard Watts, Jr., *New York Herald-Tribune*:

Although this is not one of Mr. Evans' most completely satisfying
portrayals nor Miss Webster's most brilliant staging, the current
presentation has the great and beautiful virtue of being alive, vigorous
and eloquent, and so, despite a few minor objections that I have here
and there, I would say that this is the finest production of "Macbeth"
in the modern American theatre.
   Mr. Evans' talent for combining in his characterizations both the
lyric beauty and the dramatic insight of Shakespeare by no means
deserts him in his playing of Macbeth, and his is an excellent
characterization. The one objection which I have to his portrayal is
that there is a strangely synthetic air about his interpretation of the
bloody Thane. There is a little bit of his Hamlet and a little bit of his
Richard II in his characterization, and, although it may be said with
justice that Shakespeare made Macbeth something of both those
unhappy princes, Mr. Evans sometimes fails to combine them into a
completely rounded person. There are traces of weakness in the
tortured murderer which occasionally seem weaknesses of portrayal
rather than an intended part of a portrayal of weakness. Yet much of
the time he is properly brilliant, and he handles the "Tomorrow and
tomorrow and tomorrow" speech with true magnificence.... Here,
anyway, is the finest "Macbeth" of our time.

Hardly a month of our 131-performance run had passed before the
traditionally unlucky play lived up to its reputation.... December 7 and the
Japanese attack on Pearl Harbor. In a time of such national crisis one would
have thought theatre attendance would suffer. On the contrary, people seem
to be anxious to seek relief from headlines at such times. The instantaneous
response to Pearl Harbor was to institute the law known as the Draft, which
operated on the principle of names being picked out of "the goldfish bowl."
The personnel of *Macbeth* included quite a number of youngsters of military
age, but the first names to be selected from the bowl at the local Draft Board
were the head electrician, Kelly, and mine. I didn't take this too seriously,

BECOMING AN AMERICAN & BECOMING MACBETH

because I was told it represented merely a way of getting names in some sort of order in anticipation of conscription. About midway through the New York run of *Macbeth*, however, I was ordered to report for a medical examination. Even so, I refused to believe that the doctors would pass an old gentleman of forty with fallen arches. My optimism was further fortified when the doctor I was assigned to turned out to be an enthusiastic fan of mine. Since he was so engrossed in theatre recollections instead of the state of my heart, lungs, and so forth, I smugly assumed he would mark me down as "4-F" as a sign of his admiration. Not a bit of it! What's more, he seemed to think he was paying me yet another compliment by reporting that I was in A-1 condition in all departments—in other words, topnotch cannon fodder.

I couldn't have agreed less with the doctor on account of my particularly exhausting schedule at the time. In addition to the eight performances a week of *Macbeth*, on Sundays I flew all over the country giving lectures in aid of British War Relief. One of these tiring expeditions took me to Washington, D.C., enabling me to get in touch with some influential military people with whom I had, until then, only spoken on the telephone. I managed to convince a general in the Army Special Services Branch that the kind of army that was being hurriedly recruited from all walks of life would be receptive to entertainment of an adult nature. To prove the point, I offered him the services of my company at the end of our *Macbeth* tour if he would arrange for a stage to be available at one of the camps for our use. A few weeks later I received confirmation that he wished me to go ahead.

The tour of *Macbeth* added another ninety-four performances to the record, which, though gratifying, did not dispel the frightful distress about the bombing of England and America's readying for war. In a very small way it gave us a feeling of being part of the action when eventually we gave our three experimental performances for the G.I. audiences at Fort Meade, Maryland. During the intermission of each performance an army questionnaire card was given to each man, soliciting his approval or otherwise. At the final count of three packed houses only five negative responses were found. Even more telling than the cards, I thought, was the night a G.I. stagehand joined the ranks of Macduff's followers. He had been told to gather up an armful of banners and spears and to transfer them backstage, from right to left; instead of using the doors at the rear of the stage, he marched solemnly with his load between the footlights and the first row of the audience seats. That the G.I. audience remained silently intent upon *Macbeth* was a tribute that warmed my heart.

We disbanded the company and I made my way to Washington, D.C., the next day to hear the top-brass reaction to the Fort Meade experiment. It was most favourable! It was then explained to me that amongst plans for assembling a military machine was the formation of a corps of specialists from all professional branches of civilian life—lawyers, accountants, engineers, and the like. For this purpose volunteers were being rounded up to be inducted, with the rank of captain, into what was to be known as the Army Specialist Corps (A.S.C.). Until then the organisers had not considered entertainment as one of the fields to be included, but after what they had seen at Fort Meade they remedied this by offering me a commission.

All through the tour, younger members of the company had been receiving their Draft notices and it seemed that mine would eventually arrive. I couldn't see myself fitting the role of a draftee; neither did I feel inclined to pull strings to obtain a sinecure in something vaguely connected with the war effort. Thus it was that, although it would put a halt to a career that was at a peak, I really had no option but to accept the invitation to enlist in the Army Specialist Corps. I turned down offers of a cushy post in the Washington headquarters, saying that I preferred to be sent out into the field to evaluate the needs and practicalities of troop entertainment and to inspect the facilities. So on August 15, 1942, I donned my A.S.C. uniform in the sweltering heat of Washington. I spent a month at headquarters being indoctrinated into the mysteries of army practice and protocol. Temporary wooden buildings had been erected all down Pennsylvania Avenue, providing office space and living quarters for various branches of the services. The heat was so appalling that by noontime, war or no war, we knocked off, to return to our offices in the evening and stay on the job until the wee hours.

I had asked for it, so I had no right to complain when on September 14 I was ordered to report for duty at Fort Leonard Wood in Missouri. This camp was the remotest, the hottest, and the most desolate dump imaginable—and the morale of the troops was at its lowest ebb. However, a pair of soldier-actors, who had run their own civilian summer theatre up north, had obtained their colonel's permission to start something of the same sort within the camp—with no funds to speak of and minimum cooperation from their superiors. Nevertheless, this enabled me to get a glimpse of what might be done. To escape the heat of the Ozarks I made it a very fleeting glimpse, however, and moved on to various camps throughout the Seventh Service Command. I was the first officer from the A.S.C. to be seen in these parts, and my strange green uniform bewildered the individuals to whom I reported. Actually the unfamiliarity of my clothing caused me to be treated in a guarded manner, some wrongly guessing that the A.S.C. letters on my collar stood for some important official of the Air Service Command. There was a marked diminution in their respectful attitude once I explained my mission, but wherever I stopped the need was apparent for the kind of program that was growing in my mind.

When I reached Fort Francis E. Warren in Wyoming on my tour of inspection, I found a War Department order directing me to report on the morrow to, of all places, Fort Meade, Maryland. I was green about military orders, and was peeved that no transportation had been arranged and that no travel allowance had accompanied the order. I paid my own way on civilian flights to comply with the command and hitched a ride from Washington, D.C., to Fort Meade. Arriving there a half-hour before midnight, I checked in with the major on night duty, feeling rather pleased with myself. During our *Macbeth* visit to the Fort we had been given the V.I.P. treatment; on this occasion I was told brusquely to bunk down and to report in the morning at 8:00 o'clock. Bunking down obviously implied a bedroll on a barracks floor, and I was in no mood to be trifled with at that time of night. It doesn't take long to catch on to the dodges in any army, so, after ascertaining that the major would be definitely on duty all night, I told a waiting Jeep driver to take me to the major's quarters in the original brick-built part of the Fort. I slept in the old boy's bed that night and left it unmade early next morning.

It was typical of the army that we who had been teaching in the field were then brought together at Fort Meade to be taught how to teach. Amongst the experts was the famous band-leader Glenn Miller. One uninspired experiment was an "impromptu concert" to take place in a wooded grove somewhere in Maryland. It was an odd assortment of actors, musicians, stagehands, and so forth, who got into file for that cross-country hike. At the alfresco gathering it was very funny to see Glenn Miller struggling to produce from an army-issue trombone the seductive tones for which he was so famous, and, for that matter, to listen to me spouting "Once more unto the breach" to an audience of G.I.s and Baltimore Orioles—the birds that is. Neither of us envisaged ourselves continuing to be performers while in the service, but the A.S.C. seemed to have other ideas.

It was during those disagreeable weeks at Fort Meade that the War Department decided to dissolve the Army Specialist Corps, but at the same time to offer us the choice of discharge or of transfer, as captains, into the United States Army. It was a real poser for me. Being discharged would put me back in the Draft melting pot, but transfer to the army meant I was in for the duration of the war. After much cogitation, I opted for the latter in the mistaken belief that the obvious posting for me would be England as liaison officer between the American and British Special Services branches. I was so certain of the outcome that I had a tailor make me heavy winter uniforms and an overcoat to be in readiness.

I felt the most awful fool when, finally, I received my orders, which were to report to A.P.O. 982 in San Francisco, California. No one on the West Coast would identify this postal code for me, but it was a fair guess that it would be somewhere in the Pacific. I was issued gas mask, revolver, and ammunition, and for the first time I felt like a real soldier—although I was a bit hazy about army rules and had no idea whatsoever how to fire my revolver. There were frequent occasions in the ensuing couple of years when I felt tempted to get my own way with the aid of that deadly weapon, but discretion prevailed.

III

1942–1947

"... then a soldier ..."

1. THE ENTERTAINMENT SECTION

**T WASN'T UNTIL** our convoy of inadequately escorted ships zigzagged its way westward that I learnt that our destination was Hawaii. Visions of hula-hula girls, surf-riding, and exotic music were rudely dismissed when we docked at the port of Honolulu. The whole island of Oahu was in a state of siege for fear of a second Japanese attack. All the beaches were ringed with barbed wire. Coastal guns were everywhere and military police much in evidence. Worst of all, a total blackout was rigidly enforced and, since it was November when I arrived, the nights were to seem interminable. The tropical climate of the Hawaiian Islands is tolerable owing to the trade winds, which blow incessantly. Consequently, living accommodations are designed to encourage the circulation of perpetual draughts. In normal times all doors and windows would be left wide open, the occupants spending most of their home life on screened porches, or lanais; but in blackout conditions, when not a single light could be shown, one had the choice of sitting in the dark and keeping cool, or shutting doors and windows, turning on lights, and slowly melting in the heat.

In some ways we fared better than the civilian population because the army constructed barracks and office buildings with louvered windows, which deflected the light to the ground. Our prewar officers' quarters, however, had no such amenities; so, at the end of a long day in the office, there was nowhere to go to read a book except back to the louvered office—hardly the ideal surroundings in which to relax. After an evening in the brightly lit office one was faced with the problem of finding the way back to one's sleeping quarters in the inky darkness, an exercise that tickled the perverted sense of humour of the sentries. Each of our quarters had on the doorstep a sandbox and a fire bucket. Leaving the office with one's pupils still dilated, one looked skyward to get a course between the fronds of palm trees overhead, then kicked and counted the fire buckets until kick number five indicated one was safely home.

159

The first time I went through these gyrations, a sentry popped out from behind an oleander bush with a gruff, "Halt! Who goes there?" It scared me out of my skin, and I let out a piercing high-pitched scream. The sentry shone a pencil flashlight in my face as I tried to recover my poise and identify myself. I couldn't see him, of course, but as I proceeded on my bucket route I distinctly heard him wickedly chuckling to himself.

The Pineapple Paradise was full of disagreeable surprises for this wandering minstrel, not the least of them being the shortage of the wherewithal to drown one's sorrows. At some time in the murky past the powerful lobby of the Daughters of the American Revolution (D.A.R.) had bullied the Congress into passing a statute prohibiting the sale on "military posts, camps and stations of intoxicating liquors." Our Fort De Russy commander bent the rules to the extent that each officer had a locker in the mess hall in which there was room for precisely the one bottle-a-month to which he was rationed. The only liquor to be had was an unpalatable rye whisky, which was known to us as "Schenley's Black Death." The shore-based navy had no qualms in averring that the word "military" did not apply to them, and since they provided the only existing surface transportation they could wallow in booze. It goes without saying that with unseemly haste I made friends with a couple of Admiral Chester Nimitz's fellows, who ministered to my thirst.

Another facet of the war in the Pacific struck me most forcefully as soon as I arrived. Immediately after the attack on Pearl Harbor, the civilian government of the Hawaiian Islands was suspended and replaced by the Hawaiian Command of the U.S. Army. However, the U.S. Navy establishment at Pearl under Admiral Nimitz was a law unto itself, resulting in considerable friction between the services. One constant bone of contention was the matter of the Honolulu prostitutes. The red-light district was strictly army territory, but who was to conduct the Wasserman tests remained a moot point. These kinds of Tom Tiddler's Ground arguments led to a situation in which three wars were in progress. In order of priority, war number one was between the army and the navy; number two, the air force versus both; and in third place, incidentally, a small fracas with the Japanese. There was little fraternization with the civilians, but, thanks to Louise Dillingham, the pineapple heiress, the hatchet of the interservice rivalry was buried each New Year's Eve when she threw a top-brass party at her mansion on Diamond Head. I was invited on one of those occasions and was much amused by the forced attitudes of bonhomie on the part of the big shots. I suspected that in the backs of their minds they were already composing sizzling memoranda to be exchanged on the morrow.

Leafing through the *Who's Who* about my contemporaries, I notice that mostly they confine themselves to the bare statement that they absented

THE ENTERTAINMENT SECTION

themselves from their profession during the war years. I would be making the same statement here were it not for the fact that, for me, those were the busiest professional years of my life, only incidentally as an actor, but unremittingly as an organiser and enabler. Whereas I never kept scrapbooks of my civilian theatrical activities, my personal files still harbor my army papers. The first document, dated August 15, 1942, informed me that I received "Appointment made for duties involving arduous physical exertion." In the light of what happened, that paragraph should have included amongst other qualifications, "guile," "chicanery," and "moonlight requisitioning." All of these I practised unashamedly when it became obvious from the start that cooperation by my superiors was in short supply. In the army lexicon, the sort of program I wished to establish had no right to exist. That meant no funds, no personnel, and no rations. I doubt whether I should have got to first base had it not been for an appeal that came to the office signed by Major General Ralph E. Smith, commanding officer of the so-called New York Division. His troops were headed for Alaska when they left the States, only to be reported to Hawaii, which, like Alaska, was a territory, not yet a state, in those days. The arctic clothing with which they had been outfitted for Alaska did nothing to improve troop morale in sunny Honolulu, where no proper preparations had been made for their arrival. Something had to be done in a hurry about recreation, and that was where I came in.

I was given access to the personnel files at General Smith's ramshackle headquarters and found one card that had the word "theatre" to describe the individual's civilian occupation. He was Technical Sergeant Howard Morris and immediately I met him I recognised him as pure gold. He had a buddy in the outfit who was a song composer and the two of them had outlines for a soldier-musical show, which conditions had aborted. I told them to get it down on paper and to let me hear some of the songs. I liked what I heard and read, although *Hey, Mac!* as it was entitled was no classic. What I like best, however, was that in General Smith I had a powerful ally. His enthusiasm resulted in the necessary facilities and manpower being made available to realise my goal to institute a program of shows by soldiers. I was greatly helped, too, by the president of the University of Hawaii. He not only made over to us the college's theatre, but permitted us to build on the parking lot the barracks to house 120 men, a rehearsal room, a workshop, and a scenery storehouse. With these encouraging prospects on the drawing board, their realisation depended on a successful production of *Hey, Mac!* We went to work with a vengeance, and the outcome was better than I dared to hope. The plot, such as it was, concerned the adventures of a group of G.I.s trying to adjust to army life in the Pacific—typical jokes at the expense of their officers, the bullying top sergeant, and the rest of it. General Smith made one error in judgement which very nearly wrote *finis* to my scheme for the future.

He was so delighted with the effect the show had on his men that he invited a handful of prominent Honolulu civilians to attend a performance. Someone should have warned him that the Athertons and the Cooks had their roots in stern missionary stock and that anything even faintly suggestive would shock them to the core. There was one harmless scene in the show that centered around a very naïve recruit who was determined to continue his vocal studies while in the army.

> Scene I: A barroom in the disreputable part of town. Innocent Ernie tells his mates about his singing resolve ... and his mates lead him on to believe that the best singing teacher in Honolulu occupies the rooms above the bar.
>
> Scene II: Curtain rises [to the accompaniment of "Frankie and Johnny" music] on a boudoir, which is recognized at once by the G.I. audience as being located in the red-light district. Ernie paces the floor nervously. Enter, through the bead-curtained doorway, a gorgeous blonde female, Corporal Keane in becoming peignoir.

The dialogue that followed was all in the nature of double entendre. Ernie talks about his desires (as a singer). She (thinking he wants something more intimate): "Do you want to try it in the bedroom?" He: "We can do it on the piano if you like." This so offended the prudish civilians that they went over the head of General Smith to the Hawaiian Command's top officer. A battle royal ensued between the two generals—the resident one ordering me to excise the scene and Smith countermanding with an order to keep it in. I rode the storm until my immediate superior told me that headquarters ordered that from that night onwards Ernie and Corporal Keane were to be banished. There was no time to write and rehearse a substitute scene, so to get even with the brass the curtain rose on the forbidden boudoir and received its customary guffaws. The blonde beauty, however, entered through the bead curtains carrying a placard reading: "This scene censored by order of Henry B. Holmes, Brigadier General." It was not surprising that my promotion was delayed.

Hey, Mac! had proved that entirely amateur soldier-actors could acquit themselves provided they had a few "pros" to guide their steps. It also, quite fortuitously, made it possible for me to move the program into a somewhat higher key. Before the censorship fiasco, I was contentedly watching the show one night when a hand grabbed me by the shoulder and a voice barked, "Outside!" One did not disobey anyone wearing the insignia of a full colonel, even when, as in this case, he belonged to the Army Corps of Chaplains. Poking his finger into my ribs in the most uncharitable manner he demanded, "Are you responsible for this filth?" I tried to reason with him that the main trouble with troop morale was sex, and that if he'd ever listened to the average conversation between soldiers he must have reached the same conclusion. Whereas it was his job to inveigh against moral turpitude, it was mine, I said, to make audiences laugh the subject out of their systems.

I realised I was getting nowhere on this tack with a professional advocate of cold showers and a cosy chat with the padre, so I changed my tune. Would he rather see us doing something more uplifting—something by an author such as Shakespeare, for instance? "Infinitely preferable," said the colonel. I saluted him smartly, saying, "Thank you, sir. I'll report that to my superiors." So it was with the church's blessing that we plunged into a play about the powers of darkness, murder, and violence. The *Hey, Mac!* playbills were shortly replaced by those for *Macbeth*. If that is what the Corps of Chaplains considered to be good clean fun, let 'em have it, I thought.

Washington headquarters had already approved Shakespeare's "Mac," so it was not too difficult to obtain their consent to arrange for Judith Anderson to join us in the enterprise. Judy was game and agreed to come to Hawaii on the first available ship. This meant, of course, that I had to overcome my disinclination to do any actual acting while in uniform, but the obvious hostility of the chaplain's attitude put my whole plan at risk. A production of a Shakespearean play with two Broadway stars would be a big event even in prewar Honolulu, so under war conditions it was bound to arouse the attention we needed for a secure future. I was authorised to requisition from other units any personnel with show-business backgrounds. Amongst them was a graduate from the Yale Drama School named George Schaefer. He was appointed as director of *Macbeth*, the first of many productions we have done together over the years. My immediate superior was delighted by all the advance publicity that accompanied the announcement of *Macbeth*, since he, like most officers, was smelling out a promotion. Our barracks were built on the university site and motor transport assigned to what was thereafter to be called the Entertainment Section. Having purloined Howie Morris and Bob Harding (his song-writing chum) for permanent duty with me, I was eventually to have a staff of sixty-eight men and five officers on regular assignment.

My Entertainment Section attended to the organisation of small, highly mobile shows with titles, of which I blush to say I approved, such as *Four Jerks in a Jeep* and *Shape Ahoy*. To begin with, our choice of material was much limited by the almost total dearth of young English-speaking females—their families having been evacuated to the mainland. In one instance, however, the famine worked to our advantage in a very offbeat production of *The Mikado*. Instead of the traditional D'Oyly Carte Three Little Maids, ours were three genuine Japanese schoolgirls, who sang well but whose looks left much to be desired. Someone had the bright idea of making capital out of this by having them wear thick horn-rimmed spectacles, gym tunics, and bobbysocks. Then, of course, there were interpolated G.I. pet hates to the Lord High Executioner's "little list." Pooh-Bah, the Lord High Everything Else, wore enormous sergeant's stripes on the sleeves of his kimono. It was topical and very popular with our audiences all over the Islands.

My own background of touring in the States stood me in good stead when it came to keeping such shows on the night-by-night move. Following the same system that I had learned from the United Booking Office in New York, I had two big charts in my office; one listed the shows available for routing, and the other the various units that requested them and had suitable facilities. Since we usually had as many as six shows and several dance bands on offer, it was no mean jigsaw puzzle. Without permission I started a liaison with the navy, who were doing absolutely nothing about recreation for their shore-leave personnel. The official view was that all the boys in blue needed in that respect was plenty of beer, baseball bats, and girls. They eventually capitulated when I told them they could include themselves on our circuit provided they would assign a couple of men to our outfit to take care of their own booking and transport. One of the sailors so appointed was young Farley Granger and the second, a chap who had been on my staff in New York, Bud Williams. Bud was part of the crew of a ship that was on a battle mission when it called at Hawaii; nevertheless, his sympathetic admiral listened to my plea and struck him off that roster.

Along with all this organisational activity, we managed to squeeze in enough time to hold preliminary rehearsals of *Macbeth*. Costumes were being made out of remnants donated by helpful civilian women who had responded to our appeal that they scour their closets and attics on our behalf. There were times when I felt I was in the Salvation Army rather than Uncle Sam's.

Word came from Washington at last that Judith's transportation arrangements had been made, but that for security reasons no dates could be mentioned. Our plan was to put the show on at the Honolulu High School auditorium and for truckloads of troops to be brought there over a period of several weeks. However, no final announcement could be made until Judith had actually disembarked. Immediately upon her arrival we plunged into rehearsal and it seemed like old times. We decided to do a one-night tryout in a remote camp in the mountains on the north of Oahu. The big night arrived and with it an enormous tropical rainstorm. It was a fractious audience that awaited us, sitting on benches, still in their soaking-wet ponchos. Once the curtains opened they calmed down and paid rapt attention up to the moment of Lady Macbeth's entrance atop a stairway, whereupon all hell broke loose. She was the very first woman to set foot in this particularly isolated post and the G.I.s, in their fashion, wanted her to know how they felt about it. To

THE ENTERTAINMENT SECTION

Judith's discomfiture their welcome took the form of cheers and wolf whistles. She demanded the curtains be closed and insisted that I call on the troops to behave themselves or she wouldn't continue that evening. We failed to convince her that their reaction to her appearance was complimentary and that the time for her to worry would be when they didn't whistle. However, with more discretion than valour I went before the curtain and conveyed Miss Anderson's thanks for the warmth of their greeting, but suggested we now settle down and get on with the show. It was all plain sailing from then on, and Judith gave one of her very best venom-tongued performances that night. She was duly impressed at the end of the evening when she saw King Duncan, Banquo, and Macduff loading up the scenery on trucks being driven by the three witches.

The strict army rules prohibiting fraternization between officers and men in the ranks were necessarily suspended when, as in the case of *Macbeth*, I was one of the G.I. cast. It gave me a better insight into my fellow actors' personalities and problems; above all, I was given first-hand proof of the pride my associates took in their work and the Entertainment Section as a whole. They carried out their regular military duties as well, even though it meant the touring units put in double the time of the average soldier they were entertaining. They also requested and were given permission to convert one of the buildings into what was known as the Hambs Club, despite the overcrowding that was caused in the remaining barracks. In the evenings, hotdogs, hamburgers, coffee, and so forth were regularly on the menu, and there were tables for the card and chess players. The operation was voluntarily staffed and equipped by the men themselves and became a highlight in Honolulu hospitality.

When visiting V.I.P.s came to the Command, they were invited to drop in—people as diverse as Joe DiMaggio and Yehudi Menuhin. Those were the only occasions when staff officers invaded the club, and I shall never forget Yehudi's fascination with the violin-playing of one of our entertainers—a chap who was a forerunner of today's exponents of Country Music. "Rusty" was not only a mean fiddler, but also gyrated the instrument into extraordinary positions without interrupting his bowing. Yehudi asked for several encores, not believing such dexterity to be possibile. He himself caused me some wonderment because, as he was watching his fellow fiddler, I noticed his left hand was constantly in motion, exercising his fingers. He showed me later half the leg of a small Queen Anne chair on which he had grooved simulated violin strings and frets. This strange object he carried with him at all times in order to retain the calluses on his fingertips.

The blackout curfew was in force when we were playing *Macbeth* in Honolulu—a situation that was very nearly knocked on the head by Judith's paying no attention to the regulations posted on the door of her hotel room. Guests were warned that it was forbidden, on pain of imprisonment, to open any of the blacked-out windows after dark. Judith had flung hers open, lighting up the whole area. She had to be sternly reprimanded by the military when she grumbled about her stuffy bedroom. Actually she adapted surprisingly quickly to the restrictions, though she was not too happy about being driven about, as were all the girls in our shows, in a bumpy Jeep. Spotting a sparkling limousine in the parking lot she asked the driver to whom it belonged. He named a general, telling her he was in the mess hall at that moment. From then on, Judith arrived at the auditorium each night flying a one-star flag on the bumper and with the general at the wheel.

In her breezy Australian way Judith was a good sport, but I had to curb one of her favourite habits, a custom that we still indulge in. We used to address each other as "Mum" and "Dad" during the New York run, but in front of my enlisted men I knew that appellation would stick forever unless she bit her tongue. Her admiration for the Entertainment Section knew no bounds, particularly for the inventiveness my men displayed in the face of shortages. I think her chief pet was our supply sergeant, Rappaport. He had the sole use of a weapons carrier into which he deposited the day's loot. One of his most productive sources of supply was the navy's Pearl Harbor scrapyard. All kinds of unobtainable electrical items salvaged from the sunken ships would be included in his haul. I had to veto Judith's suggestion that he carry a bell and cry "Rags and Bones" as he went on these surreptitious forays, but I shut my eyes to his conquests.

It was from Rappaport's depredations that our swords and helmets were forged, though our crowns were fashioned out of saucepans nicked from somebody's kitchen. The troops who had signed up for tickets to the show were given a free ride to Honolulu. Not surprisingly there were those with romantic ambitions who dropped off the trucks when they reached town, but for the most part we played to full houses, and the men in khaki gave us rousing receptions.

The Macbeths' dirty deeds being done, Judith left for home smothered in leis and bouquets, which she richly deserved. After seeing her off, I returned to the section to be greeted by a look of reproof on the face of Lonsbery, my invaluable but precise company clerk. In tallying the account books he had found that our meagre funds had become exhausted by a last-night party for the cast. This put me in a dilemma because my pockets were equally bare. When I joined the army I had made a resolve to treat my civilian past as though it had never existed. I left my checkbook at home and managed to scrape by on a captain's subsistence allowance of $200 per month and, if I was very careful, I could just afford a once-a-week decent meal at the Moana Hotel.

THE U.S.O. APPEARS

In order to replenish the section's coffers, I wheedled permission to give a lecture program at theatre prices of admission. The Honolulu public turned out in fine style and the proceeds were devoted to buying a lot of scaffolding that could be assembled in the form of a portable stage. This enabled our bigger shows to tour the outer islands—Maui, Kauai, Lanai, Molokai, and the island of Hawaii—none of them having alternative facilities.

The lecture matinee produced one incident that caused much merriment amongst the gossips of Honolulu. Most of the audience had been forced to come on foot, since their automobile tires had either been stolen or had become worn down to the rims. The only source of supply for these precious objects was the army, and a civilian needed illicit military connections to obtain replacements. Two such persuasive ladies were observed sitting next to one another in the audience: one of them the famed Mrs. Dillingham and the other an equally smartly turned-out matron. Although obviously not acquainted, they were exchanging pleasantries while waiting for me to start my talk, but during the intermission they were seen to be conversing animatedly. At the end of the lecture a friend of Mrs. Dillingham's asked her if she realised to whom she had been speaking. "Haven't the faintest idea," said Louise. "But *everybody* knows about *her!*" said her friend. "She's the madam of the Nuuanu establishment providing solace for Officers." They watched with envy as the Madam drove away in her Cadillac with its brand-new army tires.

2. THE U.S.O. APPEARS

After a time conditions became more normal in Hawaii. The High Command finally reached the conclusion that their earlier fear of the Islands being invaded by the Japanese was unfounded. The blackout was terminated and the barbed wire removed from the beaches. A new and in some ways more potent enemy began to take charge—sheer, unadulterated boredom. The Hollywood moguls did nothing to relieve the tedium. We begged for something other than the out-of-date "B" movies they were sending for us to distribute, and even those were small in numbers. They weren't about to give us current releases because they were reserved for Honolulu movie houses, which, of course, did a thriving business from G.I.s on leave. The pressures for more and more from the Entertainment Section were beyond our capacity until I got the consent from Washington to send us a half-dozen actresses to fill out the soldier casts. Evelyn Helmore, my onetime yachting companion, was then doing war work in an aeroplane factory outside Los Angeles. She bravely undertook to audition and vet likely candidates, and in due course the girls were flown out to us. Housing them was a problem, but an unoccupied and dilapidated officers' building was made available at Fort De Russy, provided the section was prepared to make it habitable. My fellows went to work with a will and the last lick of paint was applied on the morning of the girls' arrival. The red tape involved in requisitioning beds and blankets, to say nothing of cooking utensils, was of formidable proportions. But the real crisis arose over the subject of army-issue toilet paper! In spite of there being miles and miles of the commodity in the warehouses, any request for some to be issued for the comfort of civilian actresses was frowned upon in a manner peculiar to the military mind. My request for this vital necessity went through channels, finally being returned to me with the adjutant general's disapproval in large red letters: "THIS IS DYNAMITE!" Even the stony heart of Lonsbery was touched by this abrupt ultimatum, so much so that he made no protest when I told him to release enough money from the remains of the lecture proceeds to fill the tissue gap.

The presence of our Hollywood girls gave us far more scope in the choice of plays and enabled us to expand the touring circuit to meet the ever-increasing demand for our shows. One such plea came from the distracted commander of an armoured-tank outfit recently arrived from the mainland. His outfit had been relegated to the only area on Oahu large enough to accommodate his vehicles—a sandpit miles from anywhere, and devoid of any recreational facilities whatsoever. As I recalled my first and only exposure to Theatre in the Round, at the Penthouse Playhouse in Seattle, it struck me that the same convention would be ideal under alfresco conditions such as the formidable sandpit. A tarpaulin was spread on the sand and makeshift bleachers erected on all four sides of it. The first row of seats consisted of orange-boxes and Coca-Cola crates. The second row, Jeeps. The third row, weapons carriers. And the fourth row, the caterpillar monsters.

The action of the slight comedy *Personal Appearance* took place in a surburban sitting room. One item essential to the plot was a magazine, which was placed on a stool close to the front row of our Theatre in the Square before the play began. During the course of the performance this gave rise to a crisis, for when the heroine went to pick up the magazine she saw that it was in the hands of an occupant of one of the orange-boxes. Since the periodical contained the key to the situation, the gentle heroine was obliged to snatch it from its engrossed reader, ad-libbing as she did so, "You can have it back later." The show resumed its course in the presence of at least one reluctant listener.

Our next important step was made possible by an air service finally being started between California and the Islands. The first visiting star to take advantage of this was Boris Karloff, who joined our soldier cast of *Arsenic and*

THE U.S.O. APPEARS

Old Lace with great enthusiasm. My secretary, Mary Adams, was one of the old girls and a colonel's daughter was her sister. We set a gruelling schedule for Boris—travelling by air (lying on top of the scenery) to islands as distant as Midway, Johnson, and Christmas, the latter being three degrees above the equator. It was not only a furnace but, apart from sinister-looking land crabs, it was populated solely by army personnel of all ranks who, for a variety of reasons, had been incarcerated there by the authorities. One would have thought that Frankenstein's monster would have felt quite at home in such company, but, on the contrary, he seemed mild in comparison with some of the individuals in the audience. Nevertheless, when Boris made his first entrance in *Arsenic*, the camp mongrel dogs attempted to attack him and had to be forcibly restrained.

Midway Island, under navy control, was also not without unusual interest. The entire island was a solid mass of nesting gooney birds (albatrosses), so that our Jeeps had to pick their way among nests at a maximum speed of two miles per hour. The penalty for disturbing these strange creatures was a night in the brig, so we tiptoed our way with caution. There was a different species of feathered friends at Johnson Island aptly named "moaner birds." Sleep was out of the question when a covey of them gave voice to their heartrending moans, sounding, as Boris remarked, like "rape in a nunnery."

Our hopes of continuing to call on selected stars to join in our activities were hampered by the formation in New York of the U.S.O. (United Service Organizations), and of its subsidiary called Camp Shows. In practice, Camp Shows added up to any Honolulu schoolgirl's being able to earn $5 a night if she was willing merely to show her legs. The insult to the troops by that sort of condescension was mollified, somewhat, when the U.S.O. sent out a few shows that had been hastily put together in New York. However, the responsibility for booking, transporting, and housing the performers fell to my already busy existence. I had become so accustomed to issuing orders and having them obeyed that my patience was exhausted by the myriad of petty complaints, late reporting for work, and so forth. Oahu was already much overcrowded and those theatrical invasions only created further problems. On one occasion I had difficulty in extricating an actor from the clutches of the U.S. Navy Shore Patrol, who had run him in for propositioning sailors on leave. Much later in the game, Moss Hart brought his U.S.O. troupe, starring himself as Sheridan Whiteside in *The Man Who Came to Dinner*. I told him of the poor track record of preceding performers and, with his concurrence, read his group the riot act in advance of their first appearance. I must have laid it on pretty heavily because they behaved as though they were soldiers in danger of being court-martialed. I was happy to see that their conduct was exemplary.

An even bigger headache was when the "name" performers began to descend upon us. The main trouble with these people was that their film and radio commitments in the States limited the amount of time they could devote to our widespread audiences. Concurrently, they wished to cover as much ground as possible, since that made better publicity for the home newspapers. Bob Hope, for example, bylined a daily column in the Hearst papers, whose editor required his bulletins to come from a wide diversity of locales. This provision was most inappropriate because it called for constant island- and atoll-hopping, with only the briefest stops at each.

The Central and South Pacific being war zones, one half of the troops or navy personnel had to stay at their posts while the other half got to see their distinguished visitor. I could well understand the disgruntled feelings of the neglected half of the too short visit. I had made it a rule for the visiting artists partaking in our soldier-shows that before each performance they were to serve behind the counters in the enlisted men's mess halls, dishing up the grub. It gave the men something to write home about—to be able to say that Boris Karloff served him a ladle of soup and not elderberry wine. When a Hope or a Benny was the visitor, I was overruled by the hosting commanders, who made demands on their time. They overlooked the fact that these luminaries were there to entertain not to be entertained. I hasten to add that the visitors themselves had no choice, and it was also understood that the officers were entitled to their share. In the case of Bob Hope, I had been warned in advance that he was to be wined and dined at the Officers' Club prior to his outdoor performance at a camp on Oahu, known as the Jungle Training Center. Suspecting that hospitality by the brass might delay his appearance before a huge crowd of G.I.s sitting on their haunches, I took the precaution of having a band and a soldier concert party on hand just in case. Sure enough, Hope didn't show on anything like the scheduled time and a chorus of hostile hand-clapping started. The band struck up and my lads came on what served as a stage to go through their routines. The tap-dancing M.C. of the troupe was a youngster named Herky Silverman, who also told jokes with a flair. His stories delighted his hearers and put them in a more receptive mood by the time Hope's tardy arrival was announced. He was greeted by thunderous applause and then he started delivering the comedy monologues of which he is such a master. One after another they fell as flat as the proverbial pancake. "What's eating those guys?" he asked me as he left the platform. I thought it would not be tactful to tell him that in preceding the famous comedian, Herky Silverman had used material culled from a jokebook that featured some of the same jokes Hope had told.

Jack Benny's troupe came through Honolulu, homeward bound, after a tour mainly of South Pacific stations, mercifully staying with us very briefly. Jack himself was thoroughly cooperative throughout, but the same could not

THE U.S.O. APPEARS

be said of one of the members of his company. Earlier in the tour at a party given for them on a small atoll under navy control, the blonde singer Carole Landis, having mislaid her gold Dunhill cigarette lighter, demanded that all the officers present be searched for suspected theft—hardly a morale-building gesture on her part. I had not yet heard about the incident when she came to Honolulu and, having a soft heart where gorgeous blondes are concerned, I agreed to lend her a couple of hundred dollars (my months's army pay) so that she could go on a souvenir shopping spree. Two days later she flew back to the States and so did my $200. Jack Benny, being the gentleman he was, later reimbursed me with a personal check and an apology.

In contrast to the visits of some radio and film comedians, Yehudi Menuhin's visit was a delight. By the time he arrived, the Americans were on the offensive—Iwo Jima, Guam, and Saipan were under attack, and casualties were being flown to hospitals in Hawaii. Yehudi and his accompanist said they felt that a tour of the hospitals would suit them best, so we constructed a wheeled platform, which could just squeeze through the doorways between wards, to carry a small upright piano. Yehudi walked beside it, playing his violin as he went, and stopping now and then at some particular bed. He made one such pause at the bedside of a lad who had been operated upon that morning and was just emerging from sedation. Yehudi started to play. The boy slowly opened his unbelieving eyes, to see and hear his idol. It had to be a delusion that he, an aspiring violinist, was actually in the presence of the virtuoso. The doctors told me later that their patient made a spectacularly swift recovery, though, sad to say, that meant he would soon be back in the fighting.

I think the most awkward of the U.S.O. situations concerned my old friend Gertrude Lawrence. She had already been on the cover of *Life* magazine (in full battle dress) during her visits to the troops behind the lines in Europe and was now about to settle the hash of the Japanese. In advance, Washington sent details of the composition of her show. Her teammates consisted of John Hoyt (sophisticated Noel Coward songs at the piano), a female accordion player, and lastly, Georgie Tapps (not surprisingly, in view of his name, a noted tap-dancer). Gertie was to charm the G.I.s out of their foxholes with songs from past shows ("I'll See You Again" as her finale, of course) and Coward duologue with John Hoyt. This seemed to me gourmet fare for troop entertainment, but when she heard that Moss Hart was already blazing the trail in the forward area of Guam, she said she wished to go there, too. Once there, she was humiliated to discover that her name meant nothing to the average G.I., and that her material was not the majority's idea of entertainment. It made matters worse when the blonde accordion player was rapturously welcomed and, except on one occasion, so was Georgie Tapps.

The U.S.O. had made it a universal condition that all entertainment groups were to be given one free day each week. When, as in the case of Guam, two of their shows were simultaneously on the circuit, it was the custom for the cast of one show to pay a visit to the other on their night off, in consequence of which the Moss Hart performers paid a courtesy call on Gertie's show. Before leaving the States, Georgie Tapps had reluctantly promised to eliminate from his dance routines his *pièce de résistance*, but when he heard that Moss and Co. were to be out front he couldn't resist reinstating the forbidden *pas de seul*. In doing so he aroused the ire of the chaplains by giving his all in a tap dance set to the music of Gounod's "Ave Maria." The first I knew of the contretemps, back in my Hawaii office, was when a message from the War Department was handed to me. It was brief and to the point. "Gertrude Lawrence company are to be withdrawn from your Command immediately." It was providential that close on the heels of this order came the news that the blonde accordion player's husband had just been repatriated to England from a prison camp in Germany. I was able to use her desire to be reunited with him as the excuse for breaking up the U.S.O. unit. Both she and Georgie Tapps were dispatched home on the first available flight, but I was able to arrange for Gertie and John Hoyt to come to Honolulu for a conference.

In the meantime, I succeeded in convincing the commanding general that it would be virtually an international incident for Gertie to be sent home at such short notice, and was given permission to make a face-saving proposition to her. I sat her down on the sands of Waikiki beach and told her that if she and John would agree to stay on I would put together a production of a play that Noel Coward had written especially for her, but that she had never appeared in, namely, *Blithe Spirit*. To my enormous relief they both said Yes, and Gertie's endorsement of the plan made it relatively easy to obtain Washington's consent to send us Mildred Natwick, whose Madame Arcati had made history on Broadway. An elegant production resulted, which was a feather in the Entertainment Section's cap and at the end of the run sent Gertie home with another triumph to her credit.

None of these U.S.O. chores affected the operation of the section, which grew with the addition to our ranks of people now famous, such as Carl Reiner, Hal David the popular composer, and the late Allen Ludden who made such a name for himself as the quizmaster of *Password*. We were frequently called on to perform duties not strictly within our ken, one of them being to save an ill-conceived army recreation building from being demolished. Some idiot up top decided that what the G.I.s needed was a dance hall. He proceeded to erect an elaborate building for the purpose on the grounds of Fort De Russy. Known as "Maluhia," it possessed an absolutely priceless dance floor of Philippine mahogany on which the troops were to dance the light fantastic. What was overlooked, however, was that, except for a handfull of chippies well known to the police, there were no available dancing partners. I assembled a topnotch dance band from the best musicians in various regimental bands and was told to have them ready for the grand opening day. Only a week prior to this auspicious occasion was I informed that hundreds of soldiers from all parts of Oahu were to be brought in truckloads to Maluhia for the opening. I was so alarmed at the thought of something like a thousand booted troops trying to fight their way into the building at one time that I sought out a circus entrepreneur whom I knew to be living in Honolulu. How much space, I asked him, did he allow per person under circus conditions. "One square yard," he replied. Obviously something drastic had to be done to avoid a riot, so I called an emergency meeting of my junior officers and sergeants. If I remember correctly it was Sergeant Howie Morris who volunteered the best idea. To draw the men away from the threatened Maluhia, he suggested we organise a country fair or fete in the grounds. For once the chaplains came to our assistance with the loan of tents normally employed for more devout purposes, and in each of them we had some sort of sideshow. If ever I had my doubts about the loyalty of my men it was thoroughly dispelled by their readiness to save the day for the section's reputation. They manned the improvised sideshows, which included Sergeant George Schaefer impersonating the Fat Lady, thus keeping the customers amused and constantly circulating instead of crowding into the one building. I was not a little miffed when the only comment on this herculean effort was a reproof from the chief of staff for my being in sweaty coveralls instead of uniform.

One bonus accrued to us from this caper is that I was able to pluck from the dance band five really hep instrumentalists and an arranger to form a combo, which we named the Jive Five. They were not strong on military discipline but, musically, they were really sensational. They were much in demand for late-night parties at the various Officers' clubs, for which I suspected they were paid, but I decided it was politic to turn a blind eye to this, and I housed them in a separate barracks. It wasn't until years after the war that I discovered what those characters had got away with. I was on tour in Kansas City when a note was delivered to my dressing room signed by one of my ex-G.I.s, named Mysted. I remembered him as the only man in the section who could be relied upon to cut the grass under the stilted barracks and keep the area tidy enough to pass inspection. At the end of the performance Mysted, who by then was a prosperous farmer with a plump wife and several little ones, came backstage. Recalling the old days in the section, I asked him why it was that, whereas he had faithfully shorn the grass and weeds under all the other barracks, he had noticeably neglected to apply his sickle to the ground beneath the building reserved for the Jive Five. His answer provided my favourite example of G.I. deception. Mysted explained that by omitting to inspect the contents of the musicians' footlockers we were ignorant of the fact that they contained blocks of ice, and that holes had been drilled through the bottom of the footlockers and through the floorboards beneath them. The melting ice could thereby drip onto the ground below, providing the right amount of moisture to nurture what I had thought to be grass, but, according to Mysted, was a healthy crop of marijuana.

3 . *HAMLET* IN HAWAII

Even though I had been promoted to major, I was getting restless in Hawaii. By December 1944 I had been stationed there for upwards of two years and had seen many changes. A dramatic development took place in the type of men being drafted into the army. Married men, university graduates, and cultured individuals of all sorts were being added to the forces. We also had a change of the chief commander of the whole Central Pacific Area in the person of Lieutenant General Robert C. Richardson, Jr. He was an ex-cavalry officer of the spit-and-polish school and prior to coming to us had been the superintendent of West Point, where his nickname was "Nellie"—the result of his habit, when crossing one leg over the other, of spreading a delicate cambric handkerchief on the receiving knee so that it was protected from boot-polish stain.

I was summoned into the presence one day and was pleasantly surprised to hear words of encouragement expressed by this strict military man. It was his view that in running a conscript army in a time of war, the commanders needed constantly to remind themselves that only a very small percentage of the men in uniform would ever be engaged in actual combat. Nevertheless, the possibility of many more being so involved could not be neglected. It was a matter of grave concern to the authorities at one stage of hostilities that our men had no spirit comparable to the fanatical faith of the Japanese. In spite of all attempts to whip up a bloodthirsty attitude, the men in the Pacific at any rate remained impervious to propaganda—and that was not surprising, nor was it seriously to their discredit. Most of them, after all, had been drafted into the army and had never become thoroughly adjusted to the loss of personal freedom. For all the drilling and discipline, the American soldier remained very much an individual throughout the war, and the only way to get him to respond favourably was to treat him as an individual. This belief governed our planning in the Entertainment Section. By treating the soldier not as a moron, as was too often the case, but as an adult male who needed a little spiritual refreshment now and again, we believed we indirectly improved his efficiency as a fighting man. We gave him a chance to laugh at things that he, in particular, found amusing, or to get a lump in his throat about things he found sad, thereby doing something obliquely to relieve the intellectual desolation that was the companion of life in the army.

That talk with General Richardson proved to be just the sort of springboard I needed for my next plunge into the unknown. I had become heartily sick of the succession of light entertainments we were putting out— *Campus Capers* and *Mainland Follies* to name only two. Equally nauseating, one might have thought, having already played it here and there 380 times, would be to contemplate yet another revival of *Hamlet*. Yet, nothing else I had done in the past seemed as appropriate, and in refreshing my memory of the play I was to discover one facet of the story that had escaped me until then—the constant reference to military matters. Claudius refers to Denmark as "this warlike state." Sentries are keeping watch on the battlements in the opening scenes and there is much soldierly discussion throughout concerning the incursions by Fortinbras *père et fils* on Danish soils. To judge by his ghostly apparition, it would seem that Hamlet's father went to bed in full armour. In this martial atmosphere Hamlet himself must surely have had some appointment in the army to account for young Fortinbras's order at the play's conclusion:

> Let four captains
> Bear Hamlet, like a soldier, to the stage;
> . . . and, for his passage,
> The soldiers' music and the rites of war
> Speak loudly for him. . . .
> Go, bid the soldiers shoot.

Professor John W. Draper, in his *The Hamlet of Shakespeare's Audience*, went so far as to insist that "Shakespeare's Hamlet is a soldier in training, in ideals, and in execution"—a far cry from the dyspeptic Dane of tradition.

I am of the opinion that the short shrift given to the military background of the play has been the fault of theatrical presentations that have compressed the tragedy into a more fashionable length. By having played it widely in its entirety, I was more conscious of the importance of emphasizing that Mars plays an intrinsic part in the proceedings. How to go about implementing that conviction was the subject of long and frequent consultations with my staff. Sergeant George Schaefer was to direct. Sergeant Paolo D'Anna was to give free rein to his imagination where the costumes were concerned, as were Sergeant Frederick Stover as scenic designer and Private First Class Roger Adams for the incidental music.

1942—1947

Somewhere between the ancient and the modern we had to invent a style of production that would be consistent with the theme and would at the same time fulfill our aim of stressing the contemporary parallels. It would not be enough to design a vaguely palatial interior and put crowns on the heads of the King and Queen to indicate their station. That would inevitably thrust the play back into other times, inviting from the audience a detached regard for things happening long ago.

I was sauntering down a Honolulu street one evening, pondering the costuming problem, when an officer emerged from one of the buildings. He was wearing the full-dress uniform of a South American naval attaché—resplendent in high, polished boots, silver sword, and long, flowing cape. I was struck with the oddity of the fact that, although here was as startling a period costume as one could possibly imagine, it did not seem in the least incongruous because of its military associations. Might not the comparative timelessness of uniforms be valuable to us and further enable us to remove the play from any specific period? Polonius could rightfully wear knee breeches and swallowtail coat, which are worn by the Court chamberlains on state occasions to this day. The uniforms of the guards at the play's opening could be so close in general design, if not in colour, to a modern soldier's greatcoat and forage cap that one would think for the moment that events were taking place in present times. That we succeeded in devising a production without intellectual trimmings—a straightforward exposition of the play—was testified to by one G.I. who was heard to say, "Gee! They must have done a lot of rewriting to bring this up to date."

Our greatest difficulty was to make the cuts needed to stay within the time limit imposed by army regulations. It required reading over possible deletions with stopwatch in hand, but when totalled up we were still ten or fifteen minutes too long. I refused to bluepencil Fortinbras as so many of my predecessors had done, so the bold step had to be taken to eliminate the graveyard scene entirely. There were no critics whose wrath had to be feared—and no Yorick to be alased over. We gained the extra time we required to keep the theme of revenge rushing to its bloody conclusion.

In addition to his painstaking qualities as a director, George Schaefer had acquired some knowledge about stage lighting when he was at the Yale Drama School. We were woefully lacking in proper equipment—the only way of throwing light in a fixed direction was to house the bulb in a Chase and Sanborn coffee can, which served as a reflector. One day a bespectacled private told George that he knew where the salvage from the sunken battleship *Oklahoma* was stored and that it included all the essentials he needed to build us a dimmer board. He was put on Detached Service and told to go to work on his invention. We tested it before moving into the high school auditorium, where *Hamlet* was to be staged, and to everyone's amazement it worked—at least, until the first dress rehearsal, when the whole box of tricks went up in smoke. If our electrical genius was put out of countenance, I too had my qualms about matters. I felt that I could be justly criticised for appearing in an elaborate production to which the troops had to be transported, whereas other entertainment units of the section had to go into the field. We were able to move *Hamlet* to only one location other than the high school, and that was to the biggest camp on Oahu, Schofield Barracks. Even there we ran into electrical problems. At one performance the main fuse blew, but we ploughed ahead with nothing but hand-held flashlights for illumination. At another performance we had a mysterious mishap with the sound equipment. To illustrate Horatio's reference to "The cock that is the trumpet of the morn," we had a turntable record of a single cock-crow. For reasons no one was able to explain to me, instead of "cock-a-doodle-do!" the loudspeakers blared forth the voices of the Andrews Sisters! To drown out the anachronistic crooners, Horatio fairly bellowed the ensuing poetic lines:

> But look, the morn in russet mantle clad,
> Walks o'er the dew of yon high eastward hill.

He needn't have bothered to exert himself, because the audience was already caught up in the magic of the play. Had the intrusion been today's lugubrious rock and roll, the spell might well have been broken.

Not content to have proved beyond question that *Hamlet* was indestructible, I decided to put us to an even more stringent test on the last night of our seven-week run. We took the play to a military staging area on the north shore, having discarded all the scenery and special lighting. The men's costumes gave place to army fatigues and the stage was nothing but a narrow platform backed by a blank movie screen. The audience consisted of a mixture of troops brought back for rest from the fighting in forward areas and those preparing to be shipped out as their replacements. Chalked on a blackboard at the gate was the legend "Tonite Hamlet," with nothing to indicate it wasn't just another "B" movie. With a full moon as the only lighting for the battlement scenes, it wasn't easy to attract the attention of the G.I.s, but when a searchlight, mounted on a tower, lit up the opening Court scene we found that we had a fascinated crowd sitting on the ground before us. When I was in the midst of the "To be or not to be" soliloquy, one battle-weary youngster detached himself from his buddies and, with his elbow propped on the edge of the platform, listened intently to the words. When I reached the passage, "Thus conscience does make cowards of us all," I heard him murmur, "Boy, you ain't kiddin'!"

It was then December 1944, and it had taken two years of hard slogging on our part for Washington to become aware of the possibilities of self-entertainment in the services, but their way of showing their approval was typically obtuse. They impressed a number of New York actors, singers, and dancers, who were put together as a touring production of *This Is the Army*, and sent them, at vast expense, all through the Central and South Pacific areas. Unlike my own men, who built and painted their own scenery, drove and serviced their own army vehicles, stood inspection, and acted in their own shows—the New York visitors had no duties except to perform in their show. I did my best to keep them well apart from my own hardworking fellows by arranging barracks for them in a downtown Honolulu park with a fence around it. Even so, for the first time I noticed a spirit of discontent creeping into the Entertainment Section—caused, no doubt, by a feeling that their efforts, might be supplanted by favoured groups sent from the mainland. I had to admit I shared their resentment to an extent, and I began to think that the time had come for me to take stock of myself in relation to the army.

May 1945 brought V.E. Day, but there seemed little prospect of a speedy end to the hostilities in the Pacific. I would be forty-four in June, and I was advised that the War Department was beginning to unload aging warhorses like me, and that, although technically I was in for the duration, I stood a good chance of being discharged if I applied. I didn't need much prompting to take the step; nevertheless, a communication I received at about that time helped me to make the decision. It came from my immediate superior, on orders to him from on high, and read as follows:

Subject: Reprimand
To: Major Maurice Evans, Entertainment Officer, SSO, CPBC

1. Prior to the production of "Hamlet," you wrote to the local Musicians Union requesting opinion whether or not it would be necessary to be granted a waiver in order to utilize the services of soldier-musicians in the presentation of "Hamlet" to three (3) civilian audiences. You are hereby informed that this action was in direct violation of established policy (Par. 4, Section, II, Circular 291, WD 1942), resulting in adverse criticism of the Commanding General by the War Department.

2. In no instance will you communicate with civilians on interpretations of War Department policies.

J. J. Doyle
Colonel, FM
Special Service Officer, CPBC

I couldn't help wondering what would have happened to my scalp if I had failed to check with the Musicians' Union in advance ... a picket line outside the auditorium, perhaps! One didn't expect gestures of gratitude for doing one's duty, so it was particularly thoughtful of the Regents of the University of Hawaii to make me an Honorary Doctor of Letters by way of expressing their pleasure in having been invited to see *Hamlet*.

Any feeling of having given personal affront to General Richardson was quickly dispelled by a communication dated 28 June 1945, informing me that by his command I had been awarded the army's highest noncombatant medal, the Legion of Merit. The ceremony took place in his office and I was told to stand smartly to attention when he entered. Unfortunately, at the moment the door opened, I happened to be standing half *on* and half *off* the thick carpet on the office floor. I jumped to attention, as instructed, but when the general advanced toward me to pin on the decoration I began to teeter back and forth. What, for me, was probably the most solemn moment of my life turned into sheer farce with the general attempting to reach my bosom as I rocked in the opposite direction.

In the preceding pages I have been able to report journalists' opinions of my activities. The Honolulu paper had no such scrivener, so I feel impelled to do the next best thing by quoting the contents of the army's citation concerning the years that I was in its clutches:

The Commanding General
United States Army Forces, Pacific Ocean Areas
By Authority Of
The President Of The United States of America
Awards
The Legion of Merit
To
Major Maurice Evans
United States Army

For exceptionally meritorious conduct in the performance of outstanding services from 27 November 1942 to 18 June, 1945. Despite many difficulties, Major EVANS organized and directed the activities of the Entertainment Section, Special Service Office, Headquarters Central Pacific Area and Headquarters Central Pacific Base Command. With the westward progress of our combat operations, he created theatrical units which accompanied Army and Navy forces into battle zones of the Western Pacific. The high standard of his productions was unsurpassed in the annals of troop entertainment in the field. Major EVANS on notable occasions enhanced by his personal appearances the success of several classic dramatic presentations. The high professional and executive ability and devotion to duty displayed by Major EVANS were of immeasurable aid to the morale of our troops in the Pacific Ocean Areas.

Captain Allen Ludden drove me to the ceremony in my battered old army Chevrolet, but when it was over he strangely refused my invitation to stop somewhere in Honolulu that we might lift our elbows in celebration of the occasion, claiming a pressing appointment back at our treadmill. As we drove into the section, our Master Sergeant Kramer's voice rang out with the command "A-ten-shun!" For the first and last time in my tour of duty every single man in the outfit was in formation, shoes shined, rifles stiffly at their sides, and every one of them looking dead ahead. I had such a lump in my throat that I had difficulty in giving the order, "Stand at ease." I'm afraid I then proceeded to make one of those dreadful mock-modesty speeches that are the hallmark of the Oscar awards, but at least I made it brief. I handed over my command to Allen Ludden on June 30, 1945, and with it the nonfraternization rules. George Schaefer, Howie Morris, and a handful of my key associates were all patrons of a Chinese laundry in town, where they arranged a party for me in the back room. We sat on the floor, upright to begin with, but as the evening wore on and the beakers of rice wine emptied, our postures became universally horizontal—all of a drunken heap.

4. *THE G.I. HAMLET* IN NEW YORK

How good it was to be back in San Francisco, and to be informed by the paymaster general that, because I had not taken a single day's leave during my time in the Central Pacific, I was entitled to several months off duty. This meant I was free to go my own way while my application for discharge was being processed. One of my prewar "angels" was the rags-to-riches millionaire, Louis Lurie. He arranged for me to stay at the famous Bohemian Club, where for the first time in three years, although still in uniform, I had a reminder of what it was like to be one's own master. Meeting again with a few old friends in that hospitable city caused me to reflect upon the acutely lonely period I had been through. The buddy system common in all armies affords, at least, a semblance of social contact for the enlisted man, but an officer's lot can be a very solitary one. I was never able to accustom myself to the petty jealousies and the constant vying for promotion that was the prevailing concern of most officer personnel. On the other hand, many of the enlisted men in my outfit have become fast friends with me in the postwar years—one of them even married my secretary in New York.

I continued the thawing-out process by spending some time in Los Angeles, meeting with my agent, Leland Hayward, and paying a surprise visit

Calling on George Bernard Shaw (1946).

As Jack Tanner in *Man and Superman* (1947–48).
"Marriage is the most licentious of human
institutions! I say *the* most licentious of human
institutions; that is the reason for its
popularity."

As Dick Dudgeon in *The Devil's Disciple* (1950).

In Santa Barbara, California, with Penny and Tuppence (1951).

As Sullivan, with Robert Morley (*left*) as Gilbert,
in *Mr. Gilbert and Mr. Sullivan* (1951).
"A policeman's lot is not a happy one."

As Tony Wendice,
up to no good in the New
York production of *Dial M for Murder*.
(1952)

As Petruchio in the television
adaptation of Shakespeare's
The Taming of the Shrew (1956).

As King Magnus in *The Apple Cart* (1956).

THE G.I. HAMLET IN NEW YORK

to Judith Anderson at her home in the Pacific Palisades. The door was opened by her mother who eyed this uniformed stranger with suspicion:

"She's not in," said Judith's mother in her strong Australian accent.

"If you're expecting her, I'd like to wait if you don't mind," I said, noticing that she had one foot bracing the door against the intruder. "You don't know me, but I'm Maurice Evans."

"Maurice Evans! Oh, you 'ave got fat!" she exclaimed.

On my last night in Hollywood before heading for New York, I dined with Herbert Marshall at Romanoff's. As we left through the revolving doors, the doorman handed me a note, which read, "Congratulations on the job you've been doing. Give me a ring when you come to New York." It was signed "Mike Todd." What the notorious entrepreneur of girlie shows would want with me was puzzling, but in due course my curiosity got the best of me and I went to lunch with him at his Park Avenue penthouse. The sight of me, still in uniform, appeared to disturb my host, but what civilian raiment I possessed was somewhere in storage and had to remain there until I was sure of my army discharge. He took me into his bedroom and, throwing open cupboard doors, invited me to help myself to shirts, trousers, ties—the whole wardrobe. That was typical of the generous, wayward man-child that was Mike Todd. Over lunch he asked me what I planned to do once out of the army, at the same time expressing his personal wish to expand his reputation in the theatre. I told him that I narrowly escaped being labelled "the Mike Todd of the Pacific" by mounting a production of *Hamlet*.

"Great idea!" said Mike. "Let's do it on Broadway and call it *The G.I. Hamlet*."

"Must have a big theater," I hedged.

"I'll get you one," he replied.

"But the St. James is tied up with *Oklahoma*," I reminded him.

"Listen, Moishe, I tell you I'll get one," he fired back.

"How about an office?" I asked.

"You've *got one*, come with me!"

We drove across town like maniacs and I was whisked into his palatial headquarters on 56th Street. The building had once been a fashionable couturier's establishment—all very Marie Antoinette—but Mike's personal office resembled something to do with outer-space rocket control. His all-embracing horseshoe desk groaned under the weight of every conceivable gadget—dictaphones, intercom systems, and at least a half-dozen telephones, all of which, judging by their flashing lights, had callers awaiting his attention. "Hold on," he barked into the first receiver; "I'll call you back," into another; "Tell 'em to go to hell," into a third; "Fifty smackers on Jocko in the 3:30," to his bookie, and so forth.

Noticing a man sitting quietly in the corner, I signalled Mike to desist long enough to introduce us. "Jesus," he said, "don't you know each other! . . . Damon Runyon meet Maurice Evans." We shook hands and an embarrassing silence ensued while Mike hurled abuse at his fifth and sixth callers. Practically vaulting his desk, Mike then took me by the arm, propelling me to the door. "Come on, I'll show you your office," he said. Once outside he explained that as a result of a cancer operation Damon Runyon's vocal chords had been removed. "Poor fellow. Had to buy his lunch today." It was typical of Mike's generous nature to devote lunchtime each day to counteracting the feeling of deprivation that that cruel handicap caused the witty author to suffer. Those luncheons must have been largely a soliloquy on Mike's part, though Runyon's scribbled notes were probably priceless. On a later occasion one such billet-doux succeeded in halting Mike's telephonitis; it read, "This is the tenth time you've introduced me to Maurice."

The whirlwind atmosphere of the Todd office was not conducive to calm thinking, and it soon became apparent that as far as production chores were concerned Mike had no intention of putting his finger in the *Hamlet* pie. So, there I was, once again being made responsible for all the complexities of producing the show under conditions that had changed for the worse since I had last endured the torture. I had severe doubts about the wisdom of the whole project. Granted, by 1945 five years had passed since I was last seen as Hamlet; but, for the most part, the same critics were still around. They had already expended themselves on my three revivals and to expect them to be even faintly polite about a fourth dose of the same seemed optimistic. I was on the verge of abandoning the idea when, providentially, two of the most important men from the army production returned to civilian life—George Schaefer, the director, and Frederick Stover, the scene designer.

Technically, I was still on leave and determined to make the best of it, but word soon came that I was to report for severance at Fort Dix, New Jersey, in October. Like myself, neither George nor Freddie had anywhere to live in New York, so it took little persuading for them to join me at Norway Island, where we could work out the physical production of *Hamlet*, and at the same time get the rest we all desperately needed. Ex-yeoman Bud Williams joined us, as did my prewar assistant, Emmett Rogers. The summer weather was perfect and the healing woods wrought wonders with our spirits. With the capitulation of the Japanese, it was also a matter for mutual satisfaction that we could pick up our lives where, earlier, they had been brought to a halt. With *The G.I. Hamlet* in the offing, my team, at any rate, could look back on their service days as having helped them to make a new start. After a few weeks I packed them all off to New York to put things in the works. During the early part of September I followed the example of a one-time resident of the village of Saranac Lake,

THE G.I. HAMLET IN NEW YORK

Robert Louis Stevenson, and contented myself with fishing, hiking, reading, and thanking my lucky stars for their guidance.

That little matter at Fort Dix had to be attended to before I was officially separated from the army—a ceremony that lacked dignity, since one was stripped stark naked to wait in line for a physical examination, the grand finale of which was to be jabbed in the bottom with a needle. The lieutenant ahead of me in the line was telling me of the hair-raising war he had somehow survived when his turn came. Decorated for bravery in combat, that warrior passed out cold at the sight of the needle.

One might think that, once one was out of uniform, any hint of nostalgia would be ridiculous; but when we were faced with the changed conditions in the New York theatre we three ex-soldiers pined for the freedom from trade-union restrictions that we had become accustomed to in Honolulu. The overmanning and departmentalisation of stagehands, the overtime, to say nothing of a wage scale higher than that of actors—all these had to be swallowed manfully. For me personally there was the grim fact that I had disappeared from Broadway four years earlier and, for all I knew, might have been presumed dead and buried. Others who escaped military service might, I thought, have stolen a march on me, although fortunately none had revived *Hamlet*. On the other hand, under the guidance of John Haggart, Peggy Webster had directed a record-breaking *Othello* with Paul Robeson and José Ferrer, thereby putting PAID to my Iago ambition. It was only by reminding ourselves that, whereas in the army we had a ready-made audience and no box office, the challenge ahead of us demanded hardheaded calculation that we might succeed in catching up with the times. That we managed to put on a creditable production was borne out by the astonishing fact that between New York and the road we achieved a total of 425 performances.

No one was more elated by that outcome than Mike himself; of all the framed poster-cards hanging on his office wall (*The Hot Mikado, Star and Garter, Something for the Boys, Up in Central Park*), the one that was given pride of place was "Michael Todd presents ... *The G.I. Hamlet.*" Strange company for the Prince of Denmark, but the billing promised something out of the ordinary. A more knowledgeable producer would have shared my own fear that the absence of the graveyard scene might be regarded as an outrage. The curtailment that the army curfew imposed on the earlier production did not apply in this instance, but the equally pressing prospect of stagehand overtime meant short shrift for Ophelia's corpse. Quite apart from the time element, in our deliberately swift, somewhat melodramatic production, the graveyard scene caused a hiatus in the action besides making an insurmountable difficulty for the scenic designer.

I have always sensed a strange incongruity of structure in the play at this point. At the opening of the scene Horatio leaves Hamlet in total ignorance about Ophelia's death while his friend exchanges badinage with the gravedigger. The funeral cortege enters, but still Horatio makes no effort to enlighten him. It is left to Laertes to identify the dead body as "my sister," whereupon Hamlet is required by the dramatist to utter the embarrassing question, "What, the fair Ophelia?" followed by speeches of uncharacteristic ranting and raving. Seven short lines later (Act V, scene 2), Hamlet is back in the castle giving Horatio a breezy account of his adventurous trip to England, and the two of them are poking fun at Osric. I find it inconceivable that the graveyard scene and the latter scene were both included in any presentations at the Globe. It is even possible to speculate that the company's chief clown, Tarleton, complained so bitterly of having no part in the play that the graveyard scene was added to give him something to do.

We introduced several innovations elsewhere in the play, which made their contribution. Instead of the awkward business of Ophelia distributing actual or imaginary flowers in her mad scene, in our version she carried a child's illustrated alphabet book, going from one person to another and turning the pages as she pointed to drawings of rosemary, pansies, violets, and "there's a daisy." In addition, the overall Graustarkian visual concept made it possible to depart from the traditional costumes of the actors in the play-within-a-play scene. Our Gonzago was dressed as for the formalised King in a deck of cards, his wife as the Queen of Hearts, and the villain, Lucianus, as a sinister Jack of Clubs. I was also rather proud of one effect in the opening scene on the castle battlements. We managed to overcome the usual inappropriateness of the ghost's clanking armor by having *two* wraiths instead of one. The accompanying lines, it will be remembered, are:

HORATIO: Stop it, Marcellus!
MARCELLUS: Shall I strike at it with my partisan?
HORATIO: Do if it will not stand.
BERNADO: 'Tis here!
HORATIO: 'Tis here!
MARCELLUS: 'Tis gone!

Provided our electrician was on the alert, the illusion of the first ghost's disappearance was completely believable. The switch controlling the pin-spot focussed on the retreating figure of the talkative apparition was flipped "on" and "off" for one second ("'Tis here!"), followed immediately by switch number two illuminating the head of the ghost's "double" on the opposite side of the battlements ("'Tis here!"). Since the pin-spot was focussed solely on his helmeted head, the "double" required no nether garments, but for warmth a cloak was draped round his shoulders. However, on that one memorable night of the electrician's slipup, for a fractional moment the first switch revealed the "double" from head to toe, his cloak casually open down the front revealing his jockey shorts. My understudy, Alan Shane, besides playing Fortinbras at the end of the evening, was also the ghost's "double." He told me afterwards that he had not realised before that it was possible to blush all over.

Fortunately there was no such mishap on the snowy opening night in December 1945. The rest of the cast were full of confidence, including Lili Darvas, Thomas Gomez, and Frances Reid, but I was suffering from cold feet. It was an odd sensation to be apprehensive about being unfavourably compared with standards previously established by oneself, but the risk was inescapable. Both for Mike Todd's sake and for my own peace of mind, I prayed that the gamble would come off. Whereas American audiences are quick to embrace a newcomer into the theatrical arena, they can just as quickly forget the person. Almost four years out of public sight could easily mean also out of mind; so it was with much foreboding that I unfolded my newspapers next morning. Within minutes I heard myself singing for joy. Here are some samples of what the scribblers had to say:

John Chapman, *New York Daily News*, December 14, 1945:

If anybody wants to establish a rule that Shakespeare can be spoken only by Maurice Evans, I shall have no objection, for Maurice Evans makes things clear and alive and exciting. His new "Hamlet," which Michael Todd presented last night at the Columbus Circle Theatre, is a case in point.... Its chief interest could be its novelty—its speed, its belief that Hamlet was neither melancholy nor a nut. But its chief interest is none of these things; it is Mr. Evans himself, for he is an actor. He has enthusiasm, intelligence, judgment, and a way of speaking which makes you think how silly you were not to think of talking Shakespeare this way before now.

Robert Garland, *New York Journal-American*, December 14, 1945:

It is the greatest show in town because of the greatness of the central figure in Maurice Evans' hands. His Hamlet, like any other genius, is the result of an infinite capacity for taking pains. His sweet Prince of Denmark is no mere melancholy Dane, but a sensitive, tortured, sardonic human being with all the weakness and shame to which mankind is heir. And all the strength and glory!

Ward Morehouse, *New York Sun*, December 14, 1945:

As I wandered out into the snows of Columbus Circle at 11:20 last night, it was my impression that I had just witnessed a performance by the best actor in New York.

1942–1947

The magazines followed up in like vein, although expressing a preference for the earlier "Entirety." In the article "Yankee Doodle Hamlet," John Mason Brown wrote (*Saturday Review of Literature*):

> If anything, the Hamlet Mr. Evans presented in his new version is more virile than was his Dane when he employed the uncut text. He is all male, a man who, in Mr. Evans' fashion, is fresh from the Army.... Glancing at his person, one could swear that, instead of specializing in Freud when he was at Wittenberg, he had taken courses in military science. And what is more, enjoyed them. No wonder soldiers are his friends. They hale from the same outfit; belong to the same post. In Mr. Evans we are confronted with a player who gives us one of those chances, which at present so rarely come our way, of sampling the theatre when it is really being itself. Proudly. Unashamedly. Successfully. Then, of a sudden, we rediscover what it is that we have been missing. And are the more grateful for it.

In *Life* magazine:

> Compared to old-time conceptions the G.I. Hamlet is a rough-and-ready extrovert, delayed in avenging his father's murder more by force of circumstances than by his own pigeon liver. The result is a walloping good show which has, however, lost none of Sheakespeare's poetry and power.

Obviously sick of his colleagues' approbation, Burton Rascoe of the *New York World-Telegram* had these sobering reflections:

> The whole point of "Hamlet" seems to have been lost in this production. But it is a bizarre theatrical experience anyhow, and I recommend it, pretty much as I would recommend Ringling Bros. Circus or Billy Rose's Aquacade, to those who had never seen either.

Mercifully for me, Mr. Rascoe occupied his seat of judgement very briefly.

There was no question but that the "Ayes" had it, but what stuck in my craw was the opinion of the one and only dissenter. Was it possible, I found myself wondering, that the cascade of praise from Mr. Rascoe's colleagues was merely their gracious way of saying to me, "Welcome back to Broadway!"?

To contradict the accusation that the so-called G.I. *Production of Hamlet* was merely a stunt, I decided to publish the text of our version. It was to be embellished with illustrations and photographs, and, what was more important, the precise directions to the actors concerning their attitudes. Not content with the gallons of ink that had been spilt upon the topic of *Hamlet*, I elected to add to the torrent by writing a preface to the book, which was published in 1947 by Doubleday. I felt justified in doing so because most of the wordage on the subject has come from the pens of academicians, whereas

THE G.I. HAMLET IN NEW YORK

actors and stage producers have been responsible for a comparatively negligible amount. My apology, if one were needed, was that, unlike my learned predecessors who have concerned themselves with theoretical premises, my approach was a statement of a task actually accomplished in the theatre, for which *Hamlet* was written.

The accepted test of a classic is its readability by succeeding generations. The test of a classical play (in terms of sustained popularity in the theatre) is its capacity to yield to the contemporary customs of play presentation no matter how these customs may alter with the development of new mechanical techniques or changes in styles of acting. One of the evidences of Shakespeare's great genius is that every age has found in his thoughts a responsive echo. It has been able to stage his plays according to the fashion of the moment without departing materially from the original text or intention. Garrick played Hamlet in a tiewig and Mrs. Siddons played Lady Macbeth in a sweeping picture hat without in the least disturbing the sensibilities of their audiences. The Victorian giants—Irving, Terry, and Booth—interpreted the plays in the overdecorated and sententious fashion of their era, and delighted their audiences. There is no such thing as the oft-quoted "tradition" of presenting Shakespeare—only a timorous hesitation to depart from the manner of the immediate past.

Because of the nature of their composition, the old stock companies were guilty of perpetuating tradition for many years. The constant change of bill and interchange of actors made it convenient to adhere to a rigid formula for all the stock plays in a company's repertoire. Thus when Edwin Booth was the visiting star in a score of provincial stock companies, it was a certainty that the Oshkosh Horatio would be in the identical spot for Hamlet's dying words as had been the Mountain Bluff Horatio of the preceding week. Audiences became so used to the details of stage "business" that it took a bold performer to risk any innovation. One reads in *The Theatrical Observer* of May 18, 1824, of the absurdity of Macready's being hissed by a member of the audience because he chose to retreat from the apparition of Banquo rather than advance upon it as had hitherto been customary.

To those of us who are called upon to make these departures from our predecessors, the penalties are sometimes severe and the criticisms scathing. Nevertheless, it is my belief that if we are to prove ourselves worthy of retaining the envied honour of being one of Shakespeare's mouthpieces, we may claim that distinction only so long as we speak in a voice understandable to our own time and bring vigour and originality to our interpretations. That is not to say, as is so often the case, that directors determined to leave their imprints on productions should resort to irritating incongruities. Granted that in *Hamlet* Shakespeare was writing a thoroughly contemporary play. As a poet, of course, his vision was timeless, but as a playwright he deliberately emphasized the modernity of the theme in order to illustrate the universality of the tragedy. Unlike *Antony and Cleopatra* and *Macbeth*, in which Shakespeare took pains to create the illusion of locale, *Hamlet* is set in a royal Court such as Queen Elizabeth's, where doublet and hose were *de rigueur* for the gents, and farthingales and stomachers for the girls.

Seemingly, the dramatist wanted nothing to detract from Hamlet's character originating from the roots of human nature—a thoroughly normal though sensitive man waging the eternal struggle of the individual against society. For us to have followed his example by clothing our actors in contemporary civilian dress would have merely served to emphasize those anachronistic features, encouraging us to whittle down Shakespeare's greatest glory—his verse—into colloquial prose. In doing so, our staging would have taken on an air of pretentiousness far more foreign to the play than the most ornate period production. Taking into account that our production had originally been designed to appeal to soldier audiences, it was imperative to avoid making the production appear to be an historical chronicle of events. Instead, our watchword was that it should be great drama in the Greek sense of the word—"the art of doing"—or, as Horatio sums up the plot in the play's last scene:

> Of carnal, bloody and unnatural acts,
> Of accidental judgements, casual slaughters,
> Of deaths put on by cunning and forc'd cause,
> And, in this upshot, purposes mistook
> Fall'n on the inventors' heads.

We were not obliged, as are today's producers, to pay primary attention to the esoteric aspects of a classic, very often at the expense of the basic values of the play. Nowhere is the hesitation to innovate more apparent than in the case of *Hamlet*. So familiar is the story to the habitual theatregoer (to say nothing of the satiated drama critic) that any emphasis on the theme of the play seems superfluous to the point of being ingenuous. Instead, interest is focussed on the finer shadings of interpretation, more particularly those executed by the actor playing the central character. Too often the result is all nuance and no fibre; such qualities would probably have been hooted off the stage at the Globe in its early days.

For more than a century Hamlet himself was depicted by actors within the same general framework: a princely philosopher so filled with fineness of feeling and poetic brooding that his being is incapable of wrecking the revenge urged by the ghost. One can only surmise that advancing age forced popular performers to abandon any attempt to be convincing as "the glass of fashion and the mould of form," a soldier, and an expert fencer. It has always escaped me why so many scholars insist that the hero's failure to indulge in premeditated bloodletting is proof of his mental instability; after all, this was taking place in Elsinore's Castle, not in Dracula's.

More recently, Hamlet as the prince-philosopher has yielded to the Freudian portrait of a man whose will to act has been paralyzed by the sudden nervous shock of his father's untimely death and his mother's "o'er hasty marriage" with Claudius. These events, it is argued, reduce Hamlet to a state of neurosis, the principal symptom of which is a lethargic melancholia. Would such a "gloomy Dane," we were bound to ask, get a sympathetic hearing from our soldier audiences? In wartime a G.I. who brooded too much or had too thin a skin to withstand "the whips and scorns of time" soon found himself in a psychiatric ward. Using the same yardstick of audience-consideration, would Shakespeare or his public have accepted such a view of the Prince?

The Elizabethans employed "melancholy" in a sense quite different from modern-day usage, implying a physical disorder proceeding from frustrated passion and having outward manifestation in the form of violent behavior. "Melancholy" did not paralyze the will, but enforced *inaction* was often considered the *origin* of the malady. Admitting this premise, the whole theory of Hamlet's innate incapacity to act falls apart, and in its place we have a normal, sensitive man caught in a web of circumstances that denies him the *opportunity* to act.

Whatever shortcomings there may have been in *The G.I. Hamlet*, it was heartening to know from the reviewers and from the reception by widely differing audiences that our approach to the play came through clearly. We were seeking to be truthful to the temper of our own age and to restate Shakespeare's eternal verities in the spirit of these times. *Hamlet* is perhaps the theatre's greatest heritage, and it behooves us who are its servants to serve it well.

The long tour that followed the New York run of *The G.I. Hamlet* very nearly did not take place owing to some kind of financial pickle in which Mike had become embroiled. Several changes of cast occurred, including Doris Lloyd as Queen Gertrude (replacing Lili Darvas) and that fine character actor, Miles Malleson, as the definitive Polonius. Morton Da Costa joined our ranks to play Osric. (He was to be a tower of strength in a number of my later activities.) Several more of my ex-G.I.s were rounded up, and it promised to be a happy band of brothers who awaited their call to report to rehearsal. On the appointed day, I received an alarming telephone call from my attorney, Lloyd Almirall, the guardian of my financial affairs. He informed me that, whereas my basic salary had been paid regularly, my percentage of the gross receipts of the

1942–1947

New York run was still outstanding. Since this percentage represented the most substantial portion of my remuneration, I was forbidden by Lloyd to attend the rehearsal. Instead, the two of us had the humiliating experience of sitting in Mike Todd's outer office for hours waiting for him to settle his debt. Eventually a Todd henchman arrived carrying a sizeable suitcase containing the many thousands of dollars owing to me, in bills of varying denominations. Lloyd left posthaste for the bank, and I for the rehearsal hall to quell the anxieties of the assembled actors. Anybody but Mike would have been grossly affronted by this episode. He, on the contrary, seemed to be proud of his ability to conjure large sums of money out of thin air—and we remained the best of friends.

In 1946 the nearest attempt to establishing a national playhouse took place at the old Mecca Temple, renamed the New York City Center. It was the home of the New York City Opera Company and George Balanchine's New York City Ballet. For drama they were dependent on the odd touring company being available—a strictly intermittent affair, but better than nothing. It was with great reluctance that I agreed to help them out by promising them the final two weeks of the *Hamlet* tour, on the condition that no drama critics would be invited to cover the occasion. The gentlemen of the press, I'm sure, were entirely in accord with the ban, since it would have been their fifth exposure to this recurring Dane. By then I had passed my forty-fifth birthday—getting too old for the part, and weary beyond description.

During my comparatively short sojourn in the United States William Shakespeare and I had been in each other's company for a staggering total of 1,875 performances, yielding seven-figure returns to our backers for their investment. It had been a great experience, but at times I felt it was rather like riding a tandem bicycle—the one up front doing most of the work. As we dismounted from our trusty steed, I couldn't help doubting that I would ever again be lucky enough to have as a partner such a rarity as a dead author with no surviving relatives. In the meantime, I scanned the horizon for a worthy successor.

IV

"... this strange eventful history ..."

1. *MAN AND SUPERMAN*

AVING SHED HAMLET'S inky cloak, I was not to step onto any stage for the next six months. This was a period of reassessment of both my professional and my private life. I had begun to notice that when I was mentioned in the columns I was referred to as "the noted Shakespearean actor." Theatrical history is full of sad stories of the decline and fall of actors and actresses who have been similarly labelled, and I made up my mind that it wasn't going to happen to me. A prerequisite to changing my image, however, was to put an end to living out of a trunk and being constantly on the move. Norway Island was the nearest thing to home for me, but, being habitable only during the summer months and the early fall, that did not fill the bill. I therefore started house-hunting in the beautiful countryside that is within commutable distance from New York City.

I finally lighted on a property on the Connecticut border—a typical white-clapboard house standing in nine acres of attractive woodland. "Mountbrook," as I named it, dated back to the late 1700s and had not been very well kept up. It had that forlorn look of a house crying out to be restored—a plea that I have fallen for over the years with sickening regularity. Being of Welsh extraction myself, I should have known better than to believe a local fellow taffy contractor, who estimated $5,000 as the cost of making the house liveable. In the end it became necessary to replace all four walls and the roof, to drill a well, and to rebuild the stables. All things considered, I thought it best to leave my personal assistant, Emmett Rogers, to supervise the undertaking, and I decided to pay a long overdue visit to what remained of my family in England. Both Mother and Father had passed away in their eighties,

1947–1963

but my sister and brother were there and had children who were growing up. I was beginning to fear I wouldn't recognise the youngsters.

Over two years had passed since the last bomb had fallen on London, but the scars were distressingly apparent, and the people, including my own relations, seemed still to be in a state of shock. I was made conscious of this by a rather touching incident on my birthday, which, incidentally, was also the official birthday of the reigning monarch. I was walking in Mayfair on that sunny June day when the customary gun salute was fired in Hyde Park in honour of the King. As the salvo rattled the windows on Mount Street, a very frail, white-faced old lady stopped me, saying anxiously, "Can you tell me what all that banging is about?" Perhaps the poor soul thought it was another air raid. The evidence of the destruction caused by those raids was all around me as I walked the familiar streets of London during the rest of my stay. The St. James's Theatre, where I had once played in Molnár's *The Swan*, was just a large hole in the ground, but a surprisingly decorative crater because it was carpeted with masses of wildflowers. My club had disappeared and my tailor gone into limbo. I was glad to notice, however, that the famous suppliers of bathroom fixtures (By Royal Appointment), Thos. Crapper & Sons, had survived unscathed. All the same I felt a stranger in my native land and not altogether welcome.

One's old friends seemed hell-bent to forget that the war had ever happened, whereas having a taste of what they had endured made me feel very humble. It was one thing to have kept abreast of the happenings in one's homeland, but quite another to see the results with one's own eyes. If the face of London had changed, it was not really surprising that as far as my professional activities were concerned my acquaintances remained stolidly indifferent.

Actually I had them to thank for arousing me from artistic torpor, and reviving in my consciousness a thought that had struck me during the *Hamlet* tour. Although I had for years been a Bernard Shaw devotee, for some reason or other I had never before read *Man and Superman*, let alone seen a production of the play. The prefaces to many of his plays are often more entertaining than the plays themselves, but the tub-thumping introduction to *Man and Superman* apparently had discouraged me from going any further. When I finally got around to reading the play while on the *Hamlet* tour (with the exception of the scene in Hell, which Shaw himself describes in the preface as being extraneous), I felt sure this was the perfect vehicle to conduct me across the bridge from Shakespeare. I had written to G.B.S. asking whether he would reserve the American rights for me until my touring *Hamlet* was ended. He replied by one of his favoured postcards: "Yes, you may postpone for a season, but don't let this give you the idea that you have any exclusive rights to *Man and Superman*.

MAN AND SUPERMAN

The part of John Tanner is open to all actors just as the part of Hamlet is—only I get fifteen percent of the gate money."

I envisaged much difficulty in surrounding myself with a cast drawn from the sparse pool of English-born actors available in postwar New York. Therefore, while on this trip to London I set about looking for suitable candidates. I did a lot of theatregoing in search of the ideal Ann, and even flew to Paris to try to interest Edwige Feuillère in playing the part. She was scared that her English, though almost perfect, would not stand up well against mine. I supposed she was right but hated missing the opportunity of working with that entrancing and very talented lady. The spider-and-fly theme of the play called for both those qualities in generous measure. There was also the question of age. I had to remind myself of the warning once pronounced by a famous actor of a past generation, Sir Squire Bancroft, who said, "In the theatre, the love affairs of middle-aged people are either dull or dirty—and usually both!" It was going to be quite a strain for me to appear youthful enough, but with the aid of a toupee I thought I could just about get away with it. Even more important was that Ann, the spider, should weave her web with the impetuosity of youth, never for a moment giving the impression of being Jack Tanner's maiden aunt.

I found exactly the qualities I was looking for in the actress Frances (Fanny) Rowe—stylish, provocative, and an experienced Shavian. She had been seen in four different roles in *Back to Methuselah*, but Ann was the one part she had set her heart on for years. Although my production date in New York was considerably in the future, she declared herself willing to wait indefinitely for the opportunity to fling her coils around my soul and body. As her apoplectic joint-guardian, Roebuck Ramsden, the actor Malcolm Keen was equally cooperative and in his way just as brilliant. We had known each other when he was in New York playing Claudius in the Gielgud *Hamlet*, and he couldn't wait to get back to the bright lights of Broadway. Now that I had found the missing links in the casting, it was up to me to pull up my Edwardian socks and get things rolling in New York.

Summer in Manhattan was no time to look for actors. Except for the musical comedies, the marquees were mostly dark and the performers were largely doing the rounds of out-of-town summer theatres. Also, I had the pressing need of the security of a proper home, and Mountbrook, still an empty shell, had to take precedence over all else. My intentions regarding *Man and Superman* were a closely guarded secret known to a very few close associates, so the risk of someone else getting the same idea was minimal. Lacking a home was no circumstance to be in once the pressures of preproduction raised their menacing heads.

All my possessions had been destroyed in the London bombings, so I hadn't a stick of furniture to my name. Thus I became an habitué of any auction room that came within my ken. One unfortunate experience, however, taught me to refrain from indulging in two double martinis during an auction lunch break. On that occasion a careless gesture by me resulted in my having unconsciously bid for an enormous Spanish armoire, riddled with woodworm and too big to go through Mountbrook's doors. Another aspect of the furnishing problems had an unusual twist. The sponsors of a popular radio program, which went on the air on Friday nights, were worried that the content of their script for the coming Good Friday might give offense to people in the Bible Belt, and they were likely buyers of Philco appliances. The sponsors proposed, therefore, that I should lend dignity to the program by reading the Twenty-third Psalm. In return for that I was to have the choice of receiving a handsome fee in cash or of being supplied with any of their products that took my fancy. Needless to say, I opted for the latter and although when the day came, I was sick with the flu and had a temperature of 103 degrees, I struggled through my biblical poem with thoughts only of Mountbrook's barren kitchen and its about-to-be air-conditioned bedrooms.

It seemed to take forever and a day to make the place habitable, but eventually I was able to move in, and to luxuriate in the services of a Bavarian couple as cook and gardener. For the first time in America I had the companionship of a pair of West Highland Terriers and became something of a country squire, riding horseback and revelling in the great outdoors. Thoroughly refreshed, and with a house capable of accommodating guests, my conscience began to bother me. One by one I lured various victims of my *Man and Superman* ambition into my lair at weekends. My old chum David Ffolkes was to create the costumes, and my army scenic designer, Freddie Stover, the settings. I had decided, since the play is so ultra-British, that I ought to direct it myself. George Schaefer, however, was nominated as associate director and was to acquit himself as a resonant sounding board.

Long before we were properly organised, I was obliged to set a date for our Broadway opening and to sign a contract for the Alvin Theater, which bristled with penalties for delay or default. At that point my cautious attorney, Lloyd Almirall, stepped in. It worried him that I was making commitments for months ahead on the assumption that G.B.S. would still be in the land of the living in October 1947, at ninety-two. He also strongly doubted whether the equivocal consent expressed in Shaw's postcard would protect my financial backers and my personal investment against prying executors. Thus I was advised to make another trip to England to beard the lion in his den. While waiting for the appointment to be confirmed, I made a thorough research concerning the background of the play so that I had the facts and figures at my fingertips.

MAN AND SUPERMAN

My research revealed that, to begin with, the play had been shunned by the commercial theatre and was given, instead, a series of one-night experimental performances by the Stage Society in 1905–7. The play had to wait until 1911 to be presented at the 600-seat Criterion Theatre in Piccadilly Circus, where it had 191 showings. As an author, Shaw had been even more thoroughly rejected by the American critical fraternity, who in those early days demanded that the legitimate stage and its morals be protected from the curse of the Irish dramatist. "There is no worthy motive in any of his plays," wrote one critic. "Most of his characters are vile, with detestable views of life." Shaw's rebuttal came in the form of a magazine interview: "My plays advocate moral reform. I don't care what is said about me. I do not complain when my plays are prohibited by the police. I simply tell the American people that they are making themselves ridiculous in the eyes of the civilised world. What I fight against is the old morality, and I look upon as *immoral* what 'good people' think right." It was encouraging to find that in spite of the prudish attitude, *Man and Superman* had found favour with the American theatregoers six years before London managements dared to present it. It was given in 1905 at the Hudson Theatre in New York, where it achieved 184 performances.

Even with that crumb of comfort, I found it somewhat intimidating as I realised that the play had been published in 1903, when I was at the tender age of two, and that, forty-four years later, I was about to discuss the play with its author. More formidable was the attempt I was determined to make to browbeat him into modifying his royalty terms—as the saying goes, "Nothing ventured, nothing gained." An old acquaintance of his tipped me off, before I left for England, with the surprising information that Shaw had an incurable sweet tooth—a weakness he had been unable to indulge during the war years—and that a gift of chocolate might put him in a receptive state of mind. Thus, I set forth with a goodly supply of Hershey bars in my luggage, and a carefully composed protest regarding his "gate money."

After arriving in London, Shaw's secretary, Blanche Patch, drove me down to the country for my appointment. On the way, I told her that, in addition to securing a licence for *Man and Superman*, I was going to ask Shaw for his consent to allow me to commission the writing of a musical-comedy treatment based on his *Pygmalion*. "Don't even hint at such an idea," said Blanche. "He really sees red on the subject and you'd risk coming away empty-handed on both counts." She added that he had never forgiven the Americans who, in the precopyright days, had helped themselves to *Arms and the Man* and turned it into the highly successful musical *The Chocolate Soldier*. When others succeeded with *My Fair Lady* after his demise, one distinctly heard a sour note being plucked on a harp from on high.

It was a blessing to be driven by someone who knew the way. Otherwise

I should have been obliged to follow the printed directions that G.B.S. had sent me when the appointment was made:

> Go out the Finchley Road through Swiss Cottage. Keep on northward, avoiding a fork to the left at the Bull Inn. After passing Ayot Station, turn right under the railway bridge. Follow the lane until you come out on a main road. Turn left along it for a short bit, then turn right at a sign post marked Ayot St. Lawrence. Drive through the village past the ruined church; and at the end, where the road divides, Bernard Shaw's gate is facing you in the angle. Time from London, about an hour and a quarter.

Before Blanche Patch had offered to act as my guide, I had visions of starting off from London on my own with my host's printed route sheet firmly clasped in one hand. After two and a half hours of hopeless meanderings through every byway of Hertfordshire, the suspicion would strike me that this nerve-wracking experience had been purposely devised to put the author's visitors out of countenance.

Any such thoughts would have been immediately dispelled, however, by the warm, welcoming smile of a very tiny, very Irish maid who hoped the rain "didn't spile your journey." As we entered the front door, I noticed a strange man stealthily slip through the door on our heels. To my horror I saw he was carrying a camera and other paraphernalia. It was the London photographer whose request to accompany me I had turned down the day before. I was about to whisper a fierce reprimand when a firm voice rang out from the study, "Is that you, Maurice Evans?" Blanche swiftly disappeared into the sanctum; after a brief but anxious pause, the voice pealed out again, "Sure, let him take some pictures, but tell him he must be quick."

That is the first thing that struck one about the Sage of Ayot St. Lawrence—the vigour and beauty of his voice. I hadn't seen him since he was an active youngster of seventy-nine, and I was a little apprehensive over the possible changes in him on the threshold of his ninety-first birthday. I needn't have worried. He emerged from his study, his white beard bristling like the quills of a porcupine. Leaning lightly on a cane, he advanced slowly and offered me his hand in greeting. The famous eyes, more sunken than I remembered, still had a mischievous twinkle under those bushy brows. The red pigment that used to adorn his hair and beard seemed to have concentrated itself in his nose, giving him a faint resemblance to the clown he so often declared himself to be at heart.

Leading the way into the living room, G.B.S. cross-questioned the photographer, displaying an amazing technical knowledge of lenses and apertures and so forth. His preoccupation gave me a chance to take in our surroundings. I was surprised at the smallness of the house and the air of comparative discomfort. The living room was littered with bric-a-brac and a hodgepodge of furniture, suggesting an owner who was indifferent about his environment and scornful of luxury. Shaw moved about the room looking for a suitable spot for us to pose for pictures. He decided we should sit beside an old Spanish writing desk, one of those ornate pieces with metal-bound corners and a drop front. The handle had long since become detached, and impatient fingers had, at some time, bent back one of the metal corners to act as a substitute. Following my host's example, I pulled up a chair and rather sheepishly produced a copy of his play from under my arm. "No, no, no!" said G.B.S. "That will look as though I'm trying to teach you something. Put the beastly book down!"

The photographer disposed of, tea was served by the Irish maid and a mammoth cup of some peculiar brew was placed before Mr. Shaw. It was a raw, cold day and the only heating in the room came from a diminutive portable electric fire. What a comment on conditions in Britain, I found myself thinking, that probably her most famous son is allowed this crumb of warmth by special permission, and only on account of his advanced age. Miss Patch told me that he was in the habit of carrying that same miserable fire to his garden house, where he preferred to do his writing, and that, in spite of being warned, he would place it so close to his blanket-enshrouded knees that it was a marvel he didn't go up in smoke.

I had been put so much at my ease over the tea table that it came like a bolt from the blue when my host suddenly asked, "Which of my plays is it you want to do?"

I was speechless for the moment, my thoughts flying to the many commitments already entered into across the water. "*Man and Superman*," I breathed barely audibly.

"Very well," he said, "you may do it, but remember this—you will have to do it soon. The play is always a success, but even I know my limitations and I won't have it done in America during a presidential election year—too much competition!" As an afterthought he added, "Why on earth are you in management? It is the ruination of actors. Instead of putting money into the theatre, you should be taking money out of it."

I thought it prudent to change the topic of conversation and did so by asking him what he thought of the tentative competition for the executive office in 1948. "It's hard to judge," said he. "Truman, like Attlee, is turning out better than any of us thought. But the only American who has been over here since the war and hasn't talked with the intelligence of a villager is Henry Wallace." This sounded like an echo from a passage in one of his provocative early writings: "I have been particularly careful never to say a civil word to the United States . . . and they just adore me."

We may adore you, but the same can't be said of your royalty terms, I thought, plucking up my courage to raise the subject. The aged figure suddenly became tense in his chair and the voice took on a more noticeable Irish burr. "Everyone else has skyrocketted his demands on the theatre. I have not changed my terms in fifty years. They must be regarded as unchangeable!" This had become a do-or-die situation—nothing to lose if I failed to be understood, but much to be gained if my point of view could be stated. I asked him to be good enough to read my one-page brief about the vital need of some flexibility. He took his time to digest what I had written, munching on his gums the while. It became clear when he handed me back the figures, reluctantly grunting his assent, that no one had previously convinced him that it was in his own interest to agree to a sliding scale of royalties tied to the gross weekly income. When the play was a sellout, he would get his 15 percent, but in the less prosperous weeks of summer heat, Holy Week, and so forth (weeks that can sound the death knell during a long-running play), he would take less.

Much relieved, I trotted out the Hershey bars, which disappeared into my host's capacious pocket as though by magic. Knowing my time to be nearly up, I promised him I would do my very best to give a performance of Jack Tanner that would at least be articulate. He responded with a piece of advice in most definite terms. "The trouble with my plays is modern actors are afraid to act them." I believe he meant, rather, that we are afraid to *speak* them, for Shaw wrote a rhythmic prose that was almost poetry. It calls for the same careful phrasing as Elizabethan blank verse. To illustrate his contention, Shaw bounded with unexpected alacrity from his chair, and, standing with his back to the empty fireplace, starting to declaim a passage from *Hamlet* in the manner of the great Irish tragedian of his boyhood days—Barry Sullivan. I noticed when he finished that this effort had tired him, so I felt it was time to take my leave.

Our business was concluded and a contract, in Shaw's own writing, promised in the morrow's mail. We made our way to the hall and, as we passed the bathroom, the old boy had the courtesy to enquire, "Do you want to pump ship?" G.B.S. insisted on walking bareheaded in the rain to open the gates of the drive and, preceding Blanche and me into the lane, he stood giving traffic signals like a policeman on point duty. As our car drove past him, he waved a cheery good-bye to us; and when we were about to turn the corner, I looked back and saw him leaping a large puddle in the road. "I do wish he'd stop that!" said Blanche. "He's already broken one leg doing his jumps."

By the time the Atlantic Ocean once again separated us, I realised that I

MAN AND SUPERMAN

had to do something about the play's inordinate length. If the so-called Hell scene was to be included in my production, the play would take longer than the Entirety *Hamlet*, which meant that a matinee and a night performance on the same day would be out of the question, and the loss of revenue quite disastrous. G.B.S. had told me that the play always failed if the Hell scene was omitted, but that was nonsense, as we were about to prove. Nevertheless, I thought it prudent to anticipate critical censure by having a printed slip inserted in the opening-night programs (white for the orchestra seats, and green for the balcony) inviting members of the audience to indicate their desire, or otherwise, to witness a special matinee presentation of the missing scene, if it could be arranged. This spiked any guns that might have been levelled at us for omitting it in the first place, and the critics dutifully filled in their affirmative ballots as did the majority of the audience. The response was so good that we kept up the practice and, although the matinee was never given, my staff were overjoyed to have been given a valuable mailing list of supporters who could be kept abreast of this and all subsequent productions.

Where my business sense failed me, however, was when I overlooked the possibility of extending my licence with Shaw to include a possible presentation of the Hell scene as a separate entertainment at a later date. In any case, I doubt that I would have had the brilliant idea of staging it as a reading, as did Paul Gregory. There being virtually no action in what amounts to an entire play in itself, reading it was the logical way of treating the Hell scene, especially when the performers were Charles Boyer, Charles Laughton, Cedric Hardwicke, and Agnes Moorehead. Although the scene is really the meat of the play, full of philosophical argument and witty though it is, it seems an intrusion into the sparkling comedy of the rest of the play. That one critic didn't object to the omission was made clear by a knowledgeable out-of-town reviewer, Elliot Norton, in the *Boston Post*:

> Man and Superman succeeds enormously as a gay comedy. It is gay.
> But it is also propaganda for an idea which many playgoers might still
> consider alarming, if they understood. Not laughter, but the
> philosophy of the Superman is the deep purpose of the play. Not girl-
> chases-boy but the Life Force working through Creative Evolution. The
> Life Force strains to unite strong men and women and when it asserts
> its strength through a woman, as in Man and Superman, the man had
> better submit. Even though he runs away, as does Jack Tanner, the
> women will get him, not out of love, not out of romantic desire, but
> because the blind and powerful Force will not be denied.

1947–1963

Shaw used to complain that the theatregoers persisted in laughing at his plays so uproariously that they ignored the serious purpose of their themes. He really had only himself to blame for so sugarcoating his philosophic and political pills that he obscured the specifics they contained. *Man and Superman*, however, judging by the chilly reception it received initially in New York in 1905, would seem to have been an exception. The outspoken exposure of the huntress woman and the hunted male was no laughing matter at the turn of the century; but by the time we started rehearsing the play in 1947 it had become a period piece and its mores had a quaintness about them that was irresistibly comic. As director, I hammered at my fellow actors to play with the utmost gravity, letting the absurdities of the situations speak for themselves—comedians yes, but straight-faced ones at all times. As actor I had set myself the difficult task of erasing my classical past, an obstacle I was not entirely successful in negotiating, as witness Brooks Atkinson's review in the *New York Times*:

> As the voluble Tanner, who considerably outsmarts himself, Mr. Evans is at his best in a holiday mood. The speeches are long and the phrasing complex, but Mr. Evans keeps them refreshingly intelligible and he does not forget that "Man and Superman" is very funny stuff. To people familiar with Mr. Evans' career, there are shadows of Shakespeare chasing across the performance, particularly in the scenes between Tanner and his chauffeur. Perhaps it is only the architecture of Mr. Evans' performance which makes them seem like a Shakespearean monarch bantering words with a jester. Or perhaps this is the way Shaw conceived them. Whatever the reason, they are thoroughly enjoyable in the wittiest play in town.

Richard Watts said in the *New York Post*, October 9, 1947:

> Mr. Evans' production is excellent, going in for just enough stylization and period artificiality to add to the humor without making it seem burlesque, and his acting has a delightful note of mock-seriousness that is never overdone.

John Chapman's review in the *News* made a reference to the play's ending, an ending that became the subject of a reprimand I received from the author. Chapman wrote:

> As the spokesman, Mr. Evans carries a huge conversational burden with the greatest of bounce and ease. When, finally, he succumbs to a woman after a hopeless struggle, and the curtain comes down on her line, "Never mind her, dear. Go on talking," one feels like echoing her plea.

MAN AND SUPERMAN

Shaw's stage direction at that point is "Universal laughter." In practice, I was pretty sure no such response would be forthcoming from the audience even though the actors were splitting their sides. In fact, the customers were more likely to think the stage manager had jumped the gun on lowering the house curtain. I therefore arranged for Ann to be seated on a garden swing during Tanner's long tirade about marriage. Swinging almost imperceptibly to begin with, she increased the pendulum motion as Tanner grew progressively more vehement. By the time he reached the peak of his oration, she was laughing uncontrollably, her heels and her lacy skirts flying gaily in the air. Obviously that departure pleased Mr. Chapman, but the same could not be said of G.B.S.

A nosey English actor named Esmé Percy, who at some time had played Tanner himself, reported the innovation to Shaw. In nothing flat I received another of the famous postcards, which read: "Someone tells me you have changed the stage business at the end of my play. Why don't you stick to acting about which you are supposed to know something. My plays are ruined by duffers like yourself who think they know better than I do. G.B.S."

In my capacity as an actor-manager it is not surprising that I should have a soft spot for a universal characteristic of drama critics—their penchant for seeing their names in big print. It is one thing for them to byline their reviews week by week, but quite another to see themselves quoted in a half-page advertisement in all the principal newspapers. In attending the first night of a new play, presumably they come to the theatre with an open mind, but in the case of revivals of famous plays it is only human for them to do a bit of homework in advance, making sure that they have a pithy comment in readiness should the revival please them. The pressures of a close deadline are apt to prompt the critic to jot down two such quotations on separate pieces of paper—one a rave, the other a pan. Provided he doesn't get the papers mixed up by the time he reaches his desk, this can bring joy to the heart of the producer, and, as in the case of *Man and Superman*, result in a busy box office. Here are some typical extracts from the various reviewers:

> Wittiest play on Broadway [*Life* magazine]
> Superb Comedy [Barnes, *New York Herald-Tribune*]
> A comedy of superlative brilliance [Chapman, *New York News*]
> Vastly entertaining [Atkinson, *New York Times*]
> Resounding hit, so brilliant and so fresh [Watts, *New York Post*]
> The gayest, the brightest, the most original and delectable comedy to
> be seen in New York [Brown, *Saturday Review*]

Although she couldn't be quoted with the first-night reviewers, since Rosamund Gilder's article was in *Theatre Arts*, a monthly magazine, my sternest critic had this to say:

Setting aside for a moment his Shakespearean mantle, Mr. Evans has settled into the comfortable, if unromantic, garb of modern man. He finds himself very much at ease in a play which he has both produced and directed himself and which provides him with a leading role that he can take easily in his stride. John Tanner's witty diatribes against the female of the species flow easily from his lips, occasionally with a singing note that is a reminder not only of Mr. Evans' long service in the employ of the Bard but also of the fact that Mr. Shaw is not himself averse to Bardian periods. Mr. Evans treats the whole affair with a light touch. He is gay, detached, indifferent, but always exact.

It was left to a member of the Cincinnati audience to pour cold water on all the plaudits, when we were touring, following the 295th performance in New York. I had just made an appeal for the March of Dimes and, descending from the stage to the auditorium, I thrust a collection box before a substantial-looking dowager. She made a handsome contribution, but, while stuffing the money into the receptacle, made this remark: "Mr. Evans, I want you to know that I went twice to see this play when it was done in New York over forty years ago and I hated it on both occasions. I've come to see it again and I still hate it just as much." As long as there are people like that in this world, I thought, even an invalid as fabulous as the theatre may have hopes of eventual recovery.

The touring aggregation trouped its way through some 15,000 miles of the United States, playing fifty-seven cities in thirty-two states. It was during this pleasurable jaunt, loyally supported by Fanny Rowe and Malcolm Keen, that our publicity man discovered that the 93rd birthday of G.B.S. was approaching. Though with much misgiving, I wrote to the Sage asking whether he would consent to taking part in a transatlantic radio interview to celebrate the occasion and to mark the longest run that any of his plays had achieved anywhere in the world—575 performances in all. It was postcard time once more:

> I don't like birthdays and you shouldn't give interviews. Those people are paid for doing them while you fill in the time. In any case, you are ruining me. For every hundred pounds you send me, I have to give the Government one hundred and twenty. I can't wait for the beastly play to come off. G.B.S.

There was a note of irony in that communication, that one of the world's foremost proponents of Socialism should be hoist with his own capitalist petard. But he had his wish when the "beastly play" made its farewell two-week engagement at the New York City Center in May 1949.

2. DIAL M FOR MURDER

One would think that by the time we played our farewell engagement of *Man and Superman* at the New York City Center, I would have become proof against siren songs in any key, but such was not the case. During our brief City Center appearance I became easy prey to the wiles of the governing board of that struggling institution. Artistically the opera and ballet companies had grown in strength, but there was no continuity of dramatic attractions. The audiences were composed mainly of young people whose pockets couldn't stretch to the Metropolitan Opera House or Broadway, and I became convinced that drama should be represented on a more solid footing. I was happy to advise the board how to go about this, never dreaming that they would take it seriously or that I had unwittingly opened a trapdoor.

The breath was barely out of my mouth before the City Center board made me the Honorary Artistic Supervisor of a new Drama Department, with total control of its operation. The prospect was terrifying, but I had to admit that the American theatre had been so good to me that it was about time I did something for it by way of acknowledgement. By then my associates had become scattered all over the place, but George Schaefer, true to form, agreed to throw in his lot. Between us, we managed to round up other past stalwarts, enough to form a skeleton staff.

Our policy was to present revivals of established works for short engagements and to decorate the billing with equally established performers. That enabled us to offer prominent Broadway and Hollywood actors a chance to exercise their artistic limbs for a spell short enough to avoid interference with their serious business of earning a living. There was a ready response from the acting profession, even though everyone received only Equity minimum salaries for their pains. Thanks to that spirit of cooperation, we had enough money in the till to build our own scenery and to mount the productions quite impressively, but it took months to get everything organised before it became a reality. At the prevailing cheap prices of admission, we knew precisely what our maximum income could be to meet operating costs, and I was determined that we should either make it pay its way or throw in the sponge.

My strict Nonconformist religious upbringing had taught me that it was wicked to beg, borrow or steal, and, although I think I have obeyed those precepts as far as personal enrichment is concerned, when it came to a cause like City Center I had no scruples. In the beginning, I deluded myself that the "Honorary" in my title indicated that my job would be something of a sinecure, instead of which I found it was very much like being in the army once more—the watchdog and the enabler, while my staff had most of the

1947–1963

satisfaction. Much of my time had to be devoted to cajoling actors into believing that we were worthy of their trust and that there was a chance that some of the productions might be transferred to Broadway. To practice what I preached, I had to assure the disciples of my missionary work that I had given an undertaking to appear myself in at least one production each season. However, having been absent from Broadway for eight months of touring, it was high time I was seen again in the regular commercial theatre; so, apart from promising to make an opening night dedicatory speech at the City Center, my appearance on its stage would have to wait a while.

For an actor whose reputation has been founded entirely on his appearances in costume of one sort or another, his first step into the present day is not necessarily along any primrose path. *Man and Superman* had made a fortunate halfway house en route, but my total turn from ancient to modern had still to be negotiated. That the time had come for such a change was inescapable for reasons of theatre economics if nothing else. Nevertheless, I was anxious to make the transition as gentle as possible for my faithful public. I therefore decided to produce a double bill of two playlets by Terence Rattigan, *Harlequinade* and *The Browning Version*. The first of these was a spoof of a pair of quarrelsome actors rehearsing the balcony scene from *Romeo and Juliet* (presumably a takeoff of those superb artists, Lynn Fontanne and Alfred Lunt), a situation that would be a reminder of my own classical past but in jocular terms. It was *The Browning Version*, however, that I wanted to get my teeth into in order to demonstrate that I was acceptable as a contemporary individual. In what is unquestionably one of Rattigan's finest achievements, I played the sensitive, withdrawn professor of Greek, torn between his dedication to the classics and his carnal and voluptuous wife (Edna Best). We were both of the opinion that the sharp contrast between the tragedy of blighted marriage and the cartoon treatment of the balcony scene would stretch our powers of deception to their limit. We might not be entirely convincing, but, by golly, we were determined to be *different!* Not, alas, in the opinion of one good lady, who, not realising she was witnessing two entirely unrelated entertainments, was heard saying as she left the theatre, "I can't understand why that dear old professor ever decided to go on the stage."

Apart from my admiration of *The Browning Version*, I thought it would be a salutary experience to be directed by Peter Glenville, who had directed the successful London production. As the time came for me to move towards contemporary drama, the time was also approaching when playwrights would insist on nominating their own choices for directors—and inevitably my own preferences would not necessarily prevail. Peter had already proved his worth to the plays, besides being a charming person; so over he came from London for conferences and casting. I feared our first meeting might be strained because I was determined to extract from him his solemn word that at no time during the rehearsals would he refer to the performance of Eric Portman, who had triumphed in the part in London. "I wouldn't *dream* of it—absolutely out of the question!" he assured me. On the first day of rehearsals, however, when I uttered my opening line, "Is Taplow here?" Peter pounced on me, saying, "Yes. But that isn't the professor's character in the least." From then on I became his obedient slave and puppet. I can't pretend that I enjoyed the experience, but I surprised myself by being able to adapt to that school of acting and to bring it off satisfactorily. The press were somewhat divided, and it soon became obvious that Broadway theatregoers had little appetite for a double bill, so up went the shutters after twelve weeks. I hated to give in, particularly since it was wonderful to be working again with Edna, for whom my heart still missed a beat after an interval of nineteen years. In those days I had played a very different professor—Professor Agi, her fencing instructor— to her delightful Princess. We recalled a performance of a love scene in *The Swan* when, in addressing her by her title, I employed an excess of plosive on the letter "P," resulting in a direct hit in her eye. The little minx had a fit of uncontrolled giggles, which she hid behind her feathered fan while I stood helpless, like the original spitting image.

Whenever I found myself in the professional doldrums, my motto seems to have been "Back to Bernard Shaw." This time it was also back to City Center for a production of *The Devil's Disciple* and a reunion with Peggy Webster on the directorial throne. According to *Who's Who*, for some inexplicable reason the play had not been seen in New York since 1923. The only possible explanation seemed to be that the leading part of Dick Dudgeon (the Disciple of the title) is not as showy as the witty role of General Burgoyne, and if one were up against competition in that part, as I was, that was reason enough to pass it by. I managed to prevail upon Dennis King to join us, and what an irresistible, sly, and richly impudent performance he gave! Once again, my situation as manager outweighed any feeling I might have of envy, since anything that was good for the show was good for the books. The trial scene is Shaw at his very best, and it was almost a pleasure to be condemned to the gallows by such a gentlemanly redcoat. It was not surprising that the production was snapped up for Broadway by producer Richard Aldrich (Gertrude Lawrence's husband), and given a respectable run at the Royale Theater.

We opened there on a Monday night. On Tuesday I played with a temperature of 103 degrees, with my doctor in attendance. On Wednesday morning he informed the management he had forbidden me to play at that day's matinee, and, probably, for the remainder of the week. In my entire career up to then I had never missed a performance, but I was too ill with a particularly virulent flu bug to protest. As is the way with the theatre, the miracle happened. My understudy was totally unprepared and quite incapable of going on in my place, but to have to close the show during its opening week would have jeopardized its future. My assistant, Emmett Rogers, whose only familiarity with my part was gained from hearing me say my lines during rehearsals, nobly volunteered to go on stage in my stead, and by some magical inspiration he got through the matinee. That inspiration came in part from the capacious fireplace in the Dudgeon household, where Peggy Webster crouched, script and flashlight in hand, ready to rescue with a prompting if needed. Emmett received a standing ovation and well he deserved it. It was ironic that the unprepared understudy, James Daly, went on to Hollywood fame and fortune while Emmett remained loyally with Maurice Evans Productions, Inc. for several years to come.

Touring once more, this time as a hired hand, under the management of the West Coast producers, Lewis and Young, our halfway house en route to Los Angeles was Central City, Colorado. As usual, cast changes had to be made, since neither Victor Jory nor Diana Lynn could stay beyond the New York run. With Emmett trying his hand as director, we rehearsed in the famous Opera House of that restored gold-mining village way up in the skies above Denver. We were to be part of their summer festival, alternating with ballet and opera, and although the altitude of over 6,000 feet caused us some discomfort, it was nothing compared to what the dancers and singers had to endure. The ballet company members had to be given oxygen before their entrances, and Mozart would hardly have recognised the breakneck tempi of his opera. Nevertheless, despite puffing and blowing, we thoroughly enjoyed the unusual surroundings. One novelty at the house I stayed in was a down-the-garden-path two-holer perched on top of an abandoned mine shaft—up-draughty!

It was springtime in Los Angeles when, much to my surprise, I was offered my first concrete Hollywood film job. I had flirted with previous blandishments in the past and at one low moment in my career had actually signed my future away to Hollywood. At that time Irving Thalberg was the boy-genius of the Metro-Goldwyn-Mayer factory and, as the husband of Norma Shearer, possessed a decorative property coveted by the studio. They therefore consented to his putting actors of his own choosing under personal contract to himself instead of their being tossed into the talent pool.

This arrangement was much sought after by performers because Thalberg, besides being a talented motion-picture producer, had something of a Napoleonic personality. Those whom he hand-picked *had* to succeed in order to satisfy his own ego. Irrespective of monumental budgetary excesses and miles of discarded film littering the cutting-room floor, he would not rest until he got the one "take" that would enhance his reputation. My agent, Leland

Hayward, finally convinced me that an offer to become one of the favoured few was a once-in-a-lifetime opportunity, and I had to admit that the names already under the exclusive contract were most impressive. I was assured that, besides playing Napoleon opposite Greta Garbo in *Conquest* and Louis XVI opposite Norma Shearer in *Marie Antoinette*—parts that eventually fell to Charles Boyer and Robert Morley, respectively—if all these prominent performers (Charles Laughton was another one) had seen fit to sign up, who was I to say No? Then the unforeseen happened with the premature death of Thalberg. Since I barely knew the man, I'm afraid my chief concern was in regard to my personal contract with him. MGM claimed that the Thalberg stable automatically became their property, conferring on them all rights to my motion-picture future. I wasn't about to agree to this because it would put me into the rat race with hundreds of actors already controlled by the studio. Their lawyers kicked up an unholy row, but I said good-bye to Hollywood and went my way.

Fortunately for me, Hollywood memories are notoriously short, so that thirteen years after the Thalberg affair no one at MGM realised I had once earned their censure. I accepted the lead opposite Ethel Barrymore in their remake of *Kind Lady* and made pretend I'd never set foot in the studio before. Amongst those so blissfully ignorant of my earlier misdemeanour was the boss man himself, Louis B. Mayer. His executive, Benny Thaw, and I had just signed and exchanged the *Kind Lady* contracts when Benny asked whether I had ever met the boss. I said I'd never had the pleasure, whereupon I was ushered into the inner sanctum and there behind acres of desk sat a gnome-like figure. He jumped to his feet and, offering his hand—which I had difficulty reaching across the mahogany barrier—he proceeded to shower praises on my head. He had seen everything I had done in New York and was delighted to meet me. In the midst of this effusiveness, Benny Thaw mentioned that I was to start working for MGM on the morrow. Never has a torrent of cordiality been so suddenly dammed. Next morning, when we passed each other in a corridor of a studio building, a nod and a grunt was all he vouchsafed to what was another of his slaves.

Angela Lansbury was also in the picture, and I had great fun playing the villain of the piece. I seemed fated to tread on MGM's toes, however, Ethel became ill when we were two-thirds through the filming, so that shooting had to be suspended. That put me in a fix as I had a guaranteed termination date in my contract, which made it possible for me to have promised City Center previously to be with them for a two-week revival of *Richard II*. By the time this obligatory date arrived, Ethel was recovering and shooting was about to be resumed. I had to tell the front office that it was my bounden duty to keep faith with the City Center and that there was nothing for it but to extend the

1947–1963

picture's suspension until I was free to return from New York. What a hullabaloo that caused, including an offer by MGM to bear the expense of City Center's cancelling the *Richard II* engagement—a compromise I rejected out of hand.

I flew back to Hollywood after the closing of *Richard II* on a Sunday night at the center, knowing that I had to start filming early on Monday morning. Sleep eluded me aboard the plane, so to be sure I was ready for bed on arrival, I took a sleeping pill. That the soporific had done its work was demonstrated when, shortly after dawn, I was apologetically shaken awake by an officer of the MGM Fire Department, who had climbed a ladder to gain access to my bedroom through a window. It seemed that the blowing of horns and the ringing of doorbells had failed to coax me from my groggy slumber. It was a sleepy-eyed actor who reported for work that morning. I explained that the house I had rented had once been occupied by Judith Anderson and that the spirit of Mrs. Danvers had played tricks on me. "Oh, yeah?" was the typical response of those doubting Thomases.

The year 1951 was not exactly a banner one for me, because I was mainly occupied with the administrative duties at City Center besides being elected to the council of the Actor's Equity Association. The union was in poor shape at that time, the council being dominated by chorus boys and girls who were concerned only with that branch of the entertainment field. Their beefs about wages and working conditions were supported by a coterie of more mature discontented members who were themselves out of work. They jointly formed a pressure group within the council to force through policies that were at variance with the wishes of the fully assembled governing body. Their tactic was to talk items on the agenda into the ground, knowing that if they could string out the afternoon meetings long enough, the working actors would have to depart for their theatres, leaving the field open to the pressure group to win its motions.

One result of this strategy was the passage of a total ban on the importation of alien actors, which, even when it was modified later on to a percentage ratio, was nevertheless a severe handicap to producers aiming to present plays of foreign or classical origin. Having myself joined the ranks of the unemployed, I felt it incumbent upon me to sit out these meetings to the bitter end, constantly raising my voice in protest. Before I knew what was happening to me, the president of the union, Ralph Bellamy, was whisked off to Hollywood and I found myself appointed vice president. During Ralph's extended absence, I had to chair all those dreary meetings besides putting in regular hours at the union's office.

During this same period I was co-opted by the Board of Governors of the Actors' Fund of America to join their charitable work; after Actors' Equity it

DIAL M FOR MURDER

was a model of sober and efficient administration. In addition to operating a home for the aged, the Actors' Fund is able to assist the needy and to endow hospital beds for the sick. Another most unusual benefit comes from a bequest made years ago, which designated its purpose to be to supply shoes to actors pounding the pavements in search of work—a very popular and much-called-upon charity to this day.

The demands of these public services put a heavy strain on my personal life, since they required my constant presence in the city. For that reason, and because I had found it impossible to find domestic help content to endure the remoteness of Mountbrook, there was nothing for it but to exchange the estate for a more accessible and manageable country weekend cottage and to become principally a city dweller. Emmett set about hunting for suitable premises, eventually discovering the ideal solutions. An old carriage-house on West 10th Street in Greenwich Village was the perfect answer to the city requirements. It provided garage space and, on the floor above that (which in days past had been the hayloft), office accommodations. On the top floor were spacious living quarters and a terrace for the dogs and the soot. Leaving the last commodity behind, with Emmett at the wheel, we'd all pile in the car and make for the cottage at Wilton, Connecticut, where later on Emmett was able to pursue his hobby as a breeder of West Highland White Terriers under the name of Whipstick Kennels. Maurice Evans Productions, Inc., having become dormant, his main assignments as my personal assistant were practically at a standstill, but the dogs kept him from fretting unduly and there were still scripts to be read and ideas to be tossed around as to what my next professional move would be.

By December 1951 City Center was clamouring for me to make another appearance there, suggesting that I try my hand at Ibsen. Morton Da Costa and I put our heads together and decided that the least indigestible of the Norwegian's dramas was *The Wild Duck*, an opinion, I regret to say, that was not to be shared by the theatrical gourmets. I remembered seeing a production in London in 1930 when an actor named Milton Rosmer gave a very florid performance in the part of Hjalmar Ekdal, which, I fear, unconsciously led me to model my interpretation on his. My lapse into being a copycat resulted in a chorus of spiteful meows from the critics, who declared that I had fallen flat on my face. To this day I don't really know what went wrong. "Tec" Da Costa directed an excellent cast, which included Mildred Dunnock, Diana Lynn, and Kent Smith, and George Schaefer's choice of young Peter Larkin as the scenic designer was inspired. Of course, an actor can always dream up an alibi in the face of adverse notices, and I was no exception. The City Center schedule demanded that our opening take place on Christmas Eve, a circumstance which, from my point of view, could conveniently explain the critical thumbs-down. It is cause for suspicion that, whereas my staff has religiously saved all my positive clippings, the negative *Wild Duck* ones are nowhere to be found.

Although I had reason to bemoan my personal chastisement, the Theatre Company of City Center was by then firmly established and had built up a large following of regular subscribers; so, despite my red face, our financial column was of a different hue. It was not on account of that acting hiccup that I turned over the Theatre Company operation (including the forum for fledgling playwrights) to George Schaefer and his staff at this point. Following my conviction that unless such institutions pay their own way they don't deserve to exist, we not only came out even but made a handsome profit during my tenure of office. However, this happy state of affairs was largely due to the willingness of actors to work for a pittance.

It had been my understanding with the Board of Directors that should we ever be operating at a profit, the money would be earmarked towards increasing the prevailing miserable salaries. However, both the ballet and opera companies were in such desperate financial straits that the board withdrew from its undertaking. This left me in the hypocritical position of continuing to plead poverty when it was quite obvious to the actors that the Theatre Company was by then demonstrably able to remunerate them properly. I felt I could not face another season under those conditions and I handed in my resignation. In retrospect I am glad that, indirectly, I played a small part in the survival of what has become a splendid ballet company, and that I am able to count among many souvenirs a commemorative cigarette box, bearing the inscription: "To Maurice Evans with the personal gratitude of the Board of Directors of the City Center of Music and Drama Inc. and the deep appreciation of the entire City of New York."

It suited my situation that I was once again beckoned to Hollywood, this time to play Caesar in producer Gabriel Pascal's film of *Androcles and the Lion*. The "hungry Hungarian" was under contract to Howard Hughes at R.K.O. with an open completion date. Consequently, he lived in great style in Beverly Hills with no intention of starting the film until he was driven to it by murderous threats. I was the last actor to be signed up, but the others—Jean Simmons, Alan Young, Robert Newton, and Victor Mature—had been sitting idle for months at a time, drawing salaries with no more idea of a starting date than had "Gaby" himself. Those were the days, in both England and America, when a Mittel-Europa accent was the open sesame to the coffers of the Prudential Insurance Company and others for the financing of film productions. Gaby had an additional brand of magic all his own. Shaw's secretary, Blanche Patch, had told me years earlier that Gaby knocked at the door at Ayot St. Lawrence one memorable morning, to have it opened by Shaw himself. Whereupon

DIAL M FOR MURDER

Gaby prostrated himself on the doorstep and proceeded to kiss the sandal-shod feet of the dramatist. Somewhat embarrassed by this show of affection, Shaw drew him inside the hallway out of the sight of passersby. Drawing a half crown from his pocket, Gaby declared in his halting English that it represented the last of his capital, but that he would die happy in the knowledge that his ambition to set eyes on his adored author had at last been crowned.

Blanche explained that this extravagant display took place shortly after the death of Mrs. Shaw and that, in a fit of loneliness, G.B.S. invited the Hungarian to help himself to a spare room in the house. There was a smile on the face of the tiger when, a week or so later, the half crown nestled in his pocket side by side with a contract conferring upon him the film rights to several of Shaw's plays. The successful *Pygmalion* was one result of that extraordinary transaction and *Androcles* was to follow, but with Gaby very much as king of the castle. At least he thought he was until I joined the pensioners, when he really had no excuse for delaying the shooting any longer. He was supposed to direct the film in addition to producing it, but by the time I arrived the front office had called in an outside director, named Chester Erskine, with orders to get something in the can pronto.

To make sure Erskine was not interfered with, Gaby was forbidden to set foot on the sound stages, and guards were posted at the doors to enforce the ban. It was rather pathetic to hear him engaged in conversation with the horse wranglers, outside the barred studio doors, telling them that the design of the Roman saddles was inaccurate and that, having been an officer in the Hungarian Royal Guard, he knew whereof he spoke. The only time he was invited to visit the set was the day an untamed lion from the zoo was scheduled to appear in a chase scene. Seeing that the cameras were all behind wire fences and the director on a crane overhead, poor Gaby realised he was being subjected to a malicious joke on the part of the front office and he beat a hasty retreat.

Androcles was, for me, fun to be in except for the necessity of having my hair curled each morning a la Romana. There was no escaping the hairstylist even on the days when I was on camera in long shot for only one fleeting second. I confess I was quite testy on the occasion when, having mutely endured the curling iron, the production assistant told me to go home because the scheduled scene had been scrubbed for that morning. The explanation was that Bobby Newton had spent the whole night on the set reciting Shakespeare to the night watchman. "Relax" is the command most often given to the actors on any film set, and on this occasion Bobby had obeyed it somewhat too literally, no doubt quaffing from time to time something to soothe his vocal chords.

I did my share of relaxing by reading in my dressing room a novel that

1947–1963

Emmett had sent me with an eye to its potential in play form—its title, *The Teahouse of the August Moon*. The lesson taught me by my youthful acquaintance with *Journey's End* was that a substantial time lapse must occur following the cessation of hostilities before the subject of warfare is acceptable as theatrical fare. In the case of *Teahouse*, although the protagonists were the military government, on the one hand, and its oriental subjects, on the other, Vern Sneider's novel dealt amusingly not with war itself but with its fruits, both sweet and sour. The book had instant appeal for me because the story revolved around an offbeat character, Sakini, whom I dearly wanted to play in the theatre. Whether or not the novel could be successfully dramatised remained to be seen, but I was sufficiently optimistic to arrange to acquire the dramatic rights from the author.

It was obvious that an adaptation of *Teahouse* would take many months to become reality and that, apart from the then current *Androcles* film, I had no theatre prospects to fill the gap. I therefore took off for London when the filming was finished to survey any plays suited to my personal need. Amongst them was *The Little Hut* starring Robert Morley, which was nearing the end of a long run in the West End. I was familiar with Bob's eccentric behaviour, but even I was flabbergasted when I entered his dressing room after the show and he opened his arms, saying, "Welcome, Sir Arthur!" Seeing my bewilderment, he explained that when he had received my card at the stage door it had struck him that here was the answer to his and Alexander Korda's prayer. They had been searching for months, with no success, to find an actor who resembled Sir Arthur Sullivan enough to match Bob's look-alike to W. S. Gilbert. But for this vital piece of casting, the film *Mr. Gilbert and Mr. Sullivan* was ready to proceed, so I was immediately hired and had barely time to make a quick round trip to New York before shooting began.

A slight delay occurred, however, owing to some hassle with British Equity, which turned out to be most fortuitous. It gave me a free weekend to visit an old friend of my Cambridge Festival Theatre days, at his Elizabethan cottage in Kent—Rodney Millington. He had a group of guests on that sunny spring day, amongst them an actor, new to me, named Emrys Jones. Emrys was rehearsing for a play at London's equivalent of an off-Broadway theatre—situated cheek by jowl with Buckingham Palace and known as the Westminster. Rodney's guests were sprawled out on the grass after a typical Sunday roast-beef-and-veg luncheon, and Emrys, instead of studying his part, had fallen into a deep sleep with his script half concealed under his recumbent form. My curiosity aroused, I eased the script from beneath him and, opening it, read the title page: *Dial M for Murder*. Even a cursory leafing through the manuscript intrigued me no end—so much so, that I begged to be allowed to finish reading it in bed that night.

DIAL M FOR MURDER

I was jubilant about the play and Emrys's part in it, and determined then and there to be the first in line to obtain the American performing rights. There turned out to be a snag in that line of thought, however. Unable to find an interested producer in the past, the author, Frederick Knott, had resigned himself to allowing it to be seen on television. An agent of Alex Korda's saw the television production and persuaded his employer to buy the screen rights to it. In doing so a tricky clause in the contract included a proviso that any licences for a stage production of the play would include an undertaking to withdraw it from its run if and when the movie was ready for release. No West End management was willing to take the risk of producing under that condition, but a North Country business man, J. P. Sherwood, decided to take a chance with the very moderate cost of staging it at the Westminster, where it prospered for a long run.

Fortunately for me, knowing Korda as I did and being about to work in his Gilbert and Sullivan film, I was able to persuade him to waive the offending close-the-shop clause as far as the United States was concerned. Thereupon, I acquired the right to present the play in America, looking upon it mainly as a temporary substitute for the yet unassigned adaptation of *Teahouse*. Since I was to be tied up with filming I would not be able to attend the dress rehearsal of *Dial M*, so I brought Emmett back to England with me, from the States, to cover the occasion. He called me on the telephone after the event, full of enthusiasm about what he had seen. I authorised him to tell Mr. Sherwood that we had a deal and that I was ready to exchange contracts. The opening night at the Westminster was a triumph and on the following morning, after the reviews, the Shubert Brothers and the Theatre Guild were falling over each other to snap up the American rights, only to be told that we had beaten them to the post. It is one of the pleasures of doing business in England that a mere "handshake" over the telephone is regarded as sacred.

One doesn't associate performers with occupational hazards; actors seldom sprain a ligament, just as ballet dancers are usually immune to laryngitis, but the unexpected sometimes happens. It certainly did during my stint as Arthur Sullivan, for, of all the unlikely complaints, I was smitten with neuritis, which in musical circles is called "conductor's cramp," since it afflicts the arm and shoulder of its victim. It makes even the slightest movement of those regions indescribably painful, yet a great deal of my work in the movie consisted of conducting orchestras and massed choirs. The Shepperton Studio doctor made matters worse by his prognosis that the affliction would continue for six weeks and then disappear as quickly as it had begun. I protested that the filming would be over by then and that an instant cure was imperative. I refused to believe him when he said that there was no such relief known to the medical profession and decided to telephone my New York physician for confirmation. His advice was in the same dismal grin-and-bear-it vein, although he thought there was a faint chance that deep-ray diathermy might be beneficial. To my dismay no hospitals adjacent to the studio were permitted to use such equipment because it upset the radar at Heathrow airport. The nearest diathermy installation was finally traced to the Holloway Mental Hospital at Virginia Water. Although that institution is, strictly speaking, reserved for National Health unfortunates, the superintendent kindly agreed to arrange for me to receive treatment during my lunch breaks at the studio. That decision may have been influenced by the fact that my Arthur Sullivan mutton-chop whiskers and tailcoat would not prove untoward to other patients, themselves living in the past as Napoleon and so forth, but the permission depended on my signing the hospital register as an outpatient. I trust this abortive search for a cure is explanation enough to discourage any speculation about my sanity on the part of the writer of my obituary.

I had to admit that on my final day before the cameras, I myself suspected my wits had left me. It was a scene set in the Albert Hall with Sullivan conducting an oratorio (Queen Victoria's favourite), with full orchestra, organ, and a hundred voices. Before the conductor's podium rose a steep bank of sopranos and contraltos, all of them dressed alike in white, with blue sashes across their bosoms. After what seemed to be as many retakes as there were bosoms, the faces of the warblers were becoming familiar to me. However, towards the end of that exhausting day, I noticed a new face atop an extremely portly body in the very back row—a face that showed no lips in motion during the tremendous finale, thereby calling attention to herself. "You in the back, there, why weren't you singing?" shouted the director. From the mouth of the dumb chorister came the unmistakable voice of Robert Morley "Sorry, old chap, no ear for music"—and away he flounced, white dress, blue sash, outrageous blonde wig, and all.

Michael Korda, in his candid book, rates *Mr. Gilbert and Mr. Sullivan* as one of Uncle Alex's less notable productions, but in America, at least, it is constantly repeated on television, whereas Alex's more notable ones are less frequently shown. The expert team of Launder and Gilliat were responsible for the script, in the writing of which it is true they were much hampered by being contractually bound to stick to the outworn D'Oyly Carte traditional interpretation of all excerpts of the operettas. Bridgett D'Oyly Carte haunted the production to make sure that Martyn Green did exactly what he had been doing for ages, and Peter Finch, as D'Oyly Carte himself, had to pretend that he approved of the heavy-handed comedy conventions. During the filming, I was staying at the famous Great Fosters Hotel, and was driven back there from the studio each night nursing my sore arm in a sling. Dining in the hotel's unheated Elizabethan banqueting hall did little to alleviate my aches and pains. Neither did the noisy entrance of Margaret Rutherford, another of the hotel guests, add to my comfort. Stalking towards her table, she exclaimed, "Oh, what a terrible fug!" and threw all the windows within her reach wide open. One by one the rest of us slunk away for coffee in the cosier Buttery, cursing the ruggedness of Rutherford.

As the doctors had predicted, the sixth week went by and so did the neuritis—no more pain pills or sleeping draughts, and the luxury of shaving without assistance was restored, so life once more seemed worth living. I rented a little house in Chelsea to which I hesitantly lured the author of *Dial M for Murder*, Frederick Knott. In spite of its unqualified success in London, certain changes, I felt, had to be made for New York. The letter "M" in the title is a reference to the villain's Maida Vale telephone number and would be quite meaningless in America. This was overcome by changing the name of the wife, from what it had been in the London production, to "Margo." While we were about it, and because the writing emphasized the wife's helplessness, we thought she would gain more sympathy if she spoke with a foreign accent. To these changes Freddie Knott readily agreed. I was also bothered about the implausibility of the villain's former schoolchum agreeing to throttle the wife simply because of a threat that, if he refused to cooperate in the mayhem, a crime committed in their schooldays would be exposed. The outrageous felony occurred when the chum had sunk to the depths of stealing a trifling amount from the cash box of the school's football club—a revelation that would make him a social outcast for the rest of his life. That anyone could dream of such a dastardly act seemed to raise the hair of English audiences, but we couldn't envisage it disturbing any coiffures on Broadway; so a new form of blackmail, involving drug peddling, was suggested in the interest of believability.

Freddie Knott is a peculiarly meticulous writer. The fascinating web of clues, counterclues, and red herrings that so intrigued theatre audiences is typical of the way his mind works. Not surprising, really, because as a young man he had been a member of the Oxford-Cambridge tennis team that played the Harvard-Yale squad at Newport in 1937, and, like the form of his tennis-playing villain whom I portrayed in *Dial M*, every detail of his plot is placed with the deadly accuracy of a stroke in a championship tournament. Before consenting to drop the schoolboy cash-box motive, he characteristically demanded time to examine the alternative to satisfy himself that it contained no loopholes.

I had begun to be aware that, whereas no authors had been breathing down my neck as a producer of revivals, *Dial M* and *Teahouse* were going to make very different demands on my limited powers of diplomacy. I needn't have worried in the case of Freddie Knott, who was the first to admit that, since this was to be his trial run on Broadway, he would accept advice on

American tastes and colloquialisms. Even so, I was not 100 percent sure that the play would find favour. Its definite English atmosphere was apt to be a handicap, and the fact that it didn't fit into any of the conventional categories was awkward. "Melodrama" would certainly have been a misnomer (Webster's definition is "any romantic and sensational drama with both song and instrumental music interspersed"). "Whodunit" would have been equally misleading because *Dial M* makes no secret of the crime or the perpetrator. "Chiller" and "thriller" didn't apply; neither did "mystery." The best description we were able to find for the purpose of advance advertising was a "howdunit," the big HOW being how is the criminal going to explain his acts when his perfect murder goes wrong.

Even though my faithful followers were accustomed to witnessing my demise in Shakespearean roles (the stabbing of King Richard, Hamlet's fatal wounding, Macbeth's decapitation, and Romeo's suicide), I was by no means certain they would tolerate Tony Wendice's instigation of mayhem. Although he is the kingpin of the plot, the actor playing Tony has to look to his laurels, for it is the police inspector who has the really juicy part. Tony faces a double hazard when, as in our production, his opponent is played by an actor as winning as John Williams. His Inspector Hubbard was a marvellous invention of a seemingly bumbling character, beneath which, for all his waffling, was an acute investigator.

Looking for a director to guide me through the niceties of uxoricide, which I was about to perpetrate, I lighted upon Reginald Denham, an old hand at that kind of jollity. He had to his directorial credits the dark doings of *Rope* and *Ladies in Retirement*, making him the logical choice for our caper. However, I was faintly apprehensive when I learnt that many years previously, when piloting Vivien Leigh through her first film, he had the doubtful distinction of firing Emlyn Williams and Ralph Richardson as supporting players. One of the few advantages of being an actor-manager was that no such fate could befall me.

The fascination of acting in a play of this sort is the bond it creates between the actor and the audience even when, as in the case of *Dial M*, the husband's guilt is known to the spectator right from the start. Whether or not he will get away with the crime causes everyone "out front" to become a self-appointed detective. At one performance this spirit of audience-involvement almost caused a riot at the Plymouth Theatre. A man in the audience had obviously worked out in his mind exactly how the perfect murder plan was going to succeed and had boasted to his wife that he had it all down pat. However, just before the final curtain when the inspector reveals the true solution of the puzzle (making a pause for dramatic effect), the amateur sleuth, his infallible solution torn to shreds, was heard to say in a voice loud and clear:

DIAL M FOR MURDER

"Well, I'll be a son of a bitch!" It was that sort of reaction that made advance preparations for the production as much mischievous fun as the performances themselves.

It became a kind of game to outwit the audience's guesses, constantly leading them up the wrong garden path, but, at the same time, nurturing their sneaking hope that the villain would escape the noose. It was a freak success that we succeeded in creating the right atmosphere of tension in the play's final scene, and this was thanks to the low scenery budget allotted the London production. The Maida Vale flat was a rehash of scenery from another production stored in the basement. With a new coat of paint it served its purpose, except that the main door to the outside passageway had a three-inch gap at its bottom panel. This became apparent only when the lighting rehearsal was in progress. With the living room in total darkness, the electricians were rigging up lights in the passageway, whereupon a stagehand's feet could clearly be seen through the slit of light under the ill-fitting door. In both the London and New York productions this fluke effect was way beyond anything the author had envisaged and had everyone in the audience holding their breath. Would the villain fall into the trap awaiting him in the darkened room? The street door was heard to slam. Footsteps were heard in the passageway and a pair of feet seen under the door. They hesitated, then retreated slowly towards the street door. A change of mind and the footsteps returned to the flat entrance. That time and with a change of keys, I entered. The inspector switched on the lights, picked up the telephone, and said, "Give me Scotland Yard." *Curtain!*

The accidental footstep gimmick was wonderful and, of course, was to be retained for our production at the Plymouth Theatre. However, when our scenic workshop delivered the set they had carefully rectified what they scornfully decided was a mistake in our designer's measurements and provided a perfectly fitting door. Our own carpenter thought us crazy when he was ordered to saw three inches off the bottom panel, but was told it was not for him to reason why. Visual moments like these create a tension that in its special fashion cannot be duplicated in the movies. Even such a master as Alfred Hitchcock in his film version of *Dial M* entirely missed that tense moment. He followed the villain with his camera in the passageway, even had him leaving the house, then changing his mind, thus destroying the "will he, won't he?" excitement of the stage business caused by that strip of light under the door.

In all my experience there has been no play which so forcefully demonstrated, as did *Dial M*, the superiority of theatre over film in terms of collective entertainment. When I first saw it in London, everyone in the audience, including me, was rivetted to the happenings onstage; so much so that one could have heard the fabled pin drop. The expressions of mixed disbelief and puzzlement in the faces of the spectators were wonderful to behold, and the atmosphere in the playhouse was veritably electric. Whether or not we were going to capture the same mood with a Broadway public was a question that was answered on the morning of October 10, 1952, when the critics greeted us with a universal paean of praise, some samples of which follow:

Brooks Atkinson, *New York Times*:

Dial M for Murder is remarkably good theatre, tingles with excitement.

Richard Watts, *New York Post*:

Excellent fun . . . a good murder drama at last. The answer to our prayer.

Walter Kerr, *New York Herald-Tribune*:

It couldn't be more welcome. A happy cat-and-mouse melodrama which establishes a wonderfully innocent belief in macabre and complicated goings on.

Gilbert Coleman, *New York Mirror*:

Holds your attention like a vise.

And then the weeklies:

Life magazine:

A hit! More melodramatic excitement than Broadway has had in years.

Walter Winchell:

Terrific notices . . . terrific hit.

As if this weren't enough to bowl one over, Brooks Atkinson, in a mood rare for his customarily sober reviews, really let himself go on the matter of my own performance as the tennis-playing rotter:

In case the external world is not frightening enough, you are respectfully directed to Frederick Knott's "Dial M For Murder." It is a British thriller which Maurice Evans has had the wisdom to bring across the water and in which he gives a marvellously expert performance. You may not be thinking of Mr. Evans as a blackguard and murderer, and a swine objectionable in other aspects too. But there is no doubt that he has a talent for depravity that most of us have never suspected in one of the leading Shakespearean actors in the country. As the most loathsome husband in the world, Mr. Evans acts with a genuine intellectual agility that will get him into trouble if he behaves like this outside the theatre. The whole thing is a lark for Mr. Evans who is in fine fettle as the most odious of the theatre's monsters.

I was sorely tempted to break my rule of avoiding any contact with drama critics by writing a note to Mr. Atkinson saying, "Ah, you should have seen me as Iago, Mr. A.!"

Once the euphoria caused by that bonanza of bravos had worn off, my future was more than a little daunting to contemplate. Obviously I had been spoilt by my classical background, knowing that the drawing power of Shakespeare and Shaw, though substantial, was nevertheless limited. I had overlooked the fact that this guessing-game play was, in its genre, also a classic, but one that would seemingly have an insatiable appeal to the voracious appetites of theatregoers. Even so, it was impossible to guess that it would imprison me for two whole years—1952 through 1954—and that a tour at the end of the New York run was an inescapable obligation. This last consideration promised an elongation stretching into eternity, causing the peripatetic record of the *Man and Superman* tour to shrink into insignificance. I therefore decided, very soon after the New York production had settled down to what was patently going to be its long run, that if I were to retain my sanity I had to protect myself against the risk of being personally caught up in a repetition of our fortunes in Chicago. Consequently, we promptly set about organising a second company to have that honour. Two well-known British Hollywood personalities topped the bill—Richard Greene (Robin Hood to multitudes of viewers) and Alan Napier. They headed a cast of topnotch players. Although critically they were well received, the response at the box office was disappointing. There was nothing for it but to post the closing notice after the 100th performance, an action that automatically tossed back into my lap the responsibility of making the coast-to-coast tour myself.

Looking back on those days I find it hard to understand why I drove myself so mercilessly. If I had been hired to play *Dial M* under a management other than my own, I suppose I would have insisted on a termination clause in my contract and quit the show after a respectable time of service. Being self-employed, however, was a very different cup of tea. In the dual role of star and manager I had to bear in mind that the film rights were the property of Alexander Korda, a sweetener that in normal circumstances would have been participated in by my backers. Even with no film sale to look forward to, they had nothing to complain of. Being such a modest little show, the preproduction costs were recouped in four out-of-town tryout weeks, and the rest of the route was profit, profit all the way. Nevertheless, to make up for the lack of film income, it was necessary for us to continue the run through the summer months—a new experience for me.

The Plymouth Theatre was one of the few Broadway houses that boasted a primitive cooling system, making a summer run feasible. Huge blocks of ice were packed together somewhere in the ceiling above the audience, and electric fans circulated an arctic blast that was calculated to stiffen the necks of most of the customers. Backstage, however, we roasted in our dressing rooms and then shivered once the curtains went up. To add to my personal woes, to make my 10th Street house habitable under subtropical temperatures, it was necessary to tear the place apart to install a monster air-conditioning system throughout the premises. It was either that or revert to hotel living for the entire summer, but none of the suitable hostelries would consent to my newly acquired pair of West Highland Terriers as their guests. Thus, if my step into murder most foul did little to advance my artistic growth, it promoted a tolerable atmosphere in my bedroom. I was particularly grateful for this during the very hottest months when I had to stay on the job. To conform with Equity rules, I was bound to give each member of the cast, one by one, a two-week vacation. I, on the other hand, had no such surcease. The lucky devils came back from their holidays beautifully tanned and fresh as daisies to commiserate, somewhat hypocritically I thought, with their hardworking but wilted boss.

3. THE TEAHOUSE OF THE AUGUST MOON

After so many consecutive years of unremitting labour in the classical theatrical vineyard, the comparatively undemanding task of conniving at the murder of my wife eight times weekly was a welcome change of pace for me. Other interests were able to intrude; at the Wilton cottage I became both an avid gardener and a cook, the latter of which diversions continues to stand me in good stead. At the urging of Richard Rodgers and Oscar Hammerstein, I ventured, somewhat halfheartedly, into the troubled waters of international politics, becoming a member of a movement known as the United World Federalists. It aimed at a far more drastic breaking down of national and tribal barriers than were envisaged in the framing of the United Nations Charter and the establishment of a supreme world-governing body to replace the sovereignty of individual nations. No vetoes, no expeditionary forces, a common language and currency, and many other idealistic aims, which, had they taken root, would have made the world something other than it has become. For our pains, we were accused of being traitors to our flags and our heritages and, of course, the Soviets rejected us out of hand. Napoleon had the same trouble with his United States of Europe, so we were not alone in our defeat.

My assistant, Emmett Rogers, had another project in mind, which was a dramatisation of Elizabeth Charlotte Webster's novel about the troubles in South Africa, *The Ceremony of Innocence*. He had been working on it with Elinor Hugenir, who was a member of the New Dramatists group at City Center. I hated to discourage them both, but I felt sure the subject matter was not right for Broadway at that time. To assuage their hurt feelings, I commissioned Elinor to try her hand at adapting *Teahouse* and gave her three months to come up with a first draft, but the outline, which was all she had managed to produce by that time, made it sadly apparent that the job was beyond her. She was given her agreed fee for her valiant try and I was obliged to look elsewhere.

It so happened that the joyous time of year had come round when I was summoned to my accountant's office to sign my income-tax return—a duty which, to perform, I had the accountant guide my hand while my other hand was firmly clasped against my tightly closed eyes. Having been assured that the document was removed from my line of vision, I opened my eyes to see a duplicate of my own folder lying on the accountant's desk, obviously that of another client.

"Who's the next victim?" I asked.

"John Patrick," came the reply.

Bells rang in my head: "The chap who wrote a charming little play with a military background called *The Hasty Heart*?" I enquired.

"That's him," said the accountant.

In short, it was arranged for me to meet the author to sound him out about his possible interest in undertaking an adaptation of the novel I owned. At first he seemed reluctant to consider doing an adaptation of any sort; but on meeting him and hearing something of his firsthand knowledge of army matters, besides listening to his offbeat sense of humour, I felt pretty sure he was the right author to enlist.

Vern Sneider's novel, unlike some others, was by no means a "natural" for tranposition into dramatic form. It called for something far in excess of a scissors-and-paste job, so I was not surprised that John Patrick was hesitant to consider it. I thought it best not to press for an answer but, in the meantime, to enter into a little conspiracy with my favourite scene designer, Peter Larkin. Peter agreed to do rough sketches of the oriental background of the book, which, when he showed them to me, I recognised as being absolutely inspired. He had abjured realism and fantasised the entire atmosphere, not only of the native deprivations but of the United States military government itself.

Up to this point I hadn't really given much thought to the subject beyond being anxious to play the part of Sakini, the Okinawan interpreter and mischief-maker. Peter's imaginative approach put a whole new light on the project and had me bursting with enthusiasm. Instead of its being just another G.I.-joke play, it could become a work of art if the adaptor took his cue from Peter's whacky visual concept. I therefore took him and his portfolio of sketches with me when I was invited to John Patrick's farm in Suffern, New York, to discuss the project. Peter and I held our breath as he started to leaf through the sketches, casually at first, and then with a growing appreciation of their witty point of view. Okinawa was depicted as a sort of oriental wonderland—everything artistically distorted except for the building of the Teahouse in the last act—symbolic of the realisation of the islanders' dream and their victory over Western pragmatism. As a smile suffused the face of John Patrick and he began to chuckle, I felt pretty sure he had been won over even though he had warned us that he was far too busy to give a definite promise to tackle the dramatisation. I was able to assure him that, in my way, I was also fully occupied with *Dial M for Murder* and that there was, consequently, no hurry to start talking contracts.

For me this adaptation business was a totally new departure. Until then my skills, such as they were, had been to breathe new life into old material. Although my staff and I were inundated with new scripts by budding authors, none came our way that we considered worthy of production. Turning instead to the conversion of fiction into stage form proved to be a route beset with pitfalls and broken friendships. I found it quite impossible, in the case of derivative writing, to assess it with the same detachment as one did an original script. It was only natural that having been attracted by the basic novel one developed positive ideas as to what parts of it and what characters should be retained in the dramatisation. I was so used to having my own way with revivals, most of them by dead authors, that I found it frustrating to have to behave diplomatically with live ones, and in the case of *Teahouse* I had not then learnt my lesson. Ten months elapsed from the time I commissioned John Patrick to the actual delivery of his script—an interval that considerably alarmed me. However, I had been briefed by people who knew him not to be surprised by some erratic behaviour on his part. One such incident concerned his Suffern farm. He had applied to the local authorities for an additional electric power line to be installed. Interminable unfulfilled promises to comply so infuriated him that he was alleged to have armed himself with a chain saw with the intention of cutting down an elm tree on the front lawn of the residence of the president of the Rockland Light and Power Company. Outrageous, perhaps, if true, but I regarded the yarn as additional proof that temperament was just what made him so right for the unlikely goings-on in *Teahouse*.

Where we disagreed was over his failure to incorporate in his dramatis personae the sidesplitting character of Captain McClean, the army psychoanalyst and, incidentally, a fanatical proponent of organic gardening. I found this omission particularly strange because Patrick himself was an enthusiastic ecologist. Furthermore, the second half of his script didn't measure up to the delightful first part, and I was convinced that the absence of the offbeat analyst was the main reason. (The character was later reinstated at my insistence.) It's one thing to have a conviction, but quite another to convey it tactfully to a sensitive writer. I obviously lacked finesse to a distressing degree, with the result that in winning my point, which benefited the finished play, I had become Patrick's bête noire. Further consultation between us became impossible, and the day was saved only when George Schaefer agreed to accept the post of coproducer with me, and thenceforth George became my only means of communication with the dramatist. All playwrights, by virtue of their guild, have a standard contract conferring upon them certain rights of approval regarding casting, director, and so forth—a prerogative that in normal circumstances is largely ignored. Otherwise, of course, the producer is reduced to a mere cipher with no control of anything.

The Patrick-Evans feud threatened to reach proportions that would put my backers' investment at risk, and it became obvious that a campaign of obstruction was afoot aimed at inducing me to abandon the production. Needless to say, I wasn't about to do anything of the sort, but I was obliged to face the fact that my cherished ambition to play the Sakini role had gone with the hot wind of unseemly controversy. Only by my keeping very much in the background and giving George Schaefer full rein were we able to avoid a public scandal. As it turned out, I was able to save face quite truthfully, since *Dial M* continued to play to "standing room only." In any case, even if there had been no ruckus, I would not have been available to appear in *Teahouse* within the limited span of my options, and I sometimes wonder if that was what underlay the outbreak of hostilities.

There was no disagreement as to who should be the actor fortunate enough to play Sakini in my stead. We all thought David Wayne would be the ideal choice, and I signified my approval in a whisper to George, who set about checking on that fine actor's availability. After making a name for himself on Broadway (as the leprechaun in the musical *Finian's Rainbow* and as Ensign Pulver in *Mister Roberts*) he fell for the lure of Hollywood. Word had reached us that he was disenchanted with the way his studio was using him, a rumour that was hotly denied by his agents, the Shurr brothers. Grudgingly (with their eye on their 10 percent Hollywood commission) the New York Shurr agreed to send a script to brother Shurr in California, but prophesied that David would not be interested. Indeed, when we received no response from David we began to think he was lost to us. However, a woman friend of his, who happened to be an agent also, was about to make a trip to Hollywood and agreed to seek out his opinion of the script. She was not surprised when he told her that the script had never been delivered to him. This was quickly remedied, thanks to her intervention, when a second script was sent posthaste to David. As we had hoped, he lapped up the play and the part and, somehow or other, wheedled his way out of his film contract. We were fortunate, too, in obtaining the services of John Forsythe to play the young Captain Fisby—a long stretch from his later silver-haired mogul in *Dynasty*.

As director, the author nominated Robert Lewis and, although I was not familiar with his work for the Actors' Studio, there was no gainsaying the dramatist's preference. Bobby Lewis was in the unenviable position of having to placate his dramatist-sponsor, on the one hand, and me, on the other. It worried me when rehearsals got underway that, instead of getting on their feet, the actors sat in a circle while Bobby expounded brilliantly about the Stanislavski approach to acting. Since the bulk of the actors were either Japanese or Chinese, some of them having no English whatsoever, this seemed a curious way of directing a warm little comedy. It took some time for it to dawn upon me that this was strategy on the director's part to keep interference from the dramatist to the minimum, since, lacking any visible action, he had nothing concrete to criticise. It wasn't long, however, before the peaceful atmosphere was shattered. Without having owned up to it, Bobby and I had hired an oriental language expert to write authentic words to replace the ad libs called for by Patrick. He had the Orientals use the single word *Matamoto* when they were called on to voice crowd reactions (no doubt a device calculated to make future amateur and community productions easier to encompass), but we felt that it was a transparent convention unlikely to create the essential credibility of the Orientals. We felt strongly about this and, with Bobby backing me up, I decided to dig in my heels—and hang the consequences! It reached the height of absurdity when I was told that the adaptor had applied to the Board of Arbitrators to sit in judgement on his claim that by giving *Matamoto* its equivalent in a native tongue I had forfeited all rights to the play. Not surprisingly the board was unable to summon a quorum of arbitrators willing to consider such a preposterous brief, and that was that.

In such a disturbed atmosphere it was no wonder that the tryout in New Haven was extremely shaky. If the uncertainty about dialogue had been accompanied by similar shortcomings on the mechanical end of things, it could have resulted in a disastrous opening. However, George Schaefer protected the production valiantly by bringing from his City Center staff his wholly reliable stage manager and assistant, Tommy Sand. Two weeks in Boston were all that was needed to pull the show together, by which time it became obvious that we had a big hit on our hands.

The curtain rose at the Martin Beck Theatre on October 15, 1953, on

THE TEAHOUSE OF THE AUGUST MOON

what was to be hailed by the New York Critics Circle as "the season's best play" and to be selected for the Pulitzer Prize and the Tony Award. For the benefit of the critics, the opening-night performance was scheduled for an earlier hour than the regular time. Consequently the cheers and the applause had already taken place while I was still onstage a block away at the Plymouth. At the end of the performance I donned my Sunday best and strolled down the block to join the champagne party for the cast, which was in full swing in the lounge of the Martin Beck. A surprise awaited me as I approached the stage door. A glass of champagne came hurtling through the air to shatter on the wall behind me. Though thoroughly nonplussed, I needed only a moment to guess the identity of the attacker and to note that, fortunately, he was not also armed with a chain saw. With poorly assumed sangfroid, I beckoned the traffic policeman, who knew me as a familiar old lag on his theatre beat. He took me by the arm away from the scene of the crime and in fatherly tones advised me to ignore the incident. "You've got the biggest smash on Broadway with this show—I heard the raves from the audience as they left. You'd be sorry if you let what just happened hit the headlines. Just you go back to your Plymouth dressing room to calm down and leave it to me to get rid of that joker." He held up the traffic on Eighth Avenue until I had crossed to the other side and, following his wise counsel, I returned to my room and downed a stiff scotch and soda. Within a few minutes he knocked at my door to tell me he'd "helped" the offender into a cab so that the coast was clear. I was able, thanks to him, to greet my guests in an amiable mood and to rejoice with them about the night's reception.

Unlike its immediate predecessor, *Teahouse* was a costly production, calling, as it did, for a large cast of actors and a great deal of scenery. It required much more financing than that usually contributed by my handful of faithful backers. I had therefore let it be known that additional investors would be welcome, and, somewhat to my embarrassment, most of the members of my staff clamoured to top the list of forty-eight angels. It was, in a large measure, to protect their interest that George and I stuck to our guns in our dealings with the testy adaptor. It was walking a tightrope for George, but he skilfully maintained his balance until the show had been safely launched in New York. He was not to escape unscathed, however, when he was in charge of the London production (with Eli Wallach as Sakini). In my absence—I was still touring in the States—he became the surrogate target of a glass of bubbly and was obliged to post guards on both the stage and pass doors to deny admittance to the hostile cup-bearer backstage of Her Majesty's Theatre.

There were times when I thought nostalgically of the good old days in England when authors were kept strictly in their place. John Gielgud's actor-manager great-uncle, Fred Terry, reportedly had a technique in this respect, which, though effective, may seem excessively censorious. To break the monotony of unremitting touring (with his wife) in *The Scarlet Pimpernel*, he would occasionally stage an original play for them to appear in. On one such occasion, unbeknownst to Terry, the playwright had sneaked into the theatre during a rehearsal to voice a protest about changes in the script—made, no doubt, by Terry himself. For daring to open his mouth he found himself being frog-marched by the actor-manager out of the theatre and into the street outside. No wonder that dramatists eventually formed their own union to reverse the tide of forcible argument, even though on occasions it makes waves for those of us who try to steer an unruffled course. Neither George nor I relished the prospect of being at the helm when the time came to organise a national touring company of *Teahouse*, thereby being once more in the line of fire. We therefore agreed to lease the touring rights to those friendly and able producers, Howard Lindsay and Russel Crouse. They engaged Burgess Meredith for Sakini in their production, and, I gather, were spared the complications that had become my lot.

Recently George and I were reminiscing about those aspects of *Teahouse*, only to find ourselves hooting with laughter about experiences which at the time had seemed so calamitous. In retrospect, it is unbelievable that we allowed our almost unqualified admiration for the adaptation to be disrupted by mere personality clashes. I should have remembered the lesson taught me in my early days—that conflict is the cornerstone of both drama and comedy. The first of these was abundantly present in our bristling relationship with the adaptor, but in no way did it restrict his comic invention. He captured the precise mood and balance of the novel by Vern Sneider, an accomplishment that was illustrated by an article in the *New York Times* written by Vern and reprinted in our programs:

> People sometimes ask if the comedy, "The Teahouse of the August Moon" is not, in reality, a serious piece of work. Then I hasten to point out that they should make the "Teahouse" what they wish, for it was meant to be that way. The "Teahouse" was meant to make you think if you wish to think, or to make you forget if you wish to forget. Actually, "The Teahouse of the August Moon" contains two stories, but only one story is told directly. That is the surface story which shows the trials and tribulations of Captain Jeff Fisby (portrayed in the play by John Forsythe) in Tobiki Village, Okinawa. Perhaps it is foolery, or fantasy, call it what you wish. Yet I, for one, sincerely hope that it will bring a few smiles; or better still, a few chuckles.
> However, underlying this surface story is another one, never told but rather implied. And if anyone wishes the "Teahouse" to be serious, the seriousness will come from this story.

THE TEAHOUSE OF THE AUGUST MOON

It is somewhat difficult to explain the under story. Ultimately, it is an expression of certain ideas. One such idea being that people, the world over, are basically the same in their wants and desires, but that often we are confused by externals. As Sakini (David Wayne), the interpreter, would say, holding up his finger—"Illustration!" The Japanese might want his miso soup for breakfast; the Korean might want his pickles, called kimchi, and the American might want his ham and eggs. Yet basically they all want the same thing—namely breakfast. But a word about this island of Okinawa. The name, so I'm told, translates as "the rope that lies off shore." Actually, it is the largest island in a chain that stretches 2,000 or so miles south from the mainland of Japan. And though it is the largest island, still it is a small island—not more than ninety-five miles long and from five to fifteen or twenty miles wide.

The people of Okinawa seem to be neither Chinese nor Japanese. In ancient times they had their own language, known as the Luchuan dialect; and a few of the older people still speak it. In ancient times they had their own kingdom, known as the kingdom of the Ryukyus, the name for their chain of islands. But Okinawa was small.

First it was some dynasty on the mainland of China that demanded tribute, and Okinawa could only pay. Then the eyes of some ancient Japanese war lord fell on this island, and Okinawa had to bow. Her kings became rulers in name only. And as the centuries passed, little Okinawa at times paid tribute to China, at other times to Japan. And sometimes she paid tribute to both at once.

But on April 1, 1945, a new conqueror came to replace the Japanese who had held the island since 1895. He came off his steel ships, and he was worried, especially if he was assigned to work with the civilian population. For, technically, they were the enemy. And since the first duty of Military Government is to keep the civilian population from interfering with the military operation; and since one American would be called upon to handle perhaps 5,000 Okinawans, it was only natural that anyone assigned to such duty would have visions of bridges and supply dumps and switchboards being blown up. But then the American met the Okinawan—completely lacking in sham and pretense and filled with wide-eyed, childlike gratitude.

I would like to point out that "The Teahouse of the August Moon" is not a war story. And I hope that the reader or the viewer will not be concerned with the under story if he is not so inclined, or if he is not in the mood for such. The "Teahouse" was meant to be whatever you wish to make it.

Innumerable thousands of theatregoers all over the world were to make of the *Teahouse* what they wished it to be. Their numbers were swelled into the millions when George Schaefer included it in one of our Hallmark television programs, closely akin to the stage version and starring Eli Wallach.

Even the heavy-handed Metro-Goldwyn-Mayer film (starring Marlon Brando and Glenn Ford) added to the viewing public; although vulgar realism replaced the cartoon quality of our stage production, the fundamentals of the novel were preserved. The obscure and thinly populated village of Tobiki became, in the film version, a page from the catalogue of a travel bureau. Swarms of natives filled the Cinemascope screen from time to time, and the height of anachronism was reached when a troupe of Japanese ballet dancers just happened to have included little Tobiki in their tour-route. The perversity of Hollywood never ceases to amaze me. If the studio had been scripting the novel from scratch I suppose the unimaginative version that emerged would have been forgivable, but to ignore the style and scale that we had proved to be the correct one was just plain stupid. Granted the moviemaker must fully utilise the tools at hand and the finished product must live up to its description of being a Picture in Motion. That does not mean, however, that, irrespective of the subject matter, the camera must appear to be afflicted with St. Vitus' dance or that the visual concept must reflect the size of the scenery budget.

This "bigger-is-better" syndrome even spread to the actors. The only actor playing the part of Colonel Purdy in both our stage production and the film had obviously been directed to be "bigger and better," giving a performance that would have received stern reprimands if it had reached those proportions at the Martin Beck Theatre. One can only assume that, fearing the wide theatrical exposure *Teahouse* had received all over the world, the film at any cost had to be different with a capital D. The Marlon Brando name certainly fitted such planning—saving his proven predecessors as Sakini (David Wayne, Eli Wallach, and Burgess Meredith) the agony of being blown up to Cinemascope size.

4. DISCOVERING TELEVISION

My diaries covering these years are of little assistance to me as I write. For the most part, the memoranda are totally illegible except for historic reminders such as "pick up laundry" or "11 A.M.—Beauty Parlor" (this last had nothing to do with the bags under my eyes, but referred to the springtime stripping of the dogs' winter coats). Occasionally there are decipherable items of a personal nature. I notice that between 1940 and 1950, except for the war years, Margaret Truman followed my doings in the theatre with such regularity that

DISCOVERING TELEVISION

I wrote her a note asking her to visit me in my dressing room the next time she attended a performance. She answered the summons with such promptitude that I feared I was in for one of those glamour-seeking interviews at which I always felt I was a ghastly disappointment. On the contrary, there was no such nonsense about Margaret and we hit it off from the word "go." Independently minded and really serious about her ambitions to be a singer, an easy friendship was struck up, which I treasured, even though the distance between her base in Washington and mine in New York strained the ties.

When *Dial M* opened a refurbished theatre in the nation's capital, Margaret persuaded her parents to attend the first performance. This took quite a bit of doing on her part owing to the fact that ever since the shooting of Abraham Lincoln at Ford's Theatre, the White House security folk took a dim view of any president indulging in theatregoing, but Harry and Bess Truman, like their daughter, had wills of their own. Several rows of seats adjacent to theirs were assigned to the Secret Service and other security personnel were stationed backstage during the performance. There is a scene at the end of the play when the television writer forces an entrance into the flat by breaking the glass in the French windows. That effect was made audible to the audience by our property man, hammer in hand, smashing a pane of glass into a bucket. Unaware of the approaching action, one of the security men was dozing in his backstage chair, his hat pulled over his eyes. I was close by him awaiting my cue to enter and watched the slumbering sleuth with malicious anticipation of the moment of the break-in. I was not disappointed; for the noise, when it came, had the poor fellow very nearly hitting the roof. When the presidential party came backstage at the end of the show, the fact that they were surrounded by Secret Service men did nothing to stem their most gracious and enthusiastic comments. There was a tense moment, however, when Gusti Huber (playing my wife) dived for her autograph book, which she had secreted in advance under the couch on stage. Fully expecting her to be reaching for a revolver, a burly security officer promptly pinned her down.

We were given a tour of the White House during our weeks in Washington, and saw regions not open to the public. Margaret even took us through the kitchens, pointing out that all the refrigerators and cupboards were firmly padlocked. She explained that the responsibility for the catering was divided between two separate crews supplied by government services, neither, it appeared, trusting the other's inventory of leftovers. Margaret complained bitterly that, being something of a night owl, she was unable to extract from the kitchen so much as a glass of milk or an ice cube for her nightcap. She finally succeeded in having a small refrigerator installed in her bathroom, which she stocked up with snacks and a beverage or two. At least she didn't follow the example of Alexander Woollcott who, when a houseguest during the Roosevelt era, sent his manservant out at breakfast time to fetch a drinkable pot of coffee from the local Childs restaurant.

Our tour of the executive mansion included the Oval Room, which Margaret thought would be of particular interest to John Williams, Inspector Hubbard by night, and by day the epitome of an English military type. With a twinkle in her eye, Margaret rather pointedly informed him that the original Oval Room had been burnt to the ground by the British in the War of 1812. "Oh, I say," exclaimed John, "I'm terribly sorry about that!"

The Oval Room was the cause of a somewhat embarrassing circumstance some years later. During Lyndon Johnson's tenancy of the White House, Lady Bird Johnson arranged a big wingding for the performing arts, inviting actors, producers, and critics from all over the country. I was asked to introduce the Shakespearean entertainment. The President was able to pop into the Oval Room for the briefest of moments, explaining that he was busily engaged in a conference with the President of Brazil. Due to some mixup in the social secretary's office, my name, instead of being filed under D for Drama, was mistakenly inserted in the folder B for Brazil. Thus, as time went on, whenever a diplomatic bigwig from Brazil visited Washington, I received gilt-edged invitations to attend White House banquets, a pleasure I felt bound to deny myself since I spoke not a word of Portuguese. It could have been, also, under false pretences that every Christmas I received an enormous presidential greeting card, a courtesy that I did nothing to discourage.

The legible notations that I find in my diaries for this period suggest that all through the *Dial M* years I spent an unconscionable amount of time attending meetings of one sort or another. Presiding, as I was, over two of Broadway's biggest attractions, I felt it my duty to accept a seat on the governing board of the managers association known as the League of New York Theatres. This was, and still is, the organisation that negotiates union contracts and endeavours to foster a common code of behaviour on the part of the producers. It alarmed me, at the time, that the influx of new blood on the board was leaning to a cynical philosophy with which I was at odds. I was strongly of the opinion that prices of theatre admission had to be kept at the lowest practicable level if the younger generation were to become the regular customers of tomorrow. Newer members of the board were all for gouging the public without mercy and generally turning the theatre into a gambler's paradise. "Make hay while the sun shines" appeared to be their motto—a point of view that I did my best to counter.

I must have sounded impossibly self-righteous in claiming that my record as a producer had proved that, at prevailing prices of admission, anyone was perfectly able to run a profitable shop if he kept an eye on expenses. The opposition took the view that their policy of letting the hits pay for the failures was better for business and that the public would, perforce, pay to make up the difference. To some degree the gamblers had a point, for there seemed to be an inexhaustible pool of "angels" who never thought to examine the profit-and-loss books of the entrepreneurs. Had they done so they would have been very differently disposed, since they would have found that the duds far outweighed the winners. It was symptomatic of these operators that they couldn't be bothered to serve on negotiating committees and they refused to back up those who did when a firm stand against the unions or the city taxman was mandatory. Such new demands sounded the death knell of the $3.30 orchestra seat, which continued to escalate in price over the years to reach today's $50 per seat (tomorrow's $100?).

I was not unaccustomed to receiving flattering comments regarding my acting, but commendations for my activities as a producer were rare. In fact, hardly a soul in an audience cares a hoot about who fathers the show. That lack of interest, judging by a letter in my files, seems to have got under the skin of my trusty general manager, Richard Grayson, who was determined to see justice done. In reply to an enquiry he had made to Vern Sneider's agent regarding *The Teahouse of the August Moon*, he received this:

Dear Mr. Grayson:

In accordance with your request I am happy to confirm the earnings of the author of the original book *The Teahouse of the August Moon*. To date he has received approximately $400,000, and I believe the figure might be closer to $500,000. From the very start of *The Teahouse of the August Moon* run he received approximately $1,000 a week, and when the national companies were running he received $3,000 a week.

I should point out that the money received by Vern Sneider represented only one-third the royalties to the authors because as the author of the book Vern Sneider received only one-third royalty. The authors of the book and the play, therefore, have received approximately a minimum of $1,200,000.

On the basis of what I know to be the case, I must add my tribute to Maurice Evans personally. It was he who suggested some of the most important and most effective scenes in the play. In my opinion he deserves quite as much credit as the playwright, and I know that any production in which he is involved would receive the benefit of his great theatrical experience and talent. Maurice Evans is a creative producer and it is his creative producing which in my opinion is responsible to a great extent for the success of *The Teahouse of the August Moon*.

I had lunch recently with George Schaefer, co-producer of

1947–1963

who said that in his opinion Maurice Evans is fabulous. This tribute from one producer to another should not be underestimated.

Sincerely yours,
A. L. Fierst

I had to restrain Dick Grayson when he suggested framing that glowing testament and arranging for it to be hung on the board-room wall at the League of New York Theatres. He even wanted to write a companion piece paying tribute to the only manager in his experience who voluntarily made it a practice to raise his actors' salaries from time to time! Both well-intentioned gestures I had to veto—especially the latter because of its seeming to be a contradiction of the thrift I had been busily preaching to the League of New York Theatres.

Another disenchanted member of the league was Lawrence Langner, founder and director of the Theatre Guild of New York. An extraordinary man was Lawrence. By profession a patent lawyer, an occupation that put him in touch with an assortment of inventors and scientists, many of them seeking to patent ideas far removed from logical reason. Perhaps that kind of association prompted him to adopt the theatre as an avocation, a passion that he pursued with policies somewhat akin to those of his patent clients. Amongst other innovations he and his actress-wife, Armina Marshall, conceived the idea of subscription audiences. In the 1920s their substantial list of subscribers guaranteed a minimum run for their productions of ten weeks or so, irrespective of the tenor of the critics' reviews. Encouraged by the response of subscribers in New York, they enlarged the system to include several cities throughout the States and, in doing so, found themselves in a race to keep the voracious subscribers satisfied.

The Theatre Guild offices were a madhouse of activity that taxed even Lawrence's innovative genius. In their frantic efforts to mount sufficient productions to keep faith with their supporters, Lawrence, Armina, and Teresa Helburn were hard put to cope with the demand (which far exceeded the supply), and it is said that their production conferences were chaotic. Lawrence's absentmindedness was particularly noticeable at one such meeting concerning the casting of a stopgap play they were about to feed to the subscribers. None of the agents' suggestions for an actress suitable for an important role in the play were thought to be appropriate and there was much head-scratching by the trio. At the end of a long silence, Lawrence was suddenly inspired. Snapping his fingers in triumph, he said, "I know! That actress, what's-her-name, in that play at the what-do-you-call-it theatre, by whose-it, . . . oh, you know . . . er, er, er, Armina, er Armina, er, er . . . ." Thus his wife got the part!

It was providential for that whimsical type of management to be offset by the unswerving loyalty of the two finest actors in the land—Lynn Fontanne and Alfred Lunt. Their exemplary professionalism, discipline, and perfectionism set them far apart, yet the Theatre Guild suited them because its very existence depended upon them, and no one dared say them nay. I remember Terence Rattigan referring to them as "monsters" for the changes they wheedled out of him during the out-of-town tryout of his *O Mistress Mine*. Little by little the main emphasis of the story was shifted from the boy's part, where it belonged, to the glamorous grownups. The Lunts were right, of course, knowing that it was they whom the public were paying to see in yet another personal triumph, and naturally Lawrence remained diplomatically neutral. With the exception of the Lunts, the Theatre Guild's methods may have verged on the slapdash, but they could not be accused of getting stuck in any rut. They were in the forefront of stage producers who gradually moved into radio with their Theatre Guild on the Air and later into television with the United States Steel Hour. That activity was developed mainly by Armina, leaving Lawrence to search for some way of reconciling his love for the theatre with the changing conditions of producing plays on Broadway. Like me, he had become apprehensive about the runaway costs and the predominance of musical comedies occupying the theatres, which until then had housed the legitimate fare that was expected of us. Anything of an experimental nature had to struggle for attention in some uncomfortable cellar or loft well away from the main stem. On that account Lawrence turned his fertile mind in a direction which, he hoped, would free him from the fetters of union overmanning and the other wasting diseases that afflicted producing in the metropolis.

We were weekend neighbours in Connecticut and, over lunch one Sunday, Lawrence propounded his latest fancy, which was to follow Tyrone Guthrie's Canadian example of a rural theatre devoted to the presentation of the plays of William Shakespeare. If Guthrie had made a go of it in Stratford, Ontario, Lawrence Langner was going to do likewise in the obscure village of Stratford, Connecticut, in the good old U.S.A. I had driven to the luncheon at the Langners in my ex-army Jeep, a trusty steed that had pulled me out of many a winter snowdrift, and on this memorable day was to take us on a voyage of discovery along the banks of the Housatonic River. It's too bad that no photographers were on hand to record the sight of Lawrence standing perilously on the Jeep's front bumper, urging me to drive through the head-high rushes that lined the river's bank. Eventually we reached an area less marshy than the rest; whereupon Lawrence leapt from his perch, and like some progenitor from the *Mayflower*, knelt solemnly on the spot and in a voice charged with emotion declared that a site worthy of the Bard had at last been found by us two pioneers.

I fear I was highly sceptical about the whole concept, but once Lawrence got an idea in his head there was no stopping him. To begin with, he agreed with me that we should start, as Tyrone Guthrie had done, with a bare stage housed in a circus tent; in other words, to test the suitability of the location from every angle before embarking on a costly building program. But Lawrence was bemused by the conviction that the word "Stratford" would prove an irresistible magnet—a presumption that time showed to be erroneous. Not to be shaken in his belief, he commenced a high-powered fund-raising campaign, only to find that contributors were insisting on bricks and mortar before committing themselves. Having abandoned the tent idea, his first compromise was to offer to confine the building to a replica of an Elizabethan playhouse, modest in size, and calling for virtually no stagehands to operate the no-scenery stage. Even that failed to attract the kind of money that would be required, and it began to look as though Shakespeare would continue to be homeless. Then it was that Lincoln Kirstein came to the rescue, or to the condemnation of the project—whichever way you looked at it.

Lincoln Kirstein was, in the main, a balletomane of prodigious generosity—his patronage being largely responsible for the founding of the New York City Ballet under the direction of George Balanchine. His support of Lawrence's Stratford ambition was conditional upon the playhouse design also being capable of staging the ballets in the Balanchine company's repertoire. Thus, instead of a simple platform stage, when finally built the Shakespeare Theatre and Academy boasted a proscenium arch, a three-story stagehouse, an orchestra pit, and all the trimmings associated with the dance. Needless to say, this expansion was music to the ears of the craft unions, who moved in with full force to put Stratford in the same cost-category as Broadway, thereby negating all our economic calculations.

The Connecticut Stratfordians displayed undisguised hostility to the whole scheme, refusing to grant a liquor license for the theatre bar and complaining volubly that we had caused their local taxes to rise one-fifth of a mill per annum. Fortunately for me, I was on tour at the time of the inauspicious opening of the theatre, and although bronze busts of John Gielgud and me faced each other in the entrance lobby, they looked ill at ease on their pedestals. The man who deserved to be honoured with a life-sized statue in the grounds was none other than Joseph Verner Reed, the man whose openhandedness had been responsible for underwriting my beginnings in the American theatre.

With the exception of our successful association in 1938, Joe was destined to tangle with well-intentioned but impracticable theatrical ventures, and being a Connecticut resident made him an easy prey to Lawrence's persuasive ways. In no time at all he found himself appointed fund-raiser

DISCOVERING TELEVISION

extraordinary, besides digging into the seemingly unfathomable depths of his personal pocket.

My own connection with Stratford in its preliminary years of preparation was limited to occasional tight-lipped attendance at board meetings. I was fully occupied elsewhere, what with *Dial M* and *Teahouse*, to say nothing of my first step into the world of television. It wasn't until the spring of 1953 that I sat up and took serious notice of the new medium. Colour had not yet reached the home screens, but even the black-and-white images were enough to signal that a radical change in the entertainment field was taking place. Already there were warning signs that advertisers were calling the tune regarding the artistic content of programs—an outlook which presaged the low standards that have come to pass. Two of my associates, Mildred Freed Alberg and Tommy Sand, were eager believers in the potential of television as a cultural instrument. They had succeeded in obtaining a sympathetic hearing from Pat Weaver, the big noise of programming at NBC. They came to me with the news that if I would agree to play Hamlet for them, Pat Weaver would allot a two-hour time slot on a Sunday afternoon for such a production. In addition, they had enlisted the interest of the Hallmark greeting-card firm in the project.

One of the few dignified commercial sponsors of television, Hallmark was in the mood to expand its regular series directed by Albert McCleary and starring Winston Churchill's daughter, Sarah. I confess that at fifty-two I felt I was getting a bit long-in-the-tooth for Denmark's Prince, but, at a meeting held in New York, Al and Sarah had no such reservation, assuring me that close-ups would be suitably veiled and that I had nothing to worry about. It was agreed that Al would be responsible for all the camera work and that George Schaefer would handle the casting and the rehearsals.

Sarah, a prime minister's offspring, was practically typecast for Polonius' daughter, Ophelia, and Joseph Schildkraut and Ruth Chatterton were to play Claudius and Gertrude respectively. Except for Sarah, we were all novices at television and, although we were thoroughly familiar with the episodic nature of motion-picture making, the unbroken continuity demanded by live television drama was something else again. It didn't help matters that the only studio available to us was the old Pathé headquarters in uptown Manhattan, designed solely for the filming of Pathé News, but woefully inadequate for the castle at Elsinore. Nevertheless, in spite of our inexperience in the medium and a few "fluffs" which occurred, the performance on that afternoon in April 1953 was quite an achievement and was to mark a turning point in my career.

Although the script employed was identical to the version we used in *The G.I. Hamlet* and the decor somewhat similar, I recall one innovation that the camera alone made possible. In the play's final scene—the fencing match with Laertes—as we challenged each other we both donned fencing masks. I passed momentarily behind a large pillar, at which point my double, a professional fencing master similarly masked, stepped out from behind the pillar and proceeded to put on an exhibition of the art of fencing that neither I nor any other Hamlet could ever hope to emulate. The illusion was completely believable and no one suspected that while my double was making mincemeat of Laertes, I was already in position on the floor, having received the blow from Laertes' poisoned rapier. A quick change of cameras and there was the dying Hamlet, whose expertise on this occasion certainly didn't deserve "flights of angels" to sing him to his rest.

In those early days of television we were spared today's organised blackmail of "viewer ratings." The naïveté of advertisers who allow themselves to be held in thrall by the unscientific guesswork of these self-appointed actuaries is hard to fathom. It was understandable that a sponsor like Hallmark would be curious to know, even roughly, how many viewers were tuned in to *Hamlet* that Sunday afternoon. Since I had made it a condition that the Hallmark advertising be confined to one preliminary and one sign-off credit, plus a brief commercial at halftime, it was simplicity itself to figure that during the commercial break a large proportion of viewers would be disposed to answer the call of nature. Thus, by consulting the local water boards as to the increase of water consumption during the commercial, we had a fair idea of the size of our audience. The bladder statistics were so impressive that our sponsor signed up George, Mildred, and me to do a series of programs under the banner of the Hallmark Hall of Fame and to be aired by NBC as "spectaculars."

At that time a kinescope of the live performance was recorded on black-and-white 16-mm film while we were on the air. It was a sobering experience to be present at a private showing of our video baptism a few days later. I, for one, had not realised that, unlike the cinematographic camera that records only the image on which it is focussed, the video camera photographs the background as clearly as the person in the foreground. This was distressingly demonstrated in the opening line of Hamlet's self-castigating soliloquy, "O what a rogue and peasant slave am I," which, unfortunately, is prefaced by his statement, "Now I am alone." I had no sooner uttered those four words than a particularly scruffy stagehand in a dirty T-shirt appeared over my shoulder in sharp focus. Mercifully I had no idea at the time that there was an intruder stealing my thunder, but on the film it was woefully apparent. Not content with having made his entry on cue, he stood firmly rooted to the spot throughout the entire soliloquy, totally ignoring the frantic efforts of one of his colleagues to persuade him to get out of the picture.

Seeing oneself on that kinescope was a salutary, if not an entirely happy, experience. At our final rehearsal of that soliloquy, Al McCleary came bursting out of the control room to caution me that, whereas he was able to reduce vocal volume by turning a knob, there was nothing he could do to modify my facial "contortions." "You look ridiculous!" he bluntly exclaimed, "as though you are blowing up a party balloon!" We thought we had been rather clever in having Hamlet deliver his denunciation of his uncle to a framed portrait of Claudius. This, we thought, would intensify Hamlet's pent-up hatred for his father's murderer and keep it in a scale suited to the camera. However, in spite of Al's warnings and to my embarrassment, the kinescope showed me being so "pent-up" that the passage "Bloody, bawdy villain! Remorseless, treacherous, lecherous, kindless villain!" did, indeed, look as though I were burping vociferously. My only comfort was that the interloping stagehand kept a straight face, daring me to hope that the audience was paying more attention to him than to my exaggerated plosives.

Those days of live television demanded nerves of iron on the part of both the actor and the director at the control panel. Although it was painful to witness our bloopers on the kinescope, it summoned up within us determination to improve our techniques in the future. Knowing that Al McCleary was unable to stay with us indefinitely, George Schaefer and I had to buckle down to learning the intricacies of what, to us, was a new craft. The dining room at my 10th Street headquarters became our schoolroom and, with our head cameraman at our elbows, we sat for many long hours poring over the mechanics of the game. With large sheets of graph paper before us, and T-squares, triangles, dividers, and pencils at hand, we made the night hideous while we were being instructed in the camera capabilities and limitations facing us in our next production.

Providentially, NBC's reconstruction of studios with sufficient space for their "spectaculars" was way behind schedule, so we had ample time to absorb our technical instruction and to assemble a hand-picked crew of experts to guide us on our way. The Hallmark people requested more Shakespeare and, since I was still appearing eight times weekly in *Dial M*, this suited me perfectly. In fact, I felt it impossible to undertake the double duty of being nightly on the stage and at the same time studying, rehearsing, and performing in some unfamiliar work on television. Thus my old warhorse *Richard II* was chosen as our next offering. Out from storage came the sixteen-year-old costumes (mine having to receive what the wardrobe mistress described as "a dart" at the waistline) and we were ready to go on that memorable Sunday of January 3, 1954.

During the three weeks of preliminary rehearsals, it quickly became apparent that any idea I harboured of simply repeating my theatre performance was a delusion of colossal proportions. Instead of the comparatively formalised scenery I was accustomed to (which would have given the production the effect of a photographed version of a performance taking place in the theatre), television demanded far more realistic surroundings. The rehearsals took place in premises markedly unsuited to the atmosphere of the fourteenth century. On the ground floor was a well-known downtown Jewish restaurant, Ratner's, and above it a series of banqueting rooms that served as our rehearsal accommodations. Chalked marks on the floors indicated the various locations and dimensions of the scenery then under construction. It must have been puzzling to the sundry occupants of those rooms, hot on our heels in the evenings, to find themselves celebrating bar mitzvahs and weddings in areas clearly marked "London, the Palace," "The Lists at Coventry," "Windsor Castle," not to mention "The Prison at Pomfret Castle."

Instead of breezing through a part that I had played so many times and under such varying conditions, I found it extremely difficult to adjust to the intimacy of the television medium. The final week of rehearsals was particularly agonising. George and his camera crew, pointing their viewfinders within inches of my face, were at such close quarters that the royal fondness for garlic had strictly to be eschewed. The chalk marks on the floor enabled them to compose the "shots" as far as the actors' footwork was concerned, but other massive problems awaited us when we emigrated to the Bronx studios for the full-dress rehearsals. For instance, one glance at the scenery erected for the battlements of Flint Castle was enough to make my blonde wig stand up on end. Whereas in the stage production ingenious lighting gave the illusion of a lofty perch (actually I was only about six feet above the courtyard), our television designer's impressive castle walls were a full twenty feet in the air. The scene, it will be remembered, takes place after Richard's return from the Irish wars, to which, earlier on, he had set forth with such optimism ("We must supplant those rough rug-headed kerns, / Which live like venom where no venom else / But only they have privilege to live"). On arrival he learns that his cousin, Bolingbroke, has raised a rebellion against him in his absence. Virtually a prisoner in Flint Castle, Richard has no option but to agree to descend from his crenelated tower to parley with his disaffected cousin:

KING RICHARD: "Down, down I come, like glist'ring Phaethon,
Wanting the manage of unruly jades.
In the base court? Base court, where kings grow base,
To come at traitors' calls and do them grace!
In the base court? Come down? Down court! down king!
For night-owls shriek where mounting larks should sing.
(Exeunt from above)
BOLINGBROKE: What says his Majesty?
NORTHUMBERLAND: Sorrow and grief of heart

NO TIME FOR SERGEANTS

Makes him speak fondly, like a frantic man.
Yet he is come.

(Enter King Richard attended, below)

("That's all very well, Mr. Shakespeare," I thought, "but even your actors at the Globe had to look lively to make it to the ground level in time to enter with any dignity.")

As for me, wearing a crown and dressed in a heavy ankle-length robe, it was out of the question for me to negotiate the twenty-foot ladder which, though out of camera range, was the only means of egress from the battlements. Thus a fireman's pole was set up by the carpenters (also unseen by the camera) down which, crown and all, I slid unceremoniously to terra firma.

Unfortunately, the rapidity of my appearance through the castle's downstairs gateway gave the impression at rehearsal that I could have achieved such a hasty descent only by a nonstop fourteenth-century elevator. Thus, to lend credibility to the time lapse, we decided that Bolingbroke should be astride a horse and consume several valuable moments dismounting from the beast. At the same time we thought that Northumberland, to explain his presence, should also be on horseback. That proved to be a mistake, as we were to find out at the final rehearsal. One of the horses (Northumberland's mount) obviously had a grudge on me, for I had only to open my mouth for him to whinny at maximum lung power, whereupon his equine mate echoed his lament with equal emphasis. There was nothing for it but to banish the leading chorister and for the Earl of Northumberland to make his entrance "on shanks' mare" as the English describe hiking. If such setbacks seem trivial, it must be remembered that live television, unlike a motion picture, had no way of editing out the bloopers, and blooping and the Bard were not compatible.

It is interesting to speculate whether or not the Bard himself would have thought his tragedies suited to this newfangled medium of presentation. It seems probable that he was expressing his personal summation of an actor's job when he caused Hamlet to remind the strolling players to observe the cardinal rule, "To hold, as 'twere the mirror up to nature." What we were up to in television was substituting a magnifying glass for the mirror, thereby exaggerating the human visage to the naked eye. Shakespeare was writing broadly for performances in semioutdoor conditions and would have written in quite a different key if, in his wildest dreams, he had foreseen the coming of the home television set. "Speak the speech, I pray you, as I pronounc'd it to you, trippingly on the tongue" would have had to be transposed to "Speak in whispering tones, I pray you, and in your close-ups, don't move a muscle."

One would have thought that the ancient soliloquy and the modern close-up would be comfortable partners, but in practice others besides me have found them awkward collaborators. In the film *Hamlet*, Laurence Olivier's offscreen voice accompanied his restless, brooding image—a technique that I thought failed to solve the soliloquy problem. It took me many hours of wasted rehearsal time to be convinced that movement on the part of the actor is not the answer. Unless his legs are visible in the picture, it is not the actor who appears to be moving, but the scenery, which apparently moves behind him. It was my good fortune that King Richard is given only one soliloquy—in the prison scene where he is murdered—and even that is only in part a solo. That he should be musing out loud about his incarceration and misfortunes does not seem unlikely for a prisoner in solitary confinement; and the fact that the latter passages are directed to an unseen musician outside the cell's barred window further removes the speech from pure soliloquy. Whether by design or by budgetary limitations I don't recall, but we firmly abstained from the moviemakers' habit of disguising their actors' shortcomings by elaborate musical accompaniment under dialogue. And I'm proud that we did. What a full symphony orchestra would have been doing in the prison of Pomfret Castle would be hard to explain.

5 . NO TIME FOR SERGEANTS

"More of the same" came the word from the Kansas City headquarters of Hallmark, following our television *Hamlet* and *Richard II*. I was unable to oblige, since in March 1954 (three months after the presentation of *Richard II*) I had to proceed on a long tour in *Dial M for Murder* besides supervising arrangements for the London production of *Teahouse*. A long and blissfully restful summer holiday at my Norway Island followed, and by October I was ready to face the television cameras once more—this time in *Macbeth*, with Judith Anderson again "sleepwalking" superbly. Those were still the days of live television with all the pressures that involved, but one would have thought that it would hold no terrors for a pair of actors who had played *Macbeth* in the theatre more times than any of their predecessors.

Accustomed as Judith and I were to performing in a unit setting, we were completely baffled by the totally unrelated television scenery that bore no resemblance whatever to our cosy castle in the theatre's Scotland. The courtyard, the banqueting hall, King Duncan's bedroom, the "blasted heath" were all in separated areas dotted about the studio. At the end of a scene we would find ourselves absolutely bewildered about what was to follow. Costume changes had to be made on the run from one location to another, and both of us had to be propelled by force to our correct areas for the ensuing scene. At one point, I remember, we met, panic-stricken, in the wilderness between the sets, simultaneously saying to each other, "What the hell comes next?" It is a cliché, but at the same time true, that these unseemly marathons of live television had an immediacy and impact which today's stop-and-go filmed programs seldom achieve. At the same time they provided no margin for error. I remember seeing Boris Karloff acting his heart out in a live mystery show oblivious of the fact that one-half of his moustache had become detached from his lip. It was an exhausting experience in the case of *Macbeth* and one that was not made any easier for me when, at the end of a punishing run-through rehearsal day on camera, I arrived home to find the outside of my 10th Street house festooned with electric cables and the remote-control wagon of NBC causing a traffic jam outside the place.

I had rashly agreed to do a televised promotion interview with Ed Murrow on his popular *Person to Person* program, assuming that it would consist of a cosy chat in my living room. Instead of this, his crew had descended on my residence with a view to recording on film "a day in the life of Maurice Evans." My house was a shambles—carpets pulled up, spotlights and cameras on every floor, and the dogs furious at being shut up in their kennels in the garage. To add to the insult, I was told that Ed Murrow was to perform his part of the interview from the comfort of his farm in Connecticut, and that my task was to reply to his questions being flashed onto a monitor in my sitting room. At the end of the session we had to set up a bar in the basement where the crew refreshed themselves liberally while the Thane of Cawdor staggered to the upper regions to catch some sleep before an early morning call to report at the studio.

In spite of all the inconvenience, the *Person to Person* interview gained an enormous viewing audience for *Macbeth* on the following Sunday afternoon. In fact, it was calculated that in order to reach a comparable number of spectators in the confines of a modern-sized theatre, appearing eight times a week, the play would have had to run for forty-three years, and Judith and I would have been in our late nineties by then. As it was, we were to discover that the preparation for live television demanded as much, if not more, concentration than rehearsals for a stage presentation.

Although the opening night of a theatrical production is always a nerve-wracking affair, the knowledge that live television was a now-or-never exposure created an unbelievable atmosphere of tension. It also, of course, produced a distressing sense of letdown once the final words were spoken—no applause, no bravos, no curtain calls. Instead we actors were required to stand stock-still while Hallmark's announcer reminded the viewers that there remained only forty more days to Christmas and that their greeting cards were on sale everywhere "if they cared enough to send the very best." There was little point in reflecting that, even though a large proportion of the viewers wouldn't be able to recall the names of the actors, there was hope that Shakespeare's reputation had received a posthumous boost as a result of our gut-busting efforts. The sponsors were delighted, attributing a bumper sale of Hallmark Christmas cards to the brief "commercials" that anachronistically peppered the plot, and they were sufficiently encouraged to confirm their desire to continue our association.

I was not averse, personally, to getting deeper into television, but the staff of Maurice Evans Productions, Inc., were becoming discontented with the lack of activity in the office. I would show up on Fridays in my dressing gown to sign the checks for the *Teahouse* operation, but otherwise seldom made an appearance there. Instead I spent weary hours glued to my television set in an effort to learn from other producers' mistakes what not to do. I was rewarded for my patience by looking in on a Theatre Guild program one evening when they included an excerpt from a recently published novel by Mac Hyman entitled *No Time for Sergeants*. I jotted down the name of the adaptor, Ira Levin, and sent Emmett Rogers out to obtain a copy of the book. I found it an amusing tale of the peacetime military establishment seen through the eyes of a deep-dyed Southern boy possessing no respect for authority but at the same time being endowed with a personality of irresistible earthy charm. The book critic Bennett Cerf summed up my own reaction to the story—"I always thought 'I laughed until I cried' was just a figure of speech until I read this book! It's a four-star, one hundred per cent wowser!" My tears, however, did not stem from the comic inventions alone, but also from the realisation that there was no character in the novel for which I was even remotely suitable. Vivien Leigh had made a go of it as a Southern belle in *Gone With the Wind*, but I felt it unlikely that fortune would smile on me in the same manner if I attempted to be convincing as a hillbilly hero. I put the book aside with a sigh, only to see it snapped up by Emmett, who enthusiastically circulated it amongst the other members of my office staff. It soon became apparent that a cabal had been formed by my employees to force me to purchase the dramatic rights to the book even though there was nothing for the old man to do in it as an actor. After the disagreeable experience with *Teahouse* I was loath to become involved once again with an adaptation, but in the interests of my staff's morale I decided to explore the possibilities.

Emmett went to work with a will, discovering, amongst other things, that the writer of the Theatre Guild script happened to be the author of my then current bedtime mystery story. It was the highly successful debut of a young novelist named Ira Levin who hit the jackpot with his first book, *A Kiss Before Dying*. A bit of detective work revealed that this talented youngster was an army draftee for the Korean War and that he was stationed in the environs of New York City at Governors Island. Bluffing my way into the Signal Corps headquarters by introducing myself as Major Evans, it was arranged for me to meet the budding young author in the island canteen. Although he had dabbled in writing television sketches, he frankly admitted that he'd never tried his hand at a full-length play but was willing to attempt an adaptation, on which I was to hold an option. After my experience with the established adaptor of *Teahouse*, I was glad to be working with a tyro at the game. I immediately put *Teahouse* designer Peter Larkin in touch with Ira, and left them to kick around ideas. Another ally was my old friend Morton Da Costa ("Tec"), who, I felt, had enough years to his credit to keep the two youngsters in line, and who was to direct the show if a usable script emerged.

Ira's tour of duty in the army was drawing to a close, but until it was over he was unable to make much progress with *Sergeants*. Tec and I were satisfied that in his television script he had shown that there was ample material in the novel for a one-act play, but could he invent entirely new situations to fill out a whole evening's entertainment? Well, to put it in a nutshell, he couldn't or, rather, he hadn't when he eventually submitted his first draft. In the meantime, the novelist's literary agents were being bombarded by Hollywood for an assignment of the film rights and, since I owned only a limited option on the book, drastic action had to be taken. The agents further complicated matters by telephoning me to say that a young actor was in their office at that moment wanting permission to use material from the novel as part of a program that he and his wife were touring in down South. When I demurred, the agent urged me to interview his caller, saying the fellow was a natural for the character of the hillbilly, Will Stockdale. If I were willing to take a chance on an unknown it would be an inspired piece of casting, if and when our adaptation was ready. The agent didn't say it in so many words, but he strongly hinted that, in view of the Hollywood offers for the property, his conscience would not allow him to recommend Mac Hyman to renew my option, which had only a few more months to run. No point, I thought, in throwing in the sponge prematurely, and in any case I was curious to meet the agent's nominee.

The following day I was to do the biggest "U turn" of my managerial career. Into my office stalked a tall, gangling youth by the name of Andy Griffith, good-looking and boasting a Southern accent you could barely cut with a sharp meat cleaver. He was such a dead ringer for Mac Hyman's hero that, in ushering him into my office, my secretary announced him as "Mr. Will Stockdale." But could he act and what was his experience? He whipped out of his pocket an eight-inch phonograph disc, the label of which bore the imprint "Andy Griffith recites 'What it was, was football.'" Explaining that this was one of the monologues he delivered in Baptist Church halls ("to liven things up between my wife's solos on the gee-tar"), he said that he was anxious to do something of the same sort with Will Stockdale's conquest of the U.S. Air Force. Andy had such a winning way with him that I found it hard to refrain from making him rash promises. Although I felt pretty certain that in him I had struck pure gold, I managed to contrive a noncommittal countenance, saying I would give the matter due consideration. I had to kick Emmett under the table to dampen his too obvious enthusiasm. Andy had barely left the premises before the two of us were sitting on the floor beside the phonograph, splitting our sides over the "Football" recording.

Any thought of abandoning the *Sergeants* project had been dispelled by Andy's visit, but "proceed with caution," I told myself, "don't get in the same pickle that you did with the authorship of *Teahouse*." Step number one was to become a dues-paying member of the Dramatists Guild, thereby acquiring equal status with the playwright. Number two was to have Andy Griffith in to read the first act of Ira Levin's script in the presence of Tec Da Costa, Emmett Rogers, and members of the office staff. The reading exceeded my highest expectations, and consequently there was no question that I was firmly hooked to go ahead with the venture, provided we could somehow invent a second act for the play. Tec and I put our heads together during many agonising sessions, finally deciding that Tec was to conjure up the situations for a new Act II and I was to write the dialogue, but neither of us was to disclose publicly the fact of our collaboration. In due course, and in no mood to budge from our position, I called a conference between ourselves and our lawyer, and Ira Levin and his understanding agent. We had to be brutally frank in saying that unless the adaptor would agree to the collaboration we were not prepared to proceed with the production. It was a protracted meeting, from which Ira and his agent retired to the drawing room for a private powwow, and our lawyer had to leave us to catch the last train to his home in the country. Minutes after his departure, Ira's agent descended from the upper regions, having reluctantly reached the conclusion that they had better go along with our collaboration plan. Emmett was immediately dispatched to Grand Central Station with orders to intercept the lawyer and beg him to return to the office to formalise the agreement in writing. It was a rather grumpy Lloyd Almirall that, true to his colours, reappeared in our midst and, in spite of the inconvenience and family complications, obligingly dictated a contract enabling us to get the show on the road.

Neither Tec nor I quite realised what we had let ourselves in for, but once Ira had got over the initial shock he became most cooperative and helpful. He thoroughly approved our framework, which established that the performance was taking place in some little church hall, enabling Andy to saunter onstage

In the theatre at Epidaurus (1958).

As Captain Shotover, with Diane Cilento as Ellie,
in *Heartbreak House* (1959).

As the disguised Reverend Dr. Brock in
Tenderloin (1960).

With Judith Anderson, being directed by George
Schaefer in the filming of *Macbeth* (1960).

Alan Foster, guide, philosopher, and friend.

Norway Island (1961).

Westies in the launch off Norway Island (1961).

With Wendy Hiller in *The Aspern Papers* (1962).

Taking a break from work on *The Aspern Papers* with Margaret Webster (1962).

With Helen Hayes, on tour in *A Program for Two Players* (1962–63).

to chat with the audience and explain the action of this amateur-theatrical evening. From the word go he had the jaded Broadway audience in the palm of his hand and their ears attuned to the verbal dipthongs with which they were about to be assaulted. To be fair to Ira, it should be stated that had he submitted a script calling for the elaborate production which resulted from Tec's and my rewriting, I would have been scared off for that reason alone. As it was, we were digging our own graves by calling for a military plane in flight, special rigging to fly the parachuting Andy and his buddy, Roddy McDowall, and a brilliantly designed scene in the latrine. Once again Peter Larkin excelled himself.

The episode concerned Andy's way, as latrine orderly, of impressing the inspecting colonel with his efficiency. As the officer entered, Andy stamped on the floor, whereupon both he and all six toilet seats came smartly to "Attenshun!" Peter's seats were like none ever seen, the irregularity of their contours being unlikely to encourage the occupant to perform in the regularity expected of him. The mechanical contraption that caused the seats to rise (supposedly a simple contrivance of Andy's fertile mind) was originally electrically operated, but when the stagehands' union delegate demanded that we hire an extra man to press the switch, I rebelled. If the pop-up effect could be achieved manually with equal precision it would be more reliable than the electrical gimmick and would become a duty to be performed by one of our many property men. I bethought me of my army Jeep sitting in the garage at Wilton, remembering that its suppliers had furnished it with a quite super-fluous crank handle. Thus the costly electrical gadget was dispensed with and, thanks to a flick of the wrist, the obedient toilet seats regularly got a round of applause.

The opening night of *No Time for Sergeants* at the Colonial Theatre in Boston was a new and crucial test for me. It was the first—and last—time that I would be "out front" at any production for which I was responsible, and goodness knows I had reasons enough to be apprehensive. For one thing, Tec and I, travelling by train from New York the day before, had rewritten one scene, which received only a single rehearsal prior to the opening, and that in the theatre's lobby. To add to the butterflies in my tummy was the sight of the electric sign atop the theatre's marquee, which read "Maurice Evans presents No Time for Sergeants." This had been done without my knowledge, the theatre's owners feeling that mine was the only "name" that might attract the curious to the box office, even though we had excellent actors, such as Myron McCormick (the sergeant of the title) and Roddy McDowall. Andy Griffith's name, I had to agree, could be nonproductive.

As I paced nervously up and down the back of the Colonial that

1947–1963

memorable opening night and heard the audience responding to Andy's comedic personality, I began to gain confidence. At intermission it became evident that the audience was thoroughly enjoying itself, which allowed me to dare hope that the critics would also be favourably inclined. As I listened in on the audience's comments in the lobby, I was hailed by a New York agent who rather dampened the theatre's owners' view by saying, "Maurice, what on earth are you doing in Boston?" Such is the fame redounding to a producer even when he's up in lights! I needn't have worried, for when the reviews came on the streets next morning they were so ecstatic about Andy and the play that I could return to the anonymity that I preferred. That Andy had scored a personal triumph there could be no doubt.

It was now essential that his presence in the play be secured for its entire run. At the time we signed him up for Will Stockdale it was anybody's guess whether or not our hunch about him would be widely shared; consequently his contract was a standard one-season agreement. After his rapturous reception in Boston, it was obvious that New York audiences, always generous in their praise of a deserving newcomer, were going to turn handsprings about him—which indeed they did.

The play also garnered bravos in the press, both the *New Yorker* and *Life* magazine calling it a "wildly funny hit." As one of the authors of what we ourselves considered to be a somewhat fragile script, I was positive that its success was in large measure due to Andy's glowing performance. And here we were, putting our most valuable asset in great jeopardy eight times a week by suspending him twenty or more feet above the stage floor in a parachute harness, moving him up and down and left to right in simulation of an aeronautical jump. His partner, Roddy McDowall, similarly harnessed, confessed to me that he was nightly in mortal fear of being castrated by the uncomfortably located straps. He took little reassurance from my assertion that speaking in the treble clef would not be out of character for his already splendid Ben Whitledge. But for a similar misfortune to befall Andy would not be appropriate. I toyed with the idea of taking out special insurance against such an eventuality in Andy's case, but not even Lloyd's of London were prepared to discuss such a delicate matter, let alone assume the risk.

A vigorous effort had to be made to at least be assured of Andy's services for an extensive run. Since I was about to be immersed in two years of television, and because Emmett's enthusiasm for the property had, from the start, been more positive than my own, he was moved up a peg to become the associate producer, with me, of *Sergeants*. As such, he was instructed to think of ways of inducing Andy to commit himself for a second season. To that end Emmett had the electricians of the Alvin Theatre prepare a sign reading "Andy Griffith in No Time for Sergeants." However, no amount of persuasion on

NO TIME FOR SERGEANTS

Emmett's part or mine could nudge Andy's pen toward the dotted line, so, sad to relate, that electrified acknowledgement, instead of being proudly displayed above the marquee, remained in the cellar gathering dust. The true reason for our star's disinclination became apparent when word leaked out from Hollywood that Andy had agreed at the termination of our brief association to play the lead in Elia Kazan's movie *A Face in the Crowd*. Only then did I recall my astonishment at having noticed "Gadge" Kazan's presence at the Boston opening, never guessing that he had designs on our leading man. It was early to start thinking of someone to replace Andy, and there was always the possibility of the film being delayed. However, Andy finally left and other actors (Jim Holden, for one) were able to acquit themselves satisfactorily during the long New York run.

As for me, I was up to my ears preparing and occasionally appearing in the Hallmark television series during the *Sergeants* years and was glad to leave its welfare mainly in Emmett's hands. In addition to launching a national touring company to visit the major cities across the country, there was also the London production to be supervised. Although much of this work could be delegated, masses of details did require my own attention. The day of realisation finally came that, whereas all this diversification was rewarding for my backers and stimulating for my colleagues, for me personally it was stultifying.

Due to a series of hits overlapping each other (*Dial M*, *Teahouse*, and then *Sergeants*), a sizeable fortune was flowing into the coffers of Maurice Evans Productions, Inc. However, the lovely green dollars from Hallmark, which would swell my own bank account, had an unfortunate habit of finding their way into the hungry jaws of the Internal Revenue Service of the United States government. Thus I came to the conclusion that I was treading "the steep and thorny way" of management at the expense of "the primrose path" of acting. It was really *faute de mieux* that I had become involved in the business side of the theatre and television while never, in fact, having any particular appetite for figures. Only because nobody would do the things I wanted to do in the way I wanted them done had I been forced to do them myself. My professional life, it seemed, was becoming as convoluted as the preceding sentence, but by then I had committed myself to go ahead with the Hallmark series. It was no substitute for the glamour of theatrical footlights, perhaps, but at least it was a good excuse for getting away from my office desk.

The prospect promised to be no picnic, although the main burden was to be borne by George Schaefer and his associates, Mildred Alberg and Tommy Sand. Apart from introducing each of the programs in the Hallmark series, my tasks consisted of starring in one of them from time to time. It was good to be in double harness with George once more. He had returned to the fold following several years of valuable indoctrination in the tricks of the trade in

Hollywood under the capacious wings of Alfred Hitchcock and David O. Selznick. He also managed to find himself a wife in the course of his directorial chores at the Dallas musical-comedy summer theatre. It was understood between us from the start that, although I was to be the front man in getting the Hallmark series off the ground, once it was securely airborne, it was into his capable hands that I would surrender the controls. Little did I think that sixteen years later George would still be piloting what was considered to be the most distinguished television program of its time.

We made our debut in 1955 with *Alice in Wonderland*, to be followed shortly by *The Devil's Disciple*, in which I appeared once again with Dennis King. Ralph Bellamy, Margaret Hamilton, and Teresa Wright joined the cast, setting the high standard of acting that was to prevail throughout the coming years. In the same season we produced a really stunningly original version of *The Taming of the Shrew*, with Lilli Palmer as the man-eating Katharina and Diane Cilento as her complaisant sister, Bianca. It was twenty years earlier at the Old Vic when I had swaggered my way through Petruchio's rough-and-tumble courtship of Kate (Cathleen Nesbitt), but here I was somewhat the worse for wear taming another shrew in very different surroundings. The adaptation and decor of the television production was devised by Billy Nichols, a young actor who had been a member of my Shakespearean companies. In the interim, together with the choreographer, Tony Charmoli, each had made a name for himself on the artistic staff of the television series *Hit Parade*—hardly, one would have thought, the appropriate background for collaboration with the Bard. On the contrary, since more or less anything goes in the case of the comedies, these two certainly *went*, and in doing so turned the rather confusing plot into a zany romp. They overcame the improbabilities of Bianca's three suitors failing to recognize each other by having them wear domino masks, flipping them up for their asides to the viewers. It was sheer genius on their part to set the first meeting between Katharina and Petruchio in a boxing-ring put up in the village square. Cheered on by the villagers, the two of us played the scene as if sparring for a fight, retiring to our "corners" periodically to be revived by our "seconds."

Anyone watching the black-and-white kinescope (copies of which are in the film libraries of both the National Television Library at U.C.L.A. in Los Angeles and the corresponding collection at London's National Film Archive) should note one unintentional visual blooper in the final reconciliation scene between Katharina and Petruchio. The two of us, decked out in our wedding finery, were the spectators at a ballet pas de deux, the story of which recapitulated our turbulent wooing. The choreography was purposely a caricature of our stormy relationship—my dancing "double" plying a bull whip and forcing Katharina to jump through hoops and so forth. The cameras were trained principally on our dancing alter egos, but occasionally they focussed on me, grinning my amusement from ear to ear. This being "live" television, one such glimpse caught me in the act of mopping my sweating brow with an unsavoury-looking towel, obviously in the last stages of total exhaustion. Otherwise the program was a model of accuracy, greatly enhanced by the adaptor's use of Marcel Marceau-like clowns posing with placards describing the whereabouts of the ensuing action.

I received a fan letter from the Mother Superior of a Pennsylvania convent saying how greatly her charges enjoyed, in particular, the billboard that read "Meanwhile Back at the Ranch." She observed a discreet silence, however, regarding their reaction to the wedding interpolation. The scene was the exterior of Padua's cathedral, the voice of an unseen priest mumbling the sacraments of holy matrimony, and Petruchio's "I do" delivered in contrasting clarion tones. More priestly mumbles, directed presumably to Katharina, the only distinguishable word being "obey." Whereupon an enormous explosion erupted, the cathedral's facade collapsed, and general turmoil prevailed—the bride hotfooting it, the groom pursuing her with equal alacrity, cheers from the townsfolk, and a reminder from Hallmark that they had greeting cards suited even to occasions such as these.

The highly favourable public response to the *Shrew* confirmed Hallmark's determination not only to proceed with the series but to expand its frequency in the next season. That decision, of course, involved a substantial increase in their investment, so much so that the Kansas City headquarters came to the unfortunate conclusion that they should retain the services of an advertising agency to represent their television affairs. Whereas artistic control of the initial season had been vested solely in me, thenceforth it was to be subject to consultation with a Chicago-based purveyor of expertise. Consequently, George and I were summoned to the Windy City to lay before them our program selection for the 1957–58 season. Since our past policy had been to tailor our choice of material to the "name" performers available, we hadn't the faintest idea that far in advance what or who would be involved in the ensuing season.

Nevertheless, we had to put in an appearance at the agency's office and pretend that we were bursting with inspired proposals. In fact, the only preparation George and I made was accomplished on our flight to Chicago. We leafed through French's catalogue of published plays, jotting down at random titles that we thought might be familiar to our inquisitors, also plucking out of the air the names of popular actors and actresses calculated to whet their appetites. A hush fell upon the mahogany-panelled board room of the agency as George solemnly quoted from the notes he had made from the L to Z half of the alphabetical catalogue, and I chipped in from time to time with titles from the A to K section. One of my suggestions, Dumas's *Camille*, met with the unanimous approval of the assembled agency experts as they scribbled down the title on the foolscap pads before them. I couldn't resist asking them whether they remembered that the heroine of *Camille* was a French whore with consumption? Much vigorous scratching out on the yellow pads quickly settled the hash of la mademoiselle as George piped up with the less controversial goings-on in *The Yeoman of the Guard*.

It was fortunate that the individual nominated by the agency to act as liaison with us trusted our judgement and confined himself to supervising the commercials. As a result, we were able not only to develop original material by authors drawn from our New Dramatists operation (e.g., James Costigan's *The Little Moon of Alban*), but to overcome the hesitations of many first-rank performers to venture into the new medium. Among such luminaries were the Lunts in *The Magnificent Yankee*, Helen Hayes in *The Cradle Song*, Katharine Cornell and Charles Boyer in *There Shall Be No Night*.

Unlike British Actors' Equity, who, in spite of my being one of their founder members, refused to permit me, as an alien, to play the ghost in Richard Chamberlain's *Hamlet*, AFTRA (American Federation of Television and Radio Artists) in the United States erected no barriers to the importation of British performers. There was no spirit of reciprocity on the part of British Equity, who took the view that "any British actor could play the ghost." True enough, but I thought it lacking in respect so to describe the actor who replaced me, namely, Sir John Gielgud. Amongst those to receive the American union's blessing were Dame Edith Evans, Dirk Bogarde, Trevor Howard, and Peter Ustinov. They alternated with American stars of similar stature, such as Dame Judith Anderson, Greer Garson, Alfred Drake, Jason Robards, Lee Remick, and many others. With such freedom of choice in casting, we were able to tackle a wide variety of dramatic material irrespective of its nationality.

My personal appearances in the programs were strictly limited by Hallmark's insistence that I continue to be the so-called "anchorman." At the end of each production I was required to give a sales pitch on camera for the next offering of the series. It caused me great discomfort, having spoken the final lines of *Man and Superman*, for example, to be required to step out of character to urge the reviewer to tune in again on a given date for our coming production, which in that case was to be *The Little Foxes* starring Greer Garson, Franchot Tone, Eileen Heckart, and E. G. Marshall. Thus, at the end of our second year, I hauled up the anchor and handed over the tiller to George. He formed his own producing company under the name of Compass Productions Inc., and, having purloined my invaluable television secretary, Sybil Trubin, to be his first mate, set a course that circumvented the rocks right through the year 1970. During those intervening years I was merely a passenger who dug into his steamer trunk for tattered scripts from his theatrical past, making repeat appearances in *Dial M for Murder*, *Macbeth*, *Twelfth Night*, and *Saint Joan*. The only novelty for me as an actor came in 1959 when, for the first time in my Shakespearean career, I played Prospero in *The Tempest* in company with Lee Remick as Miranda, Richard Burton as Caliban, and Roddy McDowall as Ariel.

The elaborate production of *The Tempest* was in another sense a "first" for me, since I had never previously taken part in colour television, and I was therefore totally unprepared for the roasting effulgence of the lighting needed to reproduce colour faithfully. Since Prospero spent most of his time in a dank, cold cell, it was thought appropriate that I should be warmly clothed—a decision that, on account of the temperature in the studio, was very nearly the death of me. I perspired my way through the dress rehearsal, which preceded the final taping, after which my dripping costumes were hung in the studio boiler room in the vain hope that they would be dry by the time of the taping. In the meantime, I enviously eyed Roddy McDowall, whose Ariel was stark naked except for a fig leaf here and there.

Many mechanical problems bedevilled the dress rehearsal, resulting in the briefest of intervals between it and the actual taping. Those precious moments were spent in frenzied efforts on the part of the hairstylist to restore my wilted wig and beard to their pristine condition. I had taken particular pains in designing those adornments that they should be in accord with my concept of Prospero's physical appearance and character—the kind of hair that springs from its roots like fine strands of wire. That, it seemed to me, was the sort of thatch likely to endow the cranium of this complex personage—philosopher, magician, and fond parent—one who could, without inconsistency, utter such contrasting images as:

> I have bedimm'd
> The noontime sun, call'd forth the mutinous winds,
> And 'twixt the green sea and the azured vault
> Set roaring war; to the dread rattling thunder
> Have I given fire . . . ,

and, in the same magnificent speech, speaking of his enchantment:

> Ye elves of hills, brooks, standing lakes and groves
> And ye that on the sands with printless foot
> Do chase the ebbing Neptune . . . .

One of these days, I suppose, someone will do a modern-dress production of *The Tempest* and I shall get the blame for having originated the punk hairdo. My coiffure was not that extreme, but it bore out my conviction that in Shakespeare's company (the King's Players) Prospero was in all probability played by the same actor who undertook the part of Polonius when *Hamlet* was requested by their royal patrons. The key to that old fussbudget is to be found in his colloquy with Reynaldo (Act II, scene 1)—a duologue that is invariably, and regrettably, omitted in most stage presentations:

> POLONIUS: And then, sir, does 'a this—'a does—
> What was I about to say?
> By the mass, I was about to say something!
> Where did I leave?"

That passage surely suggests the part was played originally by the company's foremost comedian whose forte was the humour of non sequitur—a quality also noticeably present in many of Prospero's utterances. With that conviction in mind I was able, in studying the role, to avoid the tendency (inherent in the part) to give him the mien and sonority of a rather boring Nonconformist minister. Having never acted in *The Tempest*, nor even having seen it performed, for some obscure reason, I was not likely to be guilty of "improving" on some other actor's Prospero.

Our aim in this production was to preserve the diaphanous atmosphere of magic so poetically described by Caliban:

> The isle is full of noises.
> Sounds and sweet airs that give delight and hurt not.
> Sometimes a thousand twangling instruments
> Will hum about my ears; and sometimes voices
> That, if I then had wak'd after long sleep,
> Will make me sleep again.

The airy charm of the play was captured by the cameras in a manner quite impossible in the theatre and, in particular, enhanced Ariel's magical comings and goings. Summoning my obedient sprite, I extended my hand, palm upwards, and issued the command, "Approach, my Ariel. Come!" Whereupon a four-inch figure of Roddy landed gently on my hand with his "All hail, great master!" At least he did after apparently making several false landings to begin with during the dress rehearsal—not his fault, of course, since the illusion was simply a camera trick calling for delicate precision on the part of the operator. Once that chap got the mechanics right, the effect was delightful, but time was marching on and, at that point, we were barely halfway through the rehearsal. It has to be remembered that those were the experimental days of colour television, and that occasion was fraught with time-consuming surprises. The majority of the action took place in a spacious area representing "The Island before Prospero's Cell." To create a feeling of fantasy the designer, Rouben Ter-Arutunian, had a profusion of strips of translucent plastic hanging from above. To the eye the effect was mysteriously enchanting, but alas, when the

Maurice the Warlock, with Elizabeth
Montgomery as his daughter, Samantha, on the
set of *Bewitched*.

As Maurice the Warlock, with Agnes Moorehead
as his wife, Endora, in *Bewitched*.

As the Prime Minister (before rejuvenation) in
The Man from U.N.C.L.E.

As the Prime Minister (after rejuvenation) in
The Man from U.N.C.L.E.

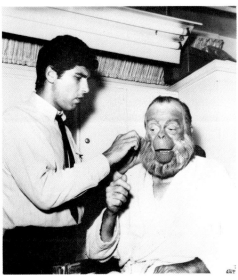

With Kenny Chase, working on the orangutan transformation (1967).

As Dr. Zaius in *Planet of the Apes* (1967).

Taking a break from *Planet of the Apes* with Charlton Heston, cinematographer Leon Shamroy, Kim Hunter and friend, Linda Harrison, Roddy McDowall, and director Franklin Schaffner (1967).

As Norman Thayer in *On Golden Pond* at the
Showboat, Clearwater, Florida (1981).

cameras were called upon to change position not only did they become entangled with the hangings, but the accompanying microphones picked up and magnified the collisions. Consequently, the sound track gave the impression that Prospero's magic island was being subjected to heavy artillery bombardment.

Sorting out these and other mechanical problems took an unconscionable amount of time, but one and all bore up bravely in spite of the delays. Roddy was the chief sufferer, since his "costume" consisted (apart from the fig leaves) of plastic spines stuck to various parts of his anatomy. A particularly vicious bunch of such thorns were attached to his rump, making it impossible for him to sit down without sustaining severe injury in a sensitive area. Sympathizing with his dilemma, I sent a distress call for a shooting stick to be brought from my home so that he should have something to perch on during the long hours of waiting.

With the clock ticking inexorably onwards, we were finally ready to tape Act I, with little margin for error. Errors there were in plenty, as our overseers discovered when they reran the tape in the viewing room while the actors and crew took a desperately needed breather. There was nothing for it but to reshoot the whole act. After the dinner break the taping of Act II began, and upon its completion the same repetition became necessary because of errors.

It was very late on Saturday night when the preparations were completed for the second taping of Act II. By this time I was not at my brightest or best. Rather like a clergyman friend of mine who has a terror of drying up when reciting the Lord's Prayer, I had an attack of nerves when I started on the most familiar speech in *The Tempest*. I was able to give "The cloud-capp'd towers, the gorgeous palaces" their due, but when I came to the final valedictory "We are such stuff as dreams are made on, and our little life is rounded with a sleep," I made an unfortunate slip of the tongue. To my horror I heard myself say, "We are such *things* . . . er . . . *stuff* as dreams are made on." George relieved my mind by telling me that they could electronically remove my heinous hiccup of "things," and that the tape showed that I had slightly lowered my head (from shame, I'm sure) and that that movement would cover the slight hesitation that would result. About the time of this writing, George transferred *The Tempest* to regular 35mm film for public release, and he assures me that in the course of the complicated process he succeeded in further smudging the error. Thus only those who read this confession will be aware of my guilt.

It was symptomatic of my growing dissatisfaction with television that, whereas to this day I can spout without prompting almost any of Hamlet's or Richard II's speeches, Prospero's eloquent pronouncements have long since left my memory. Perhaps it is because of the fleeting one-shot nature of the medium that, in spite of the intensive preparation required, it leaves little impression on the brain. Or could it be that technological advances and experiences in photography have so far failed to eradicate the basic flatness of the image appearing on the screen, be it in Video, 3-D, Cinemascope, or whatever? One of these days a third dimension will be added to the cinematographer's art, resulting in the kind of realistic pictures I used to drool over when, as a boy, I looked at picture postcards of bosomy girls through a stereopticon viewer. Until something of that sort comes to pass, the death knell of the fully-rounded actor on a stage will not be tolled, and the only true art on our screens will continue to be Mickey Mouse, Tom and Jerry, the Pink Panther, and their like.

At the time of the television *Tempest* I was being sought after to return to the theatre in a revival of Shaw's *The Apple Cart*, in which I would play King Magnus. The producers were new to Broadway and deserved better than to be confronted by Equity's ban on the importation of alien actors. Shaw's spoof of a monarch proving himself more democratic than his cabinet ministers cried out for recognisable British types, but due to Equity's embargo, many compromises in casting had to take place. Nevertheless, I thoroughly enjoyed playing the offbeat King, particularly his flirtation scene with Orinthia (cunningly depicted by Signe Hasso), but the theme of the play was a mite too British for American appetites. In spite of that, it had quite a respectable run both on Broadway and on tour and, incidentally, brought into my orbit a young enthusiast named Martin Tahse, who joined my 10th Street staff.

Martin's midwestern origins gave him a special concern regarding the shrunken capability of the railroad systems to provide access to thousands of towns across the nation with the consequence that touring, as we had once known it, had become a thing of the past. At his urging, I agreed to his canvassing the neglected territory with a view to discovering how many communities would be willing to guarantee one, two, or more performances in their bailiwicks—in the event we mounted a production capable of travelling by road instead of by rail. The response was so overwhelming that I felt it had to be given a try with a portable production of *No Time for Sergeants*. The office became a hive of industry with the adrenalin flowing in Martin and my secretary, Elizabeth McCann. (No wonder that he is now a successful Hollywood producer and she a formidable producer of successive Broadway hits.) Their desks and mine were snowed under with maps of almost every state in the Union, as we endeavoured to link up a chain of towns, sufficiently close to each other, to permit what became known as our "bus and truck tour."

After months of these preliminaries, we were ready to assemble a company to go into rehearsal—and then the crisis arose. Guaranteed employment for a season mightily appealed to all the actors interviewed—all, that was, except a likely candidate for Will Stockdale. I was really at my wit's end, knowing that the entire town route had been firmly booked, and we still lacked a leading man. Then it was that I caught a look at my troubled visage in a mirror, which showed that I badly needed a haircut; so round the corner I went to the nearest barber, whom I had never patronised before.

In spite of my tousled locks, the barber recognised me and, in the course of his very chatty ministrations, told me that an ex-army buddy of his had been transferred to my army outfit in Hawaii during the war. Fearing that I probably would have long since forgotten whoever he was, I nevertheless asked, "What was his name?"

"Charlie Hohman," came the reply. I think I knocked the scissors out of the barber's hand as I seized it in mine, imploring him to tell me if he knew where Charlie Hohman could be found. "Last I heard from him he was running an antique business in Kansas City—believe I've got his phone number in my book." Moments later he returned with his address book in hand, and he *did* have the telephone number. In spite of my impatience to get to a telephone, I felt I owed him not only a handsome tip, but an explanation of my behaviour. Hohman, I told him, had played the part of the Hollywood cowboy, Larry Toms, in my soldier-show production of *Boy Meets Girl*, and I might have a job for him in professional theatre if he were available.

I tore back to the office and miraculously got Charlie Hohman on the line at the first try. After my preamble, which rather stunned him, I told him that he was to come to New York at my expense to read for the part of Will Stockdale, and that if he passed the test he could look forward to starring in the Broadway company for a few weeks before setting forth on the "bus and truck" safari. "I want you here in a week's time, soldier, and that's an order!" I concluded. Like Julius Caesar he came, he saw, he conquered—and in doing so set a new record for the totally lunatic chances that sometimes go hand in hand with theatrical fortunes.

Our advance agent had hit the trail a week ahead of the company in order to alert the various communities, to distribute announcements for their newspapers, and to book accommodations for a busload of actors. Equity did its best to draw up a new form of contract suited to its members' peculiar wanderings—one proviso of which stipulated that the bus be halted at four-hour intervals, for what the all-male cast referred to as "a piss stop." For their first journey out of Manhattan, the company assembled outside the Alvin Theatre where they boarded our private Greyhound bus, in which for the next several months they were to spend the majority of their daytime hours. As they bowled downtown towards the Holland Tunnel, the company manager addressed his charges regarding the day's routine, and in doing so made the fatal mistake of mentioning the "piss-stop" clause in their Equity contracts.

1947–1963

The bus had barely reached the New Jersey side of the tunnel, when a dozen or more hands were raised insisting that the urgent needs of their bladders made a stop imperative as soon as they surfaced on the Jersey shore. The stern discipline that was thereafter imposed had to be relaxed, however, when the troupe were headed westward on long hauls through desert country. On those occasions, the Greyhound juggernaut disgorged its passengers—one and all performing at the roadside in a manner that must have deeply shocked the native jackrabbits.

The mid-1950s saw much turbulence in my affairs. Emmett Rogers, having directed the London production of *No Time for Sergeants*, and not being involved in either my television activities or *The Apple Cart* production, decided with my blessing to become a producer in his own right. His replacement, Richard Grayson, according to his credits in *Who's Who*, was an unlikely candidate for the job—since his stage debut in 1932 was as the Cheshire Cat and Humpty Dumpty. However, by 1955 he had graduated from such community capers to become executive coordinator of the Stratford, Connecticut, operation, where he first came into my ken. He was to change hats frequently during our association, between stage management and general managership of Maurice Evans Productions, and he was invaluable in both capacities. As stage manager of *The Apple Cart*, he accompanied me on tour, leaving Martin Tahse to cook up other schemes in our New York office.

Martin decided that, in view of my disinclination to plunge further into theatrical producing, diversification was the answer. Amongst several ideas, a rather adventurous proposal was agreed upon, which led us to set up a subsidiary corporation under the title "Maurice Evans Industrials." Its function was to provide shows to entertain visitors to exhibitions set up to promote sundry manufacturers' products. To our surprise a giant of industry came knocking at our door in the guise of General Motors. It was the custom of that august institution (before switching to television advertising) to usher in its new models annually with an automobile show in the ballroom of the Waldorf-Astoria Hotel. This was to be the last such extravaganza introducing in spectacular manner their new models. A massive piece of machinery, set up on the ballroom's bandstand, brought at the flick of a switch each model, one by one, to the front of the stage, rotating it seductively as it retired to make room for the next chariot. With the arrival of the new Cadillac, the music swelled in a deafening crescendo and the salesman's amplified voice rose to new heights of passionate admiration. Finally, in unison, the six new cars made an entrance as though parachuting from paradise—trumpets, fanfares, drums, and recorded applause and vociferous cheers! All very impressive except for the jeopardy in which it placed our singers and dancers. Their raptures over the pirouetting vehicles was necessarily curtailed if they were to avoid being firmly "impressed" into the few inches of stage remaining to them. No casualties occurred in any of the four-a-day performances, but so intrigued were the ambulatory audiences that ways had to be found to persuade them to keep moving. Harking back to my army days when I was faced with a similar problem, I sought out again a circus entrepreneur for advice. At his suggestion we erected a large sign with a direction-arrow on it, and words reading "Don't Miss the Egress." He assured me that natural curiosity would lure people through the turnstile that was, in fact, the exit into the street. It had worked for P. T. Barnum at his American Museum and it worked like a charm for us. However, it took only this one exploration into the world of industry for me to decide that a huckster's life was *not* for me, so the new corporation was hastily wound up.

6. FROM *HEARTBREAK HOUSE* TO *TENDERLOIN*

With Maurice Evans Industrials and its somewhat whimsical activity out of the way, I found that, except for occasional television appearances, for the first time in many a long year I had time on my hands. I decided to pack my bags for a sightseeing tour of Europe, with no business targets to spoil the view. *No Time for Sergeants*, after 796 performances, had finished its Broadway run, releasing from its clutches an actor friend who, like me, was planning a similar tour. Van Williams has since become one of the foremost photographers of the Broadway scene, but at that time he was learning his craft by recording on film his wanderings hither and yon. He joined me in Rome, a first visit there for both of us, and later we trotted off to my favourite Italian city, Florence. I was not to see the results of his superb photography until much later, in New York, but in the meantime I dutifully followed in his wake, loaded down with photographic equipment of various sorts. From Florence, with so many wonders to see and so many museums and art galleries that my metatarsal arches were crying for mercy, we went to Athens. For as long as I can remember I had yearned for the day when I might climb that steep hill and actually find myself inside the Parthenon. It exceeded all expectations when we made our first pilgrimage there. The sense of ancient history, the breathtaking vistas from the Acropolis made it a memorable experience. At least, that is what I thought until Van insisted on repeating our visit at sunrise the following day and again at sunset the day thereafter. One does not argue with a photographer who knows about light meters and other paraphernalia, but inwardly I was wishing we were sitting comfortably in the British Museum admiring the better-preserved Elgin Marbles.

A remarkable highlight of one of our picture-taking side trips was when I found myself standing in the center of the Greek open-air theatre at Epidaurus reciting lines from *Hamlet*. Van and his camera were at the very top of the fifty-five tiers of stone benches and, although I spoke at my normal decibel delivery, Van assured me that even from his elevated position he could hear the words distinctly. Fortunately, it being January, there were no other tourists around. What a sight it must have been in the fourth century B.C. when a "full house" consisted of 14,000 spectators! (At 10 percent of the gross, that would have been a tidy sum of drachmas for Aristophanes or whomever.) I cherish the photo Van took on that occasion showing me, in that vast arena, scaled down to the size of a peanut. It jolted me into mentally turning the clock back to the time that I first stepped on a professional stage. Thirty-two years previously had seen me getting my teeth into the part of Orestes in *The Oresteia* of Aeschylus, and although in the meantime my choppers had assumed a somewhat telltale sparkle, the replacements afforded no excuse for my being absent from the theatre.

My main preoccupation, however, after my return to New York, was to sort out my domestic affairs, which with Emmett's departure to greener pastures had fallen into disarray. Having finally decided to abandon the actor-manager role, I closed up the office at 10th Street, thus ridding myself of aggravating business matters. It was a stroke of luck for me, though distressing for the patient, that a friend of mine was stricken with a miserable complaint for which his doctor had prescribed total bed rest. Alternating with other friends of his, I would join the good Samaritans in tending to his needs.

On one such visit the door of the patient's apartment was opened by a personable young actor named Alan Foster. He was about to leave to attend a rehearsal and I had just come from one, so there was time only for the briefest of exchanges ending with "see you here tomorrow." After his departure our invalided chum filled me in on Alan's background while I rustled up something for supper. Like all his contemporaries, Alan, he told me, spent his summers acting in stock companies (which Tallulah Bankhead referred to as "the citronella circuit"), gaining priceless experience in a wide variety of plays. The rest of the year, unless Broadway or television beckoned, he was to be found guiding tourists through the historic spots of the Hudson valley. Although this afforded him an audience of a sort, it was no substitute for the theatre in which he wanted to work steadily. In addition, I learned that Alan was about to terminate his apartment lease and was looking for alternative accommodation. This was my cue, when we met again, to offer him house room at 10th Street with a prospect of becoming my assistant in the event that

FROM *HEARTBREAK HOUSE* TO *TENDERLOIN*

current rumblings of a theatrical project came to something. Some twenty-five years later I am firmly of the opinion that it was the best decision of my life, since Alan continues to be my indispensable assistant and, through thick and thin, a loyal and jolly companion.

Alan soon let it be known in theater circles that I was available for hire. Almost immediately I was contacted by Bobby Griffith and Hal Prince, the current successful producers in the field of musical comedy under the guidance of director George Abbott. That highly profitable collaboration had resulted in such hits as *Damn Yankees, The Pajama Game,* and *Fiorello,* and was to be followed by a period piece about the red-light district in New York City in the late 1880s, entitled *Tenderloin.* From the time we had our first discussion the best part of a year elapsed before an adaptation of Samuel Hopkins Adams's book was completed by Jerome Weidman, and the music and lyrics by Jerry Bock and Sheldon Harnick (the team later responsible for *Fiddler on the Roof*) had been sketched out. Leaving them all to come up with a concrete script, I agreed to "put on my dancing shoes," as Bobby Griffith expressed it.

That extended hiatus allowed me an interval long enough to become involved in the production, referred to earlier, of Shaw's *Heartbreak House.* Although I was credited with being coproducer with Robert Joseph, in actuality, apart from having a veto over casting, it was my ex-production manager Dick Grayson who represented me in all other aspects of the presentation. Between them they succeeded in breaking down Equity's restrictions on alien actors, which resulted in what was probably the nearest to an ideal aggregation of actors the play has ever received. Even my own performance of Captain Shotover was not to be sniffed at, but the others were so splendid that their contribution needs recording:

Lady Utterword	Pamela Brown
Mrs. Hushabye	Diana Wynyard
Ellie Dunn	Diane Cilento
Mazzini Dunn	Alan Webb
Hector Hushabye	Dennis Price
Boss Mangan	Sam Levene
Randall	Patrick Horgan
Nurse Guinness	Jane Rose
The Burglar	Sorrell Booke

The omens for that production were all good. Five top stars of the British theatre plus Sam Levene and me, highly imaginative scenery by Ben Edwards, and the ultimate in costume design by Freddy Wittop—all added up to a strong attraction indeed. Also in our favour was the fact that the play was to be housed in the theatre (the National) where I had played for so long in *Macbeth*, but which, for our opening, had been renovated by, and renamed, the Billy Rose. The play had not been seen in New York since Orson Welles revived it twenty years earlier, thus odious comparisons were unlikely; so there was an atmosphere of optimism, at least until our director, Harold Clurman, came on the scene.

On the first day of rehearsals, seated around a table, we were treated to an illuminating lecture about the works of George Bernard Shaw in general and *Heartbreak House* in particular. Harold Clurman was extremely erudite, but as the week wore on we had not progressed beyond reading the play still seated on our derrières. Finally, one of the leading ladies, in sheer exasperation, demanded that we get to our feet and rehearse. She would have done better to remain dumb, because, once upright, it became apparent that we were all sheep without a shepherd, or rather, a herd of bewildered actors getting in each other's way. When we appealed to the director to sort out the tangle, he claimed that spontaneity was his aim, and was best achieved by leaving us to our own devices. This, of course, besides revealing his own lack of directorial ability, resulted in utter chaos. And so it was that Lady Utterwood (Pamela Brown), revisiting her childhood home, made her majestic entrance from the kitchen instead of the front door, because nobody knew which door was which! Having fought her way to a chair to deliver her two-page introductory speech, she then found herself entirely obscured from view by the rest of us gathered around.

Accustomed as they were to strictly disciplined rehearsals, the five British actors demanded that I, as coproducer, dismiss Harold Clurman and appoint a substitute director. I was completely in sympathy with their dissatisfaction, but as the junior of the producing partners I had no such power. Harold was Bob Joseph's unalterable choice. Bob regarded him personally as a kind of surrogate father. The Britishers were not to be silenced, however—but poor Harold *was!* It was finally agreed that the stage manager, Harry Young, should take charge and should use Shaw's extremely detailed stage directions, thereby restoring order to our chaotic stumblings. Harold's tearful acceptance of his demotion was extremely distressing, but he realised that it was either that or the Britishers were going to quit in a body. We promised that the contretemps would remain secret and that he would continue to be credited with having directed the play. Needless to say, this fuss put a damper on our initial enthusiasms, but after a few tryout weeks, out of town, all was forgotten and the show was in good shape for its New York opening on October 18, 1959.

For the souvenir program of the production I wrote a piece about both the play and Shaw, which I feel is worth repeating:

FROM *HEARTBREAK HOUSE* TO *TENDERLOIN*

I sometimes suspect that Shaw deliberately used the technique of interlarding *the pale cast of thought* with comedy in order to build up his reading public. The average theatre-goer comes away from a Shaw play aware that he or she has been thoroughly entertained, but equally conscious that too many brilliant ideas poured across the footlights to absorb in one sitting. His instinct is either to re-visit the play or to buy a copy of the printed version. In both events Shaw was the richer by virtue of his royalties and more likely to communicate his full meaning thanks to the double exposure to his work. His credo of being irritating and funny while dealing with serious subjects is nowhere more strongly exemplified than in *Heartbreak House*. Our stage manager has clocked the laughs in this present production. The astounding fact emerges that in spite of its being a play which symbolizes the end of the world, our audiences split their sides no less than 189 times in the course of each performance. To those who regard Shaw as a demi-god or a prophet, this uproarious laughter is unseemly. The idolators among the critics have taken us to task for tampering with the play. In fact, all we have done is to heighten the paradoxical humor inherent in the script and to invest the play with scenery which is as topsy-turvy as the happenings it surrounds.
Hardly a single Shaw revival has escaped the critical epitaphs usually reserved for fledgling playwrights—"SHAVIAN GABFEST AT THE SO-AND-SO THEATRE." It seems so naïve, after all these years, to complain of Shaw's garrulity. Of *course* he was verbose, and gloriously so! But for all his verbosity he remains the finest writer of dramatic prose in a century or more and it is chiefly for this reason that we actors adore appearing in his plays.
If you see a tall gaunt bearded man in a hurry on 41st Street headed for the Billy Rose Theatre, look twice, because it may be the spirit, if not the person of the greatest dramatist of our age, George Bernard Shaw, ready to laugh at his own jokes and generous with his praise.

The out-of-town tryouts produced an ominous warning bell from at least one of the critics, Ernie Shier of Philadelphia:

Heartbreak House is a sad comedy in which nothing seems to happen while, in fact, everything is happening. Time has dimmed Shaw's satire against the apathy of nations, like those motherly warnings to wear our rubbers in the rain, but if the production is not a totally rapturous affair it still offers a rare opportunity to spend an evening in distinguished company.

Elliot Norton, the Boston critic, in order to meet his deadline wrote his critique after attending a special preview in New York:

1947–1963

A show that shines with the lustre of Shaw's wit and the gloss of many fine performances. . . . Maurice Evans plays Captain Shotover in a glowing performance. Dressed in the uniform of a sea-captain, wearing a white beard and wig that make him look like Bernard Shaw, he is curt and gruff and funny as the lines allow, and, in one scene with Diane Cilento as Ellie Dunn, wise and tender and touching; the wit is Shaw's, the warmth is Evans'.

The preview that prompted this encouraging notice was a benefit for a charity known as the City of Hope. Though well intentioned, such occasions, apart from putting a Broadway stage crew through its paces, are apt to produce audiences who have paid premium prices for their seats in aid of the charity. In this case the customers were largely bejewelled, blue-haired matrons with their sulky husbands in tow. The title *Heartbreak House (A fantasy in the Russian manner on an English theme)* was not calculated to console their male escorts for the gaping holes in their pockets, even for such a worthy cause. I couldn't resist taking a peek through the spyhole in the house curtain at what appeared to be an essentially social rendezvous rather than an assemblage of devotees of the thespic arts. As the house lights dimmed, I clearly heard one of the old gals calling out to a friend in another row, "See you at 'Twenty-One' after the first act!"

We fared better with our regular public, but there was a marked lack of enthusiasm on the part of the predominantly female audiences at matinees. That should not have surprised me because, in the course of touring in other Shaw plays, my advance men had found it prudent in ordering the billboards to specify that the name of the author should appear in what printers' jargon refers to as SMALL CAPS. Although the good ladies relished Shaw's gibes at almost everything under the sun, when he turned his sights on the fair sex, to them it was not a laughing matter. In announcing that the seven-star production was to be for a limited run of three months, we must have had our doubts about the play's popular appeal, and having not so long ago seen a revival of it in England I now realise that our caution was not misplaced. This revival, like others before it, had the benefit of a distinguished cast, headed this time by Rex Harrison, but, as had happened with us, they could not overcome the fundamental weakness of Shaw's attempt to emulate "the Russian manner." It was once explained to me by a Tsarist Russian that the feckless behaviour of Chekhov's characters was a quality indigenous to the Russian people and caused much mirth as audiences recognised their own morose outlook on life. This kind of fellow feeling was a purely national characteristic, not successfully translatable into other languages. Unlike Chekhov, Shaw sought to sugarcoat his apocalyptic sermon by caricaturing his protagonists to the extent, in some cases, of their being farcical. Our audiences, although amused by the

FROM *HEARTBREAK HOUSE* TO *TENDERLOIN*

peccadillos and dilemmas of Shaw's idle-rich puppets, lacked any sense of personal involvement with them.

It was a joy to be working as part of such an expert team even though, in deference to the distaff side, I surrendered to Pamela my customary dressing room. Instead, I was assigned a room upstairs that closely resembled a prison cell. Owing to the complexity of my G.B.S.-look-alike makeup, I had to spend a full hour ahead of each performance to achieve the illusion, in conditions of solitary confinement. The only decoration on otherwise bare walls was a stern warning signed by Billy Rose forbidding me or future occupants to deface the surfaces with telegrams of good wishes, and so forth. But the room's most depressing feature, the grimy barred window that gave onto an air shaft, was an aperture that one evening caused me to panic. I was putting the final touches to my Shavian transformation when the loudspeaker gave the five-minutes-to-curtain call. Whereupon my stomach started to gurgle in the most ominous manner. As was my custom before a performance, I had eaten very lightly at home and couldn't imagine what on earth could be responsible for this clearly audible distress. Something had to be done, and in a hurry! "Hold your breath," I told myself. "Sip a glass of water slowly!" Both to no avail. At that moment Alan came breezing into the room to announce, "Ready for Act One!"

"Tell them to hold the curtain," said I.

"What's wrong?" he enquired. "My stomach! Can't you hear it? I can't go on the stage in this condition!" Alan, roaring with laughter, pointed towards the barred window outside which, firmly perched on the sill, was a portly pigeon cooing its silly heart out.

As I stood in the wings waiting for my first entrance, I recalled sympathetically the embarrassment of the titled lady of the famous limerick:

> I sat next to the duchess at tea.
> It was as I thought it would be:
> Rumblings abdominal,
> Loud and phenomenal,
> And everyone thought it was *me!*

It is a strange quirk about our profession that, in recalling plays one has been in, it is the mishaps rather than the compliments that stick in an actor's memory. In that respect *Heartbreak House* was no exception. One's failure to improvise when something untoward occurs was exemplified when a nervous substitute property man literally jumped the gun at one performance. Mistaking Alan's "warning" signal for "go," he fired the offstage pistol that, one page later in the script, was supposed to throw all of us into a state of pandemonium. Although the sizeable explosion made the audience jump in their seats, we actors continued our desultory chitchat as though nothing unusual had occurred. Minutes later, on its proper cue, the abashed property man let go with a second bang. Instead of reacting with cries of alarm, all of us onstage broke into uncontrollable giggles. In the same final scene, on another occasion, I was the unwitting cause of unseemly mirth on the part of my colleagues. Captain Shotover's passionate prophecy that the English Ship of State is headed for the rocks is prefaced by the phrase, "The Captain is in his bunk, drinking bottled ditchwater!" Allowing my indignation to run away with me, I became entangled in a series of hopeless tongue-slippers, starting with, "The Captain is in his bunk bitching bottle drinkwater!"; then, with added vehemence, "The bunking's in the ditch ...," swiftly corrected by, "The bottles in the bunkwater drinking ditch!" Oh, well, we all make mistakes sometimes, don't we?

By the time *Heartbreak House* had run its appointed course, life at the 10th Street house was charting a new course. At long last, straight from heaven, a domestic couple had come there to roost. In point of fact, they were not professional servants, but refugees from Greece who had fled there from the Russian occupation of Romania with little but the clothes on their backs. Kimon and Zafiro Stavrepoulos were promptly stripped, by us, of those tongue-twisting names, and as "Pappa" and "Zed" became part of the family. Alan was already installed in the upstairs back bedroom-sitting room with a terrace, having airily mentioned, as he moved in, that he was to be accompanied by a pair of cats and hoped I didn't mind. Fortunately my dogs treated the feline newcomers with total disdain, an attitude that the cats, "Summer" and "Smoke," echoed with similar hauteur.

Having acquired personnel to feed the menagerie, we were in a position to lend an eager ear to a challenging request from Hallmark to remake *Macbeth* as a film, this time in colour, to be shown on television first in the United States and then on cinema release throughout the world. The cost factor was obviously a stumbling block as far as Hollywood was concerned; so it had been decided to shoot the interior scenes at London's Elstree Studios. Lacking the facilities there for the exteriors, George Schaefer learnt that a Crusader castle existed on the island of Rhodes, and that the Greek army garrison and the police could be hired as "extras" for a nominal fee. Since Alan and I were going on a trip to Europe before the filming began, George asked us to go to Rhodes and check on the details for him. The mayor of Rhodes was most cooperative and arranged for us to have a special tour of the castle. Armed with George's Leica camera, we arrived at the castle to find that the part open to the public had been over-restored by Mussolini some years before—Rhodes had been taken by Italy from Turkey in 1912 and had been restored to Greece by the treaty with the Allies in 1947. However, the original part of the castle proved to be most rewarding. Alan photographed the walls, gateways, staircases, and so on, the stonework of which was faithfully copied when finally the scenery was built at Elstree; for, on returning to Athens, we learned from George in London that due to logistic problems of location-shooting, it had been decided not to use the island of Rhodes, after all.

Returning to London, Alan and I rented a cozy mews house off the King's Road in Chelsea, waiting for word of a starting date and news of Judith Anderson's arrival. The top floor of the house consisted of two bedrooms, one of which was Alan's, and the other a guest room. Whether or not it was in anticipation of Lady Macbeth's advent I shall never know, but Alan went to bed in his room one night only to find himself next morning lying on the guest-room bed—sleepwalking, no less! At least he had the decency to refrain from crying out like her ladyship, "Out, damned spot! out I say!" Nevertheless, I made it a practice from then on to keep my own bedroom securely locked at night.

For once the English spring lived up to Browning's paean on England in April. Not only did the flowers bloom, but so did a spirit of cooperation on the part of our Elstree collaborators. Leslie Howard's sister, Irene, the head of their casting department, lined up a long list of notable actors for us to pick from and, what was the biggest feather in our cap, we secured the services of England's foremost director of photography, Freddie Young (later to do *Dr. Zhivago*, *Lawrence of Arabia*, etc.). The only menacing cloud on the horizon was the mounting estimate of the cost of the film, but as it turned out even that had a silver lining. By agreeing to defer our compensation, Judith, George, and I enabled the production to proceed and, by doing so, we are reaping our rewards to the present time without being absolutely clobbered by the tax man. The initial exhibiting of *Macbeth* on television took place early in 1961 as part of that year's Hallmark series, and it garnered a host of Emmy awards for practically everyone but Shakespeare. George was showered with honours at a ceremony at the Ziegfeld Theatre in New York, and Judith in Los Angeles and I in New York trotted up to our respective stages to be dubbed best actress and best actor of the year for our performances. An even more impressive recognition for Judith coincided with the Elstree filming. It had been announced that she was to be made a Dame of the British Empire and that her presence was requested at Buckingham Palace on a certain date to receive the accolade. Our schedule was adjusted to accommodate Her Majesty's command, and on the day after her investiture we cooked up a little surprise for Judith.

That day we were working at the banqueting hall of the "Castle at Forres," the tables groaning with every conceivable assortment of food—whole hog's heads, game birds, and luscious-looking puddings. A close look at these goodies revealed that each succulent dish bore a notice reading, "Touch at your peril!" The spread had already been sitting under the hot studio lights for about a week and was by then giving off a rancid odour, which made the warning superfluous even to the notoriously ravenous extras acting as guests at the feast. Even so, on camera, it all looked rich and mouth-watering. At a signal, all the studio lights were doused, the assistant director knocked on Judith's dressing-room door, saying, "We're ready for you, Miss Anderson." Flashlight in hand, he guided her out into the darkened banqueting hall, whereupon a band (recorded) struck up, the lights came on, and we all joined in the chorus of "There Is Nothing Like a Dame!" Although not exactly in keeping with the music popular in A.D. 1040, it was fitting for that talented lady of the theatre in the 1960s.

For the witches' prophecy that "Birnam Wood shall come to Dunsinane," it was necessary to show the army storming Macbeth's fortress. That was beyond the capabilities of Elstree Studios, so we all trouped up to the border country of Scotland, where a suitable site still existed. Known as Hermitage Castle, and though merely a shell within, the exterior walls were still standing and were the perfect background for one critically needed long shot of Judith and me at the main gate. What had been overlooked, however, was a flock of sheep grazing in close proximity to us. The shepherd did his stuff, to no effect. His dogs barked their heads off, but the sheep remained rooted to the spot. As the weather started to worsen it seemed that a crisis was afoot, but the sheep were not. We had both of us played in our time to unresponsive audiences, but none compared with the fixed, mournful gaze of those stubborn baa-lambs chewing their cud. Finally our script girl piped up that she had it on good authority that the eleventh-century Scots were wild about leg of lamb (with mint sauce?). Thus there would be no contradiction in a flock of sheep appearing in mid-distance. The cameras were in the positions they had taken up hours before. "Action!" cried the director, and after a few minutes of satisfactory footage, "Okay. Cut!" As if obeying his command, the masticating *moutons* removed themselves from the scene, rather in the manner of disgruntled critics after some boring play.

From the banks and braes of Bonnie Scotland to the bordellos of lower Broadway in Victorian New York was a far cry for me, but *Tenderloin* beckoned. Such vocalizing as I had been able to do while abroad had been confined to tiled bathrooms and showers. Consequently I had made little progress, particularly as far as vocal volume was concerned. It was something of a shock on returning to New York to be told that *Tenderloin* was not to have the benefit of microphones—Mr. Abbott had decreed that there was to be no amplification. So, I hied me to my singing teacher, Carlo Menotti, with the news that I had to make myself heard over a full brassy orchestra and that I was due to demonstrate at an audition in a fortnight that I had the lungs wherewith to do it. He wisely vetoed any attempt on my part to sing a familiar show tune at the audition. In the short time at our disposal, we concentrated on vocal exercises, increasing both their volume and their range, and, to prove that I could carry a tune, using "La la" to the music of "Drink to Me Only with Thine Eyes." Although the occasional critic had accused me in the past of being too melodious in Shakespeare, I had not consciously sung in public since *Ball at the Savoy* twenty-seven years previously at the Theatre Royal, Drury Lane. I had somehow survived that challenge and was determined to pick up the gauntlet once more, even though it really meant lifting up my voice for the edification of such a connoisseur as George Abbott. I thought it politic to forbear from reminding him that in 1938 we had occupied adjacent humble rooms on the same floor of an obscure Manhattan hotel, but that awareness nevertheless made me less in awe of him than I might otherwise have been. Seemingly I passed the test well beyond my expectations, and I had only myself to blame when that encouraged the composer and the lyricist to write additional numbers for me to sing in the show.

As a newcomer from "legit," I was bewildered by the fragmented style of a musical-comedy rehearsal—the dancers in one building, the singing chorus in another, and the unfortunate principals usually relegated to the "Ladies" or "Gents" in the theatre's lower lobby. I marvelled that any kind of cohesion could finally emerge from such a system, but, knowing that George Abbott was an old hand at the game, I decided to trust him implicitly and to keep my strong reservations about the "book" to myself. After all, the same team who had so successfully produced *Fiorello* were again in command, and it had to be assumed that their judgement was infallible. In a way there was a similarity between the political reformer, Fiorello La Guardia, and *Tenderloin's* Reverend Dr. Brock, and his moral crusade, but as we were to discover to our cost, there was a world of difference between the two men's outlooks. Whereas Mayor La Guardia's target of corrupt politicos made him the darling of New York audiences, the Reverend Doctor, in their opinion, was merely a scold of a secretly admired red-light district. I dutifully kept my mouth shut during rehearsals even though I had an inkling that all was not well, but not until the show received a roasting in New Haven, from an undergraduate, in the Yale University newspaper (to mention only one) did Abbott and the producers realise that we were in serious trouble. It came as no surprise to the performers, though we found it rather strange that, until the adverse reviews appeared in print, our employers had been oblivious of the show's shortcomings. We were assured in a managerial pep talk that everything would be ironed out during the weeks to follow in Boston and that, with our cooperation, all would be well.

Alan and I were sceptical, but having been asked to cooperate we decided to take them at their word. The dawn was breaking by the time we finished combing through the script, noting suggestions for radical substitutions for the many dull spots. It became as plain as the proverbial pikestaff that, to a large degree, the Reverend Doctor's censorious character was responsible for the leaden patches. This we felt could be remedied only by turning him into a figure of fun, with the ladies of the night getting the best of him. There was a true incident recounted in Samuel Hopkins Adams's book on which we thought a lighter mood could be set. The story told that when, at the clergyman's instigation, the sinful Tenderloin district was closed by the police, its female charmers descended in a body on his Park Avenue rectory one afternoon. Startled by what the neighbours would think, and in order to get those decorative protestors off the street, his wife invited them in for tea. From that historical premise, the possibilities were legion. For instance, in a moment of Christian charity, the Reverend Doctor could accede to the girls' offer to form an all-female choir at his church, with the Madam leading the contralto singers. As a result, there would be a marked increase in the number of male worshippers, some of them leaving their calling cards in the collection plate.

That, and other suggestions, were presented to the producers and the director in their hotel suite and, although they listened politely, their reaction was frigid. Whereas, in *Fiorello* they had felt no compunction about poking fun at the mayor of New York, they were reluctant to do likewise in the case of a man of the cloth. However, during the daily rehearsals that took place in Boston, in spite of my being the show's central character, I found myself pleading with them to eliminate the Reverend Dr. Brock from several of the sluggish scenes. They appreciated my concern, and much of the heavier dialogue was deleted, to be replaced, however, by newly written songs that I had to memorise in a hurry. The result was certainly a move in the right direction.

It wasn't only the dialogue that was giving us trouble, for in one scene, which took place by the seaside, my song was in a very legato tempo, and that also needed doctoring. We were rehearsing in the ballroom of an hotel near the Shubert Theatre and, everyone else having gone out to lunch, Alan and I put our heads together. I was idly picking out the melody with one finger on the piano and, in a gust of impatience, speeded up the tempo from the 4/4 time in which it was written to 2/2 (*alla breve*). Hearing the accelerated rhythm, Alan started to dance a polka and I rather clumsily joined in. We were caught in the midst of our capers as the others returned from their lunch break and were greeted by a round of applause in which the composer and lyricist joined. A few days later, with new lyrics and a livelier orchestral arrangement, the polka was substituted and I was to be seen dancing happily with my arm around the prettiest of the chorus girls.

FROM *HEARTBREAK HOUSE* TO *TENDERLOIN*

My admiration for the hardworking dancers and singers was unbounded. In Boston they were faced with unrelenting changes in their routines and had to overcome the grotesque costumes and unbecoming makeup that Cecil Beaton had perversely designed. Musical comedy being, to me, unfamiliar territory, I was not aware that a kind of apartheid was the accepted relationship between principals and chorus. Consequently, when the show opened at the Forty-Sixth Street Theatre in New York, the door of my capacious dressing room was propped open (except when I was changing my trousers), and anyone in the show was welcome to drop in for a chat. This raised a few eyebrows in some quarters, but it created a free-and-easy backstage atmosphere that contributed notably to everyone's performance in a piece that was obviously not going to be a world-beater. After the show one evening, I remember Noel Coward and Edna Ferber had to elbow their way through a bevy of girls and boys who were bidding me goodnight. Noel and Edna appeared to have enjoyed themselves and were particularly impressed by the *fortissimo* of the voice of the *jeune premier*, Ron Husmann. When Alan told Noel that Ron was known to us as "the male Merman," he crisply commented, "Apt!"

The show did nothing to set Broadway on fire, but it had a seven-month run and, musically, advanced the reputations of Jerry Bock and Sheldon Harnick. The Capitol album with the original cast has, I am told, become quite a valuable collector's item. I confess I am rather glad when some incredulous visitor asks me to play the record. As the overture strikes up, the intervening years drop away and I recapture the stimulating urge to get out on that stage and, even in a tricky part, show them what I could do.

With the closing of *Tenderloin* in the spring of 1961, Father Time, sickle and all, started to make his presence known more frequently. The hourglass nestling in the crook of his arm reminded me that I was about to become sixty and that if I were going to stick to my resolve to retire at sixty-five, I'd better get busy planning my brief future. Too many of my contemporaries, I felt, had made the mistake of outstaying their welcome—a fate that I was determined to avoid. Not for me those repetitive announcements: "Positively last farewell performance." Nor was I going to sanction the kind of memorial service at which surviving actors got their pictures taken.

It is strange, though, how something invariably turns up to justify putting pious resolutions aside! In this instance, it was an invitation to attend the Berlin Film Festival where our film of *Macbeth*, though not a competitor, was to be shown as a kind of bonus. I accepted without hesitation, being eager to revisit a city I had enjoyed in the pre-Hitler era. Little did I realise that our visit anticipated by a matter of days the building of the notorious wall separating East and West Berlin. The Film Festival organisation had booked Alan and me a flight from New York to connect at Heathrow airport with a Lufthansa plane, which would get us to Berlin the day preceding an important press conference. What we hadn't reckoned with, however, was the blistering heat wave that awaited us in Europe. Possibly on account of the temperature at London's Heathrow, our flight from New York made an unscheduled stop at Shannon, where perspiring colleens came aboard to sell Irish lace and whiskey to us not-so-fragrant passengers. The hour that we needed to effect the connection at Heathrow was fast slipping by and, even though the American captain radioed ahead asking the Germans to hold their flight until we arrived, by the time we landed the Lufthansa flight had already left. There was nothing for it but to spend the night in a steamy hotel room and to start out again on the morrow after enduring the passport and baggage formalities in furnace-like conditions at Heathrow. The only flight to Berlin early enough the next day turned out to be a hedge-hopping aircraft that limped its way to our destination, finally disgorging us at Tempelhof airport too late and too rumpled to show up at the press conference. The weary welcoming party did their best to smooth our feathers by pressing into our hands small bouquets of wilted roses and even smaller and far hotter splits of champagne. Those German hosts were so profuse in their apologies about our journey that we thought it a propitious moment to mention the one thing that might calm our shattered nerves. We had set our hearts on buying what was then a rarity in the States, a Mercedes automobile, but influence was needed to arrange for one to be snatched off the assembly line during the short time we were to be in Berlin. "*Jawohl*," said one of our greeters and, with German efficiency, in two days we were delighted to be told that we were the owners of a smart Mercedes, which we knew would be an envied novelty at home. It was somewhat deflating, however, when one hailed a taxi in Berlin and it was invariably a duplicate of the car that we were about to acquire.

One day during the Film Festival we made an interesting sightseeing trip to East Berlin. We had an official car with its special flags and our driver seemed to be persona grata with the Russian guards at the Brandenburg Gate, though his standing would have been diminished had they known the route he took us. Unter den Linden, now renamed Stalinallee, was flanked by impressive-looking apartment buildings, but when our driver made a forbidden detour to the rear of them one looked in vain for their interiors—rather like modern clocks, they were all faces and no behinds. Sixteen years had elapsed since the Soviets had taken over East Berlin, but from what we saw of that strictly *verboten* city, the war might have ceased only the day before. Grass and weeds were growing in the deserted cobbled streets, no private automobiles were in evidence, and in the air hung a pall of defeat. We had been joined in that tour by our production manager for *Macbeth*, Phil Samuels, and his stunning Swedish wife, Karen, who was dressed in the height of fashion. I will never forget the pathetic envy on the faces of the waitresses at the sight of Karen when we stopped at a dingy restaurant for a most unpalatable meal. It was my first, and I hoped my last, acquaintance with Communism in the raw. In spite of the boring public-relations duties that we had to go through for the Film Festival, West Berlin was paradise by comparison.

An interesting insight occurred at a reception at the residence of the commandant of the British forces currently on the roster of the Allied guardians of the ill-advised terms of the peace treaty. Charlton Heston and his Hollywood contingent had to leave for another engagement, allowing Alan and me to be given a tour of the gardens by the general in command. He called our attention to, and apologised for, the way the German gardeners had planted his flowerbeds. They resembled nothing so much as a parade ground with the plants standing stiffly at attention in military formation. He confessed that he counted it the one glaring defeat of his army career that the gardeners had flatly refused to cultivate a casual herbaceous border, adding, "Typical of this nation, though—no sense of humour, have they? No wonder they lost two wars to us." The general elaborated on his argument by describing the difficulty instructors were encountering in convincing postwar German recruits that even war has its funny sides. Those token troops were issued a manual illustrating the amusing fatalistic humour of the average British "Tommy," a state of mind, it was argued, that resulted in victory. The booklet contained samples of the war correspondent Bruce Bairnsfather's cartoons of his typical Tommy, "Old Bill," and his abrupt contempt for all things military. One such drawing depicted Old Bill crouched at the foot of a wall through which an artillery shell had obviously blown an enormous hole. The caption below consisted of the one word, "Mice!" As if that humour were not self-evident, the German army publishers had thought it necessary to add a footnote: "The aperture was not, in fact, caused by mice but by a high velocity shell."

Although the Berlin Wall had not yet been started, word had got around that it was imminent. The prospect of being cut off from their families and living under Russian masters caused those who could afford it to leave their East Berlin homes carrying with them nothing but a small bag apiece. A number of such elderly refugees were aboard the plane that flew us over the corridor that separated the two Berlins from West Germany. We were bound for Frankfurt to pick up our Mercedes at the Sindelfingen factory. On our flight it was impossible to regard those woebegone creatures as our onetime enemies or to avoid the critical reflection that it was the lack of foresight on the part of the, by then, decrepit Allied statesmen that had allowed the division of Berlin to occur. Alan's sympathies were deeper than my own, since, at the end of the war, he had been a member of the United States occupying forces in Germany, and remembered vividly the appalling devastation he had witnessed in those days—not only the bombed-out buildings but the survivors living like rodents in the rubble and existing on the contents of army garbage cans.

We made a tour in our beautiful new car to such places as Baden-Baden, Heidelberg, and Cologne en route to England, making a special stopover at Belgium's fascinating "little Venice," Bruges. From Ostend on to the White Cliffs of Dover and to family reunions. We shipped our car by sea and then winged our way to New York.

7. ONE-NIGHT STANDS

What with one thing and another I had been on the treadmill for a solid twelve months, so I decided that I would spend what was left of the summer of 1961 on Norway Island. The neighbouring island, Josephine, had come on the market a while before, and so the extra space and privacy needed to house Zed and Pappa were now available. The second island also proved handy on this occasion because my Westie bitch, Bridget Lady Tuffington, came into season on the very day of our arrival at the lake. In fact, there was a considerable amount of courting going on in the Mercedes as we made the 300-mile drive. Hamish, who normally slept soundly on automobile trips, was very hot and bothered on this one, but it was not until we embarked in the launch to cross the lake that his emotions ran away with him. As was their wont, both dogs always rode on the bow of the boat, ready to leap ashore as soon as we touched the island's landing stage. Not this time, however. Being just out of my reach, the snow-white pair proceeded to put on a performance that left nothing to the imagination, though it caused raucous laughter as we passed a dinghy with two anglers. We were momentarily expecting a lady houseguest and, although she was as broadminded as they come, we felt it a bit much to expect her to turn a blind eye to those romantic goings-on; so Bridget Lady Tuffington was banished to Josephine Island. Since Hamish was a terrible coward about water, never so much as dipping in a paw to test the temperature, I couldn't believe my eyes when next day I saw him swimming like an Olympic champion across the channel to his beloved.

An unforgettable summer and a spectacular fall in the Adirondacks had made it easy to brush aside any professional vows. Having put up the shutters and closed the camp, we were driving through Keene Valley—the maple trees a blaze of burnished gold—when pangs of conscience began to intrude on me. I had barely put my key in the door of 50 West 10th Street when I was called to the telephone. The caller was an agreeable young producer, David Black, about to try out his Broadway wings with Michael Redgrave's adaptation of Henry James's novel, *The Aspern Papers*. The original plan had been for Michael to double in brass, playing the leading man, H.J., and directing the show, as he had done for the London production. In the meantime, however, he had been engaged to appear in New York in Graham Greene's *The Complaisant Lover*, an attraction that was destined for a substantial run. Realising that he couldn't expect David Black to await his uncertain availability, Michael counselled David to go ahead without him, kindly suggesting that he approach me with a view to my playing H.J. Other casting commitments were awaiting confirmation, including Françoise Rosay and Wendy Hiller, and they could not be postponed any longer.

Earlier Alan and I had witnessed the successful London production which, in addition to Michael's own bravura performance, had the benefit of Flora Robson at her very best in the pathetic part of Tina. Even so, I had my doubts about the play's appeal to New Yorkers unless it were subjected to considerable pruning and revision. In particular the long expository scene that opened the play called for major surgery for a Broadway audience. To my surprise, Michael agreed wholeheartedly with my objections, and he and Alan set to with enthusiasm to rectify the script. How gratifying—and unusual—it was to be working with an author who refused to regard his adaptation as holy writ and who also recognised that New York audiences differed from their London counterparts. Michael was generous enough to say that he wished the changes had been made in the first production; so, with an altogether tighter script, we were ready to go into rehearsal early in December 1961.

Although I had initiated and approved the rewrites, I was not about to accede to David Black's urgings that, like Michael, I also direct the show. At David's suggestion, Margaret Webster was once again given the not altogether appetising job of directing a production and a script that had previously been decided upon. I don't think she was very happy with the assignment, since she had thought the London production faultless and couldn't understand why David had tampered with it. However, since our last association Peggy had made a study of recently introduced innovations in methods of stage lighting. The Venetian palazzo in which the play took place gave full scope for these new gimmicks; in fact, by the time Peggy had finished her plottings, the production had as many light cues as an elaborate musical. Ben Edwards's excellent design for the luxurious palace unfortunately encouraged an experiment that failed in execution. His set afforded a glimpse upstage of the Grand Canal painted realistically on a backdrop. When the scenery was set up for the first time, Peggy, quite rightly, complained that, since the canal was visible throughout the play, its waters had to appear ruffled at times, for persons arriving at the palazzo would have come by gondola which, of course, would have broken the calm of the water. Thereupon she and Ben came up with the idea of specially manufactured stainless-steel pans containing water and placed at the base of the backdrop. Into these reflecting pans was shone a series of lights and, to create the illusion of a ripple on the painted canal, the services of a half-dozen goldfish were requisitioned. These piscatorial additions to the cast did their best to obey Miss Webster's command to swim about like mad when anyone mounted the steps leading from the canal. What had not been foreseen was that in the course of a performance the lights heated the water almost to the boiling point—not the natural habitat for any self-respecting goldfish. They were given a decent burial, however, and replaced by an electric fan, which had a stronger constitution.

That same flight of stairs from the canal started in the basement under the stage and was the cause, at one performance, of a near accident. Smoking is strictly forbidden in the backstage areas of all New York theatres—a prohibition seldom observed by our stagehands engrossed in their poker games beneath the stage. On this occasion a marshal of the Fire Department dropped in to check various fire regulations. Alan, as stage manager, saw the fire marshal start down the backstage stairs to the basement, so he raced down the stairs on his side of the stage to alert the stagehands to extinguish their cigarettes. Alan beat the marshal by a short head and he and the stagehands were pictures of innocence when the marshal arrived. It seemed, however that the marshal's nose told him that someone in the vicinity was smoking. "Perhaps," the marshal speculated, "the offender might be lurking at the top of the temporary stairs," which ascended through the basement's ceiling to the stage above. He decided to investigate, and but for Alan promptly seizing him by the seat of his trousers, the audience would have been treated to the sight of a present-day New York fire marshal who, having parked his gondola, was about to make an incongruous entrance into a Venetian palazzo.

In spite of Walter Winchell's recommendation ("the best play on Broadway"), the response at the box office had not been as brisk as we had expected and, seeking the reason for that indifference, Alan consulted the box-office treasurer. "This show's not going to run very long," said that knowledgeable official, "and here's the proof." Reaching into the till he produced a wad of crisp dollar bills and, riffling through them, added, "Look'ee here—no dirty money!" The fact that there were no soiled smackers to speak of was a sure sign, in his experience, that Jewish customers were not favouring us with their liberally circulated cash, and lacking their support no play could prosper on Broadway. In spite of this curious line of reasoning, however, we fared considerably better than the previously mentioned goldfish, eking out our existence through the Easter holiday. I thoroughly enjoyed playing the plausible rogue H.J. in the company of two such distinguished actresses as Wendy and Françoise, and I was very grateful to be free of managerial chores.

Coinciding with the closing of *The Aspern Papers*, I received an SOS from my original backer, Joe Reed, who was by then deeply involved in the waning fortunes of the Stratford, Connecticut, Shakespeare operation. It was to him that I owed my early successes in New York and his request for help could not be denied, but what form it could take was a knotty problem. I confided my bewilderment to my good friend Helen Hayes, and, true to her reputation of being "the girl who can't say No," she asked what she could do to be of assistance. I assured her that I would put on my thinking cap and come up with some idea for something that we could do together at Stratford in the summer. Whatever it was to be, I firmly intended to abstain from management responsibility. With that in mind, I called upon my former associate, Martin Tahse, who by then had branched out in the "bus and truck" field that we had pioneered together.

Martin had come a long way since his scholarship at Culver Military Academy and his studies at the University of Wisconsin, from which he graduated *summa cum laude*. Even more to his credit was the giant step he had taken from his theatrical beginnings (at the Maxinkuckee Summer Theatre in Indiana!) to his own producing organisation with offices in New York, Chicago, and Los Angeles. At the time of our discussion about Stratford, he already had three star-studded attractions on tour, but lent an eager ear to the idea of a duet performance of some sort involving Helen and his erstwhile employer. I warned him that all we were considering at present was to lend a hand to the Stratford organisation, but should our venture prove to be successful we might be persuaded to go further afield under his management. Having given him his start on Broadway, I should have known better than to expect him to be content with such a qualified undertaking. Before I knew what he was up to, he presented me with a list of cities across the nation that had instantly expressed their wish to book our yet-to-be-written entertainment. The kind of informal program we had vaguely in mind for Stratford would obviously not do for a nationwide tour, so on went the thinking caps again!

The format that finally emerged was the result of painstaking experiments on the part of Alan and me. Every conceivable selection of twosome and solo material had been jotted down on slips of paper, which, rather in the manner of a jigsaw puzzle, we juggled around until a homogeneous pattern evolved. It was excruciatingly difficult to put together a program that flowed naturally, giving Helen and me balanced opportunities and, at the same time, avoiding any hint of being a lecture. Although Alan and I had succeeded in our picking and choosing of possible excerpts, we had not solved the problem of the connective tissue. At this point Alan was reminded of two of his University of

1947–1963

Oregon school chums who had since become successful in New York television: one a writer of documentaries, Jerome Alden, and the other a prominent scenic designer on the staff of NBC, Don Shirley. Together with Warren Enters, the director, they were set the formidable task of dispelling from the mind of the audience any notion that they were in for an educational exercise. Both verbally and visually, lightness had to be the keynote. That they were able to achieve that aim is clearly apparent from the following:

> (*The curtain rises to disclose a small raised platform with a single bench on it and gaily coloured draperies behind it. Downstage Left and Right are two lecterns and two tables piled with books. "He" and "She" enter from opposite sides, their spectacles at the ready.*)

HE:
O for a Muse of fire, that would ascend
The brightest heaven of invention,
A kingdom for a stage, princes to act,
And monarchs to behold the swelling scene!

SHE:
But pardon, gentles all,
The flat unraised spirits that hath dar'd
On this unworthy scaffold to bring forth
So great an object.

HE:
Can this cockpit hold
The vasty fields of France? Or may we cram
Within this wooden O the very casques
That did affright the air at Agincourt?

SHE:
Oh pardon! since a crooked figure may
Attest in little place a million;
And let us, ciphers to this great accompt,
On your imaginary forces work.

HE:
Piece out our imperfections with your thoughts;
Into a thousand parts divide one man,
And make imaginary puissance.

SHE:
Think, when we talk of horses, that you see them
Printing their proud hoofs i' the receiving earth;
For 'tis your thoughts now must deck our kings.

HE:
Which, let's face it, is an awful lot to ask even of an audience as friendly as yourselves.

SHE:
But having promised to give you some Shakespeare tonight, we racked our brains to find some kind of connecting thread for our program.

HE:
So, in search of a theme, we made the mistake of going to the library.

SHE:
(*Moving to her books and putting on her specs*): Only to find that if we were to place end to end all the books that have been written about Shakespeare they would, as Puck says, "Put a girdle round about the earth."

HE:
(*Having crossed to his books and reading from one*): Samuel Johnson said: Above all writers Shakespeare's persons act and speak by the influence of those

general passions and principles by which all minds are agitated, and the whole system of life is continued in motion.

SHE: (*Another book*): Tolstoy said: Shakespeare is an insignificant, inarticulate and not only nonmoral, but plainly *im*moral writer!

HE: (*Another book*): The sublime and genius shine in Shakespeare like flashes in a long night ... Diderot.

SHE: (*Another book*): ... he was completely lacking in good taste and had no respect for the rules ... Voltaire.

HE: (*Another book*): To Coleridge, Shakespeare was not merely a dramatist and poet, but a divine genius whose faults were not faults but inspired virtues.

SHE: (*Another book*): Quote: With the single exception of Homer, there is no eminent writer, not even Sir Walter Scott, whom I can despise so entirely as I despise Shakespeare when I measure my mind against his. Unquote. George Bernard Shaw.

HE: Yes. Remember—Bernard Shaw used to complain of Shakespeare's empty-headedness and accused him of being a nincompoop on the grounds that if he'd had any real sense he would have founded the Socialist Party in 1590!

SHE: (*Another book*): Mr. T. S. Eliot: About anyone so great as Shakespeare, it is probable that we can never be right; and if we can never be right, it is better that we should from time to time change our way of being wrong.

HE: Not a clue. So much for the experts. (*He discards book*)

SHE: Wait a minute. Here is the one authority who can put us on the right road.

HE: Meaning?

SHE: (*Picking up the collected works*): The Bard himself. Take any theme in the world and he made it sing.

HE: How sweet the moonlight sleeps upon this bank!
Here will we sit and let the sounds of music
Creep in our ears: soft stillness and the night
Become the touches of sweet harmony.
Sit, Jessica. Look how the floor of heaven
Is thick inlaid with patens of bright gold.
There's not the smallest orb which thou behold'st
But in his motion like an angel sings,
Still quiring to the young-eyed cherubim.

SHE: Now the hungry lion roars,
And the wolf behowls the moon;
Whilst the heavy ploughman snores,
All the weary task fordone,
Now the wasted brands do glow,

Whilst the screech-owl, screeching loud,
In remembrance of a shroud. . . .

HE: Look, love what envious streaks
Do lace the severing clouds in yonder east:
Night's candles are burnt out, and jocund day
Stands tiptoe on the misty mountain tops.

SHE: Full many a glorious morning have I seen
Flatter the mountain tops wtih sovereign eye,
Kissing with golden face the meadows green,
Gilding pale streams with heavenly alchemy.

HE: I know a bank where the wild thyme blows,
Where oxlips and the nodding violet grows;
Quite over-canopied with luscious woodbine,
With sweet musk roses, and with eglantine.

SHE: Here's flowers for you;
Hot lavender, mints, savory, marjoram;
The marigold, that goes to bed wi' the sun,
And with him rises weeping: these are flowers
Of middle summer, and I think they are given
To men of middle age.

HE: Therefore my age is as a lusty winter,
Frosty, but kindly.

SHE: How tartly that gentleman looks!
I never can see him but I am heartburn'd an hour after.

HE: She was a vixen when she went to school:
And tho' she be but little, she is fierce!

SHE: Well said: That was laid on with a trowel.

HE: I have words
That would be howl'd out in the desert air,
Where hearing should not latch them.

SHE: Foul words is but foul wind, and foul wind is but foul breath,
And foul breath is noisome; therefore, I will depart unkissed.

HE: I know a trick worth two of that.

SHE: My purpose is indeed a horse of that color.

HE: For mine own part—it was Greek to me!

SHE: As good luck would have it!

HE: Give the devil his due.

SHE: There's small choice in rotten apples.

HE: There's something rotten in the state of Denmark.

SHE: Lord what fools these mortals be.

HE: The naked truth!

SHE: The short and long of it!

HE: There's the humour of it!

ONE-NIGHT STANDS

SHE: Neither rhyme nor reason!

HE: You are pictures out of doors,
Bells in your parlours, wild cats in your kitchens, Saints in your injuries,
devils being offended, Players in your housewifery, and housewives in your
beds.

SHE: Zounds, I never was so bethumped with words
Since I first call'd my brother's father dad.

HE: With a hey and a ho and a hey nonny, nonny. . .

SHE: No!
It was a lover and his lass,
With a hey and a ho, an a hey nonino,
That o'er the green cornfield did pass
In springtime, in springtime, the only pretty ring time,
When birds do sing, hey ding a ding, ding;
Sweet lovers love the spring.

HE: (*Sings, then breaks off*): "Sweet lovers love. . ."
That's it, Helen! That's our theme! "LOVE"—
Young love, old love. . .

SHE: Sweet and sour love. . .! Bravo!

Somewhat giddy and breathless from that quick-fire "bat-and-ball"
introduction, we were to find that it put our audiences in a relaxed and
receptive mood for what followed—some of it grave, some gay—but all of it
within the framework of affection.

Billed as *A Program for Two Players*, the dress rehearsal at Stratford was a
sobering experience in at least one respect. The management, with an
optimistic eye on a future tour of enormous college auditoria, insisted that we
accustom ourselves to wearing microphones on our persons. Unlike today's
virtually invisible instruments, at that time the smallest microphone available
resembled a medium-sized zucchini. It wasn't too noticeable in Helen's case,
since it could nestle in her "cleavage," but hidden under my tuxedo shirt it
gave me the appearance of a pouter pigeon. In addition, it was found that any
stance closer than arm's length caused the beastly things to wail like banshees.
At the final rehearsal when Helen, alone on the stage, was rendering
Cleopatra's dying speech, "I have immortal longings in me," I was stricken with
an urgent longing to take a pee. In my haste to get to my dressing-room john
I omitted to switch off my mike; as a result, when I flushed, the theatre's
loudspeakers transmitted a deluge of rushing mighty waters, completely
obliterating Helen's big moment: "O Antony!" (Oh! Evans!!) Fortuitously,
someone stole one of the microphones after that night and we managed very
nicely thank you with nothing but our own bell-like tones for the rest of the
engagement.

It was unusual for the New York drama critics to cover theatrical happenings outside their normal beat, but they turned out in full force for us, as these quotations show:

> A noteworthy demonstration of performers enjoying a theatrical field day. A lively evening revisiting Shakespeare. [*New York Times*]

> Great words and great players make an irresistible combination. This is potent theatrical fascination. [Associated Press]

> Evans, Hayes triumph. A unique experience. These great stage personalities held an audience fascinated. [*New York Journal-American*]

> Hayes, Evans, Bard sparkle. [*New York Daily Mirror*]

In spite of that encouragement, we were hesitant about the proposed tour; so much so that when we finally capitulated, the shortness of notice made it, geographically speaking, impossible for Martin Tahse to lay out an easy route. The schedule finally decided upon resembled a fever chart and resulted in our playing sixty-nine cities in nineteen weeks, the majority of them being one-night stands. For two actors in their early sixties that was a daunting challenge, but we were to find such receptive audiences, especially at the universities en route, that we soon got into our stride. By the time our mobile caravan had completed its five-month coast-to-coast round trip, we had given 135 performances and travelled upwards of 19,000 miles. We were preceded at each stop by a minibus, carrying the stage managers and crew, and a truck with our little *commedia del arte* stage and the lighting equipment. Helen and her assistant, Vera Benlian, and Alan and I travelled comfortably in a Greyhound bus that had been stripped of most of its seats—these replaced by built-in beds for the odd afternoon nap, space for our steamer trunks, special tables, also an ice chest containing snacks and a cocktail shaker, as well as a crackling radio and other comforts of home. We found this a far more civilised means of transportation than the earlier days of train travel. Upon arrival at the one-night stands, the bus pulled up outside a waiting hotel and we disembarked with nothing but overnight bags. At show time the bus took us to whatever auditorium we were to play, and later returned us to collapse in our beds, having narrowly survived not only our demanding performance, but often some gruelling social affair that followed it.

Twenty years had elapsed since Helen and I had toured together in *Twelfth Night*, so it was not surprising that I had forgotten that to her the early hours of Sunday mornings were sacrosanct. Not until she had been shriven were we able to start on what, on the Sabbath, were usually long hauls to our next stand. The purging of her soul at Mass had the unfortunate concomitant of sharpening her ingrained sense of curiosity. Thus, search parties had to be

ONE-NIGHT STANDS

dispatched to scour the streets of Anderson, Indiana, or Knoxville, Tennessee, to rescue our wandering star. Once "all aboard," that indefatigable lady demanded that Alan produce the Scrabble set, a game that she proceeded to play in a manner that would have to be owned up to at Mass the following Sunday. On one such journey, going at full speed down a highway between Cleveland, Ohio, and Huntington, West Virginia, we ran into a terrific blizzard. Skidding into a ditch, our driver by some miracle contrived to get us back onto the road. Whereas the rest of us aboard clung desperately to our seats, Helen, quite oblivious of having just escaped a messy death, was heard to say to Alan in stentorian tones, "There's no such word in the dictionary!"

Athens, Ohio, remains a total blank in my memory, but the next evening at Lexington, Kentucky, does not. The route sheet showed that we were to play the university auditorium, which had the somewhat forbidding name of the "Memorial Coliseum." On arriving at our hotel, we were greeted by Thelma Chandler, our devoted production stage manager, informing us that, whereas the Coliseum was ideal for the slaughter of Christians by hungry lions, it possessed no stage or dressing rooms. No one but Thelma could have coped so ingeniously in that emergency. She had rounded up every trestle table on campus and had them lashed together; a couple of screens off this platform, left and right, served as changing rooms, and that was it. After this briefing, Helen and I were prepared for the worst, but when the bus dropped us off for the performance we circled the vast arena on foot looking in vain for the stage door. Students were already flocking in for our show, so we were obliged to get in the queue. Helen flashed a winning smile at the ticket-taker but it got us nowhere. "No tickets, no admittance!" was his dictum. We had taken the precaution of donning our evening clothes at the hotel in readiness for the show, and it was a glimpse of Helen's décolleté green dress beneath her fur coat that finally won over the doorman. The sight that greeted us as we elbowed our way into that vast arena with our pathetic little stage barely discernible, caused Helen to exclaim: "I'm going to look like a midget dill pickle down there!" Although on the preceding evening the pianist Van Cliburn had given a recital without incident, we fared somewhat less fortunately. We were in the middle of the second part of our program when the majority of the students made for the nearest exits. Our spirits sank to zero until we were assured afterwards that the mass exodus was due to the omission on the part of the university authorities to suspend the regular curfew.

A standstill week in St. Louis playing eight performances in a conventional theatre enabled us to regain our poise. But Michigan, ahead, had at least one surprise in store for us. In order to reach the university town of Albion, Michigan, in time for the show it was necessary to fly there. That we did on a veteran prop-plane operated by an airline with the impressive name of Lake

Central. To board that relic we climbed a ladder affair that was lowered from the plane's tail, and en route we rather lost confidence in the pilot when the hostess had to point out to him on a map our next port of call. After a number of such casual landings to deliver parcels, we made a very bumpy landing at our destination and were once more greeted by a distraught stage manageress. This time, not only was there no stage, but, she told us, we were announced as appearing in the university's Goodrich Chapel. From its name we assumed it would be one of those very simple meetinghouses, but not a bit of it. Upon inspection we found it to be a stunningly beautiful place of worship—stained glass windows, altar with gold crucifix and candlesticks, choir stalls and pews. What would have to serve as our stage was the space between the opposing choir stalls; hardly the appropriate platform for the bawdy double entendres of our Katharina and Petruchio scene or the murderous plottings of the Macbeths. To assuage Helen's delicate feelings and to avoid being accused of sacrilege, a veil, normally reserved for Good Friday, was draped over the altar cross. Nevertheless, in order to make her exit, supposedly to King Duncan's chamber, on "Give me the daggers!" Helen had to drop on her hands and knees and disappear behind the organ console. Alan, too, did his share of crawling through choir stalls to minister to my needs, but in spite of all that improvisation the "congregation" was not in the least embarrassed by their surroundings. In fact, they laughed uproariously at my impersonation of all the clowns in *A Midsummer Night's Dream* and were unstinting with their applause throughout the program.

If our peregrinations were anything to judge by, the early winter months are better spent elsewhere than in the region of the Great Lakes unless you happen to have a liking for razor-sharp, icy-cold winds and slippery sidewalks. It said something for our strong constitutions that neither of us contracted coughs and colds, though, alas, the same could not be said of some members of our audiences. Perhaps the reason we were not similarly afflicted was due to the fact that every evening we were working like cart horses in overheated buildings; consequently, both of us got up body temperatures that no self-respecting bug would deign to invade.

We were chancing our luck, however, when in December our route took us to places such as Atlanta, Georgia, and Charlotte and Durham, North Carolina. In anticipation of the caressing breezes and the comforting warmth of the sunny South, Helen and I busied ourselves reorganising our packing. To the bottom of her trunk went her fur coat, and my tickly long johns to the depths of mine. Alan, who had spent winters in and around Atlanta, did his best to discourage us, but we turned deaf ears to his dismal forecast. How wrong we were became apparent as our bus approached the outskirts of Atlanta. It clawed its way through snowdrifts and, having battled a howling gale, finally dropped us at what appeared at first sight to be a luxury motel. The forecourt through which we struggled, carrying our overnight baggage, was decorated with a series of pools, all frozen solid. At the center of each stood the statue of a naked goddess, supposedly reflected in the normally gentle waters of her pool. The sculptor's art was not improved upon by the addition to the breasts of these maidens of long pendulous icicles. Seemingly the prayers for a thaw offered up by the owners of the motel had not been granted; so we slunk into our rooms and stuffed towels and bathmats in the drafty gaps under doors and windows, and went to bed with our socks on.

Gradually we thawed out from Atlanta's cold snap as we continued on our way to Knoxville, Charlotte, and Durham, to play our last one-night stand, at Greensboro, North Carolina, on December 15, 1962, before our holiday break in the tour. Never before had the yuletide season been so welcome, since the universities dispersed for Christmas, allowing us time to get up steam for the thirty-nine towns and cities that still awaited us during the second part of the tour. Of all unlikely things, in spite of having been constantly in each other's company for over two months, we couldn't bear the thought of being separated. Helen had planned to spend Christmas at her second home in Mexico and, noticing a hint of wistfulness in my good wishes, she suddenly asked, "Why don't you and Alan come, too?" Thus did we pay our first visit to Cuernavaca, which, in later years, was to become our home for a while.

To fit in with Helen's timetable, we flew from Greensboro to New York and onwards to Mexico the next day; had we done otherwise, the story might have had a very different ending. Our trusty Greyhound bus, with only the company manager and Vinnie, our assistant stage manager, as passengers, puffed its solitary way back to its New York garage for a well-deserved rest. On one of the main highways, a passenger car, coming in the opposite direction, mounted the median and crashed into our bus at ninety miles per hour. Driven by some rejected suitor in his cups, the vehicle hit the bus almost head-on with a ferocious impact, shattering windows and dislodging our steamer trunks which, had we been aboard at the time, would in all probability have flattened us into pancakes. As it was, both our driver and Vinnie were quite badly injured and the young lothario was killed instantly. We were kept in ignorance of this happening until, a couple of weeks later, we resumed the tour in Seattle on December 31 after our blessed rest at Cuernavaca.

By then our mobile Greyhound home, for which we had developed such an affection, had been declared a write-off, so for the ensuing month we were obliged to travel by air in the northwestern states. Although we were treated to glorious views such as the Cascade Mountains and the Canadian Rockies, we sorely missed the comfort of our beloved Greyhound. Vancouver, B.C., and Portland, Oregon, were followed by a one-night stand at Alan's alma mater, the University of Oregon, at Eugene. It was at this institution, noted for the excellence of its drama department, that not only Alan, but our script writer, Jerome Alden, and our scenic designer, Don Shirley, Jr., had learnt their crafts; so we felt particularly welcome that evening at MacArthur Court.

It was at one of these hit-and-run engagements that the ever-ebullient Helen was reduced to a low simmer. A personable young student had forced his way backstage in a quest for autographs and, although we were overdue at a campus reception, Helen remained closetted with her admirer for what seemed an age. Eventually she emerged arm-in-arm with the youngster, her cheeks aglow. "Do you know," she said as we walked towards our waiting car, "this young man has taken the trouble to learn by heart the whole of my Broadway career including the names of theatres in which I appeared." Blowing him a kiss as she was about to enter the car, it was at that moment that the young Boswell called after her, "Oh, Miss Hayes, I forgot to tell you I thought you were just wonderful in *Whatever Happened to Baby Jane?*" To be mistaken for Bette Davis might be regarded as a compliment by some, but, in this instance, Helen resembled the original pricked balloon. The shoe was on the other foot when we were booked to appear in a local movie house. The posters outside proclaimed with pride the showing of a Boris Karloff horror film, and several misguided members of our audience were on the verge of demanding their money back when Frankenstein's monster failed to show up.

It was a feature of this whirlwind tour that we were usually on our way to the next engagement by the time the local drama critic had put his pen to work. In fact, I find only one review in my files, which, one hopes, was typical of the others that never caught up with us:

> Columbus was fortunate enough to have "A Program for Two Players" in town on both Wednesday and Thursday evenings. This is a mild way of saying that the glory of the living theatre at its best has shone round about us. . . . The "Program" was no mere scrap-book of big moments from a lot of plays, but an extraordinary, clever survey of representative Shakespeare material arranged with vast theatrical know-how. . . . With dazzling comedic skill Miss Hayes and Mr. Evans, in formal dress attire, impersonated Rosalind and Orlando, Katherine of France and Henry V, the shrewish Katherine and Petruchio. With greatest emotional cogency they described the macabre courting of Anne by Richard III, the "Closet Scene" from "Hamlet."
> Miss Hayes gave a fabulous account of Constance's "I am not mad" speech from "King John," of Cleopatra's death scene. Mr. Evans was wonderfully fine in "Once more unto the breach" from "Henry V" and in passages from "Titus Andronicus," "Love's Labour's Lost" and "Troilus and Cressida." And his playing of all the clowns in "A Midsummer Night's Dream" was a veritable acting tour de force. . . .

ONE-NIGHT STANDS

Great actors, great people, an enchanting show! [*Columbus Dispatch*, November 30, 1962]

With either San Francisco or Los Angeles as home bases, we made forays all over southern California in an elongated, car-sick-making limousine. Thereafter our digestive tracts were relieved to find themselves airborne once more as we winged our way to Denver, Colorado, where we were to be joined by a replacement bus, Greyhound II. Parties galore at that most hospitable of cities very nearly took their toll, though. On the last of our evenings we were delightfully and soberly entertained by Denver's famous daughter, the playwright Mary Chase, whose *Harvey* is a classic.

For me, our next stop at Colorado Springs was a nostalgic occasion, reminding me of an earlier visit when I was taken on a trek into the mountains on horseback. It had been in springtime and, as the snow had melted, the hillsides were a riot of coloured wildflowers. Our cowboy guide took us to higher altitudes to point out the spectacular views of the Rocky Mountains, and on our descent we were instructed to hang onto the pommels of our western saddles as our horses slid gracefully downwards on banks of loose shale. After an unforgettable campfire steak barbecue, we remounted our steeds with some difficulty and jogged our way further down to where duty called. On that occasion the duty was a performance of *Hamlet*, one in which, I may say, at no point was I able to sit down without wincing.

A different cause for embarrassment occurred when we appeared in our *Program* there at the United States Air Force Academy. The finale of the show was Petruchio's adieu:

> HE: Why, there's a wench! Come on, and kiss me Kate.
> 'Twas I won the wager, though you hit the white.
> And being a winner,
> > (*They both raise their arms in the victory*
> > *sign and speak in unison*)
> God give you good night!

Accustomed as we were to a thunderous applause from the audience, that time we were greeted by a tepid response. Retiring with noticeable egg on our faces, we refused to be mollified until we were told that our audience of cadets had been ordered to attend in dress uniform, one of the requirements being the wearing of regulation white gloves which, though smartening their appearance, muted their hand-clapping.

A late arrival at Lubbock, Texas, did nothing to discourage Helen's passion for sightseeing. When she was told that there was a strange geological fault in that part of God's own country, off she went with Alan to explore this rift in the ground, which surprisingly resembled a junior Grand Canyon.

Breathless but unbowed, she made it back to the auditorium only minutes before curtain time, as unconcerned as if she had been on one of her customary shopping sprees.

Our next stop was Austin, Texas, where I had last been seen in *Richard II* at the age of thirty-six, but there I was again, somewhat plumper at sixty-one, but still at it. In contrast with some of the motels elsewhere, Alan and I were housed in great splendour at the town's principal hotel, in the penthouse suite normally reserved for the favourite son of Texas, the then Vice President of the United States, Lyndon Johnson, and his charming wife, Lady Bird. Ushered in by two bellboys, one to each overnight bag, a quick inspection convinced us that the Johnsons were strangely cleanly in their habits, since the penthouse boasted no less than four bathrooms. A cause for anxiety, on my part, was that the machinery which operated a bank of elevators was situated immediately over my bedroom. Counting sheep may counteract insomnia, but speculating on which floor an elevator would come to a halt was no effective lullaby.

I was not to visit Austin again until 1982 when, as the guest of the University of Texas, I was invited to work with their drama students. In the nineteen years that had elapsed between visits, not only had one of the country's best theatrical libraries been established but also what I consider to be the most complete theatre complex in the whole of the United States had come into being. It is on a huge scale with every conceivable facility provided for the tremendous theatre, the scenery-building shops, and the wardrobe department. Rehearsal halls for dance, music, and drama abound, besides an intimate opera house and an open-space experimental theatre. To compensate for the vastness of the main playhouse, under every other seat in the big auditorium a minute loudspeaker is discreetly tucked away. I attended a student production of an unfamiliar Jerome Kern musical comedy, *Very Good, Eddie*, in that fabulous theatre. It took a little time to become accustomed to one's hearing seemingly being located in a part of one's anatomy other than one's ears, but the quality of the sound was surprisingly agreeable.

Battling our way eastwards in the appalling February of 1963 via Oklahoma and Kansas, we heaved a sigh of relief to find ourselves snuggly housed in Hallmark's V.I.P. penthouse in Kansas City, Missouri. Joyce C. Hall, the king of the greeting-card empire and my television angel of earlier years, was there to greet us. By chance it so happened that no performance had been scheduled on the night of our arrival, so we were able to gather round the jumbo colour television set to watch Hallmark's *Pygmalion* being beamed from New York. With understandable pride, Mr. Hall turned on the set at the appointed hour, whereupon the image on the screen developed an epileptic fit that no amount of knob twiddling would cure. In despair, the building superintendent produced his own little black-and-white set round which we huddled while hastily summoned engineers sought to rectify the antics in the colour set. Egged on by Joyce Hall himself, the mechanics worked like beavers, but by the time they succeeded in their efforts all that remained for us to see in colour was the final exhortation to buy a Hallmark Valentine's Day greeting card—"If you care enough to send the very best."

That most generous of hosts, amongst other penchants, was a great admirer of Winston Churchill, several of whose watercolours he acquired and, with Churchill's permission, reproduced one of them as a Christmas card. That was the beginning of a close friendship between those two captains in their respective fields, a token of which on Joyce's part was to arrange for a passenger lift to be installed in his winter home at the Malibu Colony in California so that the aging Churchill would be spared the stairs. Sad to say, Churchill never made the promised stay in California, and, as an occasional guest in the house myself, I felt it would be *lèse-majesté* to avail myself of that very personal conveyance.

The sun had only to peep through the clouds over Kansas City for Helen to be convinced that, in spite of its being February, spring was in the air. However, as our bus sped on its way to Indiana, we encountered more of the filthy weather that we vainly hoped had been left behind on our way from Texas. What Helen *had* left behind, however, was her beautiful sable coat, at the Hallmark penthouse. The risk of the First Lady of the Theatre being stricken with hypothermia in South Bend, Indiana, was overcome by prompt action on the part of the Hallmark wizards, who, by courier, restored the missing garment to its shivering owner. A further hazard awaited us the following night at Indianapolis, where we played in an obsolete movie house. Returning to our cubicles to change clothes for the second act, we were confronted by the sight of our shoes swimming around in water gushing forth from a temperamental toilet. Squelching our way through Act II, we were comforted by the knowledge that our next engagement was to be a full week of performances at the Shubert Theatre in Boston where, presumably, the elements and the plumbing would be more merciful.

For me, Boston meant I had to watch my "P's and Q's," since two years earlier I had been the recipient of an honorary Doctorate of Laws at nearby Brandeis University. At that time it seemed that someone had researched my undistinguished scholastic record and decided to play it safe by crediting me with possessing qualities unusually descriptive of members of the legal profession. What I feared might be a rather solemn occasion turned out to be quite jolly. The proceedings started with an alfresco breakfast on the recently landscaped grounds of the campus, and both Adlai Stevenson and I were called upon to make informal speeches, but not, to my dismay, in that order. It was no small challenge to precede a distinguished and witty politician whose

1947–1963

popularity had narrowly missed his winning the presidency in the Eisenhower era. What saved the day for me was my awareness that Brandeis University had been funded, in the main, by the Jewish community of the United States. Having been introduced by the chairman I was able to refer to the confusion about the pronunciation of my first name—either "Maurice" as in Chevalier, or "Morris" when in England. I went on to express my pleasure that in the present company it was appropriate for me to say, "Call me Moishe!" Not to be outdone, Stevenson regaled the bagels-and-lox breakfasters with hysterically funny stories about his own unfortunate first name of "Adlai." At election time, he could console himself, a critical margin of voters had been under the false impression that his candidacy was by a member of the fairer sex named "Adelaide"—in those days an unthinkable departure from the norm.

Nearing the end of our tour, with only one standstill week in Philadelphia to look forward to, we jumped back and forth over the Mason-Dixon line like grasshoppers. From the D.A.R.'s Constitution Hall in Washington, D.C., to the Shriner's "Rajah" auditorium in Reading, Pennsylvania, and various Masonic Temples en route, we darted back to the scene of my American debut as Romeo—Baltimore, Maryland—which had occurred twenty-seven years previously. Catching our breath at the Walnut Street Theatre in William Penn's City of Brotherly Love, there was light at the end of our touring tunnel. Leaving Philadelphia on Sunday, March 3, 1963, we travelled to Burlington, Vermont, to begin our last week with one-night stands at Burlington, Syracuse, Buffalo, and Corning, then to Wilmington, Delaware, where we were to give three final performances.

As we bowled down the Pennsylvania Turnpike to Wilmington, Alan reminded me that it was time I took the next penicillin pill, a course of which a Boston dentist had prescribed for a badly abscessed tooth. Never having been put on the wonderdrug before, I swigged it down with my customary midday dry martini. That, it turned out, was a disastrous error of judgement, for when we stopped for lunch at some wayside café, I ordered a bowl of soup, each spoonful of which ran down my chin into my lap. It was Helen, sitting opposite me, who first spotted, not only my peculiar table manners, but the fact that my face was swelling and turning beet-red. She recognised the unattractive symptoms as an allergy to penicillin. The café proprietor rushed me to the nearest hospital—Alan, seated beside me, held onto my tongue to prevent my choking to death—where they succeeded in arresting the condition. However, by the time we resumed our journey I was utterly voiceless. To have survived the punishing nineteen weeks only to be rendered dumb for the last stand was infuriating at the time, but seems comic in retrospect. If I had been able, I would have laughed out loud at the mixed expressions of sympathy and disbelief on the faces of those gathered in my

ONE-NIGHT STANDS

Wilmington hotel suite, and not until Helen came to the rescue were they thoroughly convinced that I was totally incapacitated. "Let us try our opening—'O, for a muse of fire!'" she said. Sounding like a croaking frog I uttered the "O," but *the rest* was *silence!* To my intense chagrin there was nothing for it but to cancel the sold-out evening performance. What I fear made me suspect was that by the matinee the next day my vocal chords were back to normal and I was able to breeze through the two remaining shows in my usual noisy fashion. How far that had been from a theatrical swan-song was not apparent at the time, nor at sixty-two did I realise that I was on the brink of a whole new career, which would continue for another twenty years with no end in sight.

V

1964-1985

"...the bubble reputation..."

1. BEWITCHED

HAT BLISS IT was to be back in New York, sleeping in my own bed with its multispring mattress and pillows of genuine down. In other words, home-sweet-home and the luxury of staying put for a change. But it was not to last.

Our Greek couple, Zed and Pappa, neither of them getting any younger, had received word that after many years of haggling, their claim for reparations from the Russian government for property seized in Romania after World War II was being approved. This meant that they would have to return to Greece, where the claim had been made, before another year was up. In good conscience I could not stand in the way of their wish to be repatriated, so I was faced, once more, with the daunting task of replacing them eventually.

Indirectly it was John Gielgud who brought about the major change in my situation. He was guest of honour at a supper party given by Edward Albee at his flat across from my house on 10th Street, and had suggested to his host that Alan and I be invited. John was appearing in Albee's play, *Tiny Alice*, and assumed that we were not only neighbours but friends. It was not surprising that we had never run across each other, since I had been on the road for an age and Albee spent most of his time at his house on Long Island. For him, commuting by car had become a problem because parking on 10th Street was virtually impossible. Knowing that I had a large garage, Albee asked me if he could rent some space. It was quite uncharacteristic of me to make snap decisions but, on this occasion, I heard myself saying that although the renting proposal was not practical I was prepared to sell him the entire property if he was in a mind to buy. He jumped at my offer to sell with such alacrity that by

291

the time I left the party I thought I was suffering from a mental aberration. But, next morning at breakfast, I knew I'd done the right thing.

However, not until a third cup of coffee had gone down my gullet did it begin to dawn upon me that I was letting myself into a task that made the Augean stables mere child's play by comparison. The clutter of half a lifetime would have to be disposed of, including masses of theatrical equipment stored in the garage. Then there was the matter of moving to—where? Fortunately, it being summer time, Albee spent those months entirely on Long Island, which gave me breathing space to reorganise my life.

The Wilton cottage was far too small to accommodate the furniture that I had painstakingly acquired over the years. Once more the country bumpkin in me took over, so we scoured the countryside within easy reach of New York City, settling finally on a charming house overlooking the Hudson River at Dobbs Ferry. Incidentally, I had come almost full circle: thirty years before I had stayed directly across the river at Sneden's Landing.

From my new house on Appleton Place, I was separated by a half mile of water from those haunts of my early days in the United States—days when commuting to the city was a test of one's stamina. In 1936 New York's West Side Highway had not yet been built, nor, on the Jersey side of the Hudson, had the Palisades Parkway come into being. To reach Sneden's Landing by car from Broadway a tortuous route had to be followed: first through all of Central Park from south to north and onwards to brave a zigzag course through a maze of traffic lights until one reached the George Washington Bridge. The best part of an hour could be consumed up to that point, with another hour's driving from Fort Lee still to be negotiated on the venerable Route 9-W. Since the journey was being made soon after the curtain had fallen on *Richard II* or *Hamlet*, I was not the most reliable of drivers, nor the most agreeable of passengers when a friend was at the wheel. In reverse, the driving was even more trying on the nerves, because the Hudson River valley is unpredictable in the matter of fog and, in winter, icy roads. How much time to allow was anybody's guess. In the theatre, however, come hell or high water, one does not keep the customers waiting—a precept I narrowly missed observing on several occasions.

In those days my neighbours were mainly prosperous businessmen, who told me that for many years they had scorned the automobile as a means of commuting to their city offices. Instead, they assembled on a rickety old dock on Sneden's riverside to be ferried across by an ancient mariner. Arriving at an equally unstable landing stage on the opposite shore, he deposited them within yards of the Dobbs Ferry railway station, and in something less than an hour those hearty souls had reached Grand Central Station, well disposed to go about their pursuits of Mammon.

BEWITCHED

That Appleton Place was destined to be the scene of my retirement was rudely dispelled even before the ink was dry on the transfer-of-ownership document. What had been a faint plume of Hollywood smoke became a roaring, fiery furnace. Offers for film and television shows came pouring in with the result that my travelling exceeded the gyrations of a yo-yo. At one moment I could be found playing a dotty old Druid to Charlton Heston's War Lord (with a girdle of mistletoe round my middle); the next in Munich, impersonating a crafty jewel thief in *Jack of Diamonds*; and then for *I Spy* in the mystical town of Marrakech in Morocco. That last junket to North Africa was memorable for several reasons, not the least of them being that Marion Hargrove had written a literate script for the series. In it I played a fanatical Moslem leader—turban, beard, sandals and all. Little did the author realise that he was prophesying today's turbulence in the Middle East.

The regulation Islamic footwear proved a serious problem because, walking each morning to our location in the market (or "souk"), as I did, I repeatedly left one sandal behind. Apart from the difficulty of following in the wake of a camel with a digestive disorder, the sight of a dignified Mahdi retrieving an errant sandal scandalised the Moroccans, who took me for a genuine potentate.

Unable to master the sandal technique, I decided to wear tennis shoes on my way to work, relying on Alan to see to it that I changed into the elusive sandals whenever my feet were to be seen on camera. Came a day of filming when Alan was busy on another assignment and, in his absence, I parked my tennis shoes in a dark corner at the Sultan's Palace, where the shooting was taking place. At the end of the day's filming, I went to exchange my sandals for the hidden tennis shoes, only to find that some acquisitive Arab had swiped them—arch supports and all! I felt particularly vexed when a survey of the nether extremities of Moroccans showed that my size sevens could never accommodate the feet of a single one of them. What made me almost panic over the theft was the fact that, in response to a telephone call in the middle of the night a week earlier, I had agreed to fly from Morocco to Mexico to take part in an episode of the *Tarzan* television series. That rashly made commitment could be honoured only if my arch supports could be replaced—a requirement demanding that I visit my foot specialist in New York en route to Mexico.

As it turned out, the necessary rerouting proved an unexpected blessing, because it required an overnight stay in Madrid that allowed us an opportunity to visit the Prado to view, for the first time, the magnificent Goya exhibition. Art galleries are apt to be hard even on the nimble-footed, but to those of us whose metatarsal arches have collapsed, such cultural expeditions can be sheer torture. However, on that occasion Goya had me walking on air.

It was also consoling, later on, when a sympathetic soul sent me a clipping from the *Chicago Tribune*, which seemed to indicate that my labours in Marrakech had not been in vain:

> Not many series provide memorable television moments, but Monday's *I Spy* episode, *Oedipus at Colonus*, was better than good. Guest star was the superb Shakespearean actor, Maurice Evans, who portrayed a powerful Moslem leader apparently bent on engineering a holy war. The writer wisely gave Evans center stage during much of the hour, including the dénouement when he turned upon his blood-thirsty comrades and had them annihilated.
> It might seen incongruous for an actor noted for Hamlet and Macbeth to be cast as a Middle Eastern political and religious leader, but Evans handled it as though he had been playing Sultan-and-Sheik types all his life.

That reviewer could not have known that there was a lighter side to the mayhem at the end of each day of outdoor filming, when a group of curious little Arab boys would gather around to watch me removing my beard. Being used to seeing their fathers and big brothers pluck out their chin-stubble with a pair of seashells, the kids emitted horrified "Oohs and Aahs" as I made pretend how painful it was to do likewise with my stuck-on beard.

When I had let it be known to the agents that I was interested in working-holidays, I was envisaging myself lolling about on golden beaches or becoming acquainted with parts of the world that were new to me. With such aspirations in mind, I once asked the well-travelled proprietress of a hotel in which we were staying whether or not she would recommend Scandinavia as an area to be sought after. "Sorry," she said, "I've never been there. My boyfriend and I always prefer to go to the smelly countries." Her apt description neatly fitted my recent peregrinations in North Africa and Mexico, although, to be honest, I was blissfully unconscious of the obnoxious odours about which my fellow actors complained. It was a legacy from my Shakespearean past, which, though a handicap at the time, gave me the advantage in those subtropical and tropical venues.

Though not related to my inability to savour either delicate or acrid fragrances, my schnozzle demands the constant attentions of a handerchief in cold weather. It is not hard to speculate how the Elizabethans, in their pocketless doublets and hose, coped with such emergencies. However, it would hardly be seemly for today's actors to resort to a wipe on the cuff, and it would be equally anomalous for Hamlet to flourish his *mouchoir* to stem the tide. Nor could he benefit, as did the old lady in my favourite story, by being prompted of the imminent arrival of the offending drip. When guests were present at table, her butler had orders to call attention to the situation by murmuring the

BEWITCHED

code words "Mr. Mackenzie" in her ear. On one such formal occasion he sensed disaster as his mistress raised her spoon. "Mr. Mackenzie," he whispered urgently, then, like an actor who has muffed his punch line, "Mr. Mackenzie's in the soup, Ma'am!"

George Bernard Shaw, possessing as he did a typically Irish proboscis, was almost fanatical about noses—describing at length the physiognomy of that feature in the characters of his plays. He once told me that, to achieve sonority, actors, singers, and politicians should make a regular habit of flushing out their beaks with a salt solution. I was to regret later on that I didn't follow his advice, since the nose-and-throat specialists, in whose clutches I became entangled, robbed me of my olfactory nerve, and with it my sense of smell. To begin with I was not aware of my loss, only grateful that my Hamlet was no longer heard to be saying, "To be or *dot* to be." By others—poets, novelists, and lovesick swains—I was pitied for lacking one of the body's most sensual delights. "All jolly well," thought I in my deprived condition, "but what about the alternative aromas wafting themselves on passing breezes?" By and large, I believe that on balance the stinks are paramount and that my inodorousness has proved a boon rather than an impediment. One drawback, it must be admitted, is my inability to realize that I have omitted to turn off the gas tap on the kitchen stove, thereby risking an exit from this naughty world rather in the melodramatic manner of the prophet Elijah.

As we winged our way from Madrid, I pondered the prospects of the life in the jungle that awaited me in Mexico. I recalled my schoolboy days when I spent halfday holidays in the darkness of the Bioscope Theatre in Stoke Newington, lapping up every episode of *The Perils of Pauline*. On alternate Wednesdays, however, it was *Tarzan of the Apes*, which, for me, was sheer enchantment; and Elmo Lincoln was the very pinnacle of manly heroics. Fifty years on, and almost as many Tarzans later, I was to be in Mexico making believe I was actually in darkest Africa and playing an ally of my boyhood hero.

"What a comedown!" I can hear the reader saying. If so, I was not the only person to swallow one's pride and the Hollywood producer's money. Ethel Merman, Helen Hayes, Julie Harris—all joined the band of the future Lord Greystoke's supporters. We could all claim that, since the current fashion on Broadway was leaning towards nudity (*Oh, Calcutta!* and so forth), there was nothing untoward in our playing opposite Ron Ely, decorously clothed in nothing but a loincloth. I enjoyed my first taste of life in the jungle so much that more scripts were written featuring my part as a very British general. Not only did Ron's highly professional behaviour make my involvement agreeable, but the equally disciplined performance of his adorable vis-à-vis completely

1964–1985

won my heart. I am often asked, "Who is your favourite leading lady?" To which there is only one reply—"Vicky, of course."

"Vicky who?" they insist.

"Vicky, Tarzan's constant companion—Cheeta, the chimpanzee." Clever, funny, loving, and obedient; and what's more, she couldn't answer back— more than can be said of many a leading lady of my acquaintance.

It wasn't all plain sailing in the Tarzan saga. The theatre's First Lady, Helen Hayes, had a perilous and prickly ride on an elephant; Alan had to be rescued by an animal trainer when a lioness, her paw extruding from her bamboo cage, pinned his foot to the ground; and Julie Harris somehow got through a long close-up in spite of a spider monkey, perched on her shoulder, having buried its teeth in the region of her jugular vein. I came off lightly by comparison, but one episode in which I was to appear presented a serious script and casting problem.

The story, as far as we could judge from the incomplete script that the Hollywood headquarters had sent us, concerned the plight of a young boy who was left fatherless in the jungle—Daddy having been eliminated by the villains. It was left to Tarzan, of course, to avenge the killing and to be kind to Junior. On the Sunday preceding the filming, Ron, in a business suit for a change, and the rest of us met in his hotel suite to read over the sketchy script. What emerged was that the part of the young boy called for talent surpassing Gielgud, Olivier, and Edwin Booth rolled into one. The youngster the Hollywood agents had sent us to perform that miracle was a nice-looking kid, but hardly a prodigy. What were we to do? There was much pacing of the floor with knitted brows. It was Ron and Alan who fought their way through clouds of tobacco smoke to come up with the solution. It was to be established that the boy had witnessed the brutal killing of his beloved father and, not surprisingly, had gone into a state of shock. A side effect of the experience was that it had robbed him of his power of speech. That conveniently explained why the main character in the story uttered nary a word until the final fade-out when he looked up at me and said, "Thank you, General!" The ironic outcome of that Sunday night rewrite was that whereas Ron and I took a back seat in the film, the boy, pathetic and winning, romped off with the show.

These latter years (though spent almost exclusively in filling in the time between commercials on television) have, nevertheless, been rewarding in several respects. I have special reason to be grateful to have been cast as Samantha's father in *Bewitched*, since, apart from the enjoyment of working with Elizabeth Montgomery and her merry gang of witches and warlocks, it put me for the first time on more than a nodding acquaintance with my grandnephews and -nieces. Up until then their Uncle Maurice's career in America was to them a topic of yawning dimensions, but as I began to appear regularly on the show they became eager to get to know me, insisting that I enlighten them on the magic tricks that made *Bewitched* so much more than just another domestic comedy. With the constant comings and goings between Hollywood and parts of the *real* world, my new reputation as a worker of wonders often stood me in good stead. It was particularly handy during my travels to be able to look a Customs official straight in the eye. If I detected a hint of suspicion in his manner, I had merely to ask him if he ever watched *Bewitched* on the telly. Recognition would begin to dawn, whereupon all I had to do was to remind him that as Samantha's father I had the power to put a hex on anyone obstructing my progress. It invariably resulted in my signing an autograph on request and proceeding jauntily to the exit with my uninspected luggage in tow.

My aura of invulnerability would not have convinced those Customs sleuths if any of them had been present during the filming of one of the episodes of *Bewitched*. I was supposed to be engaged in a fierce argument with my wife, Endora (Agnes Moorehead), and to become so enraged by her taunts that the jumbo martini glass in my hand had to shatter into a thousand slivers. To produce the illusion of magical explosive power, it was essential that I stand stock still, not blinking an eye, as a special effects man fired a pellet into the glass—assuming, that was, that his aim was accurate—or into *me* if it wasn't. To maintain a totally imperturbable countenance in those circumstances was not exactly easy; and only after several "takes" and several martinis was I able to trust the marksman to hit his target. Having survived this game of ballistics, I was voted "in" as a regular member of Samantha's household, and, although it involved commuting constantly between New York and Hollywood in the 1960s, it was a thoroughly enjoyable experience.

No sooner was I back in New York, busily engaged in getting in the way of the moving men, who were transferring our belongings from 10th Street to the Dobbs Ferry house, than yet another Hollywood summons came over the wire. My West Coast agents had an uncanny knack of catching me at defenceless moments, and being aware that we were immersed in our packing, they thought it a propitious time to call me. Indeed, for me, any excuse to escape the horrors of moving was a godsend. Normally I refused to consider television assignments without first reading the script, but on this occasion I told the agents that they had my unconditional approval. Knowing how particular I had been in the past, they thought it prudent at least to give me a rough idea of the story and a warning, too, that I had to be intimately familiar with the intricacies of the gambling game Chemin de Fer. I confess I perjured myself by saying that it was my favourite pastime and that I would be perfectly believable as the Maître of the Casino. In point of fact, I'd never played or witnessed the playing of the game, but my eagerness to put a gulf between me and the movers saw caution thrown to the winds. Alan was just in time to snatch the "C" volume of the *Encyclopaedia Britannica* and a deck of cards before the packers whisked them away. To their amazement they observed us sitting on packing crates solemnly reading the rules of the game and dealing out the cards. We divided the contents of my wallet between us for the betting. In a matter of minutes, Alan, in a succession of *bancos*, cleaned me out of every last dollar. This convinced me that I had a lot of homework to do to avoid the appearance of a novice in *The Game*.

One might think that, with this indoctrination into the nefarious goings-on in a casino, I would henceforth be proof against all forms of hazardous undertakings. Not so, however. I received an urgent "Mayday" call from the governing board of New York's Lincoln Center. Their commitment to provide a home for the drama had failed to materialise to their satisfaction. Would I, and could I, help them to unravel their tangled situation?

Although my back remained firmly turned against Broadway, I felt it would be an unbecoming posture to adopt towards the new uptown institution and its Vivian Beaumont Theatre. However, I approached the conference with much trepidation because, during the planning stages of the theatre complex some years earlier, I had foreseen the very shortcomings that became evident once the theatre was built. Although my old associates and staff from the City Center days were scattered all over the continent, they dropped everything to join me in New York for a conference. It was a weekend that bristled with ideas on their part, ideas which, if put into practice, would mean that I would have to abandon my flourishing television career and devote full time to the plan's execution.

The basic idea that evolved was to follow, in the main, the same policy that had proved so successful for us at the City Center: short runs of new and old plays with star-studded casts, the pick of which would transfer to Broadway and, later, would tour. In order to give Lincoln Center a national theatre status, the Vivian Beaumont would also play host to visits by the rapidly proliferating regional theatre companies. The facilities, in addition, would be available to renowned international theatre companies for brief seasons. In other words, the playhouse would be mainly a housekeeping institution for drama culled from many quarters. It would depend on an audience of subscribers and the income from the export of its offerings to larger commercial outlets, with the hope that the income from all sources would balance the books.

I presented the Beaumont rescue plan to the Board of Directors, making the proviso that, as at City Center, the entire managerial, artistic, and financial responsibility was to be vested in me, renewable on a twelve-monthly basis. One of the board members had formerly been an adviser in President Roosevelt's

BEWITCHED

White House inner circle, Judge Rosenman, and it was he who was delegated to take up the delicate matter of my personal remuneration. "Not a penny," I said. That statement brought about a change in the previously cordial attention paid me by His Honour. Although we parted amicably enough, there was little or no doubt in my mind that I had been politely relieved of an undertaking that, in all probability, would have put me in a premature grave.

Although I had escaped Lincoln Center, I was soon to have another—and novel—flirtation with the theatre, this time "in the round." The Valley Theatre was located on the outskirts of Los Angeles, in the San Fernando Valley, and the management was making a valiant attempt to change the building's reputation as the home of boxing matches plus revivalist services on Sundays to that of suitable venue for stage plays and musicals. In my time, apart from the circus I'd had a shot at almost all varieties of show business, but I had not tried "Theatre in the Round" since World War II, although I had seen it done well under Tyrone Guthrie's direction at Stratford, Ontario, so I welcomed the suggestion that I try my hand at it in a revival of *Dial M for Murder*.

The opening night was a nerve-twisting experience, due not only to the strangeness of the staging, but to the fact that shortly before the performance was to commence the heavens opened with a deluge of monsoon proportions. California residents hotly deny that such vagaries of weather ever interrupt their sunny clime, but a goodly number of locals had to change their tune on that night. Even so, battling their way to the theatre with water up to their hubcaps, and ploughing through water and mud between the car park and the box office did nothing to dampen the audience's enthusiasm once the ingenious thriller got going. At the end of the show, two ravishing beauties appeared at the door of my dressing room. They demonstrated how they had hitched up their long evening dresses to wade through the mire outside—Zsa Zsa and Eva Gabor, no less!

It had been two years since I had stepped on a stage, and though television and films had kept me gainfully employed, they had failed to generate the magical atmosphere that binds a live actor with a live audience. However, it has to be admitted that the mechanical substitute transmitted to one's home has a different though, I think, less potent intimacy. Certainly for the actor watching himself on the screen, it is a dismal experience. He spends most of his viewing time regretting his own performance and cursing the producer for cutting out scenes he is convinced were his best. Then, of course, his temperature rises dangerously when, during some of his most telling moments, the editor has decided to superimpose the roar of speeding traffic or deafening "mood music"—either of them causing the actor be blamed for being inaudible.

I had no right to complain when my agents took me at my word about being unreservedly available. Howls of protest, however, were emitted by our two cats, Summer and Smoke, who spent months at a time in boarding kennels while we were flitting hither and yon. In Puerto Rico for a weird film called *The Traitors of San Angel*, then to London for a doubtful number starring George Sanders (*Thin Air*), and finally back to Hollywood for a medley of television activities. There was no lack of variety in those years from the mid-1960s to the mid-1970s, but most of the results could hardly be described as having made history.

One or two jottings in my diaries remind me of happenings that, perhaps, merit some remembrance. The popular television series *The Man from U.N.C.L.E.* (the two-part episode I appeared in as guest star was later released as a feature film) offered a challenge to the makeup experts. They were called on to change my appearance from that of an aged politician, reminiscent of Winston Churchill, to that of a younger party leader. The plot demanded that my character undergo the transformation in a recently invented rejuvenation machine, but the exigencies of a nonsequential shooting schedule required me to be debilitated at one moment and dashing at the next. The old-man makeup was achieved by the application of latex to my face and hands. Screwing up my eyes as the sticky stuff was put on caused puckered wrinkles all over my visage, thereby creating the illusion of advanced age. However, when the time came for me to appear as the younger character and the latex was removed, the humps and hollows in my skin remained obstinately apparent to the camera. Ice packs and astringents were tried in vain, and massage and heat were equally ineffective. I felt humiliated that my uncooperative epidermis was holding up production, and the frequent close scrutiny of my facial condition by impatient assistant directors made me feel like a leper. Eventually they would decide that my wrinkles had subsided sufficiently for me to be popped back into the machine from which I was to make a radiant though belated reappearance.

The actress Honor Blackman, famous the world over for her role in the English series *The Avengers*, was lured to Hollywood to play the part of my secretary in an episode of *The Name of the Game* in 1969. It was obvious that, as her boss, I had designs on the smartly turned-out gal that had nothing to do with her efficiency at shorthand. She, on the contrary, led me a merry chase up a dead-end garden path, resulting in my suffering a cardiac arrest, right there in my office. This was exactly the moment the little minx had been waiting for. Watching me claw my way across the carpet in a desperate attempt to reach the life-saving pills in my desk, she stood there, defiantly holding the bottle aloft and mocking my prostration. Only then was I to realise that this gorgeous creature, clad in a white leather miniskirt outfit with knee-length

"APES IN YOUR ATTIC?"

boots to match, was bent on seeing me breathe my last. Not to be denied my pills, the director ordered me, still prone, to attempt to reach them by feebly clutching at Honor's white boots for support. At the first rehearsal of that spine-tingling moment, grunting and groaning and with eyes firmly closed, I laboriously seized one boot and then the other in a hand-over-hand effort to rise from the carpet. In doing so, and quite unaware of the extent of my upward progress, I heard shouts of laughter from everyone on the set as my head disappeared beneath the flare of Honor's miniskirt. Too bad that the cameras were not turning at the time and that the microphone failed to record her saying, through her giggles, "Ooh, it tickles!"

Having just written the word "miniskirt" prompts me to dwell, for a moment, on the subject of passing fads. One of the few advantages of continuing to prosper as an octogenarian is that one has a sense of history that is denied one's juniors. I cannot join with my middle-aged friends when I hear them denouncing current tastes and customs as being the end of civilization. Not that I don't abominate, as they do, such absurdities as the pretension of rock and roll to be classified as music. To those of us who remember the street-corner bands of the Salvation Army with the tambourines and the big drum, their "music" and the sentiments of their hymns—("I want to die, said Willie, If my poppa could die too, But he says he isn't ready, 'Cos he's got so much to do")—were similar to the doleful lyrics of their rock successors (the exception being that their preoccupation is mainly with carnal experience rather than Salvation).

When one has lived through the major part of a century, one's perspective calls up repeated outbursts of similar fads and fancies, with the consequence that they are dismissed as temporary aberrations. Which, for instance, was the more lunatic—the hobble skirt of 1912 or the draughty miniskirt of 1969? Are today's youths aware, as they proudly display their "punk" coiffures, that their hairstyle was the height of fashion in the time of the ancient Mayan and Aztec civilizations—extremism and extinction going hand in hand?

2. "APES IN YOUR ATTIC?"

Transience is a mark of much of what one does as an actor on television. And on one occasion I'm afraid I reached the depths of deception by accepting an accolade for a performance I had, in fact, never given. It is a very handsome replica in bronze and marble of the Lion of St. Mark awarded me at the 1965 Venice Bienniale for my participation in a teledocumentary entitled *Enter*

Hamlet. It wasn't until years later that I learned the reason for the mysterious honour. A friend told me that she had heard my voice on television reciting "To be or not to be," but on tuning in the picture, instead of my image, there was a bevy of honey bees behaving indecorously. Since the producers had purloined my recorded voice from the past, and had done so without my permission, the winged lion really has no cause to scowl at me, as he does to this day arrogantly astride my mantelpiece.

Unlike the "old soldiers" of the song, actors, having vowed to "fade away" discreetly whilst still in their prime, take very little persuading to respond with alacrity to calls of further duty no matter how fortuitous the summons. And chance encounters have on occasion lured me back into the saddle.

One such occurrence was when I was confronted with a vaguely familiar face while lunching at Paramount Studios. It eventually dawned on me that the face belonged to my former designer of the castle at Elsinore, which housed a very nervous Hamlet making his television debut. I was the Dane, and Dick Sylbert, the talented designer. He had in the interim risen close to the apex of Robert Evans's then powerful pinnacle at Paramount. He was surprised to know that I was committing various nuisances in Hollywood television at the time and wondered whether or not I would be available to take part in a movie, the scenic design of which was his current activity. Not another butler, I protested. No, Dick explained, this was to play a surrogate uncle to Mia Farrow in a film adaptation of Ira Levin's creepy novel, *Rosemary's Baby.* A strange coincidence if ever there was one that I was to go to work again, not only with my ex-scenic designer, but also with the dramatist whom I had launched in *No Time for Sergeants.*

It was in sharp contrast to those cosy days of yore, when work began with Roman Polanski, the director of Ira's spooky opus. Unlike most other directors, he possessed an extraordinary knowledge of optics, normally the sole province of the director of photography. Much emphasis consequently was laid on camera and lighting tricks, which, though clever in themselves, did little to enhance the acting. It was also somewhat off-putting that, on the set, Polanski wore a cowboy outfit complete with six-shooter, which he twirled by its trigger guard while we were attempting to rehearse a difficult scene.

We very nearly had a serious falling out over one section of the script. It was an episode in which, as the character "Hutch," talking incessantly, I was required to dish up a leg of lamb in the kitchen, carry it into the dining room, return to the kitchen for the vegetables, then back to the table with them— still talking. Now I had to carve the lamb for three persons, help them to the veg and sink into my chair precisely on cue as the dialogue ended. Polanski insisted that the action be continuous in what is known as a "tracking shot."

"APES IN YOUR ATTIC?"

In other words, as I moved back and forth, so did the camera. It was therefore up to me to time each move so exactly that the accompanying dialogue fitted the action to the second. Carving a leg of lamb, even at one's own table, is no mean accomplishment, but to do so by the numbers and at the same time to be a talkative master of gastronomy was a formidable challenge. A whole morning on camera, and six legs of lamb later, our whimsical director got the picture he wanted, but at the same time he ruined my appetite for that particular joint of meat for the foreseeable future.

The old adage that one man's meat is another man's poison had to be read in reverse in the case of my next film assignment. The misfortunes of Twentieth Century Fox in the late 1960s caused a somewhat bizarre change of direction in my career.

The enormous unrecouped cost of *Cleopatra* and the indifferent reception given to *Dr. Doolittle* were compounded by another financial problem. The studio had already shot the film version of the enormously popular stage musical comedy *Hello Dolly*, and the finished product was sitting on the shelf awaiting the termination of the run of the show on Broadway. That contractual inhibition was inviolate, so the new all-black version of *Dolly* played on to packed houses in New York. Meanwhile the film (starring Barbra Streisand) gathered dust in Twentieth's vaults. In desperation the studio turned to a script that had been shelved as impractical. It was a screen adaptation, by Rod Serling, of Pierre Boulle's novel, *The Planet of the Apes*. At long last producer Arthur P. Jacobs's persistence was rewarded by the green light to go ahead with a production in which only he had implicit confidence. Even so, I don't think he could have foreseen the tremendous audience appeal the screenplay contained. To the young generation it was exciting science fiction, but to their elders it was a sobering prophecy of a world in which apes had become supreme and humankind their slaves.

Initially the producers (Jacobs and Ackerman) invited the talent agencies to comb their files for clients considered to possess simian features; it was thought that the addition of wigs and body hair would suffice. The tests, however, did not convince those in command that the resulting images would ever be taken seriously. Edward G. Robinson gallantly protested that he could pass muster with very little assistance from the makeup artists. When it was decided to create masks for the apes, he was told that daily makeup calls would be for 5 o'clock each morning and that the application of his three-piece mask would take from three to four hours. Eddie's doctor forbade him to submit himself to such a rigorous schedule. In that event, and without being given the same daunting details, I innocently agreed to substitute for him as the wily orangutan, Dr. Zaius.

For me, the first step into the animal kingdom was the macabre experience of modelling for a plaster death mask of my face. Inches thick, the sticky stuff was slapped on and not until I was on the verge of suffocation were soda straws inserted through the wet plaster into my nostrils and mouth. To be imprisoned helplessly in that manner, praying for the plaster to dry in a hurry, was the oddest of sensations. Eventually, Johnny Chambers, creator of the ape makeup and expert torturer in chief, peeled off the beastly thing and bore it in triumph to his workshop, there to impose upon it the features that were to transform me into the philosophical orangutan. As a memento of Johnny's handiwork, I still treasure a milk-white plastic model of the death mask, and have been known to don it on Halloween to delight small children and to terrify sensitive ladies.

As the shooting began on *Planet of the Apes*, I was very apprehensive, those first early mornings, of the claustrophobic effect of the latex mask, as I sat in the makeup chair. Roddy McDowall, slumped in the chair next to mine, fell fast asleep whilst being turned into a chimpanzee. Each of the three pieces of the mask—the brow, the nose and upper lip, the lower lip and chin—had to be most exactly glued into position and every joint covered with hundreds of individual hairs. Finally, the shaggy ginger wig was put on and, for the first few days, I had no hesitation in joining in the applause so richly deserved for Kenny Chase, my personal makeup artist. As the weeks wore on, the novelty wore off, so that it seemed perfectly normal, between the scenes, to see one of my orangutan chums, pipe in mouth, poring over a game of chess with a gorilla.

What one hadn't reckoned with was the fact that the mouth of an ape protrudes much further forward than that of a human being. Consequently, when the shooting on the set broke for lunch, it was impossible for us to assimilate food in the same manner as lucky Charlton Heston. A partial solution was hit upon by Alan, who obtained a pair of chopsticks with which he administered morsels of food to this semireclining ape. Overcome by hunger, on one occasion, I demanded spaghetti with meat sauce for lunch. I may say that, for eating spaghetti, chopsticks are entirely unsuitable instruments.

From the actor's standpoint, the oft-repeated injunction to "relax" is the most frustrating order. It was usually the assistant director's polite way of saying, "Go back to your dressing room and stay there in case you are needed later in the day." Trussed up as I was in a hairy disguise, relaxing was the last thing I was capable of, and my comfortable but stuffy trailer outside the sound stage was the least appropriate ambience. Those cooped-up conditions aroused in me an intense sympathy for wild animals confined in zoo cages. Inquisitive members of groups touring the studio would sometimes peer through the open door of my trailer to see me being forcibly fed by Alan, a sight that provoked unbridled mirth in their midst, and looks from me that could kill.

"APES IN YOUR ATTIC?"

During those many hours of inactivity, one was apt to forget what one looked like to others. I would exchange my heavy leather ape-clothing for a light dressing gown and smoke a cigarette through an elongated Noel Coward-type holder, and, if I were outside the trailer, I would sport a rather racy straw hat. Garbed thus on one occasion, I stepped out of the trailer to take the air, quite oblivious of my peculiar appearance. Approaching me down the studio street was a simply stunning blonde in deep conversation with, I guessed, her agent (lucky fellow!). I automatically squared my shoulders and prepared to flash her the most winning smile at my command. Becoming aware of the advancing apparition, she stopped dead, let out a squeal of delight, and, clapping her hands, said, "You're wild!"

At the end of a day's shooting, knowing that brand-new masking pieces were awaiting me on the morrow, I would tear off the mask of the day and make a dash for the car park. No longer imprisoned in makeup, I would drive home, happily content with my restored freedom to blow my nose, if needed, and to pop on my reading glasses at will. When, leaving in a hurry, I had omitted to remove the black varnish from my primate's fingernails and the odd orange facial hair, I would sometimes get rather curious reactions from other drivers. One day, while waiting for the light to change, the occupant in the vehicle abreast of me said, "I've seen some oddballs in this town, but, buddy, you take the cake!"

Another aspect of the orangutan physique—the feet—put my life at risk on a day that I was required to ride horseback on the sands of Zuma Beach. Our director, Franklin Schaffner, casually asked me if I rode. "I haven't sat on a nag for ages," I replied. He then explained that the scene about to be photographed showed me as Dr. Zaius at the head of a posse of mounted gorillas. Although he could substitute me with a stuntman for the chase, it was essential that, as the riders came to a halt, he could come in close with the camera to see me dismount. It would be far more to his liking, he said, if he could avoid the inevitable cut in the action as the stuntman and I swapped places.

Thus I rashly volunteered to do the entire ride myself and, unaccustomed as I was to horses in general, spent what seemed to me many painful hours at full gallop with a gang of howling apes at my nervous heels. There was retake after retake, long pauses between them as the sand was restored to its original pristine condition, and not until the sun threatened to sink in the west did I pilot the bullyboys, uninterrupedly, to the place where I was to dismount. It was critical to the camera that I should rein in my fiery steed at an exact spot in the sand, marked by a sturdy stake sharpened at both ends. So far, so good. I proceeded to dismount, whereupon my oversized ape foot refused to part from the stirrup and I fell, one leg still at the horse's flank. Occupational hazards are not uncommon in the film business, but I think I narrowly missed being the first victim to be pierced through the heart by a piece of lumber. Had it been so, after a few crocodile tears and "Poor old Evans," the studio bosses would have congratulated themselves that, thanks to the store of duplicate masks, I was easily replaceable by someone with my fruity tones but a less adventuresome spirit.

The golden rule about acting is to get into the skin of the character you are playing. However, to follow that dictum when depicting an orangutan is a tall order. The encyclopedia reference on the subject seemed to suggest that in some respects I was not entirely a misfit. According to that article, I exceeded the average height of a *Pongo pygmaeus*—without shoes—by very few inches. By comparison, my arms were woefully short, since the knuckles of the ape I was aping actually touched the ground when the creature was in an upright position. On that score a modicum of poetic licence was inevitable. As far as my eyes were concerned, they were the regulation brown, and I could boast the identical number of teeth as Dr. Zaius, though some of mine, I have to confess, were courtesy of my dentist.

One of the unusual features of the film, and of its sequel *Beneath the Planet of the Apes*, was that the actor behind the disguise was not identifiable except by the eyes or the voice. Due to the vast audiences both films attracted, Chuck Heston and his fellow humans were instantly recognised in public and were obliged to toe the boring line of autograph hunters, film festivals, and so forth. We lucky anthropoids, however, being quite unrecognisable, were free to go our normal, if not entirely blameless ways. On one occasion we were, nevertheless, the cause of corporal punishment unfairly administered by a mother to her small son. The company was on location near a small town in Utah. Lagging behind his mother on her shopping trip, the boy espied an unusual sight through the windows of the local diner. Catching up with his mother, the boy, breathless with excitement, said, "Ma, d'you know what I just saw? A bunch of monkeys drinking milkshakes through straws!" For his pains he got a resounding smack on his bottom with a stern reproof for "telling wicked stories."

Never have I felt so anonymous as when the film opened in New York City. The Capitol Theatre had erected an enormous billboard displaying an orangutan likeness. The caption blazoned above my head read, "Thank you, Dr. Zaius," but nobody knew it was me. Never mind! The public flocked to see what we were up to, and the movie was hailed as a classic by the critics, which, of course, made me feel at home. It also set a new pattern for science-fiction subjects, which in later years saw the development of such films as *Star Wars*.

Early in 1968, before the filming of *Planet of the Apes*, I had a stern talk with myself. My split personality (Gemini), or was it the sheer cussedness of my nature, turned a deaf ear to the reminder that I had already overstepped by two years the date I had solemnly vowed would mark my retirement (no trawling of the Darby and Joan clubs for me). Could it be that, like so many of my New York chums, I had "gone Hollywood"? On that score, at least, I could make the excuse that I owed it to my zealous agents to accept the work they put in my way, particularly since I could do so without having to become a California resident. As the offers for television came pouring in, I began to wonder why I was maintaining a house in New York State that I rarely saw for more than a few odd weeks in a year. It was during one of the periodic lulls of television activity, in August 1968, that Alan and I made a business trip to London. I spotted an advertisement for a house in Surrey that had recently been auctioned.

Purely out of curiosity we called on the real estate agents only to be told that the reserve price had not been met at the auction and that consequently the property was again on the market. The agent offered to run us down there that afternoon to see the place although the owner would not be there to show us the interior of the house. With no intentions other than enjoying a ride into the countryside, and feeling only slightly guilty about that, we accepted the invitation.

Not far from the area where I had lived under the parental roof whilst working in London at Chappell's the music publishers, the car pulled up at the Mill House. It was charmingly situated on the edge of Walton Heath, which centuries earlier had been an encampment for Roman legions. More recently the heath had been a favourite spot for the dumping of surplus Luftwaffe bombs after abortive raids on London. The agent told us that it was only a few minutes walk to the famous championship golf course of Walton Heath, and we were also only a short car ride from the renowned Epsom race course where every first Wednesday in June the Derby is run.

The word "roots" is hardly glamorous; it conjures up remembrances of indigestible vegetables with forbidding names such as "Mangelwurzel" and "squash." But there are occasions when "roots" has another connotation, and visiting the Mill House was one of them. The ground beneath me tugged insistently at my feet whilst my brain told me to keep going, but I remained rooted to the spot. I was looking at a sadly neglected house in Tudor style standing in an acre of equally neglected garden and boasting a number of stables and an exercise paddock for horses that I was unlikely ever to own. Nevertheless, I was hopelessly enchanted, although trying to appear blasé to the estate agent. He urged me to make an appointment with the owner to see the interior of the house, to which I agreed with simulated indifference. No sooner were we back in London than I was on the telephone to my agents in

Hollywood, telling them that if it didn't presage an end to my film career, I wanted to take up residence in England. "Absolutely no reason why you shouldn't," was their reply. That was all the encouragement I needed to take the next steps towards acquiring the Mill House.

Upon inspecting the interior, I stubbornly refused to admit there were any problems. Five bedrooms and only two bathrooms, antiquated central heating and a vile kitchen—none of this fazed me. With the law's delays in conveying the Mill House to its eager new owners, it wasn't until late December of 1968 that we acquired the property. It took months of rehabilitation to create what we wanted and many weeks more to tame the wilderness into gardens and a croquet lawn. Meantime, we were back and forth between New York and Hollywood for constant television jobs, besides arranging for the sale of the Dobbs Ferry house.

Alan was the one to be saddled with the job of packing up our possessions, arranging not only for their shipment to England but for the dispatch by air of the two bewildered cats, Summer and Smoke. Little did the cats know that on arrival in England they would have to spend six months in quarantine (the British rabies regulation) and a further five and a half months in the kennels before the house was ready for occupancy.

At long last, we were able to move into our abode, which, having six chimneys, was entitled to be known as a "mansion." The truth is that it started from very humble beginnings, having originally been a small dwelling known as "Heather Cottage." In those days it was the homestead of the miller who operated two windmills across the ancient Roman road that ran through the property. Subsequent owners, mainly in the 1800s, had replaced the cottage with the imposing building we were acquiring.

Evidence of the extent of the property is contained in the old indentures, which offer striking proof of the decline in the style of legal procedures relevant to property transfers. Both documents are faultlessly inscribed on heavy parchment and bear the sealing-wax imprints of both buyer and seller. The one dated "the twenty eighth of December in the year of our Lord One thousand and eight hundred and sixty four" is a twenty-one-year lease of the premises for an annual rent of £210. Provided the lessee paid up on time, he was entitled "to peaceably and quietly have hold and enjoy the said Mills messuages buildings and premises without any interruption." A long list of equipment appended in the lease conferred upon the lessee the use of a steam engine to drive the corn-grinding machinery and "three Grinding Bed stones."

Those privileges, however, were conditional upon the lessee agreeing "to spread and bestow upon every acre of the land one ton of good rotten Stable manure." That requirement had, fortunately, lapsed by the time I stepped into the miller's shoes. The machinery, too, had long since disappeared, and across the road only one of the two "Walton" windmills remained, denuded of its sails. To my delight, while digging in the garden, I uncovered first one and eventually the other two corn-grinding stones, which became decorative and functional additions to our patio.

The "piggery" mentioned in the deed no longer existed, which was just as well, but the coach house still survived, though it was so riddled with woodworm that it had to be demolished. It was sad to watch it happen even though its massive beams provided us with firewood for the open-hearth fireplace in the drawing room for the next ten years. It would have horrified Mr. Coleman, of Coleman's Mustard fame, whose habit it had been to leave his coach and two horses in the building. He was a regular guest of his host's Sunday luncheons and loved to tuck into the gargantuan spread.

What had originally been a plot of land "three acres one rod and twenty seven perches" had shrunk by the time our deeds were signed to a manageable solitary acre. Somewhat inappropriately the document conferred upon me "the right to graze sheep on the Walton Heath," and in the same spot "to gather fagots," a privilege which, in today's slang, has a questionable connotation.

A splendid English tradition is a watchdog institution called the Department of the Environment. Its function is to preserve the amenities of the countryside and to declare certain buildings and their surroundings as sacrosanct. Although the Mill House itself was not so classified, one very old tree in the grounds came under their jurisdiction as an ancient monument. It certainly was (and still is, I hope) an extremely elegant tree—*Fraxinus pendula* or Weeping Ash. Some fifty feet in height, its branches reached to the ground, forming a natural arbor in which visiting children loved to "play house" and other suspiciously erotic games.

If the *Fraxinus pendula* was treasured by ourselves for its beauty, for Smoke, the black cat, it provided gymnastic facilities for her to limber up after the eleven and a half months of confinement. In spite of an injury to her back, which she sustained years before when she fell from the windowsill of Alan's third-floor apartment in New York, it in no way dampened her athletic prowess. With her seven toes on each front paw and her arched back, she was the very model of a Halloween cat. Her favourite exercise was to take a long running jump at the treetrunk and, clinging to its bark, she would look back over her shoulder at Summer, her snow-white brother, as much as to say, "Sissy."

It had been some thirty-five years since I had previously set up house in England. In those days domestic help was plentiful and gardeners were two-a-penny. Not so any longer, as we soon discovered while attempting to settle into our new life. In desperation we decided to add a servants' wing to the house, hoping it would attract suitable occupants. In doing so, we aroused the wrath of our neighbours, because a temporary drop in their water supply occurred when the site was being excavated and an underground pipe was accidentally broken. A rumour circulated that we were installing a swimming pool. It was inevitable, they figured, that when the time came to fill or to replenish this vulgar addition to the premises, their water supply would be reduced again. Not until the bricklayers started to erect the walls were the neighbours' fears assuaged and we were judged to be admissible into the local fold.

Since it had become apparent that professional domestic servants were obtainable only if one could offer ample private quarters, we postponed the search for suitable candidates until the completion of the new wing to the house. In the meantime, we managed as best we could with the assistance of Lily, our "daily." No longer, in the Welfare State, to be referred to as "the Charwoman" or "the Char," these treasures continued to be the rock on which smooth domesticity was founded. Our Lily was a Cockney stalwart of the old breed, pedalling her way to us on her bicycle in all weathers, whistling while she worked, and being a fund of local gossip for our eager ears.

In 1970 the bottom began to drop out of the motion-picture industry in Hollywood and abroad. Television films were obviously becoming the entertainment medium of the future and offers to appear in them were not to be sniffed at. On the other hand, how to accept them unless caretakers could be found for the Mill House? As if by magic, one day came a couple responding to an advertisement we had placed in *The Lady* months before. Throwing all caution to the winds, we hired them, relying on the fact that the husband, as a retired policeman, was an assurance that they were not just a pair of gypsies. Mercifully the gamble paid off, and the way was open for me to catch up on my film and television career before it was too late.

My first assignment in 1970 was the popular television film, *Brotherhood of the Bell*, with Glenn Ford; then came the sequel to the first planetary-ape picture, *Beneath the Planet of the Apes*. This was positively the last time I would don that hairy disguise because the script required that I blow myself up at the end in an atomic demise in which Chuck Heston also perished.

That monkeyshine reminded me of a letter to the *Times* (London), which I had preserved in my files of memorabilia. It was addressed to the editor of the *Times* and was headed "Apes in Your Attic?"

Sir:
May I on behalf of the Anatomical Society of Great Britain and Ireland appeal through your columns to those of your readers who have apes stored in their attics? This learned society is undertaking the task of compiling a catalogue of all existing skeletons of the four anthropoid apes (Gorilla, chimpanzee, orangutan and gibbon) in Great

DOWN THE DANUBE

Britain and Ireland, for purposes of scientific study. As this material is of great scientific value the society would be extremely grateful if private collectors prepared to cooperate in such a project would communicate with me at this address.

Yours faithfully,
John Napier, Reader of Anatomy
Royal Free Hospital School of
Medicine
8, Hunter Street, London W.C. 1.

Although not actually confined to an attic, my professional spirits were at a rather low ebb at the time, and it was largely due to Helen Hayes that I refrained from offering my skeleton to Mr. Napier. It took little persuading on her part to stifle my interest in anthropogenesis, and I decided instead to join her on a trip down the river Danube.

3. DOWN THE DANUBE

The port of departure for the Danube cruise was Vienna, where Alan and I caught up with Helen and her assistant, Vera Benlian. The night before sailing we were treated to one of those dreamy evenings that only the Viennese provide—a performance of *The Merry Widow* at the Theater an den Wien and a midnight candlelit supper at Stadt Krug. It was something of a contrast when we boarded our ship the next day to find that the handsome Austrian-built craft was manned by a Soviet crew. For us, this was our first contact with service Communist-style. Hardly to be recommended was the early morning bugle call piped into one's cabin, followed by the peremptory order, "Everyone in the dine-ink-room!" Helen very wisely ignored the command, but the rest of us meekly obeyed. Taking our assigned places at our table for breakfast we found that, before being served, we were each expected to fill in a long questionnaire as to our preferred choices of food for all three meals on the following day. Most of our shipmates were hearty Germans who tackled the task with relish. We, on the other hand, found it impossible to think rationally about tomorrow's menus until, at least, we had quaffed a glass of fruit juice, but that was not to be. Instead, a large plate of sausage and cabbage was unceremoniously placed before each of us, which succeeded in robbing us of our breakfast appetites to say nothing of the morrow's. Every morning we dutifully filled in the order forms, but what came to the table never once in the entire cruise bore the faintest resemblance to what we had ordered. The only consistent and delicious items were the bread rolls, two of which Vera popped into her pocket each morning to be smuggled into Helen's cabin.

The only member of the crew who spoke fluent English was the barman. He, at least, could keep us informed in our slow progress down the muddy Danube, even though that involved much time perched on bar stools and the consumption of more Bloody Marys than was advisable. Came the evening, however, when we could extract no information from him. In addition, he was in such a state of Russian melancholy that our orders for "the usual" failed to produce our customary drinks. The next day he was more his old self and we learned from him that the previous day he had gone ashore at that particular port to see his girlfriend only to find her locked in the arms of a rival admirer. Why that rejection should have robbed him totally of his knowledge of English, he didn't explain, but if, as I suspected, it was an act in the Slavic manner, it was one that would have delighted Stanislavski and his disciples.

With the exception of Budapest, none of our ports of call on the not-so-blue Danube sticks in my memory, even though there was a certain sense of excitement about being behind the Iron Curtain. After Budapest there was little of scenic interest until late in the cruise when we reached the spot where the Danube narrows into a gorge flanked by mountainous walls. This natural formation had once caused Julius Caesar's legions to about-face and go the other way. In our time engineers had been able to construct one of the world's largest hydraulic locks a short distance below the ravine. Our captain exercised great skill in steering the ship into this impressive feat of engineering. The ship was the largest up to that time to go through the new lock, and we all trooped onto the top deck to watch as the mast was lowered and the large funnel was tilted forward. To this landlubber's eye it looked inevitable that something would collide with the overhead steel beams. One held one's breath until we squeezed through with what seemed only inches to spare.

Having passed parts of Czechoslovakia, Hungary, Yugoslavia, and then through the great lock, the Danube some miles further downstream began its northward bend, with Bulgaria on one side and Romania on the other. Here were mostly dreary little riverside towns and villages, no worse, I suppose, than their counterparts along other large rivers. However, there was an air of defeat about the populace of these regions, which was most distressing. The rather gloomy atmosphere did nothing to curb Helen's nomadic instincts. Off she would go with Vera, who would cast an anxious eye on her watch for fear we'd sail without them. On one such occasion, Alan and I made a similar expedition at Giurgiu in Romania. We hired a taxi whose driver spoke quite respectable English. We were glad to be spared a long trek on foot, but at the same time we were apprehensive about making the return journey to the cruise ship on time. Arriving at the town, a quick glance was sufficient to convince us that a

DOWN THE DANUBE

nodding acquaintance was all it merited. We told the driver to wait for us and he agreed, and since it was quite hot we left our jackets on the back seat of the taxi. After a cursory look at the uninviting market place, we retraced our steps only to find no sign of our taxi. It is one thing when at home to forget one's door keys, but quite another to be in the dilemma in which we found ourselves. There we were, high and dry in a country of whose language we knew not one syllable—our passports in our jacket pockets aboard a fugitive taxi—no other means of identification on our persons—and a total of ten or so dollars between us. Visions of days and nights in a Romanian jail flashed through our minds, and just as panic set in our ephemeral driver gave a merry toot on his horn. He then discharged two other gullible shipmates about to be given *their* case of the jitters. Although private enterprise is frowned upon in those parts, our driver, it seemed, had learnt how to beat the system even though it put his passengers through the wringer.

It is generally accepted that tour brochures are the ultimate in literary deceit, yet we allowed ourselves to believe the rapturous description of Constantsa, a summer resort on the Black Sea, as not to be missed. We left our ship at Galatz, close to the Russian border. The ship went on to Yalta and we travelled by car down the Romanian coast to the advertised paradise, arriving there just before sunset. Any suspicion we had harboured was quickly dissipated by the view from our hotel windows of endless miles of golden sands. Came the morn, with swim trunks and sun cream at the ready, we stepped out onto our bedroom balcony to see, at a distance, what we thought to be an overnight influx of kelp all over the beach. Not a bit of it, as a closer inspection showed. What we had thought to be seaweed was in actuality countless suntanned Romanian bodies, so closely packed together that only the predawn arrivals had any chance of getting anywhere near the water—including ourselves.

After a short stay at the Black Sea, we were booked to travel first class by train to Bucharest. If our accommodation was first class, then the good Lord help those in third class! We made quite a comprehensive tour of Bucharest, seeing many of the buildings dating from the former monarchy and many fine churches. The high spot, however, was the tour of the fabulous Theatre Arts complex, which was still a-building. Whether it eventually was destined to house nothing but political propaganda one could only guess, but in sheer size it made our capitalistic establishments look puny by comparison. Since it was very hot in Bucharest, we took a trip into the Transylvanian mountains to the Prahova valley. We stayed at a hotel that had once been a royal summer home, and were to visit Dracula's Castle from there on the morrow. Instead it was yet another example of fudged socialist bureaucracy. Bucharest's tourist office had sent us in great style on a wild-goose chase, since Count Dracula was off on a week's blood-sucking jaunt elsewhere and had taken the key with him. It mollified Alan's disappointment somewhat when our pretty girl guide hotly refused the tip he offered her as being an insult in a communal society. No such delicate inhibitions appeared to afflict our chauffeur, however. Mistakenly, I credited him with sharing the pretty guide's indifference to money, but upon resuming our journey back to Bucharest, after a stop en route, my jacket was where I'd left it in the limousine, but my wallet was not. Heigh-ho!

The most enjoyable part of the holiday, once we got there, was our stay in Istanbul. We bumped our way by air in a Russian carrier with the sinister name of MALEV. It was unfortunate that, whereas the aisle of the small aircraft was as narrow as a Concorde's, the girth of the hostess was colossal. On each of her incessant sorties, as she came abreast of my aisle seat, I was swiped in the face by her skirt. We had been briefed that we were to be given the red-carpet treatment on arrival, so we had done our best to spruce up our appearance before boarding the plane. We needn't have bothered, since the official greeting party, having been given the wrong information about our flight, had gone back to the United States consulate. Our linguistic shortcomings were never more pronounced than when Turkish was the order of the day, but the word "Hilton" was the only talisman needed for the taxis to whisk us to our haven, where we collapsed in luxurious suites.

From our windows, next morning, the whole panorama of the wonderful city of Istanbul was spread before us—the mosques, the minarets, the markets, and the sparkling blue Bosphorus as far as the eye could see. Added to that was an apologetic emissary from the consulate, waiting for us in the lobby. Her somewhat commanding voice on the telephone did not prepare us for its diminutive owner, Betty Karp. We quickly realised that she, as the chief of public relations, was a minute fireball of energy and an absolute darling person to boot. She arranged for official cars to be at our disposal and for entrees to seemingly inaccessible places. In the ambassador's absence, Betty managed to commandeer his yacht for our pleasure. We were royally wined and dined as we sailed hither and yon.

Ashore the heat was so intense—hovering around 114 degrees Fahrenheit during the day—that to find ways to keep cool was imperative. Between visits to the various museums and palaces, we assumed devout expressions, kicked off our shoes, and entered some handy mosque to cool off. Sipping a cold beer on the terrace of the house once occupied by the author Pierre Loti, and drinking in the spectacular view from its lofty position on the Golden Horn, also served to reduce our danger of heat prostration. The house, overlooking as it did an extraordinary Turkish graveyard of considerble age, made one almost envy its occupants their shade.

Finally the time came to say good-bye to Betty, which we did at the splendid restaurant atop the Hilton. We had learned (before meeting her in Istanbul) that she had always wanted one of the golden roses of Vienna—a real rose dipped in gold. We had acquired one before we started the cruise, and that last night in Istanbul we presented it to her with our heartfelt thanks. Her joy upon receiving the rose made the perfect ending to our trip.

4. RETIREMENT?

The next few years, owing to changes in the film industry and in television, were unrewarding for me, professionally speaking. On the other hand, they afforded me much opportunity to brush up on my knowledge of gardening and, finally, to put it into practice. The horses belonging to the previous owners of the Mill House had obligingly left their visiting cards on the exercise paddock over the years, so the soil was in perfect condition for its conversion to a croquet lawn. It was a different matter, however, when the verdant carpet was ready to be staked out for the hoops and winning post. Checking with the handy *Encyclopaedia Britannica*, we discovered that there was a considerable divergence between the American and the British layout of the playing area, to say nothing of contradictions in the rules of play. Consequently I wrote to the secretary of the Croquet Association (Patron—Her Majesty the Queen) asking for details, particularly of the American plan. From the Hurlingham Club, which is the solemn arbiter of the sport, came this reply:

> I hope you really require this information for literary rather than
> practical purposes, because I think it would be *disaster* if the American
> game were to catch on in this country in rivalry to ours. In America,
> we are making considerable progress and I do not despair of our rules
> eventually prevailing.
>   (Signed)
>   Vandeleur Robinson (Secretary)

Mr. Robinson, I fear, would have been further affronted if he had seen us at play, with Smoke taking part. She had only to hear the first click of mallet on ball to come bounding out of her rose-bed retreat to chase the carefully aimed ball. She would stoutly refuse to budge from it and would have to be carried off bodily from the scene.

Having joined a club in London, Alan and I spent time there seeing friends and catching up on our theatregoing. On one occasion we were invited by the management of the Mermaid Theatre to be present at the opening night of a revival of *Journey's End*. It had been forty-four years since I had appeared in the original production, so I went there with trepidation, naturally wondering if it would stand up to the passage of time. My doubts were banished, as the play unfolded, by the empathy of the audience. I particularly noticed Christopher Plummer, seated in the row ahead, leaning forward in an attitude of rapt attention. "Wouldn't you have given your right arm to play the role of Captain Stanhope?" I asked him during the intermission."Both of them," he replied. When we returned to our seats for the second act, I found myself deeply moved by the play. It amazed me that the death scene of Lieutenant Raleigh, which I had played so many times, would move me to tears.

After the performance, Robert Morley's son, Sheridan, was to interview a selected few for their reactions to the play. It was hard for me to treat him with the deference due to the well-known broadcaster he had become. My only previous contact with him had been when he was a small boy and, his hand in mine, I had helped him aboard a river steamer during the filming of *Mr. Gilbert and Mr. Sullivan.* For the interview, assuming that one generation's meat would be another's poison, Sheridan also had two popular young British actors to support his opinion that the play was hopelessly old-fashioned and trivial in content. It did my heart good to hear both Ian McKellan and Tom Courtney hotly disagreeing with him and asserting that it was "the best damn play we've seen for years."

The period of the middle and late 1970s was for me a battleground of good intentions and greed. Gardening was my main recreation in those days, but, much as I enjoyed it, my joints refused to cooperate. It was one thing to drop to my knees to assault a patch of weeds, but quite another to regain an upright position without the aid of a skyhook. Then there was golf—a diversion whose skills had so far eluded me—but which others of my own age seemed to have mastered. Determined to conquer our faults, Alan and I spent several winter weeks each year on the golf courses in the Algarve in southern Portugal. At the end of these holidays I had to admit, as Lord Curzon once did about his game, that my golf was best described as "a certain species of gardening—more divots than dexterity." Better stick to acting was my conclusion.

So it was greedily back to California to reline my pockets with the proceeds from appearing as yet another butler in a *Columbo* television film, and as an older schoolmaster in a literate episode of *The Streets of San Francisco* series. The latter was an interesting study of the old boy's technique in taming a group of violent street urchins. Although he met his death in the effort, his teaching had succeeded in implanting in the young hooligans a sense of discipline. Interesting, too, was Karl Malden's brotherly advice to me never to sign up for a series. After slugging away for years on end as the San Francisco detective, but never showing a hint of this feeling in his brisk acting, Karl gave me some good counsel. He said the doubtful fame achieved by the familiarity of one's face on the television screen did nothing to outweigh the unremitting pattern of the labour and the stultifying effect it had on an actor's constant need to stretch his abilities. That Karl came through the experience unscathed is a tribute to his fortitude and his talent. The character he portrayed, being everybody's idea of the honest cop, if nothing else opened up fresh fields for him in the realm of television commercials. Not for a moment does the viewer question the recommendations by this pillar of the law.

As I scribble these words with my ballpoint pen, the calendar on my desk tells me it is 1985—reminding me that, quite undeservedly, I have been around for eighty-four years—a span that has included much turmoil in the world. Nevertheless, I seem to have remained pragmatic in the face of seemingly overwhelming setbacks—amongst them, wars and rumours of wars. Winston Churchill was once chided for being unmoved by dire threats of impending conflict, so he calmly stated, "There's always a war going on somewhere!"—a rather callous outlook, perhaps, but good news for some of us. Not until our fellow men start hacking each other to pieces are surgeons able to try out new techniques on casualties. Whereas advances in other branches of science all seem to be in the direction of moral and physical destruction, surgery, thanks largely to wartime experiences, has gained a legacy of repairs beneficial to the human skeleton.

In 1976 I was the lucky recipient of a total hip replacement and artificial joints to my great toes. Having seen my poor father totally crippled by osteoarthritis, I was doubly grateful to be spared a similar fate. It took quite a time to accustom myself to those large pieces of hardware, but at least I was out of pain and able to contemplate resuming my career where I had left off.

Still somewhat wobbly on my pins, I was summoned to the Mill House telephone one day for a call from New York. It was the Theatre Guild which, rather surprisingly, had gone into the business of supplying entertainment for cruise ships. They had already obtained Helen Hayes's consent, if mine was forthcoming, to resuscitate our Shakespeare duet, *A Program for Two Players*, on a Caribbean cruise. I agreed, provided we were permitted to dilute an overdose of culture by adding something in a lighter vein. Knowing that Cyril Ritchard was to be the Master of Ceremonies for the entertainments, it became possible to rope him into joining us in an excerpt from *The Circle*. Alan did a skillful blending of scenes from Somerset Maugham's play, providing wonderful comedy moments for all three of us. Helen's Lady Kitty was divinely funny. Cyril, as her first husband, and I, her grumpy second mate, did our best to keep up with her. We took one liberty with the text, which the audience gobbled up. We added to the reconciliation scene between Helen and me an exit in which we softly sang part of "I Remember It Well" from the film *Gigi*.

1964—1985

After brief rehearsals in New York, in April 1977, the company of entertainers, including Patrice Munsel, Milo O'Shea, and Josh and Nedda Logan, all travelled to New Orleans, where we boarded the cruise ship. For Helen and me this was the first time in our careers that we had been called upon to perform twice nightly, since the ship's movie theatre was too small to accommodate all our shipmates at one sitting. We were fortunate to have a millpond sea on the night of our performance. If Father Neptune was adversely critical of our efforts, at least he had the decency to hold off his fury until after our show. He was less considerate on certain nights during the two-week cruise, but it was our fellow entertainers, not ourselves, who had to summon up their sea legs.

Apart from rehearsals for the last-night gala, we had a pleasant relaxing time and went ashore to visit Caracas in Venezuela and Cartagena in Colombia. As we approached the Yucatán Peninsula of Mexico, the ship docked at Playa del Carmen where most of the passengers continued on to the island of Cozumel. Helen, Vera, Alan, and I, having visited the island some years before, elected to take the small boat to the shore of Quintana Roo, where a special bus was waiting to take us and a few others on a trip to see that part of the peninsula. We visited first a crystal-clear lagoon where we had a lovely swim, getting on intimate terms with myriads of tropical fish.

From the lagoon we travelled on the recently constructed road to the most spectacular Mayan ruin of the area. This was Tulum, an historic fortress previously accessible only on foot through this heavily jungled part of the Yucatán Peninsula. The guide book told us that the Castillo, as it is now called, was first sighted in 1518 by Juan de Grijalva as he sailed in the Caribbean. He was close enough to the shore to distinguish "a city or a town so large that Seville would not have seemed more considerable." Nowadays very little remains, the principal ruins are those of the Castillo (or "Tower")—"a pyramidal structure topped by a two-room temple, proudly perched on a forty-foot bluff above lonely patches of beach. A short distance away is the small Temple of the Descending God, with a diving god carved into a niche, and also unique in that its walls slant inward toward the base." As we marvelled at the sight before us, we were grateful that we were seeing this work of the ancient Mayans before any restoration had taken place and no fizzy-drink signs had been erected. The only concession to this century was an enterprising boy who made us sunhats, deftly woven out of green palm leaves, which provided effective shade from the blistering heat.

So it was "heigh-ho for the rolling main" once more on our way to disembark at New Orleans. We were mightily relieved that the *New Yorker* critic Brendan Gill had flown home earlier from the cruise and consequently would not be present to report on the caper in which Helen and I took part for the

RETIREMENT?

last-night gala. It was a hoary old script, which Cyril Ritchard had kept under wraps in his steamer trunk. Entitled *Violetta, an Opera without Music*, it was a parody of the typical libretto of an Italian opera, written in awful rhymed couplets. The plot resembled an absurd variation of Romeo and Juliet, with Helen playing the nurse, Cyril as Romeo (in a terrible blond wig and corkscrew tights on his skinny legs), and me as Juliet's outraged father. The downbeat of the silent orchestra's conductor was Violetta's cue to speak in a rhythm as monotonous as today's rock and roll. Here is a sample of the dialogue:

(*On the balcony*)

VIOLETTA: My lover calls, he's down below,
Oh, hurry please or he will go.
He cannot climb without a rope,
Find something please or I shall mope.

NURSE: A sheet, a sheet, now here's a sheet!
(*They have a tug of war with the tangled sheet*)

NURSE: (*As she drops the sheet*): Oh! Sheet!!

The audience fell apart to hear the First Lady of the American Theatre use that double entendre.

The late 1970s saw us leading an extremely peripatetic existence. The predatory behaviour of the Labour government of the day in England forced us to keep on the move. Currency restrictions and tax complications made continuous residence in the British Isles very tricky for aliens like Alan and me. There being no prospect of a friendlier administration taking office, we really had no option but to pull up stakes before even more stringent regulations came into force. The wrench would have been more painful if it hadn't been for the fact that both companionable cats, Summer and Smoke, had gone to their heavenly rest. Thus, in 1978, we sold the Mill House just before Christmas, put our furniture into storage, and gladly accepted Helen Hayes's invitation to think about our future in the peace and quiet of her house in Mexico.

Upon arriving in Cuernavaca, early in February 1979, our first thought was to follow Helen's example and have two homes; in our case, one in California and the other in Cuernavaca. With that in mind, we combed the local real-estate possibilities. Finally we lighted on a most attractive villa in the center of Cuernavaca. Located on a hilly street named Cuauhtemoctzin, it was within spitting distance of Helen's equally unpronounceable Netzahualcoyotl domain. The house was built in the Roman style, the main rooms surrounding a large swimming pool and boasting a garden on the roof. An additional attraction was that the owner was willing to lend us her handsome furniture for an indefinite period. That suited our purpose perfectly, because it gave us the opportunity to try out living in Mexico without being irrevocably committed.

Our house-hunting expedition to California was less fortunate, although by renting a condominium in Lake San Marcos we were able to make a thorough search of the San Diego and neighbouring areas. Somewhere within hailing distance of Hollywood was our ambition, with an eye on gainful employment thereabouts. As luck would have it, a film job turned up, giving us the opportunity to test our commuting idea. It instantly proved to be completely impractical, thereby saving us from making a wildly expensive error.

Sure enough, the film part was that of yet *another* butler, this time in service with a recently arrived star in the person of Steve Martin. In the firmament patronised by youthful filmgoers, he was the hottest property since Halley's Comet. In spite of its unappetising title of *The Jerk*, the film did spectacular business at the box office. What really persuaded me to break my vow of "not another Jeeves" was the fact that the author-director was one of my gang from army days. Sergeant Carl Reiner had cut his teeth as a brilliant entertainer out there in the Pacific, and this was his gracious way of saying, "Thank you, Major Evans." He approached me through my agent, cautioning him to warn me that the script required me to utter a four-letter word. After a few moments of deliberation, I heard myself saying, "As long as I don't have to *do* it, I'll *say* it!" In the final version, the naughty word was expunged and my reputation preserved.

Thus it was back to Mexico to take up residence in the only place we could call home. Sighing with relief to have come to rest at last, we were rather startled on our first night in the new house when the swimming pool developed waves that splashed over the terrace and we realized we were in the midst of an earthquake! Despite this occurrence, we banished from our minds all thoughts of a second home in California. We baked in the almost continuous sunshine during the next few months and wallowed in the luxury of being waited on by a cook, a maid, and a houseboy.

In April 1980 a completely new experience came my way. I was invited to the University of South Carolina for a two-week working session with the students of the Department of Theatre and Speech at that distinguished seat of learning. Helen's ears pricked up on hearing this, and she promptly declared that she would come for the second week. "In that case," said I, "we must put on a show for them." We turned again to our old standby, *A Program for Two Players*, for bits and pieces, put in the adaptation of *The Circle*, and added a scene from *Victoria Regina*, which had not been included in the Broadway version of Laurence Housman's playlets. This was the very amusing scene in

RETIREMENT?

which the Queen quizzes the Dean of Windsor concerning her heretical doubts about the veracity of the biblical story of Jonah and the Whale. Our modest little entertainment was designed to suit the small amphitheatre to which patrons of the university had been invited. What neither of us had been told in advance was that we were expected to repeat the performance on the following night for the amusement of several thousand students in the basketball Coliseum. On a stage especially erected for us, and wearing microphones on our persons, we struggled through our paces before a sea of faces, to say nothing of three television cameras. In spite of the unfamiliar conditions, we survived the ordeal, counting ourselves fortunate to be in partnership once more.

Throughout my life I have always been grateful that my parents were thoughtful enough to have conceived me so that I was born in the year 1901. As a result, and in spite of an uncertain memory, it is easy to remember my age. Conveniently I am always entering the year signified by the last two digits on the calendar. Thus in 1980 I was entering my octogenarian span, but not so ancient that I was not still in demand to work in the theatre, and not too aged to busy myself in an attempt to entertain the reader by penning these words in longhand.

The first of two summonses to put on the greasepaint came in the fall of 1980 when I was invited to play the father in a revival of Philip Barry's *Holiday* at the cavernous Ahmanson Theatre in Los Angeles. The courtesies exchanged between actors when we attend initial rehearsals are always somewhat strained, and it was never more awkward than in the case of *Holiday*. The two actresses who were to play my daughters and the young actor to portray my son rose politely to shake hands. To my dismay I found myself towered over by a pair of goddesses and an equally statuesque god. That I could ever have spawned such a trio of giants was straining credulity too far; so I rather wistfully asked the director if, at my first entrance, he would arranged for my brood to be seated—preferably on the floor. In that event, I hoped I might look slightly less like a pimple.

The second call to duty came early in 1981, after I had returned to Cuernavaca. The proposition intrigued me no end, since it was to be my professional baptism in a so-called Dinner Theatre—the Showboat at Clearwater, Florida. The play was Ernest Thompson's *On Golden Pond*, which was being presented some time before it was filmed. It was a rare opportunity for me, because I was to celebrate my eightieth birthday during the run of the play, which was exactly the age of the crusty old husband as envisaged by the author.

Earlier in this memoir, I claimed to have "not an ounce of vanity in my makeup." However, I confess that on this occasion I thought it appropriate to apply a hint of shadow beneath my eyes to achieve a convincing eighty. Sad to relate, my cosmetic improvement became abruptly superfluous when, four days before the opening night, I tripped on a hidden pipe on the edge of the theatre parking lot and took a bruising tumble on the tarmac. The producer, Maurice Shinners, rushed me to a doctor to be checked for a suspected broken rib. No fracture was detected by the X-rays, but a little "nasty" in my right lung *was!* I was warned that it would be touch and go unless I submitted to exploratory tests within a matter of days. This was hardly a felicitous state of mind in which to open the show. Never before had I worked for such a considerate management. The medical prognosis was kept a dark secret from my fellow actors; they were aware only of my scratched-up face and other minor injuries.

Two of the box-office staff were somewhat puzzled when I asked them to act as witnesses to revisions to my will, which an emissary brought from New York, but they didn't suspect that I was to be hospitalised after only two weeks of the run. The old adage of "the show must go on" was never truer than in the case of *On Golden Pond.*

Not since the early days of playing the role of Richard II had I felt so at home in a part as I did as Norman—so much so that, despite the cloud hanging over me, I was happily absorbed in winning the laughter and the tears of the audience, and I was able to face the future with equanimity. I was nobly supported by my vis-à-vis, Fern Persons, playing Ethel, my long-suffering wife. Although I am pretty good at dissembling, the ironic similarity between Norman's dilemma and my own gave me no option but to let Fern know the truth. This gave an added poignancy to our relationship in the play, of which only she and I were aware.

A substitute for me was found in the person of Lyle Talbot, who was "up in the part" as the saying goes, having played Norman elsewhere. It was an odd sensation to see his name being put in lights in place of my own, but once I had entered the Tampa General Hospital I was too busy being tested in every part of my anatomy to give it further thought. It was providential that the team of specialists, on whose skills my life depended, jointly agreed that the tumour was operable, but not until they started digging was it established that the malignant intruder was still encapsulated and had not spread its tentacles into my lung. Out the beastly thing came and with it only a third of my lung. What made it all the more miraculous was that, having been born with an elevated diaphragm, the excision of part of the lung was of no consequence.

In my time I have been the recipient of many flattering fan letters, but none so welcome as the one I received from the surgeon in charge of my fate. Referring to my tumble in the parking lot, he wrote, "Your Guardian angel must have given you a shove!"

RETIREMENT?

I headed back to Cuernavaca to be greeted by unmistakable rumblings of the imminent collapse of the Mexican economy. There was nothing for it but to get out of the country before the major devaluation of the peso occurred—more or less tossing a coin to choose where next to settle.

California was an option that did not appeal to me. Although I had made a complete recovery from the lung operation and was impertinently sprightly for my age, I hated the prospect of being regarded as a resident ghost in the film capital; thus the alternative of taking a fresh look at England was decided upon. Thanks to Mrs. Thatcher we found conditions in England to be far more favourable than previously, and after considerable searching, we discovered a penthouse above two Regency buildings on Brighton's seafront. Alan snapped up the ninety-four-year leasehold of the flat, which suited me down to the ground—the level of which, incidentally, is reached by a most dignified, mahogany-lined, Waygood-Otis elevator. Not only is the place the last word in comfort, but the flat overlooks a nudist beach, thrown in for good measure. When the Mill House furniture, disinterred from storage, arrived at our new abode, I distinctly heard it murmur in the moving-van, "Oh! Not *again!!*"

Miraculously the furniture fitted its new surroundings as though it had been chosen especially for the penthouse. An ample terrace, with a spectacular view of the shipping plying the English Channel, gives me all the space I need to potter around in a pretence of gardening. Only a short walk from our residence is a large private garden, which is reserved for the use of the key-holders of the area. The cultivation of the garden, I blush to confess, I leave to our agile neighbours.

I have dusted off my cookery books, tuned up my hearing aid the better to appreciate the splendid performances being given on television by hordes of young actors and actresses, and in one way or another find myself healthy and content. How comforting it is to be out of the limelight and, as far as my past is concerned, venture to echo Prospero's adieu to make-believe:

> Our revels now are ended. These our actors,
> As I foretold you, were all spirits and
> Are melted into air, into thin air:
> And, like the baseless fabric of this vision,
> The cloud-capp'd towers, the gorgeous palaces,
> The solemn temples, the great globe itself,
> Yea, all which it inherit, shall dissolve
> And, like this insubstantial pageant faded,
> Leave not a rack behind.

Appendix

My name appeared on the title pages of three books before this one, all of them published in New York.

The first, issued by Doubleday in 1947, was *Maurice Evans' G.I. Production of Hamlet by William Shakespeare: Acting Edition, with a Preface by Mr. Evans.* The second was Dodd Mead's 1948 edition of Shaw's *Man and Superman* "With Photographs of Maurice Evans' Production." Third was the same company's edition of Shaw's *The Devil's Disciple* "With Photographs of the Production Starring Mr. Evans," which was issued in 1950 but somehow got into the catalogue of the Library of Congress as having come out in 1941.

Before the days of the LP album, Columbia Masterworks had recorded me in excerpts from *Hamlet* and *Richard II* on several discs, and RCA Victor had squeezed *Macbeth* into five 78-rpm records, starring Maurice Evans and Judith Anderson.

My larynx made its microgroove debut in the Theatre Masterworks recording of Oscar Wilde's *The Importance of Being Earnest* (number 2506 in their catalogue), which was followed by the 1960 Capitol recording of *Tenderloin* (SWAO–1492) with the original cast. In 1955 Columbia issued selections from their earlier *Hamlet* and *Richard II* recordings (excerpts from excerpts) on their Entre label (RL–3107), and my voice was also heard on an RCA album (PRM–202) entitled *Great Moments from the Hallmark Hall of Fame.* In 1961 *Maurice Evans' Introduction to Shakespeare*, sometimes listed as *A Child's Introduction to Shakespeare*, was issued by Golden Record (AA–58). This was followed by my readings from A. A. Milne (Pathways of Sound 1032, 1034, and 1038) entitled *Winnie the Pooh*, *More of Winnie the Pooh*, and *Most of Winnie the Pooh*.

Index

INDEX

INDEX

INDEX

INDEX